Big Questions and Great Answers in Entrepreneurship Research

To Geneviève, who has been supporting me
since my first steps in the academic world.
(Alain Fayolle)

To Alain (Fayolle), venerable Jedi Master, for having given
the keys to understanding the academic world to the
Padawan that I am. To Stéphane, my eternal fiancé.
(Sandrine Le Pontois)

To my parents, for their unwavering love
and support along my journey.
(Duncan Pelly)

Big Questions and Great Answers in Entrepreneurship Research

Discussing Up-to-date Methodological and Philosophical Issues

Edited by

Alain Fayolle

Entrepreneurship Professor, IDRAC Business School, France and Visiting Professor, Turku School of Economics, Finland

Sandrine Le Pontois

Associate Professor in Entrepreneurship, Université Jean Monnet Saint-Étienne, COACTIS, France

R. Duncan M. Pelly

Cal Turner Endowed Chair of Business Administration, Fisk University, USA

Edward Elgar
PUBLISHING

Cheltenham, UK • Northampton, MA, USA

Published by
Edward Elgar Publishing Limited
The Lypiatts
15 Lansdown Road
Cheltenham
Glos GL50 2JA
UK

Edward Elgar Publishing, Inc.
William Pratt House
9 Dewey Court
Northampton
Massachusetts 01060
USA

A catalogue record for this book
is available from the British Library

Library of Congress Control Number: 2024946887

This book is available electronically in the **Elgar**online
Business subject collection
https://dx.doi.org/10.4337/9781800888661

Printed on elemental chlorine free (ECF)
recycled paper containing 30% Post-Consumer Waste

ISBN 978 1 80088 865 4 (cased)
ISBN 978 1 80088 866 1 (eBook)

Printed and bound in the USA

Contents

Contributors

Catherine Brentnall is a Senior Lecturer in Enterprise at Manchester Metropolitan University, UK. She has extensive experience in Enterprise and Entrepreneurship Education (EEE), working in the field since 2006 and developing programmes, teaching and/or research at all levels from Early Years to Higher Education. Catherine has a particular interest in qualitative inquiry and creating and supporting research which questions taken-for-granted assumptions in the field of EEE. In her PhD research she used Realist Evaluation to study competitions and competitive activities in secondary schools. Taking this approach, she illuminated various negative and unintended outcomes that measurement-focused impact studies had missed. She co-chairs the Research Methods, Practice and Inquiry/Impact track at the annual conference of the Institute for Small Business and Entrepreneurship (ISBE) and provides informal mentoring and online writing opportunities for EEE researchers.

Léo-Paul Dana is Professor at ICD Business School, Paris, France and Visiting Professor at LUT School of Business and Management, Lappeenranta University of Technology, Finland. He holds the title of Professor at Dalhousie University and is also associated with the Chaire ETI at Sorbonne Business School. A graduate of McGill University and HEC-Montreal, he has served as Marie Curie Fellow at Princeton University and Visiting Professor at INSEAD and at Kingston University. He has published extensively in a variety of journals including: *Entrepreneurship: Theory & Practice*, *International Business Review*, *International Small Business Journal*, *Journal of Business Research*, *Journal of Small Business Management*, *Journal of World Business*, *Small Business Economics*, and *Technological Forecasting & Social Change*.

Saulo Dubard Barbosa is Professor of Entrepreneurship and Director of the InvEnt Research Center at Emlyon Business School, France. His main research interests include entrepreneurial decision making, the social and psychological dynamics of entrepreneurship, and more recently, the intersection between religion and entrepreneurship. His research has been published in journals such as *Entrepreneurship Theory & Practice*, *Journal of Business Venturing*, and *Small Business Economics*. Before moving to France and becoming an academic, Saulo graduated at the University of São Paulo, Brazil, where he led the foundation of the Cursinho FEA-USP, a cause-driven preparatory school that trains over 400 underprivileged students every year with the goal of helping them to enter the university.

Alain Fayolle is Professor of Entrepreneurship at IDRAC Business School, France and CREA – Center for Innovation and Entrepreneurship Activities, University of Cagliari, Italy. He is also Visiting Professor at Turku School of Economics, Finland. He is Chair of the Strategic and Prospective Committee at IFAG, School of Management and Entrepreneurship, France. Alain has been Distinguished Professor and the Founder and Director of the Entrepreneurship Research Centre at EM Lyon Business School, France. In 2013, Alain Fayolle received the 2013 European Entrepreneurship Education Award and has been elected officer of the Academy of Management Entrepreneurship Division for a five-year period (2013–2018), a position that culminated as Chair of the Division during the 2016–2017 academic year. In 2015, he has been awarded Wilford L. White Fellow by ICSB.

Stéphane Foliard is an Associate Professor who teaches entrepreneurship from awareness to pre-incubation to diverse audiences in both French and English. He is notably the creator of the educational program "Campus des entrepreneurs" guiding students at the Roanne Institute of Technology to actually start their own businesses and thereby develop the knowledge, skills, and attitudes necessary for a future entrepreneurial career. His research focuses on entrepreneurship education, ecosystem dynamics, and the nature of interactions within these ecosystems, as well as the legitimacy of the teaching mentors. Since June 2021, he has been the Vice President for Entrepreneurship and Continuing Education at the University Jean Monnet Saint-Étienne, France. He also serves as the Vice President of the Academy of Entrepreneurship and Innovation, overseeing teaching-related matters.

William B. Gartner is the Bertarelli Foundation Distinguished Professor of Family Entrepreneurship at Babson College, USA and a Visiting Professor in Entrepreneurship at Linnaeus University in Sweden. His current scholarship spans a wide array of topics: entrepreneurship as practice, entrepreneurial expertise, the social construction of the future, varieties of value creation and appropriation, "translating entrepreneurship" across cultures and countries, the poetics of exchange, fiction and the entrepreneurial imagination, and the influence of legacy on entrepreneurial families.

Katriina Heljakka (Doctor of Arts, PhD, MA Art History, MSc Economics) researches toys, play, and playful learning with an interest in life-long and life-wide play in work life at the Turku School of Economics at the University of Turku, Finland. Previously, she has worked in the Academy of Finland research projects Ludification and Emergence of Playful Culture and at the Centre of Excellence in Game Culture Studies, and recently as part of museum teams playifying exhibitions. Heljakka's academic articles have been featured in academic journals and edited volumes, published, e.g., in the *American Journal of Play*, *International Journal of Play*, and books by Routledge and Palgrave. Currently, she works as a postdoctoral researcher in the EntrePlay project, which focuses on the possibilities of play as part of entrepreneurship education. Her areas of expertise include technologically driven play, playful environments, tools and techniques in learning and organizations, and the various cultures of play.

Martine Hlady-Rispal is University Professor in Entrepreneurship and Strategy at the University of Limoges, France. She is Scientific Director of CREOP, a bi-disciplinary law and management laboratory focusing on digital innovation, entrepreneurship and sustainable development of territories. Her current research covers a wide range of subjects, including qualitative methods adapted to the study of current entrepreneurial phenomena, traceability for sustainability in the luxury goods industry, the transmission of know-how and digitization, ecosystemic business models.

Jennifer Huntsley is a Senior Lecturer and programme lead in Initial Teacher Education at York St John University, UK. She completed her own teacher training at the University of Cambridge in 2009 and has worked in education ever since, both in the UK and internationally. She has led curriculum enrichment projects in primary schools and university settings, seeking to enhance the learning experience for children and adults alike. Her research interests are concerned with the journey of student teachers as they take up their role in the field of primary education. Her PhD thesis explores how critical reflection may support student teachers to make sense of their own learning and emphasizes the role that universities may play in providing spaces for such critical reflection.

Sandrine Le Pontois is an Associate Professor in Management Sciences at the Université Jean Monnet Saint-Étienne, France. She holds masters' degrees in psychology and educational sciences. She teaches entrepreneurship, strategy and social psychology. As part of the COACTIS laboratory's "Sustainable Innovations" division, her research focuses on entrepreneurship: evaluation of the impact of entrepreneurship education (critical approach), legitimacy of entrepreneurship educators, and more recently the place and role of emotions and cognition among impact entrepreneurs in the transition era.

Michela Loi is Associate Professor in the Department of Economics and Business at the University of Cagliari, Italy. Her research interests mostly concern entrepreneurship education, entrepreneurial university, and entrepreneurial learning. Her works have been published in high-ranked academic journals, such as *European Management Review*, *International Small Business*

Journal, *Journal of Management Inquiry* and *Entrepreneurship and Regional Development*.

Sara Maryami is currently working as a Postdoctoral Fellow in the Department of Industrial Economics and Technology Management at the Norwegian University of Science and Technology, Trondheim, Norway. Her research delves into the complexities of entrepreneurial team dynamics, exploring the interplay between team emotions and entrepreneurial behavior. Notably, her research has been published in the *Journal of Small Business and Enterprise Development*.

Jarrod Ormiston is a Senior Lecturer in Entrepreneurship in the Transdisciplinary School at the University of Technology Sydney, Australia. Jarrod's teaching activities focus on entrepreneurship, social entrepreneurship, and sustainability. Jarrod conducts research on entrepreneurial ecosystems, social entrepreneurship, impact investing and regenerative entrepreneurship. His research explores the interconnections between time, relationships, emotions, language, and place in shaping entrepreneurial action. Jarrod has worked as a consultant to the NSW Government, the Australian Government, the OECD and United Nations on entrepreneurship and education. Prior to his work at UTS, Jarrod worked as an Assistant Professor at Maastricht University, a Lecturer at the University of Sydney, as an Analyst in Growth Solutions at Deloitte, and in various management roles in the Australian and Latin American non-profit and education sectors.

R. Duncan M. Pelly is the Cal Turner Endowed Chair of Business in the Department of Business at Fisk University, USA. He received his PhD in Entrepreneurship from EM Lyon Business School. He served in the United States Army for four and a half years, attaining the rank of Captain, before beginning his doctoral studies. He holds a Bachelor of Arts degree from the University of Pennsylvania in International Relations, French, and German. His interests include entrepreneurial opportunity, the Marquis de Sade, heterotopias, autoethnography, and philosophical foundations of entrepreneurship.

Stratos Ramoglou is Professor of Entrepreneurship Studies at the University of Southampton, UK and Head of the Department of Strategy, Innovation and Entrepreneurship (DSIE). He received his PhD from the University of Cambridge, UK. Stratos's research interests include the conceptual foundations of entrepreneurship research, entrepreneurial opportunities, social issues in entrepreneurship, and analytic philosophy. Stratos has been published in leading academic journals, such as *Academy of Management Review*, *Entrepreneurship Theory and Practice*, and *Journal of Business Venturing*. He sits on the Editorial Boards of *Academy of Management Review* and *Journal of Business Venturing*, and is an Editor of *European Management Review*.

Aidin Salamzadeh is the Vice Dean of the Faculty of Business Management at the University of Tehran, Iran. His interests are startups, new venture creation, and entrepreneurship. Aidin serves as an associate editor for the *Humanities and Social Sciences Communications* (Nature.com), *Journal of Enterprising Communities, Revista de Gestão*; *Innovation Management Review* (Emerald), *Entrepreneurial Business and Economics Review* and *Journal of Women's Entrepreneurship and Education*, as well as *The Bottom Line* (Emerald). Besides, he is a reviewer in numerous distinguished international journals. Aidin is a member of the European SPES Forum (Belgium), the Asian Academy of Management (Malaysia), Ondokuz Mayis University (Turkey), and the Institute of Economic Sciences (Serbia). He co-founded the Innovation and Entrepreneurship Research Lab (London).

Kati Suomi, DSc (Econ. and Bus. Adm.) is an Assistant Professor (tenure track) of Business and Entrepreneurship at the Turku School of Economics at the University of Turku (Pori Unit), Finland, where she is a leader of EntreBus research group. She holds a title of docent from Tampere University, Faculty of Management and Business, Finland. She is a visiting scholar and a member of EMPRECOOP research group at the University of Valencia, Spain. Kati is an experienced educator with over 15 years' teaching experience from the Turku School of Economics, Pori Unit, where she is responsible for minor subject studies (25 ECTS) in entrepreneurship. Her research interests include topics such as entrepreneurial education, entrepreneurial marketing and branding of SMEs. Her research has been published in the *Journal of Business Research*, *Tourism Management* and *European Journal of Marketing*, among others.

Bruce T. Teague is currently Interim Director of the Daveler and Kauanui School of Entrepreneurship at Florida Gulf Coast University (FGCU), USA and Interim Director of the Rist Family Institute for Entrepreneurship. Prior to joining FGCU in 2022, he held the EWU Foundation Endowed Professorship at Eastern Washington University, where he created the Entrepreneurship Program, and the EWU E-ship Center. He also spent one year as a Visiting Professor of Entrepreneurship at Copenhagen Business School, Denmark. His research focuses on understanding what entrepreneurs do, and how. His research has explored entrepreneurial behavior, entrepreneurship as practice, and entrepreneurship from the perspective of expert skill. His work has appeared in journals such as *Entrepreneurship and Regional Development*, *Ethics and Behavior*, and the *Journal of Business Ethics*. His research has been presented at the Academy of Management, USASBE, RENT, and the Entrepreneurship as Practice Conference.

Neil A. Thompson is an Associate Professor in Entrepreneurship and Organization Studies in the Department of Management and Organization at Vrije Universiteit Amsterdam, the Netherlands. He received MSc degrees in International Economics and Business from the Utrecht University in 2009. In 2013 he received his PhD degree, based on a dissertation with the title "Institutional Logics and Entrepreneurship – Struggling for legitimacy in the emerging bio-energy field". His ongoing research covers topics about entrepreneurship as practice; organizational creativity; new venture creation; sustainable development; organization theory; institutional theory; organizational change; new industry development; economic sociology; and historical methods. Present research questions are: how do entrepreneurs experience and cope with anxiety through the entrepreneurship process? How has a global entrepreneurship ecosystem emerged and evolved? How can we best conceptualize and research entrepreneurial ecosystems? How does institutional work assist business historians in historiography? How is the imagination implicated in organizational creativity?

Richard Tunstall is Associate Professor of Enterprise at Leeds University Business School and University Academic Director for Enterprise at the University of Leeds, UK. He is Co-Editor of the *International Journal of Entrepreneurial Behaviour and Research* and a Director of Enterprise Educators UK. He is Academic Director of the KPMG Family Leadership Academy and has designed, developed and led a range of enterprise and innovation programmes and initiatives to develop individuals' entrepreneurial thinking and facilitate new opportunities. His research focuses on the social practices through which entrepreneurship develops in internal corporate venturing, universities and entrepreneurship education.

1. Why is "what is good entrepreneurship research" a big question?

Alain Fayolle, Sandrine Le Pontois and R. Duncan M. Pelly

INTRODUCTION: METHODS (ALONE) ARE NOT ENTREPRENEURSHIP RESEARCH

Based upon the seminal work of Cantillon (1755), Say (1861), Schumpeter (2000), and others, entrepreneurship research has grown exponentially over the last 50 years, especially during the last two decades (Rauch, 2020) – moving from a marginal sub-field of other disciplines (such as economics and management) to a legitimate field of research (Hindle, 2007). Entrepreneurship was first studied as an object by researchers from various academic disciplines during the 1970s, and then a community of researchers was formed around the first journals and conferences of the 1980s. The boom continued with PhDs being defended and a significant increase in publications and dedicated journals being launched during the 1990s. Over the last 30 years the field has gained maturity and has witnessed the rise of accompanying diversity of sub-fields (e.g. Katz, 2008), as well as legitimacy in the field of management sciences.

Scholars' Interest in the Entrepreneurship Field

There are several reasons why scholars are so interested in entrepreneurship research. Public policy's interest in entrepreneurship and the increase in resources provided to develop entrepreneurial activities has led to the launch of research initiatives to document entrepreneurial practices as well as the mechanisms that support these practices. Concurrently, new methods of data collection and analysis (both quantitative and qualitative) and quantitative datasets have been developed to understand who entrepreneurs are and how they act. This new data and their respective tools help understand the helix between actions and processes in the context of entrepreneurial ecosystems. Finally, the recent development of accessible AI-based tools seems to be reshuffling the deck. "Indeed, entrepreneurship scholars are now better equipped than ever to do research" (Dubard Barbosa, Chapter 7 in this volume). However, even though much has been achieved, many challenges remain, and more remain on the horizon.

The rapid and exponential growth of a relatively young field compared to other disciplines has led to two major issues. First, entrepreneurship research is highly fragmented (Davidsson, 2003; Gartner, 2004). Indeed, members of the community can observe a thematic treatment with its accompanying silos, each containing a great diversity of results undergoing caustic drift. Secondly, despite attempts at generalization, the results remain difficult to compare for methodological, contextual, theoretical, and conceptual reasons. Furthermore, it is still difficult for contemporary researchers to situate themselves within a time continuum, even though there is a consensus about entrepreneurship being portrayed as a process (Shane, 2012).

Quantitative, Qualitative, and Mixed-methods in Entrepreneurship

Often opposed, sometimes combined, both quantitative and qualitative methodologies contribute to the understanding of intricate entrepreneurial contexts and processes. Both groups of methodologies also capture current entrepreneurship challenges. Various improvements have been made in entrepreneurship research thanks to the co-evolution of quantitative, qualitative, and mixed research methods. Quantitative methods have used recently big data and AI as new source of inspiration (Schwab & Zhang, 2019; Jones et al., 2021) while qualitative methods found innovation from other fields of social science (Pelly and Fayolle, 2023). Quantitative research methods use various types of data and databases for empirical research and investigate the causal or correlational relationship among given constructs. The data-driven analysis addresses the real-life problems of the entrepreneurial world and its actors. Finally, quantitative approaches are more likely to be published in top entrepreneurship journals than qualitative research. Unfortunately, the non-inductive nature of quantitative methods means that hypotheses are only supported (Trafimow, 2022) which means that research questions are not fully answered (Hlady-Rispal et al., Chapter 8 in this volume). Qualitative approach, while time-consuming, helps to enhance knowledge of entrepreneurship because it is well adapted to the study of entrepreneurial processes and mechanisms. They reveal the situated nature of entrepreneurial praxes and habitus, deal with complexity and engage in sensemaking, and develop socially constructed theory (Pelly and Fayolle 2020). Finally, mixed-methods are seen as a creative way to reach a deeper understanding of a phenomenon.

But methods alone do not mean good research.

WHAT IS GOOD ENTREPRENEURSHIP RESEARCH? WHERE DOES IT START?

Expanding the Frontiers of a Collective Knowledge

The principal aim of entrepreneurship research is, like in any discipline, to expand the frontiers of collective knowledge. In the dynamic field of entrepreneurship, it is vital to produce continuous and comprehensive research to improve our understanding of phenomena that have significant implications for economic, societal (Kraus et al., 2020), and environmental areas. The corollary of this objective is to take an interest in the questions underlying the envisaged research. On the one hand, researchers are confronted with philosophical and ontological questions, i.e., questions that concern the study of the object and the attributes that belong to it by its very nature (Pelly, 2017). On the other hand, scholars need to address methodological issues, i.e., the techniques or procedures used to identify, gather and analyze data in relation to a specific research subject (e.g., how a researcher designs their study to obtain valid and reliable results, and achieve their research objectives). All research is (should be) part of an ongoing academic conversation. The aim is to contribute by supplementing, nuancing, (re)legitimizing and even challenging conventions and standards with a creative, collaborative, contributory and critical spirit.

Alignment and Contribution

The need to expand the frontiers of entrepreneurship research presupposes that academics involved in entrepreneurship scholarship communities approach the world with an open aperture, while relying upon genuine expertise, effort, humility, and rigor. In short, their aim is to define the epistemological positioning of the research being carried out and to align the subject, research question, epistemological positioning (i.e., how is knowledge constructed?), methodology, and the conceptual framework to fill a gap identified in the current conversation, with the aim of clearly identifying a contribution that will be published and/or disseminated in society.

To borrow Alain Fayolle's expression and turn it on its head, it is less a question of "producing entrepreneurship research" than of "producing (and thinking about) the right questions" in entrepreneurship research. Otherwise, researchers run two major risks: the misuse of an increasingly sophisticated technical apparatus and the production of many studies that are practically irrelevant and theoretically misleading (Dubard Barbosa, Chapter 7 in this volume). The philosopher Nietzsche (1911) suggests the use of three tools: the hammer, the pliers and the screwdriver. The hammer is not a destructive tool, but a means of awakening reflexes (like a doctor's hammer, which can be used to check knee-joint reflexes), and deconstructing presuppositions, prejudices, and doxas. In research, it is important to ask whether what is taken for granted is still true and valid in the light of the latest scientific advances. One of the roles of entrepreneurship scholars can be to offer a well-founded refutation of assertions taken for granted in the field. An example does not a proof make: not all researchers have the same a priori idea of an object. It is important to question ideas in an academic conversation to avoid assimilating concepts of limited value.

The debate of ideas in research contributes to democracy and enlightened citizenship, even more so in the context of transition. This habitus of discussion is supported by the use of pliers, which makes it possible to build, adjust or even squeeze a concept; indeed, it is important to peel back the onion and then assemble, disassemble, construct, and reconstruct knowledge (see the work of Jacquemin et al. (2017) on this line of thoughts). The screwdriver is then used to examine a concept in detail, in other words, to dissect the word. Researchers rarely trace words back to their source. The practice of etymology allows scholars to identify the roots of a word and its various historical branches – in short, the meaning it has been given over time. It is disappointing that most articles do not provide clear definitions of the concepts used. Yet that is what researchers do – they play with concepts, redefine terms, construct neologisms (e.g., effectuation, underdog, entrepreneurial emotions, etc.), pose problems, and analyze examples (empirical studies). Problems have an history, and knowing their history avoids asking questions that have already been answered (sometimes in other fields).

Researchers often find answers, and not just one answer, because of the positioning of each researcher and the differences in their respective anchoring. Additionally, the field of entrepreneurship is extremely contextualized and subject to uncertainty. Putting a "πρόβλημα" (*próblêma*: in ancient Greek, that which is thrown forward, projected) on the table is the starting point for stating a question. Asking the right questions helps counter two pitfalls that threaten academic conversation: relativism (saying everything and its opposite from a subjective point of view) and dogmatism. An enlightening example is to show how entrepreneurship researchers have moved on from the "who is the entrepreneur" question – which is a wrong question (Gartner, 1988; Ramoglou et al., 2020; Ramoglou, Chapter 3 in this volume) – to the turn to entrepreneurship as a social practice, contributing to the emergence of the field.

The Necessity to Discuss Up-to-date Methodological and Philosophical Issues

There is now a consensus that entrepreneurship is process-oriented, and that entrepreneurial action is a contextual, non-linear, interactive, emotional, and future-oriented process anchored in uncertainty (Hindle, 2004; Karatas-Ozkan et al., 2014; Suddaby et al., 2015). If scholars wish to produce research that remain rigorous and relevant to the field of entrepreneurship, then there is a need to move towards more transformational research (e.g., interactive, activity based, cognitively hot, compassionate, and prosocial) and novelty in theorizing and methods (Shepherd, 2015). This is not to say that the dominant methods should be rejected. Surveys, interviews, experiments, etc. are useful but provide only limited insights into entrepreneurial action (Dana & Dana, 2007; Zahra & Wright, 2011), are contextually situated, and contribute to the growth of fragmentation in entrepreneurship research. There is a call to further entrepreneurship research by observing and participating with entrepreneurs, policy-makers and other types of practitioners anchored in their environmental, social, and economic contexts (Chalmers & Shaw, 2017; Thompson et al., 2020). This means identifying the limitations of existing methods and innovating by expanding these tools and creating new ones to observe and study aspects of entrepreneurial action that remain obfuscated to researchers (Berglund, 2007; Shepherd & Suddaby, 2017). The ambition of this volume is to offer entrepreneurship researchers a discussion on up-to-date philosophical and methodological issues.

OVERVIEW OF THE CHAPTERS

The book is organized in three parts.

Part I: Exploring Philosophical Issues in Entrepreneurship Research

In Chapter 2, Alain Fayolle considers how an entrepreneurship scholar can contribute to research in their field. This chapter is meant above all to be a tribute to Michael (Mike) Wright (1952–2019), a prolific researcher who has had a major impact on the field of entrepreneurship. Having an influential role in this field means concurrently serving as a great contributor to entrepreneurship literature, a mentor for young researchers (and sometimes for older ones as well), an intellectual leader, and a community builder. Alain Fayolle looks back at his personal relationship with Mike Wright and how it has contributed to his professional development as editor of several international journals, coordinator of special issues/books, conferences, and as the Chair of the Entrepreneurship Division of the Academy of Management during the

2016–2017 academic year. He then invites us to reflect on the social identity of Mike Wright as an entrepreneurship scholar and to think about our own social identity as researcher in the field.

While the social identity of entrepreneurship scholars may be a marker of their vision of academic research, it is interesting to explore the resources devoted to answering questions considered as central to the field. Stratos Ramoglou (Chapter 3) takes us on an (academic) journey back in time, looking at the contributions (present/past) of the flawed question of "who is an entrepreneur?" and the fallacious nature of this question. He argues that "we should be more cautious with the questions that we ask". Indeed, philosophical reflection upon the tacit assumptions that underlie the emergence and persistence in a field of questions that seems important may simply reveal that they are only pseudo-questions and that there is no discovery to be made. The problem is therefore not methodological, but ontological. Stratos Ramoglou advocates for moving toward methodologically and theoretically sounder questions and for fighting against false assumptions to avoid fueling misleading narratives (e.g., determinism) about entrepreneurs and entrepreneurship research contributions. Finally, his chapter gives researchers the keys to shaping a good entrepreneurship research question.

Entrepreneurship (and entrepreneurship research) is a story of visions, plans, failures, and potential successes. Given these difficulties in conveying the reality of entrepreneurship, how is it possible for scholars to tell the entire story of entrepreneurship? What methodologies would be suitable to explore authentically what happens during the entrepreneurial journey from a processual lens? Duncan Pelly (Chapter 4) provides an overview of autoethnography, an embodied methodology that relies on the writer's experiences to illustrate a phenomenon. The descriptions furnish lucidity into the prosaic struggles faced by entrepreneurs. This chapter serves as a guide for prospective autoethnographers as they begin their writing journey. It may be of interest to entrepreneurship scholars, autoethnographers, and practicing entrepreneurs who wish to publish their entrepreneurial experiences in academic journals and elicit resonance with the reader. Various approaches to autoethnography are provided (including evocative and analytic autoethnographies) as well as an explanation of autoethnography's importance in the study of entrepreneurship (it is not just a method, but also a lifestyle). A "*mise en abyme*" is achieved in this chapter, providing an autoethnography of writing an autoethnography (from an isomorphism perspective), with one story by one voice. This chapter offers an opportunity for the reader to reflect upon what is their own story and their voice as a scholar.

What do entrepreneurs do? Bruce T. Teague and Richard Tunstall (Chapter 5) explore the roots of the entrepreneurship-as-practice (EAP) turn by examining seminal works that have shaped the field's emergence (including research from Pierre Bourdieu, Anthony Giddens, Sherry Ortner, Theodore Schatzki, Elizabeth Shove and Andreas Reckwitz). The EAP perspective contends that entrepreneurship is not merely an outcome but a socially situated and ongoing practice, which implies a holistic and contextual approach to understanding entrepreneurship. Exploring its fundamental tenets, theoretical foundations, and potential to develop practical understandings of this activity, the authors highlight that scholars embedded in EAP examine entrepreneurship beyond the narrow lens of individual attributes, behaviors, or firm-level processes. This chapter contributes to ongoing discourse on entrepreneurship by combining theoretical reflections with empirical evidence from diverse contexts to offer a nuanced perspective on the phenomenon needed to inspire future research and practical implications to better support the entrepreneurial journey.

Part II: Dealing Better with Methodological Issues and Challenges

Most research scholars are still using conventional research methods to investigate the constantly changing phenomenon of entrepreneurship. Indeed, there is a need to highlight the key issues in entrepreneurship research methods. After an introduction offering an enlightening summary of the contributions of qualitative, quantitative and mix-methods, Léo-Paul Dana and Aidin Salamzadeh (Chapter 6) shed light upon the primary issues in entrepreneurship research and classify them into three major categories. The first category includes contextualizing the entrepreneurial phenomena (contextual factors), which is necessary to ensure the quality of findings and for revisiting entrepreneurship research methods. The second category deals with the changing nature of entrepreneurship research methods (or the methodological factors). As contemporary entrepreneurs deal with big data analytics, artificial intelligence, and machine learning issues, the traditional entrepreneurship research methods need to evolve. The last category is focused upon theorizing and theory building (or the theoretical issues). In other words, entrepreneurship researchers must pay attention to theorizing entrepreneurial phenomena embedded in real-world situations.

As entrepreneurship research in highly ranked journals is mainly quantitative, researchers are responsible for discussing the challenges associated with the fact that entrepreneurship fits poorly within assumptions of normality, because it is a broad concept with a non-linear, path-dependent process. Saulo Dubard Barbosa (Chapter 7) highlights the main challenges entrepreneurship scholars have addressed as a field to be able to do more and better quantitative research, including: entrepreneurship panels and datasets; linking entrepreneurship-specific datasets to existing datasets not specifically related on entrepreneurship; data collection; and advances ın measurement, research design, and analysis. The author then presents the main challenges that remain – entrepreneurship is not normally distributed, is a broad concept, is path-dependent, and is not a linear or smooth process. Finally, he discusses newer challenges that have emerged over the last decades related to: (1) increased statistical power and analytic sophistication, and (2) the asymmetry between gains and losses in quantitative research.

In order to capture and analyze contextualized and flexible data, other tools are needed. Scholars recognized that qualitative methodologies fundamentally contribute to the understanding of complex and intricate entrepreneurial processes (Welter et al., 2019; Welter & Gartner, 2016). Martine Hlady-Rispal, Alain Fayolle and William (Bill) Gartner (Chapter 8) indicate why and how qualitative methods clearly and distinctively contribute to the understanding of current challenges of modern-day entrepreneurship by using examples from papers included in a special issue of the *Journal of Small Business Management* and from recent qualitative research. The authors demonstrate that qualitative methods illuminate current entrepreneurship challenges such as understanding context, dealing with complexity, sense making, and triggering action. Another intention of this chapter is to provide the benefits of qualitative studies for entrepreneurship research and to help researchers become more familiar with novel methods that enable scholars to explore "entrepreneurial action" in action, embrace co-design and collective intelligence, reveal a constructive critical attitude, and join a phenomenon-driven conversation.

To collect and synthetize existing research findings systematically, researchers use a method called the systematic literature review (SLR). Why and how is this method chosen? Sara Maryami and Michela Loi (Chapter 9) propose a study that outlines the key steps for its adoption. This chapter explains how to compile a comprehensive overview of the existing literature and identify potential research gaps or areas needing further exploration. The pros and cons of using a SLR are also discussed. Thanks to a clear example in the context of entrepreneurial teams (demonstrated as a case in practice), researchers can gain a comprehensive understanding of how to use a SLR effectively and make informed decisions about how and when to employ complementary approaches. The authors provide guidance to researchers, setting out the key steps involved in conducting a SLR: formulating a research question, establishing inclusion and exclusion criteria, conducting a thorough literature review, screening and selecting relevant studies, assessing their quality, extracting, synthesizing data, and presenting a comprehensive overview of the findings to provide a useful synthesis of existing literature on their topic of interest.

Before becoming seasoned scholars, novice entrepreneurship researchers begin with a doctoral journey to learn how to do relevant research. Sandrine Le Pontois and Stéphane Foliard (Chapter 10) explore how to combine coherence and effectiveness in an entrepreneurship doctoral article-based dissertation. To understand the rise of the article-based dissertation in entrepreneurship, the authors look back at its origins (massification of scientific production, standardization and professionalization of the doctoral path) and then identify the major issues and challenges of the doctoral pathway for doctoral students, supervisors and research laboratories in a competitive international context. Based upon an integrative literature review, this chapter highlights the reasons why the article-based thesis is a "good" answer to these issues and challenges by analyzing the semantic fields around "paper/article-based thesis" and what educational science research highlights about "paper-based writing" *versus* a "monograph". Finally, the authors suggest to both PhD candidates and supervisors key issues, guidelines – including a canva ($ABPhD^2$ Canva, license Creative Commons CC-BY-NC-ND) – and avenues for reflection to ensure the coherence and effectiveness of an article-based PhD dissertation in entrepreneurship.

Part III: Examining New Models and Methodologies in Entrepreneurship Research

Although it is new to the entrepreneurship research field, video research methods enable scholars to view entrepreneurship "in motion". Jarrod Ormiston and Neil Thompson (Chapter 11) explore current uses and future possibilities of video research methods in entrepreneurship qualitative research. As they provide a powerful yet accessible way for researchers to observe and theorize entrepreneurial phenomenon by analyzing entrepreneurship "in motion", the authors conduct a systematic review of 142 entrepreneurship research articles published in leading journals that reveals three dominant video research methods: videography of entrepreneurship "in the wild" (entrepreneurial practices), video content analysis using entrepreneur generated videos (e.g., crowdfunding, archival videos) and video elicitation in "manufactured" contexts (interviews, experiments). They propose a research agenda to understand through video the interactional, embodied, material, and emotional nature of entrepreneurial practice.

Investigating the potential of playful approaches in teaching and learning in higher education, Kati Suomi and Katriina Heljakka (Chapter 12) are wondering how playful learning as a pedagogical method supports the development of students' entrepreneurship competencies. The authors provide examples of ways in which playful learning might be implemented through experimental approaches and they introduce three major components of invitations to play – atmosphere, physical space, and materials. This chapter introduces student-centered learning design and tools for playful learning to build a culture that exposes students to entrepreneurial competencies. Since entrepreneurship competencies (Bacigalupo et al., 2016) and play competencies share several similarities and counterparts, it indicates that by employing playful approaches in university pedagogy, it is possible to support not only play and related skills but also entrepreneurship competencies – including entrepreneurial awareness and mindset. Building entrepreneurship competencies is imperative as they are seen as drivers of transformation, innovation, and growth in nations.

Echoing Paulo Freire's theory and principles of education, Alain Fayolle (Chapter 13) offers a deep analysis of an innovative pedagogical practice which is to ask learners to work in teams to create a methodology and a framework to assess new venture creation projects. This pedagogical approach involves learners in a reflexive process, in contrast to their traditional conception of education, and strongly encourages them to question and relativize the scope of management and entrepreneurship tools. Learning objectives focus upon understanding the processual development of rating a method in relation to a posture and a context of evaluation. During and at the end of the training, learners are encouraged to develop an awareness of the power and freedom available to them (and have) with respect to their choice (or design) and use of the tools of management, irrespective of the situations and the problems faced. The combination of the seminar on pedagogical methodology, when combined with Paulo Freire's educational model, highlights their close similarities: understanding the problem at hand, constructing and deconstructing, rebuilding (a contextualized management tool) by rethinking the learner-educator relationship, and the purpose of entrepreneurship education.

To close the final section of this volume, Jennifer Huntsley and Catherine Brentnall (Chapter 14) introduce a novel method – Generative Critical Conversation (GCC) – in which they develop educator and researcher reflexivity and enhance criticality in enterprise and entrepreneurship education (EEE). The authors ground this method in literature from the field of educational research and reflexivity scholarship. They hybridize three methodological elements – the self-study strategy of reflecting upon recorded material; exploring lived experiences through co-generative dialogue, and a focus upon critical questioning to facilitate the development of educator-researcher reflexivity. They use illustrations from their own conversations to show how GCC opens up space over time to access and move between levels of reflexive interpretation. The authors suggest enabling conditions which support GCC and its potential as a method for developing educator-researcher reflexivity across EEE, initial teacher education, and other fields of research.

CONCLUSION

What a long journey since the entrepreneurship as a field first emerged! But there is still much work required for scholars to achieve the understanding of the entrepreneurial phenomena. Key issues and challenges still remain despite the effort and rigor of entrepreneurship research to date. All the contributors to this volume wish to share their thoughts and contributions so that entrepreneurship research can move forward. Finally, doing a good research in entrepreneurship involves expanding the frontiers of a collective knowledge, presenting alignment between the components of the research study (research question, object, methodology, conceptual framework, epistemological positioning, inclusion in the current academic conversation) and discussing up-to date philosophical and methodological issues.

REFERENCES

Bacigalupo, M., Kampylis, P., Punie, Y., and Van den Brande, G. (2016). EntreComp: The entrepreneurship competence framework. Luxembourg: Publication Office of the European Union, 10, 593884.

Berglund, H. (2007). Researching entrepreneurship as lived experience. In J. Ulhoi, and H. Neergaard (Eds.), *Handbook of qualitative research methods in entrepreneurship* (pp. 75–93). Edward Elgar Publishing.

Cantillon, R. (1755). *An essay on commerce in general.* History of Economic Thought Books.

Chalmers, D. M., and Shaw, E. (2017). The endogenous construction of entrepreneurial contexts: A practice-based perspective. *International Small Business Journal*, 35(1), 19–39.

Dana, L. P., and Dana, T. E. (2007). Collective entrepreneurship in a Mennonite community in Paraguay, *Latin American Business Review*, 8(4), 82–96.

Davidsson, P. (2003). The domain of entrepreneurship research: Some suggestions. In J. A. Katz, and D. A. Shepherd (Eds.), *Advances in entrepreneurship, firm emergence and growth* (pp. 315–372). Elsevier/JAI Press.

Gartner, W. B. (1988). "Who is an entrepreneur?" is the wrong question. *American Journal of Small Business*, 12(4), 11–32.

Gartner, W. B. (2004). Achieving "critical mess" in entrepreneurship scholarship. In J. A. Katz, and D. A. Shepherd (Eds.), *Advances in entrepreneurship, firm emergence, and growth* (pp. 199–216). Elsevier/JAI Press.

Hindle, K. (2004). Choosing qualitative methods for entrepreneurial cognition research: A canonical development approach. *Entrepreneurship Theory and Practice*, 28(6), 575–607.

Hindle, K. (2007). Teaching entrepreneurship at university: From the wrong building to the right philosophy. In A. Fayolle (Ed.), *Handbook of research in entrepreneurship education, volume 1*, (pp. 104–126). Edward Elgar Publishing.

Jacquemin, A., Germain, O., Goxe, F., Janssen, F., Lebègue, T., and Schmitt, C. (2017). Critical approaches in entrepreneurship: Aspects and stakes for the community of French researchers. *Review of Entrepreneurship*, 16(1), 19–36.

Jones, P., Apostolopoulos, N., Kakouris, A., Moon, C., Ratten, V., and Walmsley, A. (2021). Universities and entrepreneurship: Meeting the educational and social challenges. In P. Jones, N. Apostolopoulos, A. Kakouris, C. Moon, V. Ratten, and A. Walmsley (Eds.), *Universities and entrepreneurship: Meeting the educational and social challenges*, Contemporary Issues in Entrepreneurship Research, Volume 11 (pp. 1–10). Emerald.

Karatas-Ozkan, M., Anderson, A. R., Fayolle, A., Howells, J., and Condor, R. (2014). Understanding entrepreneurship: Challenging dominant perspectives and theoriz-

ing entrepreneurship through new postpositivist epistemologies, *Journal of Small Business Management*, 52(4), 589–593.
Katz, J. A. (2008). Fully mature but not fully legitimate: A different perspective on the state of entrepreneurship education. *Journal of Small Business Management*, 46(4), 550–566.
Kraus, S., Breier, M., and Dasí-Rodríguez, S. (2020). The art of crafting a systematic literature review in entrepreneurship research, *International Entrepreneurship and Management Journal*, 16, 1023–1042.
Nietzsche, F. W. (1911). The twilight of the idols, or, how to philosophise with the hammer: The antichrist, *Notes to Zarathustra; and eternal recurrence (Vol. 16)*. T. N. Foulis.
Pelly, R. D. M. (2017). Entrepreneurial opportunity: A perspective from the theory of forms. *American Journal of Management*, 17(5), 87–102.
Pelly, R. D. M., and Fayolle, A. (2020). Ethnography's answer to the plus zone challenge of entrepreneurship. In W. B. Gartner, and B. T. Teague (Eds.), *Research handbook on entrepreneurial behavior, practice and process* (pp. 82–101). Edward Elgar Publishing.
Pelly, R. D. M., and Fayolle, A. (2023). What Marquis de Sade's literary critique can teach us about entrepreneurship. *Discourses on Culture*, 18(1), 47–68.
Ramoglou, S., Gartner, W. B., and Tsang, E. W. (2020). "Who is an entrepreneur?" is (still) the wrong question. *Journal of Business Venturing Insights*, 13, e00168.
Rauch, A. (2020). Opportunities and threats in reviewing entrepreneurship theory and practice. *Entrepreneurship Theory and Practice*, 44(5), 847–860.
Say, J. B. (1861). *Traité d'économie politique*. Calmann-Lévy.
Schumpeter, J. A. (2000). Entrepreneurship as innovation. University of Illinois at Urbana-Champaign's Academy for Entrepreneurial Leadership Historical Research Reference in Entrepreneurship. https://ssrn.com/abstract=1512266.
Schwab, A., and Zhang, Z. (2019). A new methodological frontier in entrepreneurship research: Big data studies. *Entrepreneurship Theory and Practice*, 43(5) 843–854.
Shane, S. (2012). Reflections on the 2010 AMR Decade Award: Delivering on the promise of entrepreneurship as a field of research. *Academy of Management Review*, 37(1), 10–20.
Shepherd, D. A. (2015). Party on! A call for entrepreneurship research that is more interactive, activity based, cognitively hot, compassionate, and prosocial. *Journal of Business Venturing*, 30(4), 489–507.
Shepherd, D. A., and Suddaby, R. (2017). Theory building: A review and integration. *Journal of Management*, 43(1), 59–86.
Suddaby, R., Bruton, G. D., and Si, S. X. (2015). Entrepreneurship through a qualitative lens: Insights on the construction and/or discovery of entrepreneurial opportunity. *Journal of Business Venturing*, 30(1), 1–10.
Thompson, N. A., Verduyn, K., and Gartner, W. B. (2020). Entrepreneurship-as-practice: Grounding contemporary theories of practice into entrepreneurship studies. *Entrepreneurship and Regional Development*, 32(3–4), 247–256.
Trafimow, D. (2022). Generalizing across auxiliary, statistical, and inferential assumptions. *Journal for the Theory of Social Behaviour*, 52(1), 37–48.
Welter, F., Baker, T., and Wirsching, K. (2019). Three waves and counting: The rising tide of contextualization in entrepreneurship research. *Small Business Economics*, 52(2), 319–330.

Welter, F., and Gartner, W. B. (Eds.). (2016). *A research agenda for entrepreneurship and context*. Edward Elgar Publishing.

Zahra, S. A., and Wright, M. (2011). Entrepreneurship's next act. *Academy of Management Perspectives*, 67–83.

2. Acknowledging the key contribution of a great entrepreneurship researcher: Mike Wright – a communitarian entrepreneurship scholar[1]

Alain Fayolle

Michael (Mike) Wright, who was born in 1952 and passed away on November 25, 2019, was a Professor of Entrepreneurship and the Director of the Centre for Management Buy-out Research at Imperial College Business School, UK. This research centre was founded in 1986 at the Nottingham University Business School before moving to Imperial College Business School with Mike Wright when he joined in 2011 as Professor of Entrepreneurship. A few years after his recruitment he became Head of the Department for Innovation and Entrepreneurship. Before joining Imperial College, Mike was Professor of Financial Studies at Nottingham University Business School. Mike Wright was a Fellow of the British Academy of Social Sciences and the British Academy of Management. He was the Entrepreneurship Division Chair of the Academy of Management in 2011–2012. Mike held a number of honorary and/or visiting professorship positions in international universities. He was also a member of advisory boards, notably in the private equity industry.

Mike Wright was a very prolific researcher and served as an editor or a member of editorial boards in top academic journals. For example, he served two terms as an editor of *Entrepreneurship Theory and Practice*, was a joint editor of the *Journal of Management Studies*, editor elect of the *Strategic Entrepreneurship Journal* and editor of the *Academy of Management Perspective*.

I met Mike Wright for the first time in the 1990s at EM Lyon Business School where he was regularly invited by the department of Economics and Finance. From the end of the first decade of the third millennium until his death we worked together on many occasions when we were both officers of the Entrepreneurship Division of the Academy of Management and when we developed joint research projects.

This chapter is a tribute to Mike Wright. It is organized as follows. In the first section, I will highlight the influential role of Mike in the entrepreneurship field. The second section will focus on my personal relationship with him. The third section will discuss Mike Wright's social identity as an entrepreneurship scholar. Finally, I will conclude this chapter with a few words, sharing what I have understood of Mike Wright's legacy.

In this chapter, I will quote as often as possible verbatim from Mike Wright's colleagues posted on the websites of Imperial College, the Academy of Management, Entrepreneurship Division and the Institute for Small Business and Entrepreneurship.

MIKE WRIGHT AND HIS INFLUENTIAL ROLE ON THE FIELD OF ENTREPRENEURSHIP

> Mike Wright was one of the most influential entrepreneurship scholars of our time. He shaped important debates in the field with both his research contributions and his editorial work.[2]
>
> Few individuals have done more for the field, both in terms of socialization, of pushing the boundaries, and in terms of total contribution.[3]
>
> Mike, you always exemplified what the Entrepreneurship community is all about – collegiality, mentorship, hard work, dedication and fun. Your brilliant contributions will live on the literature and in the community you helped build.[4]

Mike was a great contributor to entrepreneurship literature, a mentor for young researchers, an intellectual leader and an entrepreneurship research community builder.

Mike Wright: A Great Contributor to Entrepreneurship Literature

Mike Wright's research was impactful for scholars and practitioners, generating over 88,000 cites. He published numerous books and articles on a wide range of entrepreneurship-related topics in all the leading academic journals including *Academy of Management Journal*, *Academy of Management Review*, *Academy of Management Perspective*, *Academy of Management Learning & Education*, *Strategic Management Journal*, *Review of Economics and Statistics*, *Harvard Business Review*, *Journal of Management Studies*, *Journal of Management*, *Research Policy*, *Journal of International Business Studies*, *British Journal of Management* and *Journal of Technology Transfer*. More particularly, he published many articles in the top seven entrepreneurship journals: *Journal of Business Venturing*, *Entrepreneurship Theory and Practice*, *Strategic Entrepreneurship Journal*, *Small Business Economics*, *Journal of Small Business Management*, *International Small Business Journal* and *Entrepreneurship and Regional Development*. In 2009, Mike Wright was ranked #1 worldwide for entrepreneurship publications.[5] To the best of my knowledge, very few scholars, if any, in the field of entrepreneurship have published so many articles, in so many top management and entrepreneurship journals, with so many cites.

Mike Wright: A Mentor for Young Researchers (and Sometimes for Older!)

> Over the years, Mike Wright was also a mentor to a large number of junior scholars who benefited from his intellectual breadth and academic experience. At Imperial, he was highly regarded as the Head of the Department of Innovation & Entrepreneurship and for being an extraordinarily productive academic who always impressed with his humility and work ethic.[6]

> Mike supported and encouraged many people in his productive career. You could learn a lot from studying his style and the clarity he brought to complex arguments.[7]

> Mike was a prolific scholar, an outstanding mentor, and a friend to so very many.[8]

> Mike Wright will be remembered as a co-author, mentor, and dear friend. I am grateful and indebted to Mike for all the learning moments, laughs, inspiration, and time shared with young scholars like myself. Mike was always ready to help by providing valuable advice and referring to his experiences and war stories in the time of need. He was a treasure trove of resources and tacit knowledge about our field and always a source of inspiration and a fountain of energy.[9]

> Mike was a true friend and one of the smartest and most generous scholars I've ever met. He has contributed immensely to the development of Lancaster University's Centre for Family Business, and every year he was very generously attending the annual event of our Centre offering brilliant contributions and taking part to two days of activities.[10]

> Mike was instrumental in hiring me to my first job at Nottingham and was a kind mentor, friend, and co-author. Mike was also my performance reviewer at Nottingham and was generous in his support of my career, efforts and achievements, and especially my personal development. he always gave such insightful advice. Mike had such incredible intellect and work ethic, and he leaves us with a rich legacy. I feel so sad for his passing and especially for his family. It is a tragic loss and I can only be thankful for the time I knew him in life, and the opportunities I had to grow under him.[11]

> Mike was not only a brilliant scholar and a kind person, but also a person I could trust, always giving this bit of advice that only someone who knew the world of academia inside out could give. He knew how to work with people and was often the 'glue' of teams of co-authors that he put together. He agreed to become one of my supervisors shortly after he joined Imperial College in 2011. I was doing work on corporate governance in Russia and he was still interested in this field. I remember our first supervision meetings. Mike would sit in front of his computer, halfway turned towards me, and while I was bubbling away about my progress, he would listen, comment, occasionally refer to a JMS or SMJ article from a few years ago (he literally knew by heart the content of each issue) and AT THE SAME TIME write

editorial decision letters, edit manuscripts, respond to emails, and many other things like arranging his train rides between Nottingham and London. I learned to share Mike's time with many other people. This is how Mike worked, and this is why he was so prolific. After I graduated, I continued to work with Mike and published my first paper with him, and then another paper … We went on to organize an SMS extension on state capitalism in 2018 where he did a brilliant keynote speech (pictured after), secured a contract with Oxford University Press for the Handbook on State Capitalism, amongst other projects.[12]

Mike was a wonderful mentor to me, and I will miss him. I wrote to him at the start of my PhD, not really expecting a reply given everything he does! But he still made the time to write back, direct, and encourage me. For me, that is the one aspect I will always admire – his kindness. Mike always went the extra mile to help those around him and is a role model for those of us who were fortunate enough to have interacted with him.[13]

I met Mike Wright at the Doctoral Consortium at Babson. He inspired us with his dedication and commitment to entrepreneurship.[14]

Mike was a great co-author, mentor and friend to many, including myself and many people in our field. Despite his busy schedule, he was always willing to take the time to listen and provide support. For sure, his involvement in the entrepreneurship field will have a long lasting impact on it just as his kindness and openness will be remembered by many of us.[15]

I first contacted Mike in 2006 as a doctoral student. Mike was the leading scholar in my area (academic entrepreneurship) and his support secured me a Post Doctoral grant in Norway and the opportunity to visit Nottingham University for 6 months. He introduced me to the group and provided everything I needed for a productive stay (I even borrowed his office for a short period). Since then, I have always been impressed by Mike's responsiveness and dedication to provide feedback. Even to me as a young post doc, he was always precise and well prepared to our meetings, and in all our communication throughout the years I could trust that he always responded extremely quickly and thoroughly. Given his workload and responsibilities, Mike's ability to keep his promises and deliver above expectations was extraordinary. Working with Mike has been decisive for the development of my research career in several ways. He has been a highly active and dedicated contributor on the papers we have co-authored. Through our joint work, I have learned a lot about doing high-quality research that has been of crucial importance for all my research and an important basis for supervising my own PhD students. He has been an enthusiastic promoter of our research, sharing his network and always positive to contribute in workshops, research grant applications, and special issues. I know that Mike has promoted the careers of many researchers and acted as a networker bringing together people and opportunities. His achievements extend far beyond his scientific production. As an academic, Mike was very versatile. He was working with both young and well-established scholars from across the globe, contributing to theory as well as practice, and across many different subjects. Mike was a truly complete academic, who was not resting on his laurels, but actively taking part in and sharing his experience in all parts of academic life. By his inclusive approach, combined with hard work and dedication to research, Mike is a role model for all academics and beyond.[16]

> Mike Wright was always very generous with his time and advice. In my view and experience, Mike was very different intellectually from most management scholars in Great Britain and United States of America. He was very well read, possessed broad and deep knowledge of social science and economics literature in general … I am forever grateful for Mike for his wise advice and guidance.[17]

Mike Wright: An Intellectual Leader

Mike Wright has shaped influential debates in the field of entrepreneurship and has oriented research and researchers' mindset in several areas. For example, he made an important contribution to academic entrepreneurship literature examining issues in relation to:[18]

- Technology transfer offices (TTOs) and commercialization of university intellectual property.
- Performance of university TTOs.
- Taking stock of academic entrepreneurship in Europe.
- Technology transfer and universities' spin-out strategies.
- Science parks and incubation strategies.
- Incubator and incubation mechanisms.
- University high-tech spin-out companies.

Another research area in which Mike Wright's contribution has been very influential relates to the importance of context and contextualization in entrepreneurship research.[19] Mike Wright, and other colleagues such as Friederike Welter or Shaker Zahra, always considered that contextual (and process) issues were at the focus of entrepreneurship research. He notably wrote articles highlighting the importance of context in several instances (entrepreneurial innovation, buyouts, family enterprise).

A final important research area I would like to mention here refers to the relevance and the "raison d'être" of entrepreneurship research. Our field actually enjoys academic acceptance and legitimacy as a scholarly discipline. Entrepreneurship research has grown rapidly in its scope, rigour and impact (Wiklund et al., 2019). However, there are debates regarding what relevance in entrepreneurship research means, how to achieve it and how to best communicate research issues and results to the diverse stakeholders of the entrepreneurship field. Mike Wright and his colleagues discussed such issues and offered interesting perspectives to deal with key research challenges and improve the relevance of entrepreneurship research.

Mike Wright: An Entrepreneurship Research Community Builder

In addition to his intellectual leadership in the entrepreneurship research community, Mike Wright played a key role as a community builder, notably in the 2008–2013 period when he was an officer of the Academy of Management, Entrepreneurship Division. Mike was elected in 2008 for a five-year term starting with a PDW Chair position (2008–2009) and becoming successively, over the following years, Program Chair (2009–2010), Chair-Elect (2010–2011), Chair (2011–2012) and Past President (2012–2013) of the Entrepreneurship Division of the Academy of Management. During this time, the Entrepreneurship Division included around 2,800 members. The Division experienced rapid growth and was strongly engaged in the way to develop internationally. International membership increased by 55.6% from 2006 to 2011 and in 2011 there were 1,217 international members, almost as many as the 1,534 American members.[20]

However, "as the entrepreneurship division grew faster than ever, the governance structure was unable to keep up and the situation was exacerbated by the anti-bureaucratic culture within the division ... In addition, there was extensive confusion with the leadership of the division concerning the compilation and writing of the 2007 5-year Report".[21] Under such circumstances, the report was not finished on time and it received a very negative feedback from the AoM Division and Interest Group Relations (DIGR) committee.

Mike Wright, as an elected officer of the entrepreneurship division, collaborated with colleagues like Timothy Stearn (Chair 2007–2008), Ronald Mitchell (Chair 2008–2009), Eileen Fisher (Chair 2009–2010) and Per Davidsson (Chair 2011–2012) to solve the grave and crippling concerns raised in the 2007 DIGR committee feedback. Moreover, Mike Wright played a key role in internationalizing the leadership of the entrepreneurship division. Mike was one of the first non-US Chairs (with Eileen Fisher, Canadian and Per Davidsson, Swedish working in Australia). Carlo Salvato, Italian, was elected in 2012 (Chair 2015–2016), Alain Fayolle, French, in 2013 (Chair 2016–2017) and Christina Guenther, German, in 2014 (Chair 2017–2018).

MY PERSONAL RELATIONSHIP WITH MIKE WRIGHT

As mentioned in the introduction to this chapter, I met Mike Wright for the first time in the 1990s at EM Lyon Business School. However, our professional collaboration really started in 2010 when I was elected as a Representative-at-Large of the entrepreneurship division of the Academy of Management. At that time, we sometimes met regarding matters concerning our AoM division. From 2011, we worked together on research or institutional projects. I would like to elaborate on some of them chronologically.

FNEGE Academic Training Program: "Meet the Editors" of *JBV*, *ET&P*, *E&RD*, *SEJ*, *SBE*, *JSBM*, *ISBJ* and *IJEI*

In 2011, I was asked by the *Délégué Général* of the French National Foundation for Management Education (FNEGE), Pierre-Louis Dubois, to design and coordinate an Academic Training Program dedicated to a young entrepreneurship faculty in order to help researchers with how to write a scientific paper and get published in top entrepreneurship journals. This event, also supported by the French entrepreneurship and innovation association (AEI) was offered in January 2012, 23–26, one year after the first "Meet the Editors" seminar organized by the French association in marketing (AFM).

As keynote speakers, I invited Mike Wright (Editor-elect of *Strategic Entrepreneurship Journal*), Nicole Coviello (Field Editor of *Journal of Business Venturing*), Alistair Anderson (Editor of *Entrepreneurship and Regional Development*), Friederike Welter (Associate Editor of *Entrepreneurship Theory and Practice*), Roy Thurik (Associate Editor of *Small Business Economics*), Hermann Frank (Associate Editor of *Journal of Small Business Management*), Robert Blackburn (Editor of *International Journal of Small Business*) and Gerard McElwee (Editor of *International Journal of Entrepreneurship and Innovation*).

Mike Wright was the first speaker, addressing two key topics on Monday, January 23, 2012. In the morning he gave a lecture on: "Submitting a paper to a top journal" and in the afternoon he shared what he had learned from his experiences as an editor and an author on the "Review process". He was available in the evening and the following day to interact with some participants[22] to answer their questions or develop complementary arguments. On Tuesday morning, we had breakfast together and we discussed the possibility of working together on a book project based roughly on the main topics addressed in the seminar.

Edward Elgar Publishing book: *How to Get Published in the Best Entrepreneurship Journals*[23]

As discussed previously the idea of the book came up in a discussion Mike Wright and I had at breakfast on Tuesday 21, 2012, during the FNEGE and AEI Academic Training Program. The book project was spread over two and a half years (2012–2014) and was published in 2014. The first task we tackled was to design the content of the book and to invite (and convince) the most experienced scholars on the different topics we wanted to develop to contribute to the book. In the end 19 contributors came on board, most of them being (or having been) editors or associate editors of top entrepreneurship journals, such as David Audretsch, Per Davidsson, Robert Blackburn, Garry Bruton, Andrew

Corbett, Nicole Coviello, Dimo Dimow, Hermann Frank, Friederike Welter and obviously Mike Wright. Some of them (five) were keynote speakers at the FNEGE and AEI seminar. As editors of the book, Mike Wright and I regularly met to share the workload, and our comments/suggestions after a double assessment of each submitted chapter.[24]

Danny Miller wrote the Foreword of the book and recognized its usefulness for young researchers by claiming: "Life would have been so much easier had I had the benefit of this terrific book. It provides concrete and actionable advice on all aspects of publishing in the field of entrepreneurship, and indeed other domains of management. … There is no question that the sound advice given here by Audretsch, Corbett, Fayolle, Honig, Wright and other stars in the field will focus readers on the essentials so vital in today's highly competitive and ever more exacting publishing environment."[25]

Throughout the editing process, I was greatly impressed by at least three of Mike's skills: his high level of creativity, his speedy responses to questions, or requests or assessing papers,[26] and finally the scope and quality of his academic network.

Entrepreneurship Division Leadership Duties

As soon as I was elected as an officer of the Entrepreneurship Division of the Academy of Management for a five-year term (2013–2018), I was fortunate enough to have Mike Wright by my side. Throughout these five years, Mike shared his thoughts, gave wise advice, answered my tricky questions and provided assistance and support. I remember, in the first year of my term I had to raise money for the division, identifying and convincing potential sponsors. Mike helped me by suggesting some names and guiding me in the best way to get in touch with them and to deliver the most significant arguments depending on each specific case. More importantly, when I was Chair of the Entrepreneurship Division, I had to manage the 2017 five-year survey and write the report. Mike was greatly experienced in this kind of work, being the author of the 2012 five-year report. There was a lot of pressure surrounding this because every officer knew the negative feedback and the criticisms addressed in 2007 by the AoM Division and Interest Group Relations (DIGR) committee. First, Mike accepted my invitation to be a member of the Entrepreneurship Division Review Committee and in this role gave me very useful information and advice, notably, to conduct the membership survey among almost 3,500 of our division members, analyse the results and develop key implications. He also carefully read the draft versions of the report and suggested many changes. His whole contribution to this 2017 survey and report was extremely significant and resulted in very positive feedback from the AoM DIGR.

Visiting, Conference Invitations and Journal Special Issues

During the last decade I invited Mike Wright a couple of times, as a visiting professor, to emlyon business school. He gave keynote lectures to PhD students, faculty members and external researchers. He also reviewed research papers by PhD students and provided them with insightful comments and suggestions.

I invited Mike to give lectures in international conferences or workshops I organized at emlyon business school (for example, the 2016 ESU conference) or I co-organized with my colleague and past PhD student, Wadid Lamine, at Toulouse Business School (such as the International Research Conference on Science and Technology Entrepreneurship Education held on April 27–28, 2017). Mike was also a keynote speaker in several Professional Development Workshops (PDWs) Wadid Lamine and I organized at Academy of Management conferences.

Some of these conferences were good opportunities to discuss potential special issue projects in relation to the main topics addressed in those events. As a consequence, alongside Mike and other colleagues I edited two special issues with *Technological Forecasting and Social Change* (Klofsten et al., 2019) and the *Journal of Technology Transfer* (Lamine et al., 2018).

WHAT WAS THE SOCIAL IDENTITY OF MIKE WRIGHT AS AN ENTREPRENEURSHIP SCHOLAR: DARWINIAN, COMMUNITARIAN OR MISSIONARY?

In this section, I would like to question the social identity of Mike Wright, based on what I have learned from this review of his professional career, his role and potential impact on the entrepreneurship community and, finally, my personal relationship with him.

A fundamental concern we have at a personal and professional level relates to the question: "What is my role in society?" that can be turned into: "What is my role in society as an entrepreneur?" or "What is my role in society as an entrepreneurship scholar?" This is a fundamental concern because "An identity is like a compass helping us steer a course of interaction in a sea of social meaning" (Burke & Reitzes, 1981: 91). Social identity shapes our decisions, behaviours and professional strategies regardless of our activity. Whoever we are, being an entrepreneur or entrepreneurship scholar thinking about our role in society and acting accordingly is a key driver for our professional career.

To examine the issue of Mike Wright's social identity, I was inspired by an *Academy of Management Journal* article I read and appreciated some years ago. Emmanuelle Fauchart and Marc Gruber, using social identity theory, explore the identities, behaviours and actions of 49 entrepreneurs in the industry of sports-related equipment. Among the results of their analysis, three pure types of firm founder identities have been identified (Fauchart & Gruber, 2011).

Darwinian Identity

This is the first main type observed in Fauchart and Gruber's sample. Entrepreneurs who belong to this category focus their attention, time and energy on establishing strong and profitable firms. They are entrepreneurs who devote resources to activities aimed at ensuring the firm's success. Darwinians pay great attention mainly to their companies, competitors and businesses whatever the sport domain in which they operate.[27]

Communitarian Identity

These entrepreneurs are primarily and strongly engaged in a sport domain. Their main orientation is to contribute to their community with their innovative products and they appreciate the support from their community members. They perceive their initiatives and activities as important for the development of the community and for achieving recognition by their peers.[28]

Missionary Identity

Missionary entrepreneurs believe that their firms can be seen as powerful agents of change in society. Their engagement in new firm creation aims at establishing a platform from which they can pursue their political visions and advance particular causes, generally of a social or environmental nature. Missionaries strongly believe that their actions can positively affect the well-being of others and seek to act in a responsible, transparent and empathetic manner to make the world better.[29]

I believe that these three types of social identity could be identified not only for entrepreneurs or new firm founders, but also for other categories of profession. This is why I have tried to apply this typology when thinking about Mike Wright's social identity as an entrepreneurship scholar. To my knowledge, Mike was not a Darwinian, that is to say someone focusing mainly on his level of performance in research, his number of publications and citations and aiming at becoming the indisputable leader in the entrepreneurship field. Mike Wright was a modest and humble scholar and I never heard him engaging in somewhat self-centred or egocentric talk. Mike Wright was not a missionary entrepreneurship scholar even though he thought that the "raison d'être" of entrepreneurship research was to bring useful results and knowledge to society. He was also conscious of his own limitations in acting as an agent of change in society. To me, Mike Wright was a great communitarian entrepreneurship scholar. As I attempted to illustrate in the previous section, Mike was a mentor highly appreciated by his young and older peers; he was a research team builder and in this role he often helped his team members to grow; he strongly contributed to entrepreneurship literature; and he was an entrepreneurship community builder and a recognized leader. Moreover, Mike was someone who was always smiling and in a good mood, open-minded, benevolent and generous.

CONCLUSION

It is "what we think" and "what we write" that matters in our academic world. Moreover, we need to take care to avoid losing our way. Mike Wright, during the last decades of his career as an entrepreneurship scholar, never lost his way. He published extensively not only in his privileged area of academic entrepreneurship, and his publications will stimulate many entrepreneurship researchers for years. This is certainly an important part of his legacy. However, in my opinion, Mike Wright leaves a broader legacy. As a passionate researcher, an inspiring guide for the whole entrepreneurship community and someone with a high level of professionalism and conscientiousness, Mike inspired powerful ways to think, design and research different forms of entrepreneurship. In particular, he shared his thoughts and experiences on why and how to do research in our field and how to improve the legitimacy of our discipline, suggesting an interesting balance between relevance and rigour in research.

NOTES

1. This chapter comes from an article published in the *Revue de l'Entrepreneuriat* (Fayolle A. (2021). Mike Wright: A communitarian entrepreneurship scholar. *Revue de l'Entrepreneuriat.* DOI 10.3917/entre1.pr.0033).
2. Rod Ball, Deputy Director Centre for Management Buy-out Research (CMBOR) at Imperial College (from the website of Imperial College).
3. Julio de Castro, IE Business School, Madrid (from the website of Academy of Management, Entrepreneurship Division).
4. Helena Yli-Renko, Llyod Greif Center for Entrepreneurial Studies, Marshall School of Business, University of Southern California (from the website of Academy of Management, Entrepreneurship Division).
5. Professor Nigel Culkin, ISBE Fellow (from the website of the Institute for Small Business and Entrepreneurship).
6. Rod Ball, Deputy Director Centre for Management Buy-out Research (CMBOR) at Imperial College.
7. Professor Nigel Culkin, ISBE Fellow.

8. Dawn de Tienne, Professor, Colorado State University, Chair of Academy of Management Entrepreneurship Division.
9. Yuliya Snihur, Associate Professor, Toulouse Business School.
10. Alfredo De Massis, Free University of Bozen-Bolzano and Lancaster University.
11. Mathew Hughes, Professor of Entrepreneurship and Innovation, Loughborough University, UK.
12. Anna Grosman, Lecturer in Innovation and Entrepreneurship, Loughborough University London.
13. Siddharth Vedula, Assistant Professor, Babson College.
14. Manjula Salimath, Professor, G. Brint Ryan College of Business, University of North Texas.
15. Mirjam Knockaert, Professor, Ghent University.
16. Einar Rasmussen, Professor, Nord University Business School, Bodo, Norway.
17. Bat Batjargal, Professor, Oklahoma State University.
18. See e.g. (2004). Critical junctures in the development of university high-tech spin-out companies. *Research Policy*, 33(1), 147–175 (co-authored with A. Vohora and A. Lockett); (2005). Science parks and incubators: observations, synthesis and future research. *Journal of Business Venturing*, 20(2), 165–182 (co-authored with P. Phan and D. Siegel); (2005). Resources capabilities, risk capital and the creation of university spin-out companies. *Research Policy*, 34(7), 1043–1057 (co-authored with A. Lockett); (2005). Spinning out new ventures: a typology of incubation strategies from European research institutions. *Journal of Business Venturing*, 20(2), 183–216 (co-authored with B. Clarysse, A. Lockett, E. Van de Velde and A. Vohora); (2011). 30 years after the Bayh–Dole: reassessing academic entrepreneurship. *Research Policy*, 40(8), 1045–1057 (co-authored with R. Grimaldi, M. Kenney and D. Siegel); (2007). *Academic entrepreneurship in Europe*. Edward Elgar Publishing; (2003). Technology transfer and universities' spin-out strategies. *Small Business Economics*, 20(2), 185–200 (co-authored with A. Lockett and S. Frankin); (2005). Assessing the relative performance of UK university technology transfer offices: parametric and non-parametric evidence. *Research Policy*, 34(3), 369–384.
19. See e.g. (2001). The focus of entrepreneurial research: contextual and process issues. *Entrepreneurship Theory and Practice*, 25(4), 57–80 (co-authored with D. Ucbasaran and P. Westhead); (2014). Entrepreneurial innovation: the importance of context. *Research Policy*, 43(7), 1097–1108 (co-authored with E. Autio, M. Kenney, P. Mustar and D. Siegel); (2011). Entrepreneurship's next act. *Academy of Management Perspectives*, 25(4), 67–83 (co-authored with S. Zahra); (2014). Contextualization and the advancement of entrepreneurship research. *International Small Business Journal*, 32(5) (co-authored with S. Zahra and S. Abdelgawad).
20. ENT Division 2012 five-year Report (from the website of AoM, Entrepreneurship Division).

21. Hans Landström and Jon Lindhe (2016). A history of the Entrepreneurship Division of the Academy of Management. https://ent.aom.org/committees/history-of-entrepreneurship, 16.
22. 21 young researchers from French universities and business schools registered at this "Meet the Editors" seminar.
23. Fayolle A., and Wright M. (2014), *How to get published in the best entrepreneurship journals. A guide to steer your academic career*. Edward Elgar Publishing.
24. The book finally includes 14 chapters.
25. From the Foreword by Danny Miller.
26. Very often, Mike returned detailed and relevant comments a couple of hours after I sent him a submitted chapter.
27. Ibid., p. 942.
28. Ibid., pp. 943–944.
29. Ibid., pp. 944–945.

REFERENCES

Burke, P. J., and Reitzes, D. C. (1981). The link between identity and role performance. *Social Psychology Quarterly*, 44(2), 83–92.

Fauchart, E. and Gruber, M. (2011). Darwinians, communitarians, and missionaries: The role of founder identity in entrepreneurship. *Academy of Management Journal*, 54(5), 935–957.

Fayolle A., and Wright M. (2014). *How to get published in the best entrepreneurship journals. A guide to steer your academic career*. Edward Elgar Publishing.

Klofsten M., Fayolle A., Guerrero M., Mian S., Urbano D., and Wright M. (2019). The entrepreneurial university as driver for economic growth and social change: Key strategic challenge. *Technological Forecasting and Social Change*, 141, 149–158.

Lamine W., Mian S., Fayolle A., Wright M., Klofsten M., and Etzkowitz H. (2018). Technology business incubation mechanisms and sustainable regional development. *Journal of Technology Transfer*, 43(5), 1121–1141.

Wiklund J., Wright M., and Zahra S. (2019). Conquering relevance: Entrepreneurship research's grand challenge. *Entrepreneurship Theory and Practice*, 43(3), 419–436.

PART I

Exploring philosophical issues in entrepreneurship research

3. From better answers to better questions

Stratos Ramoglou

> As long as the alchemists merely sought the philosopher's stone and aimed at finding the art of making gold, all their endeavors were fruitless; it was only when people restricted themselves to seemingly less valuable questions that they created chemistry. (Ludwig Boltzmann, 1974: 14)

Who is an entrepreneur? Why do some but not others recognise opportunities? Why do only a few exploit the opportunities they recognise? How can entrepreneurs know an otherwise unknowable future? What makes entrepreneurs so different?

These questions about "the entrepreneur" sound important and "big" (Fayolle, Le Pontois & Pelly, this volume). It is therefore unsurprising that considerable academic resources have been devoted to answering them (Gartner, 1989; Ramoglou, Gartner & Tsang, 2020). In this quest, a multitude of state-of-the-art research tools have been utilised, and genetics research has emerged as the most promising way of deciphering the presumed "secrets" of the "entrepreneurial nature" (Nicolaou & Shane, 2009; Nicolaou, Phan & Stephan, 2021). Yet, the success of such efforts is questionable, and we still do not know what is so "special" about entrepreneurs (van der Loos et al., 2013; Rietveld, Slob & Thurik, 2021). Likewise, entrepreneurial alertness is routinely posited as a "rare gift" that enables only a few to recognise opportunities in an otherwise uncertain future (Moore, McIntyre & Lavinich, 2021; Neneh, 2019; Shane & Venkataraman, 2000). However, years of research have not revealed any special quality of alertness, and recent work suggests that mystified notions about such a quality originate in problematic questions (see Ramoglou, 2021a; Ramoglou, 2021b).

In this chapter, I argue that we should be more cautious with the questions that we ask. Rather than being on the lookout for "great" answers to supposedly "big" questions, we should be far more reflective of whether we are dealing with *genuine* – let alone "big" – questions in the first place. My argument is that philosophical reflection on the tacit presuppositions motivating the emergence and perseverance of seemingly important questions – such as the question of "the nature of entrepreneurs" – may reveal that they are simply nothing but pseudo-questions. That is, questions that promise to shed light on deeply-held secrets of reality, when there is actually no discovery to be made; only problematic assumptions sustaining impressions to the contrary.

On the face of it, the very act of silencing questions by eradicating problematic assumptions does not seem to be a sufficiently constructive contribution. But this superficial impression should be resisted. If a question is flawed, it only makes sense to look for better questions – not better answers to a flawed question. Consider, for example, questions about the detection of ether (Helrich, 2012). If physicists were only looking for ways of detecting this supposedly real substance, they would never reject what was nothing but a wrong question (ether simply does not exist).

Moreover, weeding out bad questions does not only *free* intellectual attention from misguided research enterprises; as importantly, hygienic interventions are also positively constructive. For, in the very process of understanding why a question is ill-conceived, we inevitably gain a clearer understanding of key concepts. In turn, enhanced clarity harbours the power of reorienting our scholarly attention toward better questions. That is, questions that do not only *sound* great, but questions that *are* great. For the only questions that are *really* great are the ones that promise to improve our understanding of the world.

I illustrate my argument drawing on a particularly recalcitrant question since the inception of entrepreneurship as a scientific field of inquiry, viz., how do entrepreneurs differ from non-entrepreneurs (Gartner, 1989; Ramoglou, 2013; Ramoglou, Gartner & Tsang, 2020)? Although the focus of this chapter is on this question, we will also consider other problematic questions at the core of our scholarly discourse: (1) "Why do some but not others recognize opportunities?" (Ramoglou, 2021a), and (2) "How can successful entrepreneurs know opportunities in an otherwise uncertain world?" (Ramoglou, 2021b). This will help reinforce the point that we have yet to fully come to terms with the extent to which much of our scholarship is often held captive by assumptions that give rise to misleading questions.

THE SEARCH FOR BETTER ANSWERS TO A FLAWED QUESTION[1]

The Past

The observation that it is only a handful of individuals who become entrepreneurs has motivated one of the most intractable and notorious questions in the scholarly study of entrepreneurship (Aldrich, 2005; Swedberg, 2000), viz., the question of the entrepreneur: What are the essential qualities that make entrepreneurial action possible? Logically unpacked, this question means:

what are the necessary qualities whose (presupposed) absence explains why non-entrepreneurs cannot act entrepreneurially (Ramoglou, 2013)?

The question of the entrepreneur was seminally critiqued by Gartner (1989) in his paper headed with the aphorism "'Who is an entrepreneur?' is a wrong question". Gartner rejected the view that enterprising individuals possess some "inborn natural capacity" as opposed to "the rest of us mortals" who lack "what it takes" (Cunningham & Lischeron, 1991: 46–47), effectively reorienting entrepreneurship research toward contextual and process views (Gartner, 1985; 1989; 1993; 1995) (see also Fayolle, 2007). From this standpoint, just as there is nothing to be learnt about dancers aside from the ways that they dance, there is nothing to be found in individuals who just exercise entrepreneurial action: "an entrepreneur is what an entrepreneur does" (Casson, 2003: 19). And with respect to the explanation of non-enterprising individuals, Gartner's critique encouraged the view that they would also have acted entrepreneurially had situational contingencies been favourable, akin to the non-dancing individuals who also would have danced if the song had been right or the audio fine-tuned.

Although Gartner's critique is oriented toward an unsuccessful empirical programme of the era, the notion that entrepreneurs must be endowed with "special inner qualities" also runs through important theoretical work on entrepreneurship. For example, von Mises tackles the puzzling contrast that "there are in the market pacemakers and others who only imitate the procedures of their more agile fellow citizens" by alluding to the "inequality of men [*sic*]" (1963: 255). Similarly, we may find Bentham, back in the early nineteenth century, contrasting entrepreneurs with the "common herd of men [*sic*]" who presumably lack the required "degree of courage" (1839: 23). In a similar vein, Casson addresses the fact that only a minority of people become entrepreneurs as follows:

> A scarcity of personal qualities usually occurs, not because everyone has only a little of the quality, but because only a few people have the quality and many people do not have it at all. In other words, scarcity is associated with skewness in the distribution of qualities between people. It is the possession of scarce qualities which confers an advantage on some people in becoming an entrepreneur. (Casson, 1982/2003: 29)

Gartner's (1989) critique undermined a once-thriving research genre into special entrepreneurial qualities. Yet, the question of the entrepreneur returned with a vengeance following Shane and Venkataraman's thesis that so many people fail to "respond to the situational cues of opportunities" (2000: 219). The chief reason for the resurgence of the question of the entrepreneur was the argument about the non-uniform exploitation of "entrepreneurial opportunities", since it has anticipated the (largely intuitive) concerns raised by mere attention to the non-uniform engagement in entrepreneurial activity (Mitchell, et al., 2007: 3). In an important sense, "opportunity" serves as a "controlling factor" recovering confidence in the existence of differences at the individual level of analysis. "Often opportunities are there for anyone to notice; yet, thousands or even millions of persons do not notice them. Why?" (Baron, 2007: 107). To express the puzzlement in recasting Gartner's cherished analogy of dancing: the music is on, the floor is spacious, but still, there are only a handful that dance. Why?

The Present

Entrepreneurial genes?

In response to this why-question, modern-day researchers searching for unique entrepreneurial qualities are typically quick to distance themselves from the answers yielded by researchers working in the "trait" era criticised by Gartner. Attributing earlier failures to the "lack of rigorous and appropriate research methods" (Thornton, 1999: 22), they seek better answers to the question by investing in issues of method and technique (Baum et al., 2007; Baron, 2004; Nofal et al., 2018). Most noticeably, the research programme into the biological foundations of entrepreneurial action utilising state-of-the-art research methods and techniques stands out. For example, Nicolaou and Shane (2009: 3) draw researchers' attention to "quantitative and molecular genetics" to highlight the potential salience of information "encoded in DNA and transmitted biologically ... to explain people's tendency to engage in entrepreneurial activity" (ibid: 2), calling special attention to genes DRD4 and DRD2.

It is worth mentioning that, from a philosophy of science standpoint, the search for answers in genetic mechanisms is an improvement compared to the answers typically offered during the trait era. The reason is that contemporary research marks a departure from earlier research agendas fashioned with tautological formulations, such as "risk-taking", "optimism", or "control locus". The candidate answers advanced in the pre-Gartnerian era were essentially instrumental in crafting predictive research projects but were theoretically vacuous (see also Nicolaou et al., 2008). Note that to say that entrepreneurs engage in risk-taking behaviours because they are "risk-takers" is no more enlightening than the "explanation" that "smoking opium puts people to sleep because of its dormative powers" (Lipton, 2004: 59).

In spite of the early optimism encouraged by turning the lens to genetics, results are rather disappointing and the question of the entrepreneur remains unaddressed (Kerr, Kerr & Xu, 2018; Ramoglou et al., 2020; van der Loos et al., 2013). As put by Rietveld et al:

> Despite promises that were solidly backed up with ex ante power calculations, attempts to identify specific variants underlying the heritable variation in entrepreneurship have until now been unsuccessful (2021: 1303).

Yet, in spite of the limited success of the relevant research agenda, Rietveld and colleagues argue that "this search will eventually be successful" (2021: 1303). Hitherto, shortcomings "hampering the identification of associations between genetic variants and entrepreneurship" (idem) are treated as fundamentally methodological and it is suggested that genetics research will eventually shed light on the "extent [to which] different mechanisms and cognitive processes are involved in the identification and exploitation of business opportunities" (2021: 1313).

In short, despite the repeated failures to answer the question of the entrepreneur, belief in the question's soundness remains firm and problems are identified at the level of method. What is hardly ever scrutinised is the most foundational assumption that entrepreneurs must be intrinsically different from non-entrepreneurs. The metaphysical rigidity underlying this scientific attitude has been chastised by Wittgenstein as follows: "On hunting for the phenomenon and not finding it, we say that it has merely not yet been found" (Wittgenstein, 1982: 15); "'We still don't know; but it is knowable and it is only a matter of time before we get to know it!' As if that went without saying" (Wittgenstein, 1998: 46).

We turn to explain that the question of the entrepreneur is doomed to fail regardless of the choice of method or the sophistication of our research tools. The reason is that the search for better answers is fruitless when these are meant to tackle a flawed question. As we will examine, the problem is not methodological but ontological. The deeply held assumption that entrepreneurs must be endowed with something "further" emerges as sound only against the backdrop of a fallacious mode of reasoning.

The structure of the core why-question

The question of the entrepreneur concerns the methodological ways of deciphering the presupposed distinctive qualities that enable entrepreneurial behaviour. However, the conviction that such endowments must exist in the first place emerges as a response to the following why-question:

> Much research in the entrepreneurship field has focused on the person of the entrepreneur, asking the question, why do certain individuals start firms when others, under similar conditions, do not? Asking why has led us to answer with who: Why

> did X start a venture? Because X has a certain inner quality or qualities. (Gartner, 1989: 47)

Note that the why-question does not lead directly to the question of the entrepreneur. The latter presupposes a deterministic response to the basic why-question: it is only a few who act entrepreneurially because only a few can do what others cannot. It is this tacit answer to the empirical why-question that in turn lends credence to the question of the entrepreneur. Akin to Gartner, Alvarez and Barney similarly document the logic underlying the emergence of the question of the entrepreneur using "discovery lenses" as follows:

> In order to explain why entrepreneurs [are] able to exploit opportunities while non entrepreneurs are not [that] discovery theory must necessarily assume that entrepreneurs who discover opportunities are significantly different from others in their ability to either see opportunities or, once they are seen, to exploit these opportunities. (2007: 14; emphasis added)

Once again, the mere empirical fact that only a few act entrepreneurially does not directly lead to the question of the entrepreneur. It is the deterministic answer that entrepreneurs can do what non-entrepreneurs (supposedly) cannot that makes discovery theorists conclude "necessarily" that the former "are significantly different from others".

Interestingly enough, the logical structure of this deterministic mode of reasoning has been captured by Anscombe as follows: "[i]f an effect occurs in one case and a similar effect does not occur in an apparently similar case, there must be a relevant further difference" (1993: 88). This mode of reasoning has been attacked by Wittgenstein as follows:

> [t]oday, in case we actually discovered two seeds which we could not distinguish … we should look frantically for a difference. – But in other circumstances we might give this up – give up looking for a difference. This would be a tremendous thing to do – as great as recognising indeterminacy. We would no longer look for the difference, and so we would no longer say there must be a difference. (1993: 411)

Wittgenstein's critique is far-fetched. The possibility of spontaneous actualisation of dissimilar effects despite the existence of identical causal structures is theoretically possible. However, it cannot be the most plausible mode of explanation when we deal with entities for which we have no good reason to expect spontaneous responses. For example, it would be a manifestation of extreme scepticism to say that there is no causal difference when, say, only one metal responds to the triggering presence of a magnet. In the absence of other explanations, we are simply forced by reason to infer that one piece of metal is ferrous as opposed to the other that lacks the requisite powers.

In such highly controlled contexts, the causally deterministic mindset holds water. But the context of entrepreneurship is dramatically different. In other words, the problem is not that the causally deterministic mode of inference never holds water. The problem is that it cannot be meaningfully applied in the context of entrepreneurial action. Let me explain.

The fallaciousness of the question of the entrepreneur

In the previous section, we conceded that it makes sense to infer the presence of variously ferrous entities when only one and not the other responds to the triggering presence of a magnet. But does it make sense to talk about entrepreneurial action as the causal outcome of something external? Relatedly, is it sensible to conclude that entrepreneurs must possess something "further" to explain the non-uniformity of events of entrepreneurial action? Such a mode of inference does not work well when studying the behaviour of human agents. The reason is that, unlike ferrous metals that predictably respond to the presence of magnetic forces, human behaviour is not predictable. Humans do not simply respond to external forces or triggers. They exercise agency.

If entrepreneurial action is an expression of human agency, we should recognise its fundamental contingency: (1) the individuals who acted entrepreneurially need not have acted thus; and that (2) the individuals who did not act entrepreneurially could have acted thus. The acknowledgement of the contingency of entrepreneurial action entails that we will never discover some "entrepreneurial gene" capable of answering the "question of the entrepreneur", viz., why some are able to do what others aren't. The reason is that entrepreneurs exercise a widely held human potential. To phrase this using possible world semantics, there is a possible world in which the entrepreneurs and non-entrepreneurs of our world are, respectively, non-entrepreneurs and entrepreneurs.

Besides philosophical arguments, the counterfactual nature of entrepreneurial action can be corroborated once we reflect on what might be involved when we talk about the "exploitation of discovered opportunities" (Shane & Venkataraman, 2000). Entrepreneurs may routinely talk about the discovery of opportunities in the manner in which they would about the discovery of empirical things, say, a dollar-bill on the sidewalk. Yet, what they typically mean is that they discovered a promising idea (cf. Davidsson, 2015). As suggested in Ramoglou and McMullen's (2022) linguistic analysis, when entrepreneurs say "this opportunity exists", they do not point to anything; rather, the ordinary logic of the expression is "I believe that the imagined state of the world in which I succeed by doing so-and-so can actualize". Opportunities are, quite simply, nothing more than (desirable) possibilities (McMullen et al., 2024). Once these clarifications have been made, it takes a moment's reflection to clearly appreciate that humans do not "react" to ideas. They (may) act entrepreneurially only if they believe that it is possible such and such a new venture idea will lead to desirable entrepreneurial outcomes. But such beliefs cannot be the causal manifestation of a different genetic structure.

Entrepreneurial action is not the manifestation of some "hidden" genetic or psychological "enabler". It is an expression of the normativity of intentional human action (Dimov et al., 2021; Harré & Tissaw, 2005): Humans decide whether they ought to act entrepreneurially. And pro-action decisions are not expressions of causal mechanisms obeying the regularities we observe in the natural world. They are expressions of the first-person perspective that a distanced, third-person study of entrepreneurship fails to grasp (McMullen & Shepherd, 2006; Ramoglou & McMullen, 2022). Importantly, these first-person stances are ontologically irreducible to biological or personality traits (Dimov et al., 2021; Searle, 1983). They are based on quite complex and subtle understandings, themselves made possible by what is commonly described by Wittgensteinian philosophers as grammar. This grammar involves "all kinds of schemata, conventions, rules and so on, which the people who live this kind of life use to guide their meaning-making and management, consciously or unconsciously" (Harré, 2009: 134) (Harré, 2004; Harré & Tissaw, 2005). From this nuanced understanding of human action, to "dig deeper" for the appropriate "genetic makeup" is to simply misconstrue the phenomenon of entrepreneurship – if not, more broadly, what it means to be human.

To recap, the fact that it is only some and not others that act entrepreneurially does not license the conclusion that the former must be somehow endowed. There are no "hidden" entrepreneurial genes or necessary psychological traits. Rather, entrepreneurs exercise a widely held agentic potential simply because they happen to believe that they can succeed entrepreneurially. And their belief is due to the way that they view the world – and worldviews are not rooted in genes, or traits, but in grammars.

TOWARD BETTER QUESTIONS

From the Question of Essence to Questions of Agency

While a deterministic explanation of the entrepreneurs versus non-entrepreneurs contrast encourages the search for "deep" essentialist differences, paying attention to the logic of human agency we can no longer suppose that it must be "personality factors [rooted in genes] which explain why one person will respond to an opportunity when others will not" (Casson, 2005: 424). Once we bring front and centre the experiential substratum of action-conducive beliefs, we simply can no longer presume that entrepreneurial activity is the effect of some special constitution that allows (if not compels) (only) entrepreneurs to respond quasi-automatically to the triggering presence of something named "opportunity". Entrepreneurs do not react to opportunities in the same way that (comparatively) unstructured objects respond to external stimuli. Their choices are the end-product of a wealth of underlying understandings dictating that they should not abstain from exercising entrepreneurial action: entrepreneurs exercise entrepreneurial agency, because they have underlying reasons to believe that they should do so rather than not. According to Metcalfe: "Entrepreneurs believe something that nobody else believes" (2004: 167). We need to know why it is only some who believe in more widely perceived opportunities. We ought to actively seek access to the ways through which deeper belief-strata condition the ways through which future world-states are experienced as possible or not.

Moreover, remember that the "Why only some and not others?" question channelled research attention exclusively to "some" in search for what "others" must be lacking. Having recovered the logic of entrepreneurial agency, however, we may not equally mindlessly slide into presuming an underlying isomorphism of powers. Even further, we may also discern the dawning of two independent research directions from the very same why-question: (i) Why do some believe that imagined futures can actualise?, and (ii) Why do others doubt that the non-actual is possible?

Another interesting ramification concerns the possibility of diachronic research into why some people came to adopt a positive mindset toward a possible opportunity on the occasion that they initially had been less favourably or even negatively predisposed. The very same rationale applies to the reverse experiential course (whenever exhibited) by negatively predisposed individuals. Critical incident research methods should be of high relevance in developing an understanding of such cases (see Karatas-Ozkan, 2011).

Another presumption in need of closer attention concerns the blunt idea that enterprising individuals always act (or believe in opportunities) versus non-enterprising ones who always stay inactive. Arguably, these two types of individuals may be met in the two polar extremes of a continuum that may nonetheless include many more and far more complex cases. In other words, this is not to dogmatically rule out that there may exist such individuals but to underscore that, up to now, this crude binary conceptualisation is only an upshot of careless academic thought. Needless to say, the length of this middle space, so to speak, and the precise nature of the combinations, are issues that may be settled only by empirical inquiry.

Toward Methodologically Sounder Questions

In order to address those renovated questions, we must explicitly and systematically rethink the nature of the tools appropriate to the task at hand. Most importantly, we need to substitute "scientistic" tools with research equipment better-suited to the task of delving into the structure of human experience. No doubt, research that is intelligible to the layperson and does not involve fancy techniques may sound "unscientific" to many. But this impression only betrays a misconception of what it means to be scientific. The mark of scientificity does not lie in the nature of the tool but in the relevance of the tool for the task of uncovering the nature of the phenomenon at hand (Bhaskar, 1978). In this vein, Harré stresses that "the qualitative techniques and the metaphysical presumptions that back them that come much closer to meeting the ideals of the natural sciences" (2004: 4). Alas, what should have been common sense in the sciences of human understanding seems to be significantly downplayed in favour of the formalistic techniques of inquiry espoused by empiricist preconceptions of how the scientific study of meaning ought to proceed (Harré, 2002; Sayer, 2001). Quite counter-intuitively to many researchers with a desire to study entrepreneurial cognition scientifically, it is the systematic phenomenological inquiry of entrepreneurial agency that shows the way toward a genuinely scientific study of entrepreneurial action.

Toward Theoretically Sounder Questions

It would be worth pushing the non-essentialist conceptualisation a bit further by drawing clear links between the study of entrepreneurial action and existentialist lines of inquiry. If there is any tenet defining existentialist strands of thought, it is that "existence precedes essence", a dictum in perfect line with our elaborated reorientation.

In brief, what this is supposed to mean is that what we actually become does not denote who we were meant to be. There is not some metaphysical deity or natural decree necessitating that we are who we turn out to become. And it is precisely this recognition of choice that signifies existentialism's radical departure from deterministic modes of understanding ourselves in the world, since the possibility of choice presupposes the reality of freedom (agency) (Sartre, 1957). We are masters of ourselves, and what we become is (to some extent always) dependent upon our choice to act somehow and not otherwise. Moreover, an important insight stemming from the existentialist vantage point is that the realisation of freedom raises the awareness of responsibility for our actions, an awareness that is, inevitably, a source of angst, an angst that, in turn, may materialise into guilt.

If the very awareness of freedom to choose to act or refrain from acting is a source of angst, then this should especially be the case when entrepreneurial action is at issue, since the uncertainty of the world entails the impossibility of knowing the consequences of action (McMullen & Shepherd, 2006; Ramoglou, 2021a). Had we known the future states of the world that would follow our every step, then the very concept of choice would be devoid of meaning (von Mises, 1963). It is precisely the awareness of this uncertainty with the concomitant appreciation that we can choose from a number of options without, however, knowing what we ought to choose that is an irreducible source of anxiety. Note, however, that this is not tantamount to neurotic modes of anxiety. It is akin to the existentialist angst stemming from what Kierkegaard called "the dizziness of freedom" (1980: 61).

Taking the existentialist leanings implicit in strands of entrepreneurial theory more seriously (e.g., McMullen & Shepherd, 2006; Ramoglou & Tsang, 2016), we need no longer conceive of individuals who react as pre-programmed atoms in "the presence of an opportunity" (Shane & Venkataraman, 2000). In elaborating the explanatory significance of the active interpretation of the world for bringing performances onto the world, existentialist philosophy shows the way out of the nature vis-à-vis nurture dilemma.

Finally, although the elaboration of a research agenda along existentialist lines of thought could make a paper in its own right, it is worth construing the abovementioned research question along an existentialist landscape: what sort of understandings about oneself in relation to the world and fellow human beings affect (and how) the ways through which alternative states of the world are experienced as (Heideggerian) possibilia (or not)? How illuminating may the concept of "authenticity" prove for understanding action in a world in which the entrepreneur's beliefs stand in opposition to the beliefs of the majority (Heidegger, 1962; Sartre, 1992)? Is the entrepreneur perhaps better aware of the contingency of the world? If yes, how could this provide the phenomenological underpinnings of an existentialist theory of entrepreneurial action? Obviously, the suggested research orientation is in need of theoretical fine-tuning.

OTHER WRONG QUESTIONS

The hidden analogies in the individual-opportunity nexus have not only epistemologically resuscitated the problematic question of the entrepreneur, they have further reinforced two poor theoretical notions at the very foundations of entrepreneurship theory. The first is the notion that entrepreneurs can know opportunities ex ante. The second is the idea that economic agents who do not act entrepreneurially must be "blind" to opportunities. In other words, a problematic conceptual framework has sustained the illusion that not only do entrepreneurs possess some undiscovered genetic makeup – they further possess some rare and clairvoyant quality of "alertness".

Ramoglou (2021a) explains how the notion that entrepreneurs possess a prescient capacity of "alertness" that allows them to peer through uncertainty and know what will work is an unfortunate side-effect of unreflective linguistic practices. The way we habitually discuss opportunities as "recognised" or "identified" simply commits our theoretical imagination to the illusion that entrepreneurs must have known ex ante what may happen at a later point in time. The source of this theoretical illusion lies in the untimely use of words such as "'discover', 'solve', 'prove', 'perceive', 'see' [to] describe items in the inquisitive life of human beings" (Ryle, 1949/2008: 151). For these are achievement verbs that create conceptual rigidities when used before achievements materialise. As seminally remarked by Gilbert Ryle, when we refer to processes of trying with achievement words, we end up supposing that there may exist "temporarily infallible marksmen and some occasionally infallible doctors" (2008: 153). After all, how would entrepreneurs have failed given that they "recognised the opportunity"? Even worse, this problematic representational practice sustains misconceived questions about some "mystical" quality of "Kirznerian alertness" (Kirzner, 1973; 1979) allowing some to know opportunities in an otherwise unknowable future (see Ramoglou, 2021a).

The other problematic question concerns the notion that non-entrepreneurs must be "blind" to opportunities. It is this unexamined assumption that feeds the myth of some sort of mysterious and "rare gift" (Kirzner, 1979: 148) possessed by a minority of economic agents. Ramoglou (2021b) demonstrates that the reasoning backing the Kirznerian framework is erected on a modus tollens fallacy. That is, the inference that the majority of economic agents are "non-alert" to opportunities rests on the assumption that "to 'see' an opportunity" is to inevitably "pursue an opportunity". In effect, Kirzner falls for the conclusion that only a few must have "discovered opportunities" on the basis that only a minority of economic agents engage in entrepreneurial forms of activity. "Nowhere does Kirzner allow for the possibility of a perceived yet unexploited opportunity: either alertness or opportunity must be absent" (Ramoglou, 2021b: 831). This is problematic. Even if entrepreneurs believe they have perceived a real opportunity they may simply not inhabit an entrepreneurial ecosystem that would allow them to exercise action (McMullen, 2011). But even if one can exercise action, what we now know to have been a real opportunity was previously only imaginable, thus susceptible to doubt.

It follows that, if the question "How do only a few discover opportunities under conditions of uncertainty?" is fallacious due to problematic word-use, the question "Why do only a few recognise opportunities?" (Shane & Venkataraman, 2000) rests on the false assumption that events of "opportunity discovery" and "opportunity exploitation" are constantly conjoined. This is a flawed assumption. As we saw, if "opportunity discovery" means anything at all, it may only mean that somebody imagined or believed that something (say, profit X) is possible following a course of action. And the fact that knowing whether a venture will be profitable can only be gained ex post means that we cannot reasonably conclude that non-entrepreneurs must have been "non-alert". Many may have had the very same idea yet simply doubted that it is a good one – not to mention that, even if one believes that they have found a good idea, one may simply not have the material means to pursue it.

In all, limited theoretical reflection has sustained several questions that do not remain unaddressed because we lack better answers. They are simply bad questions. To reiterate, if the "question of the entrepreneur" requires the study of what non-entrepreneurs lack in terms of genetic structures, the question of alertness presupposes the study of what non-entrepreneurs lack in terms of abilities of imagination and prescience. In the place of the question of the entrepreneur, it was suggested that, rather than researching what non-entrepreneurs do not have we can study how both entrepreneurs and non-entrepreneurs make sense of the world by deepening our understanding of their phenomenological grammars. Similarly, the question of "alertness" can be replaced by more sustained and systematic research into what prevents imaginative individuals from realising their potential (the so-called 'non-alert non-entrepreneurs') as well recognising the role of luck in entrepreneurial achievements (in the place of illusions of foreknowledge).

Up to now we have seen how limited ontological and linguistic reflexivity nurtures problematic questions. We turn to discuss further reasons responsible for letting problematic questions go undetected.

DISCUSSION

Fallacy of Possibilism: The Core Illusion?

A particularly problematic notion in entrepreneurship research is the frequent reliance on unreasonably optimistic worldviews about entrepreneurship. As noted by Brattstrom and Wennberg, entrepreneurship research is dominated by "stories of entrepreneurship as a road to salvation and means to emancipation" (2022: 1443). There is no doubt that many entrepreneurs have made it from rags to riches. Entrepreneurship can indeed be emancipatory. Yet, what is deeply problematic is our academic disposition to portray the world as rosier than it is. For, although entrepreneurship is sometimes the road to riches, the crude matter of fact is that "most [entrepreneurs] never get to cash in, and instead earn less than comparable employees in paid work" (Brattstrom & Wennberg, 2022: 1449) (see also Aldrich & Ruef, 2018).

What is important from a philosophical vantage point is the observation that the empirical realities of failure have failed to undermine the particularly rosy worldview at the core of our scholarship. For, the crude matter of fact that only a minority of ambitious entrepreneurs will ever witness their dreams materialise is not a recent empirical discovery. If so, what is preventing us from watering down our unrealistically optimistic narratives?

Bad theoretical assumptions are the culprit. In particular, the problem lies in the unfalsifiable nature of the possibilistic worldview; that is, a worldview in which "success is always possible in principle" (see Ramoglou & Tsang, 2016). Why? No experience is alone sufficient to falsify the presupposed "can". Although empirical manifestations of failures abound in the business landscape, they can always be explained away as a contingent and quite unnecessary state of the world. It is always conceivable that the opportunity was there, but something went awry on the way. The core commitment to a failure-free world is consistently maintained in making the required conceptual adjustments. Indeed, it is always possible to shield the core commitment in the existence of opportunity in ascribing the cause of failure to wrongdoings or omissions at the phase of the "exploitation" stage – e.g., by alluding to the presence of "greed, stupidity, thoughtless bandwagon-climbing, or incompetence whether in design or execution" (Drucker, 1985: 46). In a similar vein, Brattstrom and Wennberg argue that the problem is that "the Better Story Stands in the Way of the More Likely Story" (2022: 1452). But what would a "more likely" story look like?

According to Ramoglou and Tsang, moving toward more plausible stories requires that we take the realism of our theories far more seriously. Among other things, we ought to depart from the view of entrepreneurship as a "panacea to some of our most pressing socioeconomic challenges, such as poverty and employment" (2016: 429). Instead, we ought to acknowledge that "like watering soil where no seeds exist, venturing in this domain cannot be profitable regardless of the level of effort or entrepreneurial resourcefulness" (idem). Of course, there are obstacles to the turn towards more realistic accounts. Most notably, the departure from the "emancipatory story [that] assumes agency over context" (Brattstrom & Wennberg, 2022: 1458) "does not chime well with the climate of an era that elevates agency at the expense of societal structure" (Ramoglou & Gartner, 2023: 1530). But, perhaps, moving toward less popular stories is precisely what we ought to do. The reason is that making people feel optimistic is not part of our job description. This is not to deny that entrepreneurs have every reason to be optimistic in a world of opportunity. But they should be rationally optimistic and unaffected by the intoxicating and escapist culture of "positive thinking" (Brattstrom & Wennberg, 2022; Ehrenreich, 2009).

Just as importantly, making our scholarship more realistic can also contribute to creating more equal societies. In a naively optimistic worldview in which one can always get out of poverty and unemployment by trying hard enough, the failure to do so should be entirely their fault. For, one failed to do what one could (supposedly) do – leaving (inter alia) considerations of conductive entrepreneurial ecosystems aside (cf. Stam & van de Ven, 2021). This agent-centric story leaves no room for interventions that can help make the opportunities in our economies more accessible to more people. Rather, it makes us turn a blind eye to the structural problems that may not allow many individuals to exercise entrepreneurial agency (or succeed if they do so). From a neighbouring standpoint, entrepreneurs can neither create new worlds if such worlds are not already possible, nor effectuate new realities disregarding what present realities allow (compare with Sarasvathy, 2001; 2021).

Furthermore, this misleading narrative makes us less forgiving and less compassionate (Shepherd, 2019) toward unsuccessful entrepreneurs. If we exaggerate what entrepreneurial agency can achieve it is difficult to explain failures without attributing the locus of causality to the individual. It is in this spirit that Ramoglou and Gartner suggest that, as an antidote against the overemphasis on opportunities, we should also start discussing threats far more seriously and systematically:

> If anything, calling attention to the threats associated with business venturing can forge more forgiving conditions for failed entrepreneurs. It may help persuade governments and policy makers to engineer less threatening environments. This is feasible by establishing more institutional and economic safety nets for the agents who help economies prosper (Mazzucato, 2013); albeit often at an unbearable personal cost, and in spite of their best efforts. (2023: 1530)

Other Obstacles

Other obstacles standing in the way of better questions lie in philosophical taboos – particularly the ones surrounding the term "determinism". According to Ramoglou and Gartner (2023), the rejection of possibilism ought to entail the acceptance of environmental determinism. However, the problem is that, as scholars, we are inclined to instinctively reject anything that sounds "deterministic". This instinctive reaction is problematic. It is not grounded on a clear meaning of the word. Instead, it is more of an intellectual knee-jerk reaction to something that "sounds bad" (see also Ramoglou et al., 2023).

To be sure, determinism is a false metaphysical doctrine when it means that what happened was predestined to occur as if written by a "Book of destiny" (Ryle, 1954). However, determinism is not invariably a problematic way of thinking when it applies at the level of possibility. The reason is that certain world-states that humans can imagine are just impossible. For example, we know that existing technologies simply do not allow time travel. Similarly, in the context of entrepreneurship, success is not possible if the (current) structure of the world does not allow the actualisation of a desirable world-state – e.g., due to the absence of the necessary scientific knowledge – amongst a variety of factors that oftentimes make imagined world-states nothing but figments of a playful imagination.

CONCLUSION

In this chapter, I argued that, instead of being on the lookout for "better answers", we should more patiently study our questions. Drawing on previous work, I endeavoured to demonstrate that we are not making good progress with several of our "big questions" because, fundamentally, they are the wrong questions. That is, they rest on unexamined and largely problematic assumptions. As a way out of the search for "better answers" to flawed questions, I recommended that a more studious engagement with our questions may not only reveal previously unidentified errors in our thinking; as importantly, such studies can further help reorient our scholarship towards more promising questions. To be sure, such questions need not always be as exciting as the "wrong questions". With little doubt, the questions of alchemists were more "exciting" than the questions animating chemists (see also Wright et al., 2023). Similarly, the idea of a gene that may help predict who will act and succeed entrepreneurially may sound more exciting than questions about entrepreneurial beliefs, values, and attitudes. But, if we want to be genuinely scientific, we should make sure that our questions can reasonably be expected to shed light on entrepreneurial realities. To close echoing Boltzmann (1974) in the opening epigraph: in making our scholarship more scientific, it may be prudent to be more sceptical of the "big questions" and restrict ourselves to seemingly less valuable albeit more plausible ones.

NOTE

1. For more in-depth analyses, please see Ramoglou (2013), Ramoglou (2014) and Ramoglou, Gartner & Tsang (2020). This section is largely a synopsis and assortment of earlier work

REFERENCES

Aldrich, H. E. (2005). "Entrepreneurship". In N. J. Smelser & R. Swedberg (Eds.), *The Handbook of economic sociology*, 2nd edition: 451–477. Princeton, NJ: Princeton University Press.

Aldrich, H. E. & Ruef, M. (2018). "Unicorns, gazelles, and other distractions on the way to understanding real entrepreneurship in the United States". *Academy of Management Perspectives*, **32**, 458–472.

Alvarez, S. A. & Barney J. B. (2007). "Discovery and creation: Alternative theories of entrepreneurial action". *Strategic Entrepreneurship Journal*, **1**, 11–26.

Anscombe, E. (1993). "Causality and determination". In E. Sosa & M. Tooley (Eds.), *Causation*: 88–104. Oxford: Oxford University Press.

Baum, J. R., Frese, M. & Baron, R. A. (Eds.) (2007). *The psychology of entrepreneurship*. Mahwa (NJ): Lawrence Erlbaum Associates.

Baron, R. A. (2004). "The cognitive perspective: A valuable tool for answering entrepreneurship's basic 'why' questions". *Journal of Business Venturing*, **19**, 221–239.
Baron, R. A. (2007). "Behavioral and cognitive factors in entrepreneurship". *Strategic Entrepreneurship Journal*, **1–2**, 167–182.
Bentham, J. (1839). *The works of Jeremy Bentham: Part IX*. Edinburgh: Simpkin Marshall & Co.
Bhaskar, R. (1978). *A realist theory of science*. Brighton, UK: Harvester Press.
Bhaskar, R. (1998). *The possibility of naturalism: Philosophical critique of the contemporary human sciences*. London: Routledge.
Boltzmann, L. (1974). *Theoretical physics and philosophical problems: Selected Writings*. New York: Springer.
Brattstrom, A. & Wennberg, K. (2022). "The entrepreneurial story and its implications for research". *Entrepreneurship Theory and Practice*, **46**, 1443–1468.
Casson, M. (2003). *The entrepreneur: An economic theory*, 2nd edition. Cheltenham, UK and Northampton, MA, USA: Edward Elgar Publishing.
Casson, M. (2005). "The individual–opportunity nexus: A review of Scott Shane: The general theory of entrepreneurship". *Small Business Economics*, **24**, 423–430.
Cunningham, B. J. & Lischeron, J. (1991). "Defining entrepreneurship". *Journal of Small Business Management*, **29**, 45–61.
Davidsson, P. (2015). "Entrepreneurial opportunities and the entrepreneurship nexus: A re-conceptualization." *Journal of Business Venturing*, **30**, 674–695.
De Jong, H. L. (2000). "Genetic determinism: How not to interpret behavioral genetics". *Theory & Psychology*, **10**, 615–637.
Dimov, D., Schaefer, R. & Pistrui, J. (2021). "Look who is talking ... and who is listening: Finding an integrative 'we' voice in entrepreneurial scholarship". *Entrepreneurship Theory and Practice*, **45**, 1176–1196.
Drucker, P. F. (1985). *Innovation and entrepreneurship: practice and principles*, 2nd edition. Oxford: Butterworth-Heinemann.
Ehrenreich, B. (2009). *Bright-sided: How the relentless promotion of positive thinking has undermined America*. New York: Metropolitan Books.
Fayolle, A. (2007). *Entrepreneurship and new value creation: The dynamic of the entrepreneurial process*. Cambridge: Cambridge University Press.
Gartner, W. B. (1985). "A conceptual framework for describing the phenomenon of new venture creation". *Academy of Management Review*, **10**, 696–706.
Gartner, W. B. (1989). "'Who is an entrepreneur?' is the wrong question". *Entrepreneurship Theory and Practice*, **13**, 47–68.
Gartner, W. B. (1993). "Words lead to deeds: Towards an organizational emergence vocabulary". *Journal of Business Venturing*, **8**, 231–239.
Gartner, W. B. (1995). "Aspects of organizational emergence". In I. Bull, H. Thomas & G. Willard (Eds.), *Entrepreneurship perspectives on theory building*: 67–86. Oxford: Pergamon.
Harré, R. (2002). *Cognitive science: A philosophical introduction*. London: Sage.
Harré, R. (2004). "Staking our claim for qualitative psychology as science". *Qualitative Research in Psychology*, **1**, 3–14.
Harré, R. (2009). "Saving critical realism". *Journal for the Theory of Social Behaviour*, **39**, 129–143.
Harré, R. & Gillett, G. (1994). *The discursive mind*. London: Sage.
Harré, R. & Tissaw, M. A. (2005). *Wittgenstein and psychology: A practical guide*. Aldershot, UK: Ashgate.
Heidegger, M. (1962). *Being and time*. Oxford: Basil Blackwell.

Helrich, C. S. (2012). *The classical theory of fields: Electromagnetism.* New York: Springer.
Karatas-Ozkan, M. (2011). "Understanding relational qualities of entrepreneurial learning: towards a multi-layered approach". *Entrepreneurship & Regional Development*, **23**, 877–906
Kerr, S. P., Kerr, W. R. & Xu, T. (2018). "Personality traits of entrepreneurs: A review of recent literature". *Foundations and Trends in Entrepreneurship*, **14**, 1–78.
Kierkegaard, S. (1980). *The concept of anxiety: A simple psychologically orienting deliberation on the dogmatic issue of hereditary sin.* Princeton, NJ: Princeton University Press.
Kirzner, I. M. (1973). *Competition and entrepreneurship.* Chicago: University of Chicago Press.
Kirzner, I. M. (1979). *Perception, opportunity and profit.* Chicago: University of Chicago Press.
Lipton, P. (2004). *Inference to the best explanation*, 2nd edition. London: Routledge.
Mazzucato M. (2013). The entrepreneurial state: Debunking public vs. private sector myths. London: Anthem Press.
McMullen, J. S. (2011). "Delineating the domain of development entrepreneurship: A market–based approach to facilitating inclusive economic growth". *Entrepreneurship Theory and Practice*, **35**, 185–215.
McMullen, J. S. & Shepherd, D. A. (2006). "Entrepreneurial action and the role of uncertainty in the theory of the entrepreneur". *Academy of Management Review*, **31**, 132–152.
McMullen, J. S., Fitzsimmons, J., Khyati, S. & Ramoglou, S. (2024). "A temporal typology of entrepreneurial opportunities: Implications for the optimal timing of entrepreneurial action". *Journal of Business Venturing*, **39**, 106356.
Metcalfe, J. S. (2004). "The entrepreneur and the style of modern economics". *Journal of Evolutionary Economics*, **14**, 157–175.
Mitchell, R. K. et al. (2007). "The central question in entrepreneurial cognition research 2007". *Entrepreneurship: Theory and Practice*, **31**, 1–27.
Moore, C. B., McIntyre, N. H. & Lanivich, S. E. (2021). "ADHD-related neurodiversity and the entrepreneurial mindset". *Entrepreneurship Theory and Practice*, **45**, 64–91.
Neneh, B. N. (2019). "From entrepreneurial alertness to entrepreneurial behavior: The role of trait competitiveness and proactive personality". *Personality and Individual Differences*, **138**, 273–279.
Nicolaou, N. & Shane, S. (2009). "Can genetic factors influence the likelihood of engaging in entrepreneurial activity?". *Journal of Business Venturing*, **24**, 1–22.
Nicolaou, N., Phan, P. H. & Stephan, U. (2021). "The biological perspective in entrepreneurship research". *Entrepreneurship Theory and Practice*, **45**, 3–17.
Nicolaou, N., Shane, S., Cherkas, L., Hunkin, J. & Spector, T. D. (2008). "Is the tendency to engage in entrepreneurship genetic?". *Management Science*, **54**, 167–179.
Nofal, A. M., Nicolaou, N., Symeonidou, N. & Shane, S. (2018). "Biology and management: A review, critique, and research agenda". *Journal of Management*, **44**, 7–31.
Ramoglou, S. (2013). "Who is a 'non-entrepreneur'? Taking the 'others' of entrepreneurship seriously". *International Small Business Journal*, **31**, 432–453.
Ramoglou, S. (2014). *A realist analysis of the entrepreneurial worldview: Underlabouring for a scientific study of entrepreneurship.* Cambridge: Cambridge University Library.

Ramoglou, S. (2021a). "Knowable opportunities in an unknowable future? On the epistemological paradoxes of entrepreneurship theory". *Journal of Business Venturing*, **36**, 106090.

Ramoglou, S. (2021b). "Why do disequilibria exist? An ontological study of Kirznerian economics". *Cambridge Journal of Economics*, **45**, 833–856.

Ramoglou, S. & Gartner, W. B. (2023). "A historical intervention in the 'opportunity wars': Forgotten scholarship, the discovery/creation disruption, and moving forward by looking backward". *Entrepreneurship Theory and Practice*, **47**, 1521–1538.

Ramoglou, S. & McMullen, J. S. (2022). "'What is an opportunity?': From theoretical mystification to everyday understanding". *Academy of Management Review*, forthcoming.

Ramoglou, S. & Tsang, E. W. K. (2016). "A realist perspective of entrepreneurship: Opportunities as propensities". *Academy of Management Review*, **41**, 410–434.

Ramoglou, S., Gartner, W. B. & Tsang, E. W. K. (2020). "'Who is an entrepreneur?' is (still) the wrong question". *Journal of Business Venturing Insights*, **13**, e00168.

Ramoglou, S., Zyglidopoulos, S. C. & Papadopoulou, F. (2023). "Is there opportunity without stakeholders? A stakeholder theory critique and development of opportunity-actualization". *Entrepreneurship Theory and Practice*, **47**, 113–141.

Rietveld, C. A., Slob, E. A. & Thurik, A. R. (2021). "A decade of research on the genetics of entrepreneurship: a review and view ahead". *Small Business Economics*, **57**, 1303–1317.

Runde, J. & de Rond, M. (2010). "Evaluating causal explanations of specific events". *Organization Studies*, **31**, 431–450.

Ryle, G. (1954). *Dilemmas*. Cambridge: Cambridge University Press.

Ryle, G. (2008). *The concept of mind*. London: William Brendon and Son.

Sarasvathy, S. D. (2001). "Causation and effectuation: Toward a theoretical shift from economic inevitability to entrepreneurial contingency". *Academy of Management Review*, **26**, 243–263.

Sarasvathy, S. D. (2021). "Even-if: Sufficient, yet unnecessary conditions for worldmaking". *Organization Theory*, **2**, 26317877211005785.

Sartre, J.-P. (1957). *Being and nothingness: An essay on phenomenological ontology*. London: Methuen.

Sartre, J.-P. (1992). *Notebooks for an ethics*. Chicago: University of Chicago Press.

Sayer, A. (2001). *Realism and social science*. London: Sage.

Searle, J. R. (1983). *Intentionality: An essay in the philosophy of mind*. Cambridge: Cambridge University Press.

Searle, J. R. (1995). *The construction of social reality*. London: Penguin.

Shane, S. & Venkataraman, S. (2000). "The promise of entrepreneurship as a field of research". *Academy of Management Review*, **25**, 217–226.

Shepherd, D. A. (2019). "Researching the dark side, downside, and destructive side of entrepreneurial action: It's the compassionate thing to do". *Academy of Management Discoveries*, **5**, 217–220.

Stam, E. &, van de Ven, A. (2021). "Entrepreneurial ecosystem elements". *Small Business Economics*, **56**, 809–832.

Swedberg, R. (2000). "The social science view of entrepreneurship: Introduction and practical applications". In Swedberg, R. (Ed.). *Entrepreneurship: The social science view*: 7–44. Oxford: Oxford University Press.

Thornton, P. H. (1999). The sociology of entrepreneurship". *Annual Review of Sociology*, **25**, 19–46.

van der Loos, M. J., Rietveld, C. A., Eklund, N., Koellinger, P. D., Rivadeneira, F., Abecasis, G. R. et al. (2013). "The molecular genetic architecture of self-employment". *Plos One*, **8**, e60542.
von Mises, L. (1963). *Human action: A treatise on economics*. New Haven, CT: Yale University Press.
Wittgenstein, L. (1982). *Wittgenstein's Lectures: Cambridge, 1932–1935*. Chicago, IL: University of Chicago Press.
Wittgenstein, L. (1998). *Culture and value*. Oxford: Blackwell.
Wright, T. A., Emich, K., Pearce, J. L., Ramoglou, S., Ashkanasy, N., Bartunek, J. M., Kunisch, S., Denyer, D., Foss, N. J., Klein, P. G., Town, S., Hollwitz, J., Barney, C. E., Harms, P., Munyon, T. P., Seijts, G., & Tsang, E. W. K. (2023). "Advocacy and the search for truth in management scholarship: Can the twain ever meet?". *Journal of Management Inquiry*, in press.

4. Telling the entire story of entrepreneurship: an autoethnography on autoethnography in entrepreneurship

R. Duncan M. Pelly

INTRODUCTION

> Two roads diverged in a yellow wood,
> And sorry I could not travel both
> And be one traveler, long I stood
> And looked down one as far as I could
> To where it bent in the undergrowth;
> (Robert Frost, 1916)

As I read this poem, I reflect upon what it has always meant to me. The traveler ultimately decided to take the road less traveled "and that has made all the difference" (Frost, 1916). But I couldn't help but ponder: what if he had taken the road more traveled – what would that have been like? And, what made him decide to walk in the forest in the first place? What did he do after his walk? How did taking this particular path lead him to improve or change his life? Why didn't he simply make his own path instead of choosing this particular one? The paths (or stories) he recounted along with the rejected monologues comprise a complete entrepreneurial journey. Entrepreneurship is a story of visions, insights, (rejected) plans, struggles, failures, and possibly successes. What methodologies would be suitable to explore these pathways? From my perspective, the Horatio Alger (Sarachek, 1978) style of entrepreneurial narratives are unconvincing – they smack of Schumpeter's heroic entrepreneur (Boutillier & Uzunidis, 2014). Moreover, popular media glorifies stories of world-renowned entrepreneurs such as Bill Gates, Mark Zuckerberg, Steve Jobs, and Jeff Bezos – all of whom are white, male billionaires working in Silicon Valley. Their stories are so far removed from the experience of the average entrepreneur that they might as well be fiction – and, much like Horatio Alger's writings, they lack authenticity.

Although these men did take the road less traveled, how do we follow the journeys along other paths, including more mundane ones in entrepreneurship? Can we visualize the routines of ordinary people and translate them into stories (Engstrom, 2012)? If so, then we can expand upon the popular conceptions of entrepreneurship of the billionaire tech mogul, and include the small-time family entrepreneur (Colli, 2003), the entrepreneur who transforms a hobby into a business (Frith, 2007), the one who pursues entrepreneurship as a calling (Da Palma et al., 2018), and those undertaking entrepreneurship to survive (O'Donnell et al., 2020).

If we conceptualize entrepreneurship as the study of the prosaic and its accompanying narratives (Engstrom, 2012; Hjorth and Steyaert, 2004; Johannisson and Olaison, 2007), then emerging entrepreneurial organizations are the reification of elaborate stories (O'Connor 2004; Tsoukas and Chia, 2002) in that they represent complicated tales destined to aid entrepreneurs in envisioning an imagined future. As entrepreneurs pursue meaning-making, a method rife with verisimilitude (Herrmann, 2020b), numinosity (Mills, 2013), or resonance (Tracy, 2010; Bochner, 2000) is needed; in other words, one that will jump off the page and elicit the imagination of the reader (Herrmann, 2020a; López and Tracy, 2020; Brommel, 2017) to inspire all entrepreneurs. This can be achieved through understanding the paths not chosen and why. What is necessary is a fundamental shift from focusing on the starting and ending points of entrepreneurship (akin to the "erklaeren" or explaining perspective), to focusing on the processes of entrepreneurship (akin to the "verstehen" or understanding perspective) (Schurz, 1990; Chiles et al., 2007). Understanding the paths not taken, and the corresponding impact upon the imagination, requires a methodology of meaning, of deep understanding of entrepreneurship and of entrepreneurs. One method that answers this call is autoethnography.

This chapter will provide the reader with guidance on ways to pursue autoethnography and, more importantly, how to elicit resonance with the reader. Initially, an explanation of autoethnography's importance in the study of entrepreneurship will be provided, followed by an outline of various approaches to autoethnography, and culminate with an autoethnography of writing an autoethnography. Final remarks will complete the article.

AUTOETHNOGRAPHY'S SIGNIFICANCE IN STUDYING ENTREPRENEURSHIP

Most positivist methods focus on endpoints – things that can be objectively measured (Alvarez et al., 2014). This type of research aggrandizes the "who", "when", and "what". Typically, the goal is a beautifully neat dataset with equally attractive hypotheses that is to be proved or disproved (Pelly, 2017a).

These positivist data sets are unhelpful in studying entrepreneurial stories because neither entrepreneurship nor narratives rely upon model building (Steyaert, 2004). Conversely, storytelling research highlights the "how", and sometimes the "why" (Ellingson, 2009; Rosile et al., 2013; López and Tracy, 2020), flipping the logic and opening the black box of what transpires between the beginning and end points of a process.

Stories focus upon what would otherwise be, or "potentiality" (Hernes, 2014) to resonate with the reader; fortunately, autoethnography is a method uniquely suited to the exploration of stories (Holbrook, 1995) and potentiality (Gartner, 2007) via the small narrative (Fletcher, 2007; Hjorth and Steyaert, 2004). Autoethnography is fitting because the foundation upon which entrepreneurship sits is storytelling, i.e. convincing others to act (Hjorth, 2014), directing their desires, organizing resources, and focusing on anomalies (Spinosa et al., 1997), playfulness, and emotions (Hjorth, 2007).

Entrepreneurial stories are an amalgamation of observable actions as well as those that never left the "thought experiment stage". Boje's (1995) exploration of Tamara-Land offers one of the best explanations of the significance of alternative pathways, or antenarratives in storytelling. The Tamara-Land play is a unique theatrical experience because it allows the audience to shift from room to room as they search for meaning, much like an entrepreneur who floats among storytelling, action, and the socio-material environment (Pelly and Boje, 2019, 2020). Tamara-Land is relatable because there are unlimited possibilities the audience can pursue as they interact with the production. Unlike real life, this play provides the reader the opportunity to fully explore all available paths as the stories unfold, encouraging the audience to repeatedly revisit the play. It is the ability to explore the unfulfilled that gives the play its completeness.

The Tamara-Land play is an illustration of antenarratives, or bets on a series of alternative possible futures, while also reconstructing the past; the antenarrative is both prospective and retrospective (Rosile et al., 2013). These antenarrative road maps are important in autoethnography because they highlight an Aurelian-type of introspection (Graiver, 2019) that signifies what actually happens may well be less important than the courses of action that are not pursued – similar to the lessons learned from studying entrepreneurial failure (Shepherd et al., 2016). To further elucidate – individuals may not "feel" the story behind Facebook or how Mark Zuckerberg became a technology entrepreneur, but they are likely to understand why he did not become a different type of entrepreneur such as a restaurateur.

A contributory characteristic of autoethnography is its focus on the individual (Parry, 2008; Zavattaro, 2011). Many autoethnographers subscribe to the premise that an individual is uniquely qualified to describe his or her own experiences (Wall, 2006) and in the case of entrepreneurship, there is no better way than to understand than to "entreprendre" (Fletcher, 2011; Steyaert, 2011; Johannisson, 2011; Hjorth, 2007; Engstrom; 2012). This type of approach has an internal validity, or "truth" because it utilizes preexisting stories (Larsen et al., 2020).

Unfortunately, social science prioritizes the "organization" because it is visible, whereas antenarratives and emotions are less so. Left in the shadows are stigmas, cultures, identities, and experiences (Herrmann, 2020a, 2020b) – these are the cruxes of the working lives of entrepreneurs and merit further exploration (Engstrom, 2012), which can be achieved through autoethnography (Pelly, 2017a; Pratt, 2007; Alsop, 2002; Tiwsakul and Hackley, 2012), because it highlights "the subjective, empathetic, process-oriented, and inclusive sides of social life" (Neumann, 1994). These marginalized facets of entrepreneurship merit study (Webb, 2020). Up next are two prevailing schools of autoethnography and their commonalities.

TYPES OF AUTOETHNOGRAPHIES

It is important to note that autoethnography is characterized as more of an orientation in lieu of a methodology (Wall, 2006; Holt, 2003; Ellis, 1999; Johannisson, 2011; and Bochner and Ellis, 2003). However, there are basic definitions and precepts common to most forms of autoethnography.

Autoethnography is predicated upon three primary concepts. "Auto" or self, "ethno" or culture, and "graphy", or writing. Spry (2001) defines autoethnography as "a self-narrative that critiques the situatedness of self with others in social contexts. Autoethnography is both a method and a text of diverse interdisciplinary practices". Sparkes adds that autoethnography includes "highly personalized accounts that draw upon the experience of the author/researcher for the purposes of extending sociological understanding" (Sparkes, 2000).

Autoethnographical traditions typically have a place in literature, history, and the social sciences (Herrmann, 2020a). These practices frequently oscillate between social science and literary studies, and use stories that create a sense of truth for the reader (Denshire, 2014). Autoethnography dates back to the late nineteenth and twentieth century, where management scholars used firsthand experience to develop broader theoretical precepts (Pelly and Fayolle, 2020; Kirzner, 1982). Well-known examples of autoethnographies include Lorimer (1903), Taylor (1919), and Follett (1940). Although this style of study was previously discouraged, it has seen a recent resurgence (Pelly and Boje, 2019, 2020).

This use of firsthand experience enhances reflexivity because it encourages researchers to understand their identities, inclinations, loves, beliefs, feelings, relationships, provides insight into ways in which background influences impact findings (Herrmann, 2020a; Cook, 2012), and requires significant introspection (Johannisson, 2011; Johannisson et al., 2002). In lieu of concealing or manipulating these "uncontrollables", the autoethnography places them in front and center, encouraging readers to judge their relevance for themselves, since all representations are partial, partisan, and problematic (Van Maanen, 2011). The goal is to invite the reader to feel a part of the story (Tracy, 2010; López and Tracy, 2020; Bochner and Ellis, 2016; Townsend et al., 2020). The writer lulls the reader into their world allowing them to explore individual hypothetical scenarios in similar situations (Richards, 2008; Damgaard et al., 2004).

There are two main schools of autoethnographical thought. The first, evocative autoethnography, solicits research in entrepreneurship that includes opinions, hunches, intuition, and emotions (Johannisson, 2011) which are profoundly linked to articulating opportunities (Pelly, 2016). The evocative autoethnography serves as a robust narrative highlighting the co-construction of entrepreneurial stories with stakeholders (Pelly, 2016, 2017b). All entrepreneurship settings are unique, but emotionally-based responses linked to theory can be shared within alternate contexts.

Evocative autoethnography differs from autobiography because personal experiences are interwoven into broader theoretical understanding (Allen-Collinson, 2013; Ellis et al., 2011; Chang, 2007; Reed-Danahay, 1997; Bochner and Ellis, 2002). Like autobiography, evocative autoethnography strives to tell the story in totality; thus, they include acts of failure, paths not taken, and the story as it authentically transpired (Denker et al., 2020). This is germane to entrepreneurship because it is a discipline rife with stories of disappointment and defeat (Shepherd et al., 2016).

Analytic autoethnography (Anderson, 2006) is less emotional than evocative autoethnography. The main difference is analytic autoethnography is designed to benefit from active participation, and an author serves as an opportunistic Complete Member Researcher (CMR). CMR status intimates that knowledge of an entrepreneurial phenomenon is acquired through occupational and lifestyle participation, a theme reflected in entrepreneurial autoethnographic literature (Steyaert, 2011; Fletcher, 2011). This approach challenges conventional researchers who observe the environment but do not actively alter it. Analytic autoethnography includes dialogues with informants beyond the self; the point of which is to narrate the interactions between groups and individuals both internal and external to an organization, and to highlight porous institutional borders. Finally, an analytical autoethography must apply knowledge from the study to broader theoretical abstractions and provide a more practice-based example of a phenomenon (Anderson, 2006; Ellis et al., 2011; Fletcher, 2011).

Both evocative and analytical autoethnographies begin with an "auto" because autoethnographers believe that the individual is the starting point for knowledge, although we can abstract the "individual" to an organizational individual (Fletcher, 2011, Bochner and Ellis, 2003; Holt, 2003). This can include an "I", a "we", "stakeholder I" or an "organizational I" (Tomkins, 2020). This "self", broadly defined, highlights the relationships to broader cultural practices (Cullen, 2011; Kempster and Stewart, 2020), and explores how they may relate to larger and/or differing settings (Herrmann, 2017), or macro contexts (Boyle and Parry, 2007). It is not unlike Van Maanen's (2011) confessional or impressionist tales that begin with the self to create a story that includes others.

Autoethnographies can be confusing, messy, and disorganized (Goodall, 2004; Townsend et al., 2020; Hearn et al., 2020). They also require a degree of courage – they make writers vulnerable, because they expose their weaknesses, their failures, and their inner selves (Rambo, 2005; Denker et al., 2020). This can also make a paper review process particularly challenging, since reviewers are oftentimes viewed as attacking both paper and writer!

At this point in time, my preferred autoethnographical format, which can be applied to the evocative, analytical, and any other autoethnographical approach, (and one that is more palatable to entrepreneurship journals), is the layered account (Pelly, 2016, 2017b; Frandsen et al., 2020; Mendez and Pelly, 2020). A layered account has a conventional introduction, literature review, methods and discussion, and conclusion. The difference lies within the empirics. Layered accounts tell stories in a tableau vivant (Witte, 2021) format that oscillates the reader's attention of the reader from evocation to analysis. This type of writing mirrors the confessional ethnography (Van Maanen, 2011), focuses on the researcher, and uses a diary or memoir format.

The layered account follows the plus zone challenge in entrepreneurship education (Hindle, 2007; Pelly and Fayolle, 2020) that advocates telling a story and then exploring its meta and/or theoretical aspects. This writing style diverges significantly from others found in social sciences, including in entrepreneurship, because it opens the door for readers to formulate conclusions. Plus zone writing uses literary techniques to explore paths not taken in the writer's mind, and it is designed to create a looking glass for the reader to peer into the story (Tracy, 2010; López and Tracy, 2020).

The empirical section of this chapter will be depicted by writing an autoethnography about autoethnography. To exemplify the layered account and tableau vivant format, I have interwoven the storytelling and theoretical vignettes. Vignette titles in **bold** are theoretical vignettes, and vignettes in ***bold italics*** are the storytelling vignettes.

Background

In order to understand my autoethnography monomania, I have provided a brief synopsis of my professional background. My military service schooled me in a rigid thought process that dictated first-hand experience as the preferred learning tool. In other words, if I had not experienced it, I was clueless about it. This became the basis for my obsession to seek first-hand knowledge before drawing conclusions, and to use primary sources in lieu of secondary ones.

As both a doctoral student and a junior scholar, I remained frustrated by the positivist paradigms advocated in much of entrepreneurship literature. Oftentimes, the depictions of "reality" are so far removed from my personal experiences in similar empirical settings that I simply cannot believe or relate to them – despite the "rigor" of the methodology.

This led me to seek other methodologies – ones that conformed to "my" understanding of truth and matched my sagacity. I discovered that I had many entrepreneurial stories to relate based upon my military experiences. My focus on personal experiences served a two-fold purpose: they challenged existing entrepreneurship theory, and they provided the reader an in-depth, realistic understanding of the struggles encountered by individuals on their unique paths to entrepreneurial success (or failure). I had the opportunity to recount a captivating tale so that readers could "feel" present in the story. Thus, the decision was made to hone my craft as a way to illustrate theory.

What originally started as a passion project has evolved into much more. As an entrepreneurial researcher and academician, I understand the importance of recording personal experiences, struggles, and success so that others may achieve their goals by learning through mistakes and successes.

Autoethnography as More than a Method – But as a Lifestyle

The aforementioned vignette illustrates multiple key points for consideration in autoethnography. First of all, many faculty members have had careers prior to entering academia – experiences which may form rich settings for theorizing (Learmonth and Humphreys, 2012; Tomkins and Nicholds, 2017). Autoethnographers struggle with memories and antenarratives (Rosile et al., 2013) – retrospective recall is far from perfect (Pelly and Kulik, 2024), because we, as humans, engage in memory (Pelly and Kulik, 2024) and history making (Hatch and Schultz, 2017). Our interactions with previous and contemporary selves form a rich palimpsest (McMorran, 2007) where the historical and potential interact. The tension between selves further facilitates verisimilitude, because it allows the reader a glimpse into regrets, successes, and roads not taken (Rambo, 2005; Pelly, 2016; Denker et al., 2020). This research orientation differentiates autoethnography from other methodologies because stories focus upon interpretation and not observation (Chang, 2016).

Secondly, the vignette emphasizes the fact that autoethnographers perceive their work as a calling to story-tell via publication (Pelly, 2020). This means that we make a choice to expose ourselves "warts and all" (Hindle, 2007) to our readers; and, we must recognize our own vulnerability in order to pursue this path (Webb, 2020; Denker et al., 2020). We must be willing to write about our mistakes, errors, and the choices we did not make and the rationale behind those decisions (Pelly, 2017b). On the other hand, observation and interviews may result in subjects masking reality to "save face", whereas this motivation in autoethnography is less relevant. From a professional standpoint, there are much safer avenues for publication (Ellis, 2007), so this is a labor of pure passion.

The following vignettes will describe ways in which I use autoethnography to aid my entrepreneurship students to better express themselves and discover a passion for writing.

Guiding the Reader, Guiding a Student

Fast forward to today. As an entrepreneurship faculty member, I enjoy pushing my students to challenge frontiers, to question why, to seek anomalies. Most of my entrepreneurship students are not satisfied with conventional concepts of management, but they are fascinated by thought experiments and stories as a way to record and sensationalize new venture creation – which reflects the importance of antenarratives in entrepreneurship (Rosile et al., 2013).

All of my students are required to write a thesis, which in an ideal situation, is published. Since they are entrepreneurship majors, many are practicing or soon to be entrepreneurs. The educational focus requires an emphasis on the practical need for research in order to aid budding entrepreneurs as they relate to the field's meta aspects (Hindle, 2007).

Each of my students challenges the findings of the articles I present in class. They usually share a personal experience from launching a business that contradicts or extrapolates the classic doctrine in literature – and they want to replace it with something else.

I tell my students – being an entrepreneur is in many ways like being a "troll", it is by challenging, destroying, or parodying that you can create or discover opportunities. I encourage them to follow a path similar to my own – build upon personal experience and see where the road leads you. It is this alternate road that will be explored in the following vignettes

Autoethnography and the Study of Outliers

The literary turn in autoethnography follows a train of thought parallel to that of the entrepreneur – a rejection of the status quo (Spinosa et al., 1997). A good autoethnography starts with introspection – asking how to engage in self critique, subject critique, and philosophical critique (Hearn et al., 2020;

Hackley, 2020). Individuals can generate reflexive interactions, resulting in internal dialogues that create new possibilities (Gielnik et al., 2014; Lakoff, 1990; Rorty, 1989), and account for organizational voices overlooked when a traditional ethnography is written (Denshire, 2014). The process of writing an autoethnography is also one where the writer and text interact – the more the writer engages with the text, they more they will learn from it, and the greater the self-mastery (Adams et al., 2017).

A Desire to Question the Status Quo

One of my students, I shall name her "Rachel", came to me with an interesting internship proposition: she wanted to explore green washing (or using environmentally friendly tactics to hide less than sustainable practices) at a well-known local entrepreneur's place of business. Her goals were two-fold: (1) to encourage environmentally safe practices; and (2) to start a similar operation in her hometown after graduation. As part of our pre-meetings during her internship, I provided her with basic guidance on taking autoethnographic field notes with a particular emphasis on vignette generation, as found in Rambo (2005) and in Pelly (2016, 2017b). The vignettes were designed to enhance Rachel's experience as if she were a participant and autoethnographic writer. I suggested she playfully experiment with her surroundings to interact with her colleagues in a proto-interview fashion, and to think about how her observations could contribute to or refute the theories she had digested in her entrepreneurship courses. She met with me each week to discuss any issues or difficulties she encountered. Although this project was designed for a thesis, she asked to co-author and publish the findings – an interesting prospect to which I readily agreed.

Co-constructed Autoethnography, Co-constructed Field Notes

Interactions with Rachel disclose a variety of approaches to field note taking in autoethnography. Although more traditional qualitative data sources such as research diaries (Johnstone, 2007), and emails (Wakkee et al., 2007) are beneficial, they are used differently than in a narrative (Dawson and Hjorth, 2011) or critical discourse analysis (Wodak and Meyer, 2001; Fairclough and Wodak, 1997). Instead, these data sources are reviewed to promote an emotional reaction which is then recorded in an autoethnography, embodying the idea that an actor and a script are interlocking parts of an unfolding relation (Hjorth, 2014; Cooren, 2004; Steyaert, 2004).

Autoethnography differs from more science-based experimentation in that the author is not separated from the setting. This has led to occasional conflicts with respect to research ethics. Rambo (2007) addressed these concerns at the onset by explaining that, because the occurrences contained within the autoethnography are part of the reader's everyday experiences, it is not considered an experiment. As such, an Institutional Review Board approval is unnecessary – the subject of the authethnography is the author, and consent is granted through the act of writing. She further explained that anonymizing the characters protects all characters in the narrative. This technique of altering details and characters is known as a "strange account" (Rambo, 2016) where fiction protects anonymity and is used as a sensemaking device.

The next vignette will explore ways in which to incorporate emotion into field notes.

The Contents of the Autoethnography

Throughout the following year, I met with Rachel on a weekly basis to review her field notes. Her initial stories had a stiff "academic" quality taught in school. Because positivism has pervaded our educational systems, it was challenging to teach Rachel to think more like a fiction writer than a scientist. As I explained, "one of the joys of autoethnography is you no longer have to be a mere observer, you are now free to interpret, as outlined in Follett (1970)". As a follow up, I provided her with my favorite "how to" writing style guide of autoethnography – de Sade's *Reflection on the Novel* (de Sade, 1987).

"Rachel, let's take some time to read this small pamphlet together," I advised. "Do you notice that he advises us to be emotional in our writing – to encourage us to help the reader feel what we feel as we are writing it – what de Sade refers to as verisimilitude?"

"You mean I can have my own voice and say what I feel?" she asked quizzically.

"That is exactly what I am telling you to do. Help me feel like I am part of your story. I am looking forward to seeing you next week!"

Autoethnography and the Evocative Writing Style

Breaking with mainstream academic tradition is the most difficult thing to achieve as an autoethnographer for many reasons. The most obvious one is mentioned in the prior vignette. Writing that incorporates emotion violates most publishing conventions and makes it difficult to achieve acceptance as a scholarly writer. In truth, it can endanger tenure due to the limited number of publishing outlets that accept authethnographies (Lunceford, 2015). Ergo, most scholars prefer to take the "safe" route, and discourage students from exploring this different style of writing.

From a positive perspective, emotional writing forms a "space for play" (Hjorth, 2005) that creates a bond with the reader. This bond is important because autoethnographers create truth not through objectivity, but through believability in the eyes of the reader (Herrmann, 2020a). In his writings, the Marquis de Sade described this bond with the reader, and other writers profess the value of using emotion to help the reader relate to the characters of the story. Follett, (1970) stresses the importance of leaving room for readers to develop their own interpretations of the story – a meaning-making process that may trump the author's initial writing. Moreover, Follett (1940) encourages storytellers to be so relatable that the audience is free to apply the findings of a narrative for their own benefit. Even Whitehead (1933) implores scholars to embrace the power of the imagination through emotion to make stories more believable, and more importantly, more relevant.

The next vignettes will explore how to integrate antenarratives into storytelling vignettes.

Peeling Back the Onion

In our next meeting Rachel presented several polished evocative vignettes similar to the ones found in Rambo (2005) and Pelly (2016, 2017b). These were short, choppy stories that recorded her workplace occurrences. This time, she did a remarkable job of depicting her emotions and frustrations – but the vignettes were still empty. She had limited her writings to observations.

To help Rachel with her narrative, I said, "Let's go back to de Sade. The first principle for de Sade's writing is to examine people as they actually are, not as they purport to be" (de Sade, 1987). I was met with a blank stare.

"Let me elaborate. As you previously read in Rosile et al. (2013) and in Boje (2011), antenarratives are important precedents to entrepreneurial behavior and they are necessary in understanding bets on the future. But there is a big problem in research – most of what we write explores what happened, and maybe why – but almost never do we discuss what didn't happen. What were the roads not taken? As a first person observer, you have an advantage – you have access to your own thoughts, you know the paths you didn't take and why. Record these inner thoughts. Write down the fantasies that you have – think of enactive research (Johannisson and Olaison, 2007)."

"I get that, but how can I know what other people are thinking? How can I write the story if I don't have all of the facts?" she inquired.

"That is why your first person role is so important. You are an insider, you can gain that trust, and you can ask those tough questions to figure out the internal struggles of other people. You can use this insight to give voice to your characters, to help the audience connect with them as well. And absolutely don't forget to rely on and record your intuition – even if you do nothing about it."

Focusing on the Road Not Taken

As highlighted in the Robert Frost poem, sometimes readers relate best to the road not taken. In Rachel's case, she was able to wander down both roads; in other words, from person to person in a Tamara-Land experience (Boje, 1995), exploring not only the "real" (in an ontic sense) occurrences, but also in multiple possible futures, both for herself and her co-workers. Travelling many roads can be achieved through interviews and direct observation; however, her presence in the setting enabled her to engage in thought experiments (Sarasvathy, 2001) and explore the phenomena imaginatively.

An insider perspective is extremely valuable in the search for understanding a phenomenon (Boyle and Parry, 2007). Outside observers cannot fully experience the full spectrum of their setting: they will miss the sensory perceptions (De Rond et al., 2019); the subtle cues (Pelly, 2017b); and, the sensemaking that comes with status as a CMR (Anderson, 2006). Membership in a setting removes the need to justify an understanding of an experience, and enables the writer to focus on telling their story in a way that will connect with the reader. In other words, the "data" for the autoethnography has to be a setting in which an author/entrepreneur actively participates – including, but not limited to a work place, community setting, or hobby (Engstrom, 2012; Steyaert, 2011; Fletcher, 2011).

Most importantly, the analysis of antenarratives serves as a record of struggle. Autoethnography captures processes and anti-processes which are an essential piece of the entrepreneurial story. The full experience aids us in capturing these rejected paths, failures, and difficulties – after all, it is pain that makes a story believable (Denker et al., 2020; Rambo, 2005, Pelly, 2020; de Sade, 1987). Rachel was able to experience the complete nature of the phenomenon and not just what could be directly observed.

Next, we will explore how we reframe vignettes.

Ready to Begin Writing the Story

After a year of suffering through her job and taking copious field notes, Rachel and I began to sift through her writings. She had accumulated 100 pages of single-spaced notes. More data and note taking are usually anticipated in formal interviews for conventional ethnographies. Nonetheless, her written observations served her well as she told her story. I asked Rachel to comb through her notes and look for vignettes with common themes.

"How do I know which vignettes have common themes?" she asked me in a state of panic.

"Go with your intuition – go with what feels right," I prompted her.

"Sometimes, the vignettes have a common theme, but the timelines are tough – some of these things happened in a strange order and they don't naturally make sense – what do I do?" she responded.

"Your job is to be an effective storyteller. You are not a recorder of the story, you are the teller of the story. Sometimes we have to bend reality in our minds in order to make sense of what we see. Think of flashbacks or scenes that have been cut in reality TV. You can reorder your stories in a similar fashion. When you write, you are the master of the universe – rock with it."

The "Hyphen" Problem

The goal of autoethnography is to take away the "hyphen" in the literary-social domain (Bochner, 2020). In this case, it was up to Rachel to tell her story in the way she felt was most effective. This could include viewing time in a kairological order and not a chronological one (Hernes, 2014). Chronological time is frequently measured by a watch, is seen as linear, is objective, and is the dominant understanding of time. However, this form of time does not exist at the cosmic or microscopic levels (Fayolle, 2007). We can look to kairological time to guide us in autoethnographies (Larsen et al., 2020; Pelly, 2017b). Kairological time is qualitative, subjective, process based, and is not linear (Hernes, 2014). Understanding time kairologically has been used in autoethnographies previously – especially in the case of Rambo (2005, 2007, 2016) where she reorders events so that readers can understand the traumatic, confusing maze of events she describes.

This mixing of events is also used in entrepreneurship autoethnographies as a sensemaking device. Pelly (2016, 2017b) describes how entrepreneurs focus on kairological time to tell stories, and to re-order organizational timelines during the creation of adhocracies. However, the autoethnography is also told through a process of reordering events across separate time continuums. In Rachel's case, this reordering was achieved though flashbacks, allegory, and ontological shifts. The truth for the teller and audience of the entrepreneurial story lies not in discreet timelines, but in its coherence (Larsen et al., 2020; Rosile et al., 2013).

Our next vignette will explore the initial reactions Rachel experienced that helped her to write in a relatable way.

The Beginning of the Writing

Rachel chose a consistent theme in her stories – she was interested in how the owner of the store was able to create a counter narrative to support this entrepreneurial venture. This counter narrative was the tension between environmental sustainability and capitalism. She also found herself interested in how the store became a special place where this owner could make his own rules and stories. She was fascinated by her growing awareness of these occurrences, her increasing frustrations associated with these events, and her options to change the current environment.

"How did you choose this theme?" I asked her.

"As I read and re-read the text, I kind of worked with it and certain things popped out after the fact, and then I felt like I could maybe build a story around it. I can't give an exact answer, the text just kind of spoke to me. I think I can communicate how I feel – maybe others would feel the same and I could guide them in a similar situation."

"I write in the exact same way," I reassured her.

"So what do we do now?" she asked.

Potentializing the Text

During autoethnographical writings, the discourser is encouraged to work with, struggle with, and confront the text (McMorran, 2007; Herrmann, 2020b). The writer, the text, and the writer's memories all take on a life of their own as the story is being written and as the text undergoes repeated iterations (Hatch and Schultz, 2017).

Emotions aid in potentializing a narrative and encourage readers to act (Aldrich and Fiol, 1994; Lounsbury and Glynn, 2001; Hjorth, 2007). Whether fact or fiction, stories use emotions as sensemaking devices (Gartner, 2004; Campbell, 2004). A good story relies upon the writer's ability to help the audience relate to the principal characters and plots (Hjorth, 2004; Fletcher, 2007) irrespective of how fantastical the story may be, because the truth of a story lies within its meaning and not in objective criteria (Gabriel & Griffiths, 2004).

To facilitate the potentializing of a text, autoethnographers rely upon a variety of literary techniques such as poems, reflective essays, theatrical performances (Hesse-Biber and Leavy, 2010), creative non-fiction writing, (Hackley, 2007, 2020), and writing styles such as flashbacks, foreshadowing, dialogues, short stories, and vignettes (Herrmann, 2020b).

In the case under discussion, Rachel gave life to her text. She entered the field with no theoretical bias (an almost inductive approach) and simply observed the setting as it unfolded, matching the idea of reflexive stories in entrepreneurship (Rosile, 2016). Although she is the storyteller, there is a joint authorship with the events themselves, which guided her in an inexplicable way toward her tentative theory. The more she interacted with her writing, the better she understood her emotions, and the better she was able to share these emotions with the readers so they could think about how they felt and how they would act in a similar situation. Our next vignettes will explore in more depth the art of co-authorship.

Co-authorship

At this point, Rachel asked me a question that was both surprising and interesting.

"I want to tell my story to the world – it is just so wrong what happened here. I know this is for a thesis project – but what about publishing? Can I do that? The story is good, but I don't know a lot about theory."

"How would you feel about co-authoring with me? I want you to tell the story. I will provide suggestions on the theory, and we can discuss where the paper should be submitted. I will write a general theory, and you can decide if this helps to tell your story," I suggested.

"I like this idea – this can help me tell my story to people like me (practitioners), and it will become part of research."

"Indeed, this is something that can remain long after we're gone," I added.

Autoethnography or Duography?

The preceding vignette illustrates two of the greatest strengths of the autoethnography – the ability to harness the passion of the storyteller and the ability to co-author to find a single voice. This is particularly important because knowledge is co-constructed (Sambrook and Doloriert, 2020) and because entrepreneurs are rarely lone wolves (Peredo and Chrisman, 2017). Such relationality is captured in collaborative autoethnographies and in poly-vocal texts (Doloriert and Sambrook, 2012; Yarborough and Lowe, 2007; Zawadzki and Jensen, 2020).

Due to increasing pressures of tenure and promotion, we (academicians) may find ourselves increasingly locked in an ivory tower (Hindle, 2007). This means that our contributions to entrepreneurial practice may be restricted, or may be outright lost (Learmonth and Humphreys, 2012; Tomkins and Nicholds, 2017). Unfortunately, once we become academicians our professional experiences become increasingly finite. Therefore, the voices of the practitioner and the academic can be combined into a single voice (Doloriert and Sambrook, 2012; Yarborough and Lowe, 2007; Zawadzki and Jensen, 2020), which expands the possibilities for empirical exploration.

The next vignette will discuss the passion found in autoethnographic vignettes.

The First Draft

Rachel returned to my office. She had taken my advice and produced a series of vignettes detailing her experiences. Her writing was raw, emotional, and authentic – I loved it!

"Rachel – you knocked it out of the park!" I exclaimed.

"Really?" she inquired. "But I am not a 'real' writer."

"It doesn't matter – your writing speaks to me, and it's totally working."

The vignettes were unlike the writings found in business literature, but they reflected Rachel's undergraduate education in English. Her vignettes were spellbinding and read like a great novel. Each vignette was short, sweet, and totally coherent. Since we were hoping to publish an article, I asked Rachel to produce at least 15 pages of double-spaced material. Instead, Rachel wrote almost 60 pages, enough for several paper submissions for publication.

"I know this is way more than you wanted, but I wanted to tell the story of my experience, I'm crazy pissed off about what happened," she explained.

The Value of Prior Experiences and Passion

The above vignette highlights two key components of autoethnography: the importance of writing about topics that are of paramount interest to us and of taking advantage of and incorporating our prior experiences in our writings.

Autoethnographers should focus on settings that are important to us not only as scholars, but also as active members of society (Adams, 2016; Adams et al., 2017). Many scholars choose a setting for experimental purposes, or as a ticket to fast-paced scholarly publication. Purist autoethnographers write because they want to make a difference (Schein, 2008; Berry and Patti, 2015) or perhaps they are trying to expose and/or fight an injustice (Rambo, 2005; Pelly, 2020). It is this passion for writing that helps writers return to the roots of entrepreneurship research (Pelly and Fayolle, 2020) and to present a more authentic (Larsen et al., 2020) and reflexive representation of the world (Tomkins, 2011; Osentoski, 2015).

In this specific vignette, Rachel has a burning story to tell – one that might not have an audience in the mainstream media or in popular publishing; but, autoethnography and academic outlets may provide an alternative platform (Pelly, 2020; López and Tracy, 2020) in which to give voice to the voiceless in order to discuss sensitive issues such as corruption (Pelly, 2017b), resistance (Frandsen et al., 2020), rape (Doloriert and Sambrook, 2009), incest (Rambo, 2005), illness (Wall, 2006), and other distressing situations. Clearly, there is value in descanting upon these topics, and as academics we have a moral responsibility to do so. As a contrast, autoethnography can capture entrepreneurial passion and its playful spirit as advocated in Hjorth (2005).

The next vignette will elaborate upon ways in which we add theory to the story.

Adding Theory

In the next step, Rachel and I worked together to develop a theory for the paper. We agreed that her storytelling vignettes were too lengthy. Our goal was to use between 10 and 15 of the 60 double-spaced pages she had written in order to accommodate the theory, literature review, discussion, conclusion, and introduction.

We searched to discover common threads contained within the story – what were the vignettes we could pluck from this sea of 60 pages that could be used to construct a tight narrative that I could use as the basis for theory building? As we progressed through the pages, we copied all relevant vignettes and placed them into a new word document. Next we arranged the vignettes (not necessarily chronologically) into an order that made a coherent story. Contained within the messiness of these little tales, we uncovered a variety of inner thoughts, monologues, and fantasies that were not necessarily observed, but were experienced by Rachel and, thus, had a direct impact upon her actions.

As Rachel explained, "It was hard for me to piece the story together based only upon what I observed. I thought about how you probably couldn't figure out a theory because the stuff was so scattered. So, I added my daydreams to the story – my 'Bobby's World' and 'Walter Mitty' "what if's". They provide the mortar to the bricks. I think they also magnify the emotional difficulties I've encountered and may help others also in need. My actual experiences may be unique, but I'll bet my daydreams are pretty relatable. They also show a pathway of what I will do in my business when I graduate."

Observation or Interpretation?

One of the advantages of the insider observation in autoethnography is the interpretation and description of events that were contemplated but did not actually occur, (Pelly, 2017b). These can include morsels of the stream of consciousness (Vyner, 2018), antenarratives (Rosile et al., 2013), daydreams (Semler, 2001), scattered recollections (Rambo, 2005), and fantasies (Hall, 2013). There is a tremendous degree of veracity in these types of introspective behaviors (Hearn et al., 2020), and few methodologies can capture them (Larsen et al., 2020).

All of the aforementioned cognitive processes, much like enactment, can have a direct impact upon an entrepreneur's behavior (Sarasvathy, 2001). They represent the antecedents of entrepreneurial action (Pelly, 2016, 2017b), thereby making them worthy of study. Autoethnography is one of the few methodologies that focus on the transition from antecedent to action. The reading and writing of such texts can inspire any form of action (Bochner and Ellis, 2016; Townsend et al., 2020) – including entrepreneurial action (Damgaard et al., 2004; Fletcher, 2011; Hackley, 2020).

Despite the fact that it may be difficult to generalize about specific components of entrepreneurship – i.e., definitions, opportunities, and outcomes (Gartner and Teague, 2017) we should strive to create verisimilitude for our readers (Denzin, 1997; Conquergood, 1991). Alternatively stated, generalizability allows our audience to co-create meaning with the authors. The internal monologues, struggles, and difficulties that occur during the entrepreneurial process can assist readers in understanding possible pathways to "success" and "what not to do", which can lead to teachable moments for entrepreneurs (Shepherd et al., 2016).

Furthermore, the writers of an autoethnography are free to change the order and details to support a story. The veracity of a well-constructed autoethnography lies not in objective "facts" but in resonance with the reader (Tracy, 2010; Bochner, 2000) or "truth" (Larsen et al., 2020) because the story is useful to them. This is not problematic because plausibility trumps accuracy in entrepreneurship (Gartner, 2007) on the condition that plausibility prods activity (McKinley et al., 1999). Rachel's small tales streamline the imagination and serve as the basis for the reader's own thought experiments as advocated in Folger and Turillo, (1999).

The most important skill of a writer is the ability to effectively communicate the message. It is this ability that enables the author to alter settings, exaggerate, and hide details (de Sade, 1987). Alteration is considered ethical because it can provide anonymity for the subjects within a story (Rambo, 2016). The most challenging part of writing an autoethnography is not writing the tale or adding the proper theory – it is the iterative process of discussing, selecting, and narrating the stories – along with the refinement of arguments, interactions, and implications (Denker et al., 2020).

The next vignette will explain how to begin writing theoretical vignettes.

Constructing the Theory

"There is no magical theory for any story, but a few things come to mind," I told Rachel. I proceeded to provide four different theoretical explanations I thought we should consider. "Which one do you like the most – go with your gut," I told her.

After she selected one of the basic theories, I began writing the theoretical vignettes to match each of her storytelling vignettes. As I was writing, I tried to keep my vignettes short and generally free of excessive jargon, barring careful explanation.

"Rachel – one day you may wish to write an autoethnography by yourself. I am sure you remember how painful those academic papers are that you normally read. Try to write in such a way that an educated 12-year-old could follow. Write in an honest, convincing way."

An Overview of Theoretical Writing Techniques

There are varied approaches used to develop theory in an autoethnography. Some autoethnographies do not have research questions, and most shy away from coding or other qualitative data procedures (López and Tracy, 2020). Many autoethnographies focus exclusively on the story, with little or no theory development, may skip the conventional paper layout, and use the theoretical vignettes to serve as the introduction, literature review, and discussion sections (Rambo, 2005, 2007). Still, others may use a very sparse storytelling portion in favor of theory (Anderson, 2006).

Autoethnography may be used to refute theory, illustrate theory in a clearer way, or serve as a means for a replication study (Pelly and Fayolle, 2020). In the field of entrepreneurship, journals tend to favor a more conventional structure. This would mean writing a paper with a standard introduction, literature review, methods, discussion, and conclusion section. The interwoven storytelling and theoretical vignettes are designed to serve as the empirical section of the paper. The theoretical vignettes also serve as the placeholder where theory development occurs. For examples of this technique in entrepreneurship and management, see Pelly (2016, 2017b), Mendez and Pelly (2021), Frandsen et al. (2020), and Fernando et al. (2020).

Irrespective of the goal of the autoethnography, it uses theory to support the story, not vice versa. Autoethnographers are encouraged to borrow from other disciplines and traditions (Herrmann, 2020a, 2020b). This encourages writers to think more broadly about a phenomenon, and it reflects entrepreneurship's multidisciplinary roots (Gartner and Teague, 2017). This means that autoethnography can help writers explore ideas and settings that might otherwise be overlooked by more conventional methods, and it provides valuable insights into understandings of entrepreneurship (Pelly, 2017b).

The goal of utilizing these techniques is to produce texts that are engaging, meaningful, and accessible to a larger audience than conventional academic research (Hackley, 2020). This is particularly relevant in the field of entrepreneurship, because scholarship appears to have become more and more disengaged from the needs of practitioners and students (Hindle, 2007; Pelly and Fayolle, 2020). Therefore, it is essential that we write theoretical vignettes that are as engaging as the storytelling vignettes. This can be achieved through microstories (Anderson 2006), colloquialisms (Mendez and Pelly, 2021), and pop culture references (Pelly, 2017b).

The next vignette will discuss how we jointly revised the text.

Iteration of the Palimpsest

After I wove the story into a draft paper, I presented it to Rachel.

"What do you think?" I asked her.

"Some parts of the manuscript I totally agree with … but others I am not so sure. I feel that in some of these vignettes you totally missed the point of what I was saying, and in some of them you revealed insights I would have otherwise missed. Would it be ok if we changed some of the vignettes and tweaked some of the theories you mentioned?" she timidly inquired.

"Absolutely! This is the point of this conversation. Let's work together to transform this into something that you feel best represents your story," I encouraged.

We then spent the remainder of the afternoon working and reworking the text. The more we discussed it, the more we understood both sides of the story – and the text began to take on a life of its own …

One Story, One Voice

It is perhaps due to bounded rationality (March and Simon, 1993), that one author may not truly understand every aspect of their story, and similarly, may not be able to generalize about it to the same extent as could an inside observer. It is for this reason that autoethnographic writing, whether it has one or many coauthors, benefits from a palimpsest approach.

Palimpsest means that authors struggle and debate both with one another and with the text (McMorran, 2007). As interpretations and reinterpretations occur, new directions arise as new drafts are written. This struggle becomes deeper as the document is being rewritten, the tensions and emotions in the story become stronger and more apparent for the reader – who can then become part of the palimpsest and cannibalize and apply it as necessary.

Although the *Journal of Business Venturing* (22(5)) special issue is not an autoethnography in a traditional sense, it embodies this concept of the palimpsest and layered account writing. In this particular issue, Allen (2007), who is a practitioner, wrote a playful text describing his unconventional entrepreneurship journey. He included the faux pas he made, told humorous anecdotes, shared his fears, and his successes. Allen's article served as a storytelling vignette for the theoretically based articles that followed.

Several scholars provided a series of alternative interpretations of the events that Allen described via the other articles in this special issue (for examples, see Gartner, 2007; Steyaert, 2007; Fletcher, 2007; Hjorth, 2007). While Allen's angle of writing was clearly literary and praxis oriented, each scholarly contributor provided reflections based upon their own biases and research interests, resulting in a quilting of understanding (Hearn et al., 2020) that provides the reader additional room for interpretive flexibility. This special issue illustrates the fact that coauthored autoethnography serves as a two-way mirror into processes and helps to provide multiple insights into a story.

The next vignette will discuss how Rachel and I wrote the remainder of the paper.

Writing the Rest of the Paper

Once Rachel and I agreed upon the theoretical interpretations for the paper, including how the theoretical vignettes were written, we backtracked and wrote the literature review to reflect our choices.

"No one is going to accept this paper as research," Rachel told me. "I feel like all we did is write a story – there is no quantitative data, no numbers, no fancy analysis. I feel like our methods section is going to be ridiculously long to explain what we are doing."

"There is certainly a positivistic bent in research. But don't worry, autoethnography is becoming more accepted in all areas of business, including in entrepreneurship. Who knows, you may even be featured in a best-selling book, which includes a chapter on how to write an autoethnography (as I playfully wink at my reader …). The trick is not for you to spend so much time defining the basics of autoethnography, or why it is important, but rather to explain how your interpretation of this particular methodology supports the story you are trying to tell. That was some of the best advice my advisor (who is also a co-editor of this book) gave me, and I want to share it with you as well."

Next we began writing the methods section before we finalized the paper.

Rising Acceptance of Autoethnography as a Method to Study Entrepreneurship

As Rachel correctly assessed, there is a strong bias against using autoethnography. Most mainstream science favors positivism and more subjective methods still seek the visage of legitimacy provided by objectivism (Parry, 2008). This means that faculty who write autoethnographies may face ridicule from colleagues (Denker et al., 2020), and struggle with institutional review boards and chains of command that are unsympathetic to autoethnography (Rambo, 2016; Townsend et al., 2020). Moreover, writing autoethnographies can create a challenging path for publication as well as tenure and promotion (Denker et al., 2020).

The goal of composing an autoethnography is not to write for its own sake, but to be able to ask different types of research questions – the kinds of questions that require the use of autoethnography, such as those that not only study an (entrepreneurial) organization, but (entrepreneurial) individuals and identities (Herrmann, 2020a), and the antecedents behind the formation of a new business.

The next vignette will discuss composing the final thoughts of this autoethnography.

Putting the Finishing Touches on the Paper

Once we finalized the theory, storytelling, and methodology sections, the rest of the writing process was a breeze. We composed the discussion and conclusion, and polished off the paper with the introduction and abstract.

"My other faculty members told me that the paper can't count because it is based on my own experiences. I can't generalize about reality because I'm only telling my own story," Rachel told me.

"Well I don't know if you can generalize about reality, especially not in entrepreneurship – we are exploring a phenomena that is about outliers. There is no normal distribution here, and not even any agreed upon definition," I explained.

In our discussion section, we explained why the small sample size was not problematic for our study – we were simply telling one person's story and allowing the reader, not the author, to exercise the right of interpretation of the narrative.

Studying the Black Swan in Entrepreneurship

Small sample sizes can be problematic in traditional social sciences, but not in entrepreneurship. Entrepreneurs are rebels (Corbett et al., 2018), deviants (de Vries, 1977), innovators, and progenitors of creative destruction (Schumpeter, 2000). They are the black swans of human action (Pelly, 2017a), and their stories cannot easily be compared with others. The examination of entrepreneurship is more holistically conducted by the individual and contextual, and not the generalizable (Fletcher, 2007, 2011). Only through a deep dive can we create understanding, or "verstehen" of entrepreneurial behavior (Kirzner, 1982).

Despite the fact that interpretive research is seen as lesser to positivist frameworks (Tracy, 2012), it might be the most appropriate choice for entrepreneurship studies. First, entrepreneurship is the story of outliers, opportunities that rarely occur randomly, and are not normally distributed (Eckhardt and Shane, 2003). Seeking a normal distribution of the "how" and "why" would violate the underlying assumptions of most quantitative research (Pelly, 2017a). Even with qualitative methods, it may be possible to generalize about some of the processual aspects of entrepreneurship. However, chopping up a story means that it ceases to be the story of the entrepreneur; it is the attempt of the researcher to supplant his or her narrative onto the events in lieu of allowing the characters to tell their own stories (Bochner, 2001; Bochner and Herrmann, 2020).

For these reasons, scholars of entrepreneurship research methodologies are unique. We can discard rationality, and engage with the playful sides of research and human action (Hjorth, 2005). In short, we can create change through our writings and be innovative like the entrepreneurs whom we are studying (Townsend et al., 2020).

FINAL THOUGHTS

This chapter has explored autoethnography not simply by telling the reader about it, but rather by illustrating autoethnography (Denker et al., 2020; Schindler, 2015). It is my opinion that the best approach is to create a strange account (Rambo, 2016) of my experiences working with "a" co-author in order to allow the readers to insert themselves into the story, after which point they can write their own. I tried to avoid a "step-by-step" checklist, because I do not believe one truly exists or is appropriate, since autoethnography is to be followed in spirit, not in letter (Bochner, 2000; Schwandt, 1996). Although I did describe some of the different styles and formats of autoethnography, it is important to remember to mold the method to the story, not vice versa.

I provided a series of dialogues to depict the internal struggles of the autoethnographic writing processes. I highlighted some of the obstacles that I and others have encountered as we tell our stories, because these struggles make the story believable (Pelly, 2020; Rambo, 2005; de Sade, 1987), and because we as faculty have an obligation to open ourselves to criticism and allow ourselves to be vulnerable to our readers (Denker et al., 2020). I could have easily written this from a first-person account; but a dialogue, with questions, introspection, and responses can be much more convincing than a single stream of consciousness (Rosile et al., 2013).

It is my intention for this chapter to serve as a beacon of inspiration and hope for the aspiring autoethnographer. This style of writing is a lonely one (Denker et al., 2020) – even when you work with co-authors. You may not find support for your ideas, but that does not mean they are not worth developing. Remember that every paper has a home, so do not lose courage. Go out, explore, experience, and experiment in the world. Then write about it! The frontiers and fringes of entrepreneurship research demand no less. Take the road less traveled, because that may well make all the difference.

REFERENCES

Adams, T. E. (2016). *Narrating the closet: An autoethnography of same-sex attraction*. Routledge.
Adams, T. E., Ellis, C., & Jones, S. H. (2017). Autoethnography. *The international encyclopedia of communication research methods* (pp. 1–11). Wiley.
Aldrich, H. & Fiol, C. (1994). Fools rush in? The institutional context of industry formation. *The Academy of Management, 19*(4), 645–670.
Allen, T. (2007). A toy store(y). *Journal of Business Venturing, 22*(5), 628–636.
Allen-Collinson, J. (2013). Autoethnography as the engagement of self/other, self/culture, self/politics, selves/futures. In Holman Jones, S., Adams, T. E., & Ellis, C. (Eds.) *Handbook of autoethnography* (pp. 281–299). Left Coast Press.
Alsop, C. K. (2002, September). Home and away: Self-reflexive auto-/ethnography. *Forum Qualitative Sozialforschung/Forum: Qualitative Social Research*, 3(3).
Alvarez, S. A., Barney, J. B., McBride, R., & Wuebker, R. (2014). Realism in the study of entrepreneurship. *Academy of Management Review, 39*(2), 227–231.
Anderson, L. (2006). Analytic autoethnography. *Journal of Contemporary Ethnography, 35*(4), 373–395.
Berry, K., & Patti, C. J. (2015). Lost in narration: Applying autoethnography. *Journal of Applied Communication Research, 43*(2), 263–268.
Bochner, A. P. (2000). Criteria against ourselves. *Qualitative Inquiry, 6*(2), 266–272.
Bochner, A. P. (2001). Narrative's virtues. *Qualitative Inquiry, 7*(2), 131–157.
Bochner, A. P. (2020). Autoethnography as a way of life: Listening to tinnitus teach. *Journal of Autoethnography, 1*(1), 81–92.
Bochner, A. P., & Ellis, C. (Eds.). (2002). *Ethnographically speaking: Autoethnography, literature, and aesthetics* (Vol. 9). Rowman Altamira.
Bochner, A., & Ellis, C. (2003). An introduction to the arts and narrative research: Art as inquiry. *Qualitative Inquiry, 9*(4), 506–514.
Bochner, A., & Ellis, C. (2016). *Evocative autoethnography: Writing lives and telling stories*. Routledge.
Bochner, A. P., & Herrmann, A. F. (2020) Practicing narrative inquiry II: Making meaning move. In Leavy, P. (Ed.) *The Oxford handbook of qualitative research* (pp. 285–328). Oxford University Press.
Boje, D. M. (1995). Stories of the storytelling organization: A postmodern analysis of Disney as "Tamara-Land". *Academy of Management Journal, 38*(4), 997–1035.
Boje, D. M. (Ed.). (2011). *Storytelling and the future of organizations: An antenarrative handbook* (Vol. 11). Routledge.
Boutillier, S., & Uzunidis, D. (2014). The theory of the entrepreneur: from heroic to socialised entrepreneurship. *Journal of Innovation Economics Management*, (2), 9–40.
Boyle, M., & Parry, K. (2007). Telling the whole story: The case for organizational autoethnography. *Culture and Organization, 13*(3), 185–190.
Brommel, B. J. (2017). Sensemaking in the dialysis clinic. In Herrmann, A. F. (Ed.) *Organizational autoethnographies: Power and identity in our working lives* (pp. 87–106). Routledge.
Campbell, K. (2004) Quilting a feminist map to guide the study of women entrepreneurs. In Hjorth, D., & Steyaert, C. (Eds.) *Narrative and discursive approaches in entrepreneurship* (pp. 194–209). Edward Elgar Publishing.

Chang, H. (2007). Autoethnography: Raising cultural consciousness of self and others. In Walford, G. (Ed.) *Methodological developments in ethnography*, Studies in Educational Ethnography, Vol. 12 (pp. 207–221). Emerald.
Chang, H. (2016). *Autoethnography as method* (Vol. 1). Routledge.
Chiles, T. H., Bluedorn, A. C., & Gupta, V. K. (2007). Beyond creative destruction and entrepreneurial discovery: A radical Austrian approach to entrepreneurship. *Organization Studies*, *28*(4), 467–493.
Colli, A. (2003). *The history of family business, 1850–2000* (No. 47). Cambridge University Press.
Conquergood, D. (1991). Rethinking ethnography: Towards a critical cultural politics. *Communications Monographs*, *58*(2), 179–194.
Cook, P. (2012). To actually be sociological: Autoethnography as an assessment and learning tool. *Journal of Sociology*, 1440783312451780.
Cooren, F. (2004). Textual agency: How texts do things in organizational settings. *Organization*, *11*(3), 373–393.
Corbett, A., Mitchell, R., Shelton, L. M., & Wood, M. (2018). The attitudes, behaviors and cognition of entrepreneurs: rebels with a cause. *International Journal of Entrepreneurial Behaviour & Research*, *24*(5), 938–946.
Cullen, J. G. (2011). Researching workplace spiritualization through auto/ethnography. *Journal of Management, Spirituality & Religion*, *8*(2), 143–164.
Cruise, T. (2017). Are we confounding heroism and individualism? Entrepreneurs may not be lone rangers, but they are heroic nonetheless. *Business Horizons*, *60*(1), 257–259.
Damgaard, T., Piihl, J., & Klyver, K. (2004). *The drama of consulting and counselling the entrepreneur: Narrative and discursive approaches in entrepreneurship*. Edward Elgar Publishing.
Da Palma, P. J., Lopes, M. P., & Alves, T. F. (2018). Entrepreneurship as a calling: A pilot study with aspiring entrepreneurs. *The Journal of Entrepreneurship*, *27*(2), 277–300.
Dawson, A. & Hjorth, D. (2011). Advancing family business research through narrative analysis. *Family Business Review*, *25*(3), 339–355.
Denker, K. J., Rausch, K., & Williams, S. E. (2020). Learning through the process: Failure, frustration, and forward movement in autoethnography. In Herrmann, A. F. (Ed.) *The Routledge international handbook of organizational autoethnography* (pp. 353–365). Routledge.
Denshire, S. (2014). On auto-ethnography. *Current Sociology*, *62*(6), 831–850.
Denzin, N. K. (1997). *Interpretive ethnography: Ethnographic practices for the 21st century*. Sage.
De Rond, M., Holeman, I., & Howard-Grenville, J. (2019). Sensemaking from the body: An enactive ethnography of rowing the Amazon. *Academy of Management Journal*, *62*(6), 1961–1988.
De Vries, M. K. (1977). The entrepreneurial personality: A person at the crossroads. *Journal of Management Studies*, *14*(1), 34–57.
Doloriert, C., & Sambrook, S. (2009). Ethical confessions of the "I" of autoethnography: The student's dilemma. *Qualitative Research in Organizations and Management: An International Journal*, *4*(1), 27–45.
Doloriert, C., & Sambrook, S. (2012). Organisational autoethnography. *Journal of Organizational Ethnography*, *1*(1), 83–95.
Eckhardt, J., & Shane, S. (2003). Opportunities and entrepreneurship. *Journal of Management*, *2*, 209–224.

Ellingson, L. L. (2009). *Engaging crystallization in qualitative research: An introduction.* Sage.

Ellis, C. (1999). Heartful autoethnography. *Qualitative Health Research, 9*(5), 669–683.

Ellis, C. (2007). Telling secrets, revealing lives: Relational ethics in research with intimate others. *Qualitative Inquiry, 13*(1), 3–29.

Ellis, C., Adams, T. E., & Bochner, A. P. (2011). Autoethnography: an overview. *Historical Social Research/Historische sozialforschung, 36*(4), 273–290.

Engstrom, C. (2012). An autoethnographic account of prosaic entrepreneurship. *Tamara: Journal for Critical Organization Inquiry, 10*(1–2).

Fairclough, N. and Wodak, R. (1997). Critical discourse analysis. In Van Dijk, T. A. (Ed.) *Discourse as social interaction* (pp. 258–284). Sage.

Fayolle, A. (2007). *Entrepreneurship and new value creation: The dynamic of the entrepreneurial process.* Cambridge University Press.

Fernando, M., Reveley, J., & Learmonth, M. (2020). Identity work by a non-white immigrant business scholar: Autoethnographic vignettes of covering and accenting. *Human Relations, 73*(6), 765–788.

Fischer, M. M., & Nijkamp, P. (2009). The nexus of entrepreneurship and regional development. In Capello, R., & Nijkamp, P. (Eds.) *Handbook of regional growth and development theories* (pp. 198–217). Edward Elgar Publishing.

Fletcher, D. (2007). 'Toy Story': The narrative world of entrepreneurship and the creation of interpretive communities. *Journal of Business Venturing, 22*(5), 649–672.

Fletcher, D. (2011). A curiosity for contexts: Entrepreneurship, enactive research and autoethnography. *Entrepreneurship and Regional Development, 23*(1–2), 65–76.

Folger, R., & Turillo, C. J. (1999). Theorizing as the thickness of thin abstraction. *Academy of Management Review, 24*(4), 742–758.

Follett, M. (1940). *Dynamic administration: The collected papers of Mary Parker Follett.* Routledge.

Follett, M. P. (1970). The teacher–student relation. *Administrative Science Quarterly, 15*(2), 137–148.

Frandsen, S., Duncan, R., & Pelly, M. (2020). Organizational Resistance and autoethnography. In Herrmann, A. F. (Ed.) *The Routledge international handbook of organizational autoethnography* (pp. 252–268). Routledge.

Frith, K. (2007). Fickle rooster productions: Making a business from a hobby. *The International Journal of Entrepreneurship and Innovation, 8*(2), 149–153.

Frost, R. (1916). The road not taken. In *Mountain interval.* H. Holt and Co.

Gabriel, Y., & Griffiths, D. S. (2004). Stories in organizational research. In Cassell, C., & Symon, G. (Eds.) *Essential guide to qualitative research methods in organizational research* (pp. 114–126). Sage.

Gartner, W. (2004). The edge defines the (w)hole: saying what entrepreneurship is (not). In Hjorth, D., & Steyaert, C. (Eds.) *Narrative and discursive approaches in entrepreneurship* (pp. 245–254). Edward Elgar Publishing.

Gartner, W. B. (2007). Entrepreneurial narrative and a science of the imagination. *Journal of Business Venturing, 22*(5), 613–627.

Gartner, W. B., & Teague, B. T. (2017). What does "writing a business plan" mean? Paper presented at the Expanding Understanding of Business Creation: Ethnographic Approaches to Tracking Entrepreneurial Decision-making Conference, Princeton University, August 1–3.

Gielnik, M. M., Barabas, S., Frese, M., Namatovu-Dawa, R., Scholz, F. A., Metzger, J. R., and Walter, T. (2014). A temporal analysis of how entrepreneurial goal inten-

tions, positive fantasies, and action planning affect starting a new venture and when the effects wear off. *Journal of Business Venturing*, *29*(6), 755–772.
Goodall, Jr, H. L. (2004). Commentary: Narrative ethnography as applied communication research. *Journal of Applied Communication Research*, *32*(3), 185–194.
Graiver, I. (2019). The late antique history of psychology: The test case of introspection. *History of Psychology*, *22*(2), 130.
Hackley, C. (2007). Auto-ethnographic consumer research and creative non-fiction: exploring connections and contrasts from a literary perspective. *Qualitative Market Research: An International Journal*, *10*(1), 98–108.
Hackley, C. (2020). The discomfort of autoethnography in academic marketing research. In Herrmann, A. F. (Ed.) *The Routledge international handbook of organizational autoethnography* (pp. 176–187). Routledge.
Hall, M. L. (2013). Imagining neighbourhood-based community: an autoethnography (Doctoral dissertation, Queensland University of Technology).
Hatch, M. J., & Schultz, M. (2017). Toward a theory of using history authentically: Historicizing in the Carlsberg Group. *Administrative Science Quarterly*, *62*(4), 657–697.
Hearn, J., Sveiby, K. E., & Thym, A. (2020). Organizational autoethnographies of economy, finance, business and management: Reflections and possibilities. In Herrmann, A. F. (Ed.) *The Routledge international handbook of organizational autoethnography* (pp. 160–175). Routledge.
Hernes, T. (2014). *A process theory of organization*. Oxford University Press.
Herrmann, A. F. (2017). *Organizational autoethnographies: Power and identity in our working lives*. Taylor & Francis.
Herrmann, A. F. (2020a). Introduction: Organizing a handbook and how to use it. In Herrmann, A. F. (Ed.) *The Routledge international handbook of organizational autoethnography* (pp. 1–10). Routledge.
Herrmann, A. F. (2020b). The historical and hysterical narratives of organization and autoethnography. In Herrmann, A. F. (Ed.) *The Routledge international handbook of organizational autoethnography* (pp. 13–41). Routledge.
Hesse-Biber, S. N., & Leavy, P. (2010). *The practice of qualitative research*. Sage.
Hindle, K. (2007). Teaching entrepreneurship at university: From the wrong building to the right philosophy. In Fayolle, A. (Ed.) *Handbook of research in entrepreneurship education, volume 1* (pp. 104–126). Edward Elgar Publishing.
Hjorth, D. (2004). Towards genealogic storytelling in entrepreneurship. In Hjorth, D., & Steyaert, C. (Eds.) *Narrative and discursive approaches in entrepreneurship* (pp. 210–231). Edward Elgar Publishing.
Hjorth, D. (2005). Organizational entrepreneurship: With de Certeau on creating heterotopias (or spaces for play). *Journal of Management Inquiry*, *14*(4), 386–398.
Hjorth, D. (2007). Lessons from Iago: Narrating the event of entrepreneurship. *Journal of Business Venturing*, *22*(5), 712–732.
Hjorth, D., & Steyaert, C. (Eds.) (2004). *Narrative and discursive approaches in entrepreneurship*. Edward Elgar Publishing.
Hjorth, D. (2014). Organizational entrepreneurship: An art of the weak. In Hjorth, D. (Ed.) *Handbook on organizational entrepreneurship* (pp. 169–190). Edward Elgar Publishing.
Holbrook, M. B. (1995). *Consumer research*. Sage.
Holt, N. (2003). Representation, legitimation, and autoethnography: An autoethnographic writing story. *International Journal of Qualitative Methods*, *2*(1), 18–28.

Johannisson, B. (2011). Towards a practice theory of entrepreneuring. *Small Business Economics, 36*, 135–150.
Johannisson, B., & Olaison, L. (2007). The moment of truth: Reconstructing entrepreneurship and social capital in the eye of the storm. *Review of Social Economy, 65*(1), 55–78.
Johannisson, B., Ramirez-Pasillas, M., & Karlsson, G. (2002). The institutional embeddedness of local inter-firm networks: A leverage for business creation. *Entrepreneurship and Regional Development, 14*, 297–315.
Johnstone, B. (2007). Ethnographic methods in entrepreneurship research. In Neergaard, H., & Ulhoi, J. P. (Eds.) *Handbook of qualitative research methods in entrepreneurship* (pp. 97–121). Edward Elgar Publishing.
Kempster, S., & Stewart, J. (2010). Becoming a leader: A co-produced autoethnographic exploration of situated learning of leadership practice. *Management Learning, 41*(2), 205–219.
Kirzner, I. M. (Ed.) (1982). *Method, process, and Austrian economics: Essays in honour of Ludwig von Mises*. Lexington Books.
Lakoff, G. (1990). *Women, fire, and dangerous things: What categories reveal about the mind*. University of Chicago Press.
Larsen, J., Boje, D. M., & Bruun, L. (2020). *True storytelling: Seven principles for an ethical and sustainable change-management strategy*. Routledge.
Learmonth, M., & Humphreys, M. (2012). Autoethnography and academic identity: Glimpsing business school doppelgängers. *Organization, 19*(1), 99–117.
López, C. J., & Tracy, S. J. (2020). Anchoring "the Big Tent": How organizational autoethnography exemplifies and stretches notions of qualitative quality. In Herrmann, A. F. (Ed.) *The Routledge international handbook of organizational autoethnography* (pp. 383–398). Routledge.
Lorimer, G. H. (1903). *Letters from a Self-made Merchant to His Son: Being the Letters Written by John Graham, Head of the House of Graham & Company, Pork-packers in Chicago, Familiarly Known on 'Change as "Old Gorgon Graham," to His Son, Pierrepont, Facetiously Known to His Intimates as "Piggy" in One Volume* (Vol. 3684). B. Tauchnitz.
Lounsbury, M. & Glynn, M. (2001). Cultural entrepreneurship: Stories, legitimacy, and the acquisition of resources. *Strategic Management Journal, 22*(6–7), 545–564.
Lunceford, B. (2015). Rhetorical autoethnography. *Journal of Contemporary Rhetoric, 5*, 1–20.
March, J. G., & Simon, H. A. (1993). *Organizations*. John Wiley & Sons.
McKinley, W., Mone, M. A., & Moon, G. (1999). Determinants and development of schools in organization theory. *Academy of Management Review, 24*(4), 634–648.
McMorran, W. (2007). Intertextuality and urtextuality: Sade's Justine palimpsest. *Eighteenth-Century Fiction, 19*(4), 367–390.
Mendez, O. J. M., & Pelly, R. D. M. (2021). Failed entrepreneurship in a heterotopia: The story of Villa Ahumada. *Journal of Entrepreneurship in Emerging Economies, 14*(3), pp. 449–468.
Méndez, M. (2013). Autoethnography as a research method: Advantages, limitations and criticisms. *Colombian Applied Linguistics Journal, 15*(2), 279–287.
Mills, J. (2013). Jung's metaphysics. *International Journal of Jungian Studies, 5*(1), 19–43.
Neumann, W. (1994). *Social research methods: Qualitative and quantitative approaches*. Needham Heights, MA: Allyn and Bacon.

O'Connor, E. (2004). Storytelling to be real: Narrative, legitimacy building and venturing. In Hjorth, D., & Steyaert, C. (Eds.), *Narrative and discursive approaches in entrepreneurship* (pp. 105–124). Edward Elgar Publishing.
O'Donnell, P., O'Gorman, C., & Clinton, E. (2020). Rethinking the "necessity" in necessity entrepreneurship. *Academy of Management Review*, *46*(4), 827–830.
Osentoski, N. J. (2015). Changing from the inside out: Leading organizational change as an insider. *Journal of Positive Management*, *6*(3), 41–66.
Parry, K. W. (2008). Viewing the leadership narrative through alternate lenses: An autoethnographic investigation. *Management Revue*, 126–147.
Pelly, R. D. M. (2016). A bureaucrat's journey from technocrat to entrepreneur through the creation of adhocracies. *Entrepreneurship & Regional Development*, *28*(7–8), 487–513.
Pelly, R. D. M. (2017a). Entrepreneurial opportunity: A perspective from the theory of forms. *American Journal of Management*, *17*(5), 87–102.
Pelly, R. D. M. (2017b). The story of captain baby face and the coffee maker: An entrepreneurial narrative perspective on corruption. *Journal of Management Inquiry*, *26*(4), 390–405.
Pelly, R. D. M. (2020). Sadism in foreign lands: The burn pit atrocity. In *Academy of Management Proceedings*, 2020(1), 18217. Briarcliff Manor, NY 10510: Academy of Management.
Pelly, R. D. M., & Boje, D. (2019). Neoliberalism in the North American university: Toward integrating divisions in agent orientation via a Follettian differentiated relational ontology. *Communication & Language at Work*, *6*(2), 28–41.
Pelly, R. D. M., & Boje, D. (2020). A case for Folletian interventions in public universities. *Journal of Applied Research in Higher Education*, *12*(4), 561–571.
Pelly, R. D. M., & Fayolle, A. (2020). Ethnography's answer to the plus zone challenge of entrepreneurship. In Gartner, W. B., & Teague, B. T. (Eds.) *Research Handbook on Entrepreneurial Behavior, Practice and Process* (pp. 82–101). Edward Elgar Publishing.
Pelly, R. D. M., & Kulik, S. (2024). A triography on the sharing economy. In Pelly, R. D. M. (Ed.) *A World Scientific encyclopedia of business storytelling. Set 1: Corporate and business strategies of business storytelling – Volume 1: Business storytelling in entrepreneurship* (pp. 107–131). World Scientific Publishing.
Peredo, A. M., & Chrisman, J. J. (2017). Conceptual foundations: community-based enterprise and community development. In Van Ham, M., Reuschke, D., Kleinhans, R., Mason, C., & Syrett, S. (Eds.) *Entrepreneurial Neighbourhoods: Towards an Understanding of the Economies of Neighbourhoods and Communities* (pp. 151–178). Edward Elgar Publishing.
Pratt, M. L. (2007). *Imperial eyes: Travel writing and transculturation*. Routledge.
Rambo, C. (2005). Impressions of grandmother: An autoethnographic portrait. *Journal of Contemporary Ethnography*, *34*(5), 560–585.
Rambo, C. (2007). Handing IRB an unloaded gun. *Qualitative Inquiry*, *13*(3), 353–367.
Rambo, C. (2016). Strange accounts: Applying for the department chair position and writing threats and secrets "in play". *Journal of Contemporary Ethnography*, *45*(1), 3–33.
Reed-Danahay, D. (1997). *Auto/ethnography*. Berg.
Richards, R. (2008). Writing the othered self: Autoethnography and the problem of objectification in writing about illness and disability. *Qualitative Health Research*, *18*(12), 1717–1728.
Rorty, R. (1989). *Contingency, irony, and solidarity*. Cambridge University Press.

Rosile, G. A. (2016). *Tribal wisdom for business ethics*. Emerald.
Rosile, G. A., Boje, D. M., Carlon, D. M., Downs, A., & Saylors, R. (2013). Storytelling diamond: An antenarrative integration of the six facets of storytelling in organization research design. *Organizational Research Methods*, *16*(4), 557–580.
Sade, Marquis de (1987). *The 120 days of Sodom and other writings*. Compiled and translated by A. Wainhouse & R. Seaver. Grove.
Sambrook, S., & Doloriert, C. (2020). Towards a model of collaborative organizational autoethnography: The more the merrier? In Herrmann, A.F. (Ed.) *The Routledge international handbook of organizational autoethnography* (pp. 399–414). Routledge.
Sarachek, B. (1978). American entrepreneurs and the Horatio Alger myth. *The Journal of Economic History*, *38*(2), 439–456.
Sarasvathy, S. D. (2001). Causation and effectuation: Toward a theoretical shift from economic inevitability to entrepreneurial contingency. *Academy of Management Review*, *26*(2), 243–263.
Schein, E. H. (2008). Clinical inquiry/research. *The SAGE handbook of action research: Participative inquiry and practice* (pp. 266–279). Sage.
Schindler, J. (2015). Expertise and tacit knowledge in artistic and design processes: Results of an ethnographic study. *Journal of Research Practice*, *11*(2), Article M6.
Schumpeter, J. A. (2000). Entrepreneurship as innovation. University of Illinois at Urbana-Champaign's Academy for Entrepreneurial Leadership Historical Research Reference in Entrepreneurship. https://ssrn.com/abstract=1512266.
Schurz, G. (Ed.). (1990). *Erklären und Verstehen in der Wissenschaft*. De Gruyter.
Schwandt, T. A. (1996). Farewell to criteriology. *Qualitative Inquiry*, *2*(1), 58–72.
Semler, R. (2001). *Maverick! The success story behind the world's most unusual workplace*. Random House.
Shepherd, D. A., Williams, T., Wolfe, M., & Patzelt, H. (2016). *Learning from entrepreneurial failure*. Cambridge University Press.
Sparkes, A. (2000). Autoethnography and narratives of self: Reflections on criteria in action. *Sociology of Sport Journal*, *17*(1), 21–43.
Spry, T. (2001). Performing autoethnography: An embodied methodological praxis. *Qualitative Inquiry*, *7*(6), 706–732.
Spinosa, C., Flores, F., & Dreyfus, H. L. (1997). *Disclosing new worlds: Entrepreneurship, democratic action, and the cultivation of solidarity*. MIT Press.
Steyaert, C. (2004). The prosaics of entrepreneurship. In Hjorth, D., & Steyaert, C. (Eds.) *Narrative and discursive approaches in entrepreneurship* (pp. 8–21). Edward Elgar Publishing.
Steyaert, C. (2007). Of course that is not the whole (toy) story: Entrepreneurship and the cat's cradle. *Journal of Business Venturing*, *22*(5), 733–751.
Steyaert, C. (2011). Entrepreneurship as in(ter)vention: Reconsidering the conceptual politics of method in entrepreneurship studies. *Entrepreneurship and Regional Development*, *23*(1–2), 77–88.
Taylor, F. W. (1919). *The principles of scientific management*. Harper & Brothers.
Tiwsakul, R. A., & Hackley, C. (2012). Postmodern paradoxes in Thai-Asian consumer identity. *Journal of Business Research*, *65*(4), 490–496.
Tomkins, L. (2011). The myth of Narcissus: Ovid and the problem of subjectivity in psychology. *Greece & Rome*, *58*(2), 224–239.
Tomkins, L. (2020). Autoethnography through the prism of Foucault's care of the self. In Herrmann, A. F. (Ed.) *The Routledge international handbook of organizational autoethnography* (pp. 54–68). Routledge.

Tomkins, L., & Nicholds, A. (2017). Make me authentic, but not here: Reflexive struggles with academic identity and authentic leadership. *Management Learning, 48*(3), 253–270.
Townsend, T. W., Duggins, A., Bragg, B., McCoy, T., Guerrault, J., Newell, J., & Tiberi, H. (2020). The IRB's stone wall: Rollercoaster of doom. In Herrmann, A. F. (Ed.) *The Routledge international handbook of organizational autoethnography* (pp. 366–382). Routledge.
Tracy, S. J. (2010). Qualitative quality: Eight "big-tent" criteria for excellent qualitative research. *Qualitative Inquiry, 16*(10), 837–851.
Tracy, S. J. (2012). The toxic and mythical combination of a deductive writing logic for inductive qualitative research. *Qualitative Communication Research, 1*(1), 109–141.
Tsoukas, H., and Chia, R. (2002). On organizational becoming: Rethinking organizational change. *Organization Science, 13*(5), 567–582.
Van Maanen, J. (2011). *Tales of the field: On writing ethnography*. University of Chicago Press.
Vyner, H. M. (2018). *The healthy mind: Mindfulness, true self, and the stream of consciousness*. Routledge.
Wall, S. (2006). An autoethnography on learning about autoethnography. *International Journal of Qualitative Methods, 5*(2), 146–160.
Wakkee, I., Englis, P., & During, W. (2007). Using e-mails as a source of qualitative data. In Neergaard, H., & Ulhoi, J. P. (Eds.) *Handbook of qualitative research methods in entrepreneurship* (pp. 331–358). Edward Elgar Publishing.
Webb, S. K. (2020). Polypreneur: An autoethnography of owning multiple businesses, simultaneously. In Herrmann, A. F. (Ed.) *The Routledge international handbook of organizational autoethnography* (pp. 240–251). Routledge.
Whitehead, A. N. (1933). The study of the past: Its uses and its dangers. *Harvard Business Review, 11*(4), 436–444.
Witte, M. N. (2021). Inspiration for a libidinal cinema: Klossowski, Lyotard, and the tableau vivant. *Journal of Comparative Literature and Aesthetics, 44*(3), 99–106.
Wodak, R. & Meyer, M. (Eds.) (2001). *Methods of critical discourse analysis*. Sage.
Yarborough, J. P., & Lowe, K. B. (2007). Unlocking foreclosed beliefs: An autoethnographic story about a family business leadership dilemma. *Culture and Organization, 13*(3), 239–249.
Zavattaro, S. M. (2011). An autoethnographic tale of image-generation tactics on employees. *Employee Responsibilities and Rights Journal, 23*(1), 1–16.
Zawadzki, M., & Jensen, T. (2020). Bullying and the neoliberal university: A co-authored autoethnography. *Management Learning, 51*(4), 398–413.

5. Entrepreneurship as practice: philosophical implications and opportunities

Bruce T. Teague and Richard Tunstall

WHY "PRACTICE THEORY"?

What do entrepreneurs do? To appreciate the potential of practice theory in the entrepreneurship literature, it is important to recognize that a practice theory is not a singular theory but rather a collection of closely related theories that share a common epistemological perspective and some common principles. These ideas grow out of attempts to explain social phenomena. Thus, many of these ideas – especially those that form early foundations – were developed independently. To the best of our knowledge, it was not until Ortner's work in 1984 that a common label, practice theory, was applied collectively based on the underlying commonalities (Ortner, 1984). We do not intend to provide an exhaustive representation of social practice theory, but a brief introduction to a few influential perspectives will elucidate this point and lay the foundation for this chapter.

We begin with Pierre Bourdieu, as his work is the most cited motivation for entrepreneurship scholars conducting practice-based studies. Bourdieu's work on the logic of practice has influenced several fields, including sociology, anthropology, cultural studies, strategy, organizational theory, and entrepreneurship. It has helped to illuminate the ways in which social and cultural structures shape individual behavior and how individuals negotiate and adapt to their social context. Bourdieu (1977) defines practice per the following formula:

(Habitus x Capital) + Field = Practice

For Bourdieu, *Habitus* reflects the constitutive structure of a particular type of social environment. The habitus connects individual conduct to a specific milieu. In this way, even seemingly individual activity becomes inherently social (Bourdieu, 1990). Thus, if we were studying a recognized entrepreneurial activity such as pitching for investment, we would see a divergence in the unit of analysis between the focus of behavioral theorists from the positivistic perspective and practice theorists. Behavioral theorists would focus on the individual and their choices in the pitch and assume their agency as a justification for studying these behaviors in isolation. A practice theorist, in contrast, would consider how social expectations, material arrangements of the space, and power relations embedded in the practice space (among many possibilities) shape the enactment of a role within it (Teague et al., 2020).

According to Bourdieu, habitus is closely tied to social class and cultural capital. This *Capital* of an individual or group refers to the knowledge, skills, and cultural resources that they possess and that are valued within a particular social field. Individuals from different social classes and cultural backgrounds will likely possess different forms of cultural capital, shaping their habitus and practices. Capital refers, in broad terms, to anything that can be exchanged. (Bourdieu, 1977: 178). As such, cultural capital helps explain variations in qualities such as legitimacy and power.

Whereas habitus and capital interact to shape the practice, *Fields* define the spaces within which the practice is carried out. Bourdieu initially developed this concept as analogous to "fields of play", as we might witness in sports. Different fields have different rules and norms, and individuals may have different habitus and cultural capital depending on the fields in which they participate. Bourdieu argues that the struggle for power within fields is not simply a matter of individual competition – it is shaped by the larger social and cultural structures that underpin the field.

In summary, for Bourdieu, an agent's practice is shaped by habitus and their understanding of the field-specific "game" as it unfolds in time. There is no determinism in the operating of habitus: agents' practices are improvised according to local, practical, and social conjunctures. Agents continuously and recursively respond to cues from the habitus, which allows micro-strategizing within the bounds permitted by their habitus (Nicolini, 2012). Thus, Bourdieu seems to view habitus as a force that reduces variance in practice as performed by different agents. In other words, it explains why we can recognize the practice even when the location and participants are different.

Anthony Giddens's work is also commonly cited as motivation for studying entrepreneurial practice. While Bourdieu accepts certain social structures as given in that he sought to explain human agency by examining the interdependent duality of human agency and social structures, Giddens's structuration approach differs. Structuration theory posits a recursive relationship between human agency and the social structures that shape them such that human agency is capable of shaping structure, while in turn, structure serves to constrain and shape human agency (Giddens, 1979, 1991).

Giddens's theory relies heavily on both reflexivity of the individual agent and practical consciousness. Reflexivity refers to the ability of the individual to reflect upon their actions and the structures within which the actions will be enacted to select behaviors deemed appropriate in the specific situation. Practical consciousness shapes reflexivity. Practical consciousness is not just knowledge about how to perform a particular action but also knowledge about the social norms, values, and facility (a form of enabling power) that shape that action.

These concepts form the basis for his notion of the duality of structure. For Giddens, social practices are structured by social norms, rules, and institutions, and they also intentionally or unintentionally reproduce and influence those same structures (Giddens, 1991). This notion of agents as carriers of the practice continues to influence more recent conceptions of practice.

While Bourdieu and Giddens have both provided a crucial foundational understanding of the nature of social practice, Ortner's work (1984) was transformative because she was – to the best of our knowledge – the first person to explicitly offer the label of practice theory as an umbrella term for the variety of theories which emphasize understanding the social while not placing primacy on either the individual or the social context within which the practice occurs.

For Ortner (1984), the modern practice turn in sociology, anthropology, and other social science fields casts traditional issues in a new light. For example, the relationship(s) between human action and a different phenomenon called 'the system'. Like Giddens, this relationship is recursive in that practices influence the system, and the system influences the practices. It is an emergent and negotiated phenomenon that highlights human agency but also human passivity or the tendency to select behavior out of habit, which can be reinforced by elements found in the system.

According to Ortner, practice is the primary unit of analysis for understanding culture and society. She argues that cultural practices, such as rituals, customs, and social norms, are not just symbolic representations of social structures but are themselves constitutive of social structures. In other words, social structures are the product of individuals' and groups' ongoing, everyday practices.

Her work also emphasizes the importance of power in shaping practices and social structures. She argues that power is not just a property of individuals or groups but is embedded in the practices. Practices reinforce and challenge power relations and illuminate the manner in which practices reproduce or transform power relations over time. This is essential for understanding social change.

Finally, Ortner argues that practice emphasizes what people do. The focus is on understanding how and under what conditions human action is carried out and the agent's role in the production and reproduction process. This duality makes room for both an informed and intelligible agent and an organized context that shapes the field of possible and untenable action choices.

Since these early foundations, there has been an explosion in contributions to social practice theory. Modern influential practice theorists include Theodore Schatzki, Andreas Reckwitz, Elizabeth Shove, Allison Hui, and Robert Schmidt, though numerous others have also been influential. It is worth reiterating that the purpose of this chapter is not to provide an exhaustive overview of the emergence of practice theory but rather to provide a basis for exploring what practice theories generally share in common as we turn towards the topic of how a focus on practice might enhance knowledge about entrepreneurship.

Among the modern theorists, perhaps none has contributed so significantly to the logical arrangement of concepts and the precise definition of terms, as Theodore Schatzki. For Schatzki, a practice is an open-ended, spatially-temporally dispersed nexus of doings and sayings (Schatzki, 2012). As such, he emphasizes what is done performatively, as well as communicated verbally. He goes on to clearly define each part of this definition. Open-ended means that practices are not comprised of any particular number of activities (Schatzki, 2012, p. 14). Spatially-temporally dispersed means that activities occur somewhere in objective space at some point or duration (Schatzki, 2012, p. 15). Nexus refers to the idea that a group of related activities "hang together" and connect through relations such as causality and intentional directedness (Schatzki, 2012, p. 15). Finally, doings and sayings recognize sayings as a specific and recognizable subclass of doings within the practice space (Schatzki, 2012, p. 15).

Another significant contribution of Schatzki's logical arrangement is the recognition of a hierarchically nested set of activities that can be studied in relation to one another. Thus, basic activities stand alone. They are actions the individual can perform on their own. This notion of "basic activities" then allows him to broaden the focus to action hierarchies, in which basic activities are combined and related in a sequentially and temporally meaningful manner. Finally, he suggests that some activities are subunits of larger activities. A basic example might be playing a note on a piano keyboard (basic activity), which can be conceived as a subunit of a larger activity (playing a scale) that forms the basis for a still larger activity (playing a concerto). Teleological hierarchies refer to activities at such a high level in the activity sequence that they do not compose part of a still larger activity. In other words, teleological hierarchies represent the highest order of activity constituting the practice.

While Schatzki established a logic to the study and understanding of practice, Elizabeth Shove emphasized materiality as it influences the social. Her work highlights the various ways in which physical arrangements of material objects influence, shape, and channel the human activities associated with executing the practice. She encourages scholars to recognize and distinguish the different roles filled by material objects within the practice.

Shove has identified three roles for material objects in practice: infrastructural, device, and resource (Shove, 2017, p. 164). Notably, the role of an object is not fixed or objectively defined – as expected in positivist research – but rather depends on the frame of reference being employed when the object is observed. She demonstrates this through the example of refrigerator freezers to demonstrate how a material object may fill different roles depending on the frame of reference. Thus, from an industry perspective, refrigerator freezers play an infrastructural role because they are a necessary precondition to the frozen food industry. However, from a home cook's perspective, they play a device role because they are used to facilitate the practice of cooking.

Finally, Andreas Reckwitz has contributed to framing and understanding the nature of practice in research. While some might view Reckwitz as taking an opposing view to that of Schatzki when he wrote, "Practice theory does not place the social in mental qualities, nor in discourse, nor in interaction" (Reckwitz, 2002), we view this as bounding and clarifying the role of sayings and doings, or discourse, in the study of practices. For Reckwitz, individuals are carriers of practice. Agents are body/minds who 'carry' and 'carry out' social practices" (Reckwitz, 2002). He has defined 'practice' as a routinized type of behavior. It involves the interplay between bodily activities and mental activities, often involving the deployment of tacit knowledge, material objects and things and their use, the generalized background knowledge and understanding of the practice, and emotion and motivational knowledge.

He describes practices as "routinized bodily activities; as interconnected complexes of behavioral acts, they are movements of the body." Individuals engage in bodily performances that are connected with know-how. This know-how includes their knowledge of the expectations associated with the practice and an awareness of how to respond to other individuals who play different roles within the practice.

This brief review highlights the plurality of approaches that fall under the umbrella of practice theory and some commonalities that allow them to be seen as part of a pluralistic approach to the study of social phenomena. Among the commonalities is the role of individuals as carriers of practice through their replication of expected practice habits. The theories described also share an understanding that the context interacts with and shapes any particular example of the practice. While the practice will vary from example to example, identifiable elements will remain recognizable across space and time, regardless of the particular actors enacting the practice. Practice highlights the interplay between actors filling distinct and interacting roles. It casts a spotlight on the interactions between people, context, and socio-material arrangements that lead to improvisational responses in the moment. Performances will follow an almost jazz-like subtlety as actors adjust their performance in real-time – often relying on tacit knowledge.

Whether we look at Bourdieu, Giddens, Schatzki, or others, we see an emphasis on reconciling the interplay between social structure and individual agency, with neither being causally dominant in the ensuing practice (Rouse, 2007). The fact that the practice is not dependent on the presence of any particular actors, spaces, or material artifacts demonstrates the importance of understanding rules and norms within the practice. This, too, shows up across practice theories. Practice theory recognizes the roles played by individuals within the execution of the practice. However, unlike a behavioral approach, the emphasis is not on what individuals do that can be directly observed (Bird & Schjoedt, 2017; Bird et al., 2012; Bird et al., 2014; Bird, 1989). Behavioral scholars pay attention to the behaviors of specific individuals and how behaviors differ across similar contexts. Instead, practice theorists view individuals as carriers of the practice, but the practice exists beyond any individual performer.

For example, if we consider the practice of pitching to investors, we might observe several meetings of a specific angel investor group over the course of a year. We would observe similar arrangements of material elements such as chairs, tables, projector screen, computer, and podium, among other things (Teague et al., 2020). We would also observe an individual – likely the group's president – orchestrating the agenda. We would observe individuals (entrepreneurs) delivering pitches for their businesses as prospective investments. These pitches would include common elements such as a pitch deck, common information deemed critical to the investor's decision, and similar presentation styles. We would observe many attendees, some present to contemplate investment and others with other interests in the practice or the prospective businesses. Finally, pitches would typically be followed by a period in which audience members ask questions to elaborate and clarify their understanding of the business.

While roles, activities, and material arrangements will typically be recognizable across angel group meetings, the practice exists beyond any particular location or individual actors. For example, we would observe different entrepreneurs pitching in the May meeting from those we watched in the April meeting. The attendees may include different cross-sections of the membership. The location might shift to a different hotel ballroom or meeting space. However, the practice remains recognizable as pitching to angel investors.

This distinguishes the contribution of social practice theory to the study of entrepreneurship. A practice transcends individuals, locations, material arrangements, and specific sayings and doings. Moreover, we are intrigued by the fact that practices are repeated over time while the specific constituents change. Therefore, when studying a practice, it is incumbent on the researcher to observe the individuals, their performances, their sayings and doings, and the socio-material arrangements and power dynamics as means by which to understand the practice that transcends the performance of the practice on any given occasion.

In summary, a practice-based sensitivity offers an approach to the problems left unaddressed by other traditions, especially those that tend to describe the world in terms of dualisms such as actor/system, body/mind, etc. (Ortner, 1984; Schatzki, 2001; 2002; Reckwitz, 2002, and Rouse, 2007). Practice theories emphasize awareness of activity and performance in creating and re-creating social practices. They pay close attention to the role of the body and material items that shape and influence the production of a given practice (Reckwitz, 2002). While practice theorists do not focus exclusively on the actions of individual agents, practice theory carves out an important space for agency and the activities of agents. Human beings are viewed as carriers of practice, though the knowledge that guides them through their performance is often tacit. All practice theories emphasize the importance of power and conflict as each shapes and is shaped by the practice's performance and the practice space's structure. Collectively, these common elements of practice theories orient researchers towards new objects of inquiry (Schatzki, 2002), leading to new understandings of entrepreneurship, or from a processual perspective, of entrepreneuring (Steyaert, 2007). In the next section, we look at how practice theories have contributed to research in entrepreneurship to date.

THE CONTRIBUTION OF PRACTICE THEORY IN ENTREPRENEURSHIP

Practice theory has already become well-established in the field of entrepreneurship. Among the extant literature, the work of Giddens and Bourdieu most frequently motivates existing work. Structuration theory (Giddens, 1979, 1991) offered a lens through which the interplay between individual differences among entrepreneurs and extant opportunities posited by Shane and Venkataraman (2000) gets reconceived. Rather than dichotomous and independent elements of an entrepreneurial system, Sarason, Dean, and Dillard (2006) use the lens of structuration to argue for a tangled and coevolutionary view of the same nexus, such that entrepreneurs both create and are created through the process of opportunity creation. Chiasson and Saunders (2005) similarly used structuration theory to argue that the processes of opportunity recognition and formation are recursive in nature. They suggest that a more complete understanding is offered when entrepreneurial action is enabled and constrained by the business scripts of entrepreneurs.

While Giddens's work has led to important insights for the field of entrepreneurship, Bourdieu's work has offered the most frequently cited motivation. Similar to the authors cited in the last paragraph, Tatli, Vassilopoulou, Özbilgin, Forson, and Slutskaya (2014) employed Bourdieu's relational perspective to reframe the individual–opportunity nexus (Shane and Venkataraman, 2000) as irreducibly interconnected sets of relations.

Some authors have drawn upon Bourdieu's notion of capital to look for and demonstrate a strong relationship between human capital and innovation activity (Dakhli and De Clercq, 2004). Other authors were guided by habitus and fields to explore the practice of newcomers entering and becoming socialized to existing entrepreneurial fields (De Clercq and Voronov, 2009a, 2009b). They describe a process through which newcomers' cultural and symbolic capital helps them navigate the field of entrepreneurship as they strive to develop legitimacy with existing participants. However, through this process, the newcomers are also shown to shape the field that has been entered.

Bourdieu also inspired Vincent and Pagan (2019) as they explored the experiences of 25 entrepreneurial human resource consultants in the North of England. Through their work, they described the constituents of the economic fields that shaped the activity of this group. In addition, they added a deep understanding of the reflexive struggles the workers engaged in as they struggled to access resources and build relationships with other agents.

Reid (2021) also took inspiration from Bourdieu's capital and habitus in examining the practices of entrepreneurs involved with six lifestyle ventures. His work highlighted the process through which these entrepreneurs deployed capital and actively generated new processes through which capital was converted to new forms. Reid also demonstrates habitus's generative role in forming social capital within this group. This study also offers an excellent example of how practice theory lends itself to the study and elaboration of undertheorized phenomena.

As with the prior study, McKeever, Anderson, and Jack (2014) employed a Bourdieuan lens to offer a new perspective on the nature of networks and networking. Their study highlights the connective role played by social capital. From this perspective, social capital enables connection and sharing between entrepreneurs in a small town in northwest Ireland. Their description and findings contrast with and add to an extant literature limited primarily to structural, relational, and cognitive measures that could be measured and tested within a positivistic paradigm.

Dodd has used practice theory to generate deep understandings of novel contexts and practice spaces. In one study, she and her coauthors draw on Bourdieu to extend and reframe Welter's notion of entrepreneurial contexts (Drakopoulou Dodd et al., 2018). Their study of 25 Irish craft beer entrepreneurs showed how emerging habitus is enacted through the hybridization of diverse global and local field logics. In another study (Dodd, 2014), she explores punk entrepreneurship through the story of Rancid. In this study, Dodd highlights the role of power through data collected related to dominance, subordination, exclusion, control, and liberation. In each study, she and her coauthors highlight the power of the practice lens to uncover a new understanding of topics of central importance to entrepreneurship while offering deep descriptions of unusual contexts that enrich and broaden the representation of entrepreneurs studied.

While the works of Bourdieu and Giddens have inspired many researchers, others have drawn upon integrated practice theory lenses to explore and extend our knowledge of well-researched topics. For example, in one study, Teague, Gorton, and Liu (2020) spent 27 months observing the activities of an angel investment group. Prior research implicitly assumed that these pitches served the primary purpose of seeking investment in new companies. However, their exploration of the practices in this community uncovered a richer, more relational purpose served by pitches – one in which pitches morphed, depending on context and intent, to build and maintain relational capitals.

Finally, other researchers have added to the study of practice by employing the lens to generate new insights and by offering new methodological approaches useful to researchers collecting data about practices. Thompson and Illes (2021) employed video ethnography to explore and describe entrepreneurial learning as an emergent activity within the practice domain. Johannisson (2011, 2018, 2019) has used Bourdieu's theory to suggest the power of enactive research as a means of understanding both explicit and tacit aspects of practice. As conceived, enactive research involves the researcher becoming a member of the practice space – often by engaging in business creation. Collectively, these researchers demonstrate our field's power to borrow from and contribute to social practice theory.

This review is not exhaustive but selective. Studies were chosen as exemplars among myriad contributions made to the field. Each highlights the unique benefits provided by employing the practice lens. The strength of practice theory is its capacity to make the unseen visible (Reckwitz, 2002). Each study above describes, elaborates, or challenges prevailing wisdom in the broader literature. Each foregrounds aspects of the context and practice that might otherwise go unrecognized or unstudied. This brief review demonstrates the practice lens's potential, yet numerous opportunities remain for future research. The following section highlights several areas where entrepreneurship scholars may make important new contributions.

FUTURE OPPORTUNITIES FOR ENTREPRENEURSHIP AS PRACTICE SCHOLARS

It would be natural to begin this section by focusing on topics within the field of entrepreneurship. However, we suggest that entrepreneurship scholars are uniquely positioned to contribute to and answer important questions that remain within the broader topic of practice theory. For example, entrepreneurship involves the creation of new and differentiated offerings to the market. As such, entrepreneurial practice spaces are uniquely adapted to the study of variation within practices – from performance to performance within a common practice space. Variation may also be observed and studied across related or connected practices (Hui et al., 2017). The study of variation between practices would simultaneously advance the field of entrepreneurship while addressing important questions in practice theory, more generally (Hui et al., 2017).

Variation in the performance of practice involves a tension between forces driving change against those that reinforce the stability and recognizability of the practice. For practices to be intelligible to practitioners, there must be a significant degree of stability to the practice's form, structure, material elements, and performance. Thus, researchers might ask how elements of stability are reinforced within the practice space to overcome the natural variation in performance. How much stability is required for a practice to be recognizable to participants? What patterns do we see in the emergence of new practices? Patterns consistent with punctuated equilibria seem like a probable expectation. How are tolerable variations of the practice made meaningful to participants? (Hui et al., 2017). Finally, how do shared meanings play a role in defining the boundary between tolerable variations within the practice, versus those that are not?

Relatedly, entrepreneurship researchers might explore how variation in the performance of a practice influences the cognitive categorizing of someone as an insider or an outsider to the practice. How do behaviors change towards the individual based on this categorization? How are new inductees to the practice socialized? In this vein, expertise might take on new meaning. An expert in practice may primarily be a function of achieving a sufficiently narrow variation of practice performance that falls within expectations for that particular practice and setting.

A parallel inquiry might raise questions about how people move/transition between practices. Schulz (2015) examined transitions between work and nonwork practices in Norway, France, and the US, but this is an area in which much remains to be learned. How do people manage the balancing act of participating in multiple practices under conditions where performance in one practice necessarily hinders or interferes with performance in another practice? For example, motherhood and career for women have been one area of study.

Shove (2017) argues that while much has been said about material things within social practices, there is still a lack of research on the range and variety of material relationships involved or how precisely material entities figure in what people do. Shove uses the example of material arrangements associated with the practice of cooking to identify a chain of preceding material arrangements that make the practice possible. In so doing, she opens the door to the recognition of temporally arranged events and material objects related across time such that certain events must necessarily precede others to understand practices.

This raises additional questions that may be accessible to entrepreneurship scholars. For instance, how do material objects shift roles within different practices? How do we distinguish between those material objects that have a background or "infrastructural role" from those that are directly involved in the practice, and how do material objects switch between one of these roles and the other? How do we operationalize the *infrastructural roles* of material objects in practice? How do we determine that something is necessary, though it is not directly involved in the practice? Moreover, when does something become so far removed (shift so deeply into the background) as theoretically necessary but practically unimportant? Is something necessary if a substitute is available?

CONCLUSION

The first part of the chapter introduces the notion that practice is not a theory but a collection of theories that share essential commonalities. Among those, practice theories foreground the practice – a repeated and replicated social exchange dependent neither on particular individual actors nor particular times or locations. However, they remain recognizable to the observer as the same practice. We demonstrated this by reviewing some of the most influential perspectives, including those of Bourdieu, Giddens, Schatzki, Shove, and Reckwitz. While each emphasized different aspects of the practice, all shared a substantial interest in the practice rather than in individual behavior or specific contexts. Actor and context are not interdependent within the practice lens; they are relational, each shaping and being shaped by the other.

Following this, we considered the significant contributions that have already been made to the field of entrepreneurship by scholars engaged in practice scholarship. Practice has been used to reexamine one of the most influential theories of entrepreneurship: the individual-opportunity nexus. Practice research has highlighted previously unexplored aspects of entrepreneurship, including the role of habitus, capitals, and fields on the performance and success of the practice. Practice scholars have broadened our understanding of established topics such as pitching, and craft business. Others have added to the field through their rich description and understanding of unique research settings. Finally, others have used the constraints of practice knowledge to suggest new methods for capturing practice data.

In conclusion, this chapter argues that practice theories fundamentally change how researchers look for, explore, and understand topics of interest to entrepreneurship. We argue that practice theory sensitizes the researcher to look for the previously unseen and to recognize that which may not be describable by participants in the practice – that knowledge that is tacit. In this manner, practice theories hold the potential to make the unseen and unnoticed visible and observable. It offers the opportunity to reframe commonly accepted wisdom of the field by eliminating false dichotomies and instead foreshadowing the interplay in which the actor is both maker and made within the context of the practice. It offers a way for the field of entrepreneurship to move forward from individual agency in economic systems, toward richer theorizing about what entrepreneurs do in social practice spaces and the consequences for those spaces.

REFERENCES

Bird, B., & Schjoedt, L. (2017). Entrepreneurial behavior: Its nature, scope, recent research, and agenda for future research. In Carsud, A., & Brännback, M. (Eds.) *Revisiting the entrepreneurial mind*, New York: Springer, pp. 379–409.

Bird, B., Schjoedt, L., & Baum, J. R. (2012). Editor's introduction – Entrepreneurs' behavior: elucidation and measurement. *Entrepreneurship Theory and Practice*, **36** (5), 889–913.

Bird, B., Schjoedt, L., & Hanke, R. (2014). Behavior of entrepreneurs – existing research and future directions. In Chell, E., & Karataş-Özkan, M. (Eds.) *Handbook of research on small business and entrepreneurship*, Cheltenham, UK and Northampton, MA, USA: Edward Elgar Publishing, pp. 207–221.

Bird, B. J. (1989). *Entrepreneurial behavior*. Glenview, IL: Scott, Foresman and Company.

Bourdieu, P. (1977). *Outline of a theory of practice* (Vol. 16). Cambridge: Cambridge University Press.

Bourdieu, P. (1990). *The logic of practice*. Stanford, CA: Stanford University Press.

Chiasson, M., & Saunders, C. (2005). Reconciling diverse approaches to opportunity research using the structuration theory. *Journal of Business Venturing*, **20** (6), 747–767.

Dakhli, M., & De Clercq, D. (2004). Human capital, social capital, and innovation: a multi-country study. *Entrepreneurship & Regional Development*, **16** (2), 107–128.

De Clercq, D., & Voronov, M. (2009a). The role of cultural and symbolic capital in entrepreneurs' ability to meet expectations about conformity and innovation. *Journal of Small Business Management*, **47** (3), 398–420.

De Clercq, D., & Voronov, M. (2009b). Toward a practice perspective of entrepreneurship: Entrepreneurial legitimacy as habitus. *International Small Business Journal*, **27** (4), 395–419.

Dodd, S. L. D. (2014). Roots radical – Place, power and practice in punk entrepreneurship. *Entrepreneurship & Regional Development*, **26** (1–2), 165–205.

Drakopoulou Dodd, S., Wilson, J., Bhaird, C. M. A., & Bisignano, A. P. (2018). Habitus emerging: The development of hybrid logics and collaborative business models in the Irish craft beer sector. *International Small Business Journal*, **36** (6).

Giddens, A. (1979). *Central problems in social theory: Action, structure, and contradiction in social analysis*. Berkeley, CA: University of California Press.

Giddens, A. (1991). Structuration theory: Past, present and future. In Bryant, C., & Jary, D. (Eds.) *Giddens' theory of structuration: A critical appreciation* (pp. 201–221). London: Routledge.

Hui, A., Schatzki, T. R., & Shove, E. (Eds.) (2017). *The nexus of practices: Connections, constellations, practitioners*. London: Routledge.

Johannisson, B. (2011). Towards a practice theory of entrepreneuring. *Small Business Economics*, **36**, 135–150.

Johannisson, B. (2018). *Disclosing entrepreneurship as practice: The enactive approach*. Cheltenham, UK and Northampton, MA, USA: Edward Elgar Publishing.

Johannisson, B. (2019). Disclosing everyday practices constituting social entrepreneuring: A case of necessity effectuation. In Fayolle, A., Janssen, F., Le Loarne-Lemaire, S. & Maalaoui, A. (Eds.), *Social entrepreneurship and bricolage: Taking stock and looking ahead* (pp. 129–145). Abingdon, UK and New York: Routledge.

McKeever, E., Anderson, A., & Jack, S. (2014). Entrepreneurship and mutuality: Social capital in processes and practices. *Entrepreneurship & Regional Development*, **26** (5–6), 453–477.

Nicolini, D. (2012). *Practice theory, work, and organization: An introduction*. Oxford: Oxford University Press.

Ortner, S. B. (1984). Theory in anthropology since the sixties. *Comparative Studies in Society and History*, **26** (1), 126–166.

Reckwitz, A. (2002). Toward a theory of social practices: A development in culturalist theorizing. *European Journal of Social Theory*, **5** (2), 243–263.

Reid, S. (2021). The generative principles of lifestyle enterprising: Dialectic entanglements of capital-habitus-field. *International Journal of Entrepreneurial Behavior & Research*, **27** (3), 629–647.

Rouse, J. (2007). Practice theory. In Turner, C., & Risjord, M. (Eds.) *The handbook of the philosophy of science, vol. 15: Philosophy of anthropology and sociology*. London: Elsevier. pp. 499–540.

Sarason, Y., Dean, T., & Dillard, J. F. (2006). Entrepreneurship as the nexus of individual and opportunity: A structuration view. *Journal of Business Venturing*, **21** (3), 286–305.

Schatzki, T. R. (2001). Practice mind-ed orders. In Schatzki, T.R., Cetina, K.K., & von Savigny, E. (Eds.) *The practice turn in comptemporary theory*, London: Routledge, pp. 50–63.

Schatzki, T. R. (2002). *The site of the social: A philosophical account of the constitution of social life and change*. University Park, PA: Penn State University Press.

Schatzki, T. R. (2012). A primer on practices. In J. Higgs, R. Barnett, S. Billet, M. Hutchings, & F. Trede (Eds.) *Practice-based education: Perspectives and strategies*. Rotterdam: Sense Publishers, pp. 13–26.

Schulz, J. M. (2015). Winding down the workday: Zoning the evening hours in Paris, Oslo, and San Francisco. *Qualitative Sociology*, **38**, 235–259.
Shane, S., & Venkataraman, S. (2000). The promise of entrepreneurship as a field of research. *Academy of Management Review*, **25** (1), 217–226.
Shove, E. (2017). Matters of practice. In Hui, A., Schatzki, T. R., & Shove, E. (Eds.), *The nexus of practices: Connections, constellations, practitioners* (pp. 155–168). Abingdon, UK and New York: Routledge.
Steyaert, C. (2007). 'Entrepreneuring' as a conceptual attractor? A review of process theories in 20 years of entrepreneurship studies. *Entrepreneurship and Regional Development*, **19** (6), 453–477.
Tatli, A., Vassilopoulou, J., Özbilgin, M., Forson, C., & Slutskaya, N. (2014). A Bourdieuan relational perspective for entrepreneurship research. *Journal of Small Business Management*, **52** (4), 615–632.
Teague, B., Gorton, M. D., & Liu, Y. (2020). Different pitches for different stages of entrepreneurial development: The practice of pitching to business angels. *Entrepreneurship & Regional Development*, **32** (3–4), 334–352.
Thompson, N. A., & Illes, E. (2021). Entrepreneurial learning as practice: A video-ethnographic analysis. *International Journal of Entrepreneurial Behavior & Research*, **27** (3), 579–599.
Vincent, S., & Pagan, V. (2019). Entrepreneurial agency and field relations: A realist Bourdieusian analysis. *Human Relations*, **72** (2), 188–216.

PART II

Dealing better with methodological issues and challenges

6. An overview of key issues in entrepreneurship research methods

Léo-Paul Dana and Aidin Salamzadeh

INTRODUCTION

Entrepreneurship research has evolved dramatically, especially during the last two decades (Rauch, 2020). Despite the extensive use of the traditional hypothetico-deductive approach, the inductive approach has become vastly used in this domain (Dana & Dana, 2005). The co-evolution of qualitative, quantitative, and mixed research methods in entrepreneurship research has led to various improvements, such as using innovative qualitative methods, which have been borrowed from other domains of social sciences, and quantitative methods, which have used big data as a source of inspiration (Schwab & Zhang, 2019; Jones et al., 2021).

The new streams of qualitative methods in entrepreneurship research have highlighted the importance of paying attention to inductive and not necessarily quantitative research as the primary strategy to answer research questions (Hlady-Rispal et al., 2021). On the one hand, using such qualitative methods has several advantages, including: (i) learning new things about the subjects in question, reducing measurement errors of quantitative studies, (ii) providing a more profound understanding for scholars, which could help them reach a more holistic view of the research problem, (iii) reducing the Type III (asking wrong questions) and Type IV (solving wrong problems) errors, and (iv) ensuring internal validity of quantitative research. These are among the most critical issues to be mentioned, but one should note that the advantages are more than these (Dana & Dana, 2005; Dana & Dumez, 2015). Van Burg et al. (2020) argued that entrepreneurship scholars face difficulties and challenges in publishing manuscripts that follow a qualitative approach in top journals. They add that most researchers could not justify selecting a particular qualitative approach to address specific research questions. In addition, they argue that not all qualitative entrepreneurship research fit templates proposed by Gioia et al.'s (2013) grounded theory or Eisenhardt's theory-building approaches (Eisenhardt, 1989). Besides, by following such previously defined approaches, entrepreneurship scholars might lose their creativity, and therefore, many advantages of the qualitative research methods might be overlooked. Finally, generally, it could be controversial which entrepreneurial characteristics and entrepreneurship theories might fit well with the relevant qualitative approaches.

On the other hand, the quantitative research method has its own advantages, including: (i) using various types of data in empirical entrepreneurship research, (ii) addressing the real-life problems of entrepreneurs, entrepreneurial firms, and entrepreneurial societies through highlighting data-driven analysis, (iii) ability to choose various measures, different types of data, and investigating the causal or correlational relationships among a series of constructs, and (iv) possibility of using various databases to scrutinise any probable relationship. Similar to qualitative research methods (Groenland & Dana, 2020), these are just a series of advantages of using the quantitative approach in entrepreneurship research (Saridakis & Cowling, 2020). In their seminal work, Maula and Stam (2020) focused on enhancing rigour in quantitative entrepreneurship research. They believed that significant developments in empirical research and software tools could create novel opportunities for quantitative research in entrepreneurship. These have gone beyond traditional approaches and allowed researchers to analyse big data, use data science methods, and machine learning tools and techniques. They summarised their recommendations for enhancing rigour in quantitative research. These recommendations include: (i) revisiting the selected research design in order to comply with research problems/questions, (ii) comprehending the advantages, disadvantages, and limitations associated with using specific data sources, (iii) making sure that the specified measures and variables will measure what we intend them to do, (iv) choosing suitable analytical tools and techniques based on the research questions and empirical setting, (v) reporting the results and research methods transparently so as to be able to interpret the results clearly, (vi) clarifying the workflow to minimise errors and facilitate reproducibility and generalisability, and (vii) learning more about novel quantitative methods that are applicable in entrepreneurship research (Maula & Stam, 2020).

Finally, mixed methods, which are used extensively in contemporary entrepreneurship research, are sources of inspiration for entrepreneurship scholars. Many recent research questions in the entrepreneurship domain need creative mixed research approaches. It is the case when scholars need to reach a deeper understanding of a phenomenon through adding insights drawn from qualitative methods to quantitative ones or vice versa. For instance, Zhang et al. (2021) used such an approach in ramifications of effectuation on biases in entrepreneurship. They followed such an approach to unravel the relationship patterns between effectuation and biases. In another seminal work, van Ewijk et al. (2020) followed a mixed approach to explore how pedagogy affected students' entrepreneurial intentions. Such an approach helped them in answering their multifaceted research questions. Nevertheless, using mixed methods is not always flawless, and in many cases, there are some barriers and bridges, as suggested by Dy and Agwunobi (2019). As they mentioned, mixed methods research might face a series of problems in entrepreneurship research, such as criticisms about how these methods are used, lack of [methodological] rigour, and finally getting published in high-rank journals. In order to address the methodological rigour, they refer to Grace's (2014) approach. Grace (2014) believed that entrepreneurship scholars could face this dilemma by paying attention to the data collection timing, the balance between quantitative and qualitative data, how to use those two types of data, and consolidating the theoretical framework and research assumptions. Besides, Dy and Agwunobi (2019) discussed three main issues hindering entrepreneurship scholars from publishing their manuscripts. First, entrepreneurship researchers tend to focus on the object and overlook their underlying assumptions, which they might implicitly or explicitly mention in their research. Secondly, they might face challenges while handling the contradictory assumptions of positivist and constructionist quantitative and qualitative research methods approaches. Finally, the findings of the mixed method projects might not be included in a single manuscript. Then, the author(s) must make critical decisions about the content of their research.

To summarise, it is noteworthy that, similar to other disciplines in social sciences, using an appropriate research method is a daunting task that could facilitate or hinder the publication of a typical manuscript in top journals. Many editors consider it the most critical decision an entrepreneurship scholar must make (Liguori et al., 2021; Rajasinghe et al., 2021; van Gelderen et al., 2021). Then, it is crucial to provide an overview of the key issues in entrepreneurship research methods, which is further discussed in this manuscript. The paper is structured as follows. First, the authors provide a review of the research methods used in entrepreneurship research. Then, key issues in entrepreneurship research are discussed. Finally, the paper concludes with some remarks and suggestions for entrepreneurship scholars.

A REVIEW OF ENTREPRENEURSHIP RESEARCH METHODS

Despite its history, the variety and diversity of methods used in entrepreneurship research have dramatically increased during the past two decades. Like several other emerging disciplines, entrepreneurship researchers faced numerous challenges and opportunities in the same vein. Many researchers followed the constructivist approach and conducted qualitative research methods to address phenomenological questions, while other scholars used the positivist approach and designed quantitative research plans to investigate the relationships between previously investigated or sometimes poorly defined variables. In addition to these two major streams, a limited number of researchers adventurously used mixed method research designs, which mainly were criticised and became controversial. These approaches shaped an accumulation of data, information, and knowledge regarding entrepreneurship as the focal phenomenon.

However, several attempts were not successful. For instance, some expressions were coined, such as "venturepreneurship", which have never come into existence. Due to a lack of consistency and integrity in defining new concepts, the emerging field of entrepreneurship has witnessed many such unsuccessful attempts. Nevertheless, such evolutionary development is an integral part of the lifecycle of any discipline. To some scholars, qualitative research methods have further progressed this phenomenological aspect of entrepreneurship research (Litt, 1973; O'Neill, 1977; Tyagarajan, 1959). Another stream of researchers dealt with quantitative research methods and explored and investigated possible relationships between various concepts in entrepreneurship research. This group was somewhat conservative at the very beginning (Hsu et al., 2017). Therefore, they primarily focused on exploring the characteristic traits of entrepreneurs or using management theories and their logic to define what the entrepreneurship lifestyle looks like or how entrepreneurs act (Bell, 1969). Attempts such as using the Theory of Planned Behaviour (Krueger & Carsrud, 1993) or the Bricolage perspective (Nicolaou et al., 2021) are examples of such efforts. A third stream, less conservative and more adventurous, used mixed-method research designs. They accepted criticism, and in many cases, they proposed controversial approaches and creatively disrupted the previously defined structures (e.g. Cromie, 1987; Gartner et al., 1989; Belitski et al., 2021).

Several researchers have already studied the evolutionary trends in entrepreneurship research methods (Huarng et al., 2021). For instance, McDonald et al. (2015) have extensively reviewed the research methods used in entrepreneurship research between 1985 and 2013. They argued that "entrepreneurship research is dominated by positivist approaches and data gathering methods, but that this picture is changing over time". Besides, their research revealed that various research methods were used in research outputs published in entrepreneurship and small business journals. Also, in their book, Carsrud and Brännback (2014) focused on vital issues such as the challenges of [empirical] entrepreneurship research, philosophical concerns, measuring the trends, cross-cultural studies, and experimental methods. In addition to these, Hlady-Rispal and Jouison-Laffitte (2014) paid more specific attention to the trends of publishing qualitative research in entrepreneurship journals between 2007 and 2011. They criticised the extant developments, highlighted the importance of convincing journal editors to publish their qualitative studies, and challenged the existing entrepreneurship journals to a set of specific and transparent criteria for authors. In the same venue, Van Burg et al. (2020) challenged the traditional research methods frequently used in entrepreneurship research and suggested that future researchers might "broaden the set of methods they employ and use them more creatively and rigorously to advance entrepreneurship research". Considering such an approach in their mind, another group of researchers, such as Aldrich (2017) and Newth (2018), examined the contextual differences affecting entrepreneurship research methods. For example, Aldrich (2017) argued that "I have witnessed a continuing debate over the sophistication of research methods in entrepreneurship. Although change has proceeded unevenly, substantial progress has been made on many fronts". These approaches reveal the extent to which various entrepreneurship scholars have already tried to address such controversial issues.

In sum, it is crystal clear that entrepreneurship research has evolved dramatically during the last few decades (Karatas-Ozkan et al., 2014; Fayolle et al., 2016). In the same vein, many researchers took advantage of diversified entrepreneurship research methodologies and approaches to increase the chance of publishing their manuscripts (Fayolle & Wright, 2014). Nevertheless, there is a need to consider some key issues in entrepreneurship research methods. Therefore, the next section of this chapter sheds more light on this subject.

KEY ISSUES IN ENTREPRENEURSHIP RESEARCH METHODS

Entrepreneurs are change agents of societies. From the very first days of gaining legitimacy as an academic discipline, entrepreneurship has evolved dramatically. During these decades, the notion of the entrepreneur as a *self-employed risk-taker* (Cantillon, 1756) and *innovative* (Schumpeter, 1947) agent has evolved to a *super(wo)man* in charge of the socio-economic development of the nations and even the globe (De Simone & Priola, 2021). Despite their importance, these agents were marginalised in classical and neoclassical economics approaches and, after some decades, were partially included in the next generations of economic studies (Glancey et al., 2000; Landström, 2020). Nevertheless, respective scholars altered their points of view incrementally (Hébert & Link, 2009). While the practice of entrepreneurship was progressing, researching entrepreneurship initiated as an interdisciplinary field of research (Herron et al., 1992; Zahra, 2005; Kuratko & Morris, 2018). Generally, entrepreneurship scholars exploited various research methods to investigate topics including, but not limited to, entrepreneurial characteristics, intentions, behaviours, activities, incidents, structures, and contexts.

At the outset, scholars mainly focused on elaborating the personality traits and characteristics of entrepreneurs (Urban, 2010). The primary focus of this research stream was on understanding the differences among entrepreneurs, managers, innovators, and inventors (Bygrave & Hofer, 1992; Zahra & Dess, 2001). Afterwards, behavioural approaches became dominant in entrepreneurship research (Peneder, 2009). Such early approaches evolved dramatically after almost four consecutive decades, and newer approaches became prevailing. Until the seminal work of Shane and Venkataraman (2001) unravelled the concept of entrepreneurship by proposing the *individual–opportunity nexus*. In the same year, other distinguished entrepreneurship scholars like Gartner (2001) were raising fundamental questions about the ontological aspects of entrepreneurship. This new conceptualisation, which prospective researchers further discussed, continued to stay as a linking pin in entrepreneurship research (Eckhardt & Shane, 2010). While some scholars, such as Per Davidsson, have also offered concepts like New Venture Idea (NVI) as the basic idea in defining entrepreneurship (Davidsson, 2015), Shane's elaboration has remained the most popular (Salamzadeh & Arbatani, 2020; Klusmann et al., 2021). In addition to all these developments, several controversial aspects of entrepreneurship research would need further clarification. According to the authors' best knowledge of the field and based on reviewing the existing body of the literature, the following are considered the key issues in entrepreneurship research methods (Figure 6.1).

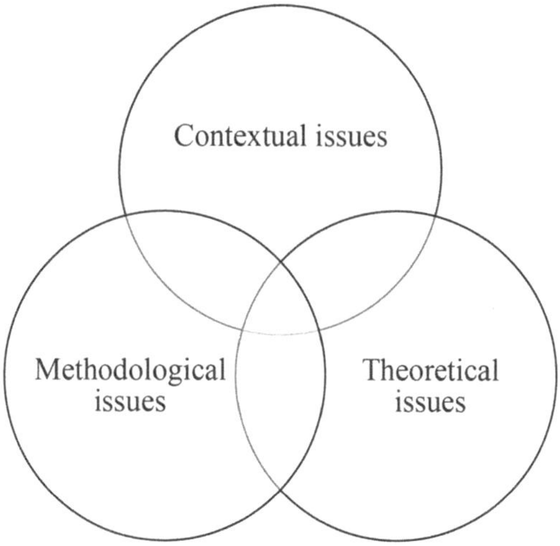

Source: Author's own.

Figure 6.1 *Key issues in entrepreneurship research methods*

Contextual Issues: Contextualising the Entrepreneurial Phenomena

Similar to most of the phenomena in social sciences, entrepreneurship is contextual. Entrepreneurs act variously in different contexts, considering contextual factors. Therefore, entrepreneurship scholars have continuously emphasised contextualising entrepreneurship theories, especially during the last decade (Gupta et al., 2020; Stevenson et al., 2020). In their seminal work, Wadhwani et al. (2020) enlisted a few approaches toward conceptualising the context. They argue that entrepreneurship scholars have investigated the context as a constraining, embedding, or constructed phenomenon. They propose that following each of these approaches could affect entrepreneurial actions. While considering contextual elements in quantitative research is possible by adding some variables, this is not the case in most qualitative researches. It is noteworthy that contextual differences could substantially change the results as some of those factors themselves might be the means to specific ends (Aljarodi et al., 2020). Also, Laveren et al. (2021) emphasised contextual heterogeneity and proposed that "entrepreneurship as a phenomenon is highly context dependent". They argued that the context generally affects the whole research process, specifically the data interpretation, assumption formulation, hypothesis development, and observation stages. To clarify what they meant, they proposed eight dimensions of the context, i.e. "(i) temporal, (ii) historical, (iii) institutional, (iv) industry and market, (v) social, (vi) organisational, (vii) spatial, and (viii) ownership and governance". Moreover, Landström and Harirchi (2019) suggested that to make their research "*interesting*", entrepreneurship scholars include specific contextual considerations and contextualising in their research.

Nevertheless, to include contextual factors in entrepreneurship research, scholars must consider a series of issues. Foremost, they must not overlook significant contextual factors. It might lead to a kind of myopia in conducting research (e.g. Smith et al., 2021). Secondly, it is crystal clear that controlling for contextual variables is not sufficient. Instead, the context and its impacts shall become an integral part of the research (e.g. Martínez-González et al., 2021). Thirdly, one should notice that contextual factors could give unique meanings to entrepreneurial events. Therefore, it is necessary to consider them to understand almost any entrepreneurship-related topic (e.g. Audretsch et al., 2021). Last but not least is to consider evolutionary contextual elements in longitudinal studies, case studies, narrative research, and the like (e.g. Laveren et al., 2021).

In sum, as mentioned earlier, contextualising entrepreneurship research is necessary to ensure the quality of findings. Without following such an approach, findings might not reveal the pure reality of entrepreneurial incidents or could even be misleading. Thus, the authors suggest that scholars consider these contextual issues when selecting and implementing various entrepreneurship research methods.

Methodological Issues: Changing Nature of Entrepreneurship Research Methods

Entrepreneurs, their nature, and behaviours have changed dramatically, primarily owing to technological advancements. While conventional entrepreneurs used to act in steadily changing environments, contemporary entrepreneurs deal with big data analytics, artificial intelligence, and machine learning issues (Obschonka & Audretsch, 2020). As the nature of entrepreneurial activities has changed significantly, traditional entrepreneurship research methods need to be altered. For instance, Lévesque et al. (2020) argued that "AI holds great promise to transform entrepreneurship into a more relevant and impactful field, but it must overcome conflicts between the AI-driven research approach and that of the traditional, theory-based research process". Besides, using big data generated constantly on various platforms, such as social media platforms, could have a disruptive power, as noted by Lackéus (2020). Such innovative approaches raise the need for more innovative and somewhat interdisciplinary research methods. In addition, Grégoire et al. (2019) focused on the validity tradeoffs in entrepreneurship research. They suggested new techniques to clarify and facilitate entrepreneurship research experiments.

Although entrepreneurship scholars have recently paid close attention to more innovative research methods, yet, a significant number of them believe that following qualitative methods could lead to novel and rich insights about entrepreneurship (Henry et al., 2018; Sassmannshausen & Volkmann, 2018; Javadian et al., 2020). Nevertheless, based on Javadian et al.'s (2020) study, some approaches such as that of Gioia et al. (2013) and the discursive approaches are underutilised. Also, they highlighted that non-interview data are marginally used as a primary source of data in the extant body of the literature. In addition, there is a need for increased transparency in reporting the data collection and analysis phases.

In addition to the qualitative approaches in entrepreneurship research, quantitative research methods have gained much attention (Weigel & Soost, 2020). Nevertheless, according to Maula and Stam (2020), there are new opportunities for enhancing rigour more than before. They suggested that entrepreneurship scholars could do the following to reach this aim: (i) matching the research problem and the design, (ii) considering various sources of data owing to their advantages and disadvantages, (iii) considering the validity of the measures, (iv) selecting relevant analytical tool(s), (v) reporting the research methods and the results transparently and interpreting the results thoroughly, (vi) using a sound reproducible workflow, and (vii) learning more about evolving quantitative methods in entrepreneurship research.

To summarise, the changing nature of entrepreneurship research methods requires scholars to consider methodological issues. Otherwise, conducting qualitative, quantitative or mixed research without paying close attention to these issues might turn into a controversy in entrepreneurship research.

Theoretical Issues: Theorising and Theory Building

Entrepreneurship researchers are criticised for failing to develop indigenous entrepreneurship theories (Suddaby et al., 2015; p. 2). Furthermore, they are cautioned about focusing on general themes and principles that "value parsimony and consistency over richness and variety" (Lévesque et al., 2020). Scholars believe that such an approach might lead to choosing a series of traditional research methods, and incremental contributions might decrease relevancy (Shepherd, 2015). Therefore, researchers must pay close attention to emerging trends and potentially disruptive innovations in terms of theory to avoid making any theoretical mistakes. Lévesque et al. (2020) went beyond this and proposed that scholars feel they need to produce an "illusion of theory development" which mostly lacks rigour. Besides, they mentioned that such an approach generally leads to incremental theoretical contributions with reduced real-world relevance. Based on their view, entrepreneurship research struggles to achieve rigour and relevance, and they called it "a grand challenge". Therefore, to address this challenge, research questions, assumptions, hypotheses, and rationale must be aligned with the practitioners' and policymakers' needs to know about current issues in the entrepreneurship field. Besides, the research results must inform various stakeholders and provide them with implications. They argued that "a closer connection between theory development and real-world relevance" is needed.

Moreover, some scholars, such as Arend (2020), believed that theory development and theorising in entrepreneurship have been "frustratingly slow" during the last decades. Stevenson et al. (2020) reviewed the experiment-based entrepreneurship research publications and mapped organisational and management theories used in those studies. They provided a big picture of the theories used in those studies and showed how entrepreneurship theories had been grounded in those theories. This study revealed how incremental contributions had dominated the entrepreneurship research methods. In addition to this study, Kerr and Coviello (2019) argued that causation or ends-driven logic is the most frequently used approach in terms of quantitative research methods and is a significant part of the extant entrepreneurship literature. Many suggest that such an approach might kill innovation, and one might find possible relationships among irrelevant subjects while using the causation logic mistakenly. Also, Van Burg et al. (2020) believed that grounded theory is the primary method of theorising in entrepreneurship in terms of qualitative research methods.

According to the issues mentioned above, entrepreneurship researchers have to pay particular attention to theorising entrepreneurial phenomena. Also, more recent approaches could provide researchers, practitioners, and policymakers with important information about real-world situations in which entrepreneurs act.

CONCLUSION

As a promising field of research and practice, entrepreneurship has evolved dramatically during the past decades. The notion of entrepreneurs as risk-takers, arbitrageurs, and innovators has changed to *super(wo)men* who could change the lives of millions or even billions of individuals (De Simone & Priola, 2021). In the meantime, entrepreneurship scholars did their best to precisely investigate various aspects of their entrepreneurial lives and their impacts. They borrowed theories from other fields such as management and organisational sciences, coined new words, redefined management and business concepts, all and all, to develop entrepreneurship as a scientific field. However, their efforts were not flawless, and there were some drawbacks and shortcomings (Stevenson et al., 2020).

The authors believed that it was time to stop and rethink the key issues in entrepreneurship research methods. Therefore, in this chapter, the authors first reviewed the research methods used in entrepreneurship-related studies. Then, three primary issues in entrepreneurship research methods are discussed. Based on our points of view, entrepreneurship scholars must pay close attention to the *contextual issues* that could make significant distinctions in the results of any research and clarify the specifications of the context in which a study is conducted. Besides, numerous *methodological issues* have been raised by various researchers throughout the past decades, without considering which one could not opt for the best research method. Finally, for theorising and theory-building purposes, *theoretical issues* must be taken into account. As theory building has changed with the advent of new technologies and techniques, such as artificial intelligence and big data analysis, following such an approach has become inevitable.

In sum, the authors advise future entrepreneurship researchers to pay particular attention to the mentioned issues in this chapter. We believe that change is an integral part of any phenomenon. Entrepreneurship is not an exception, but it is also a fast-changing field (Arend, 2020). Then, the highlighted key issues could pave the way for selecting and implementing a sound entrepreneurship research method, based on which valid and reliable findings could be proposed to practitioners and policymakers. Besides, future researchers could use different lenses to investigate this subject and provide deeper insights. Another opportunity is to investigate each of these key issues and their aspects in more detail. As the field is progressing significantly, using interdisciplinary research methods might be considered an interesting opportunity (e.g. see Lévesque et al., 2020; Obschonka & Audretsch, 2020).

REFERENCES

Aldrich, H. (2017). Learning together: National differences in entrepreneurship research. In Sexton, D. L., & Landström, H. (Eds.) *The Blackwell handbook of entrepreneurship* (pp. 5–25). Wiley Blackwell.

Aljarodi, A., Lopez, T., & Alfahaid, T. (2020). Different approaches of context in quantitative entrepreneurship research. In Welter, F., & Urbano, D. (Eds.) *How to make your doctoral research relevant* (pp. 69–79). Edward Elgar Publishing.

Arend, R. J. (2020). Entrepreneurship: A theory for no theory for now. *Strategic Organization, 21*(2), 403–415. https://doi.org/10.1177/1476127020979041.

Audretsch, D. B., Lehmann, E. E., & Schenkenhofer, J. (2021). A context-choice model of niche entrepreneurship. *Entrepreneurship Theory and Practice, 45*(5), 1276–1303.

Belitski, M., Caiazza, R., & Lehmann, E. E. (2021). Knowledge frontiers and boundaries in entrepreneurship research. *Small Business Economics, 56*(2), 521–531.

Bell, P. F. (1969). A quantitative study of entrepreneurship and its determinants in Asia. *The Canadian Journal of Economics, 2*(2), 288–298.

Bygrave, W. D., & Hofer, C. W. (1992). Theorising about entrepreneurship. *Entrepreneurship Theory and Practice, 16*(2), 13–22.

Cantillon, R. (1756). *Essay sur la nature du commerce en general.* R. Gyles.

Carsrud, A., & Brännback, M. (Eds.) (2014). *Handbook of research methods and applications in entrepreneurship and small business.* Edward Elgar Publishing.

Cromie, S. (1987). Motivations of aspiring male and female entrepreneurs. *Journal of Organizational Behavior, 8*(3), 251–261.

Dana, L. P., & Dana, T. E. (2005). Expanding the scope of methodologies used in entrepreneurship research. *International Journal of Entrepreneurship and Small Business, 2*(1), 79–88.

Dana, L. P., & Dumez, H. (2015). Qualitative research revisited: epistemology of a comprehensive approach. *International Journal of Entrepreneurship and Small Business, 26*(2), 154–170.

Davidsson, P. (2015). Entrepreneurial opportunities and the entrepreneurship nexus: A re-conceptualisation. *Journal of Business Venturing, 30*(5), 674–695.

De Simone, S., & Priola, V. (2021). "Who's that girl?" The entrepreneur as a super(wo)man. *Canadian Journal of Administrative Sciences/Revue Canadienne des Sciences de l'Administration, 39*(1), 97–111. https://doi.org/10.1002/cjas.1643.

Dy, A., & Agwunobi, A. J. (2019). Intersectionality and mixed methods for social context in entrepreneurship. *International Journal of Entrepreneurial Behavior & Research, 25*(8), 1727–1747.

Eckhardt, J. T., & Shane, S. (2010). An update to the individual-opportunity nexus. In Acs, Z. J., & Audretsch, D. B. (Eds.) *Handbook of entrepreneurship research* (pp. 47–76). Springer.

Eisenhardt, K. M. (1989). Building theories from case study research. *Academy of Management Review*, *14*(4), 532–550.
Fayolle, A., & Wright, M. (Eds.). (2014). *How to get published in the best entrepreneurship journals: A guide to steer your academic career*. Edward Elgar Publishing.
Fayolle, A., Landström, H., Gartner, W. B., & Berglund, K. (2016). The institutionalisation of entrepreneurship: Questioning the status quo and re-gaining hope for entrepreneurship research. *Entrepreneurship & Regional Development*, *28*(7–8), 477–486.
Gartner, W. B. (2001). Is there an elephant in entrepreneurship? Blind assumptions in theory development. *Entrepreneurship Theory and Practice*, *25*(4), 27–39.
Gartner, W. B., Mitchell, T. R., & Vesper, K. H. (1989). A taxonomy of new business ventures. *Journal of Business Venturing*, *4*(3), 169–186.
Gioia, D. A., Corley, K. G., Hamilton, A. L. (2013). Seeking qualitative rigor in inductive research notes on the Gioia methodology. *Organizational Research Methods*, *16*(1), 15–31.
Glancey, K., McQuaid, R., & Campling, J. (2000). *Entrepreneurial economics*. Macmillan.
Grace, D. (2014). Intersectionality-informed mixed methods research: A primer. *Health Sociology Review*, *19*(4), 478–490.
Grégoire, D. A., Binder, J. K., & Rauch, A. (2019). Navigating the validity tradeoffs of entrepreneurship research experiments: A systematic review and best-practice suggestions. *Journal of Business Venturing*, *34*(2), 284–310.
Groenland, E., & Dana, L. P. (2020). *Qualitative methodologies and data collection methods: Toward increased rigour in management research*. World Scientific Publishing.
Gupta, P., Chauhan, S., Paul, J., & Jaiswal, M. P. (2020). Social entrepreneurship research: A review and future research agenda. *Journal of Business Research*, *113*, 209–229.
Hébert, R. F., & Link, A. N. (2009). *A history of entrepreneurship*. Routledge.
Henry, E. Y., Dana, L. P., & Murphy, P. J. (2018). Telling their own stories: Māori entrepreneurship in the mainstream screen industry. *Entrepreneurship & Regional Development*, *30*(1–2), 118–145.
Herron, L., Sapienza, H. J., & Smith-Cook, D. (1992). Entrepreneurship theory from an interdisciplinary perspective: volume II. *Entrepreneurship Theory and Practice*, *16*(3), 5–12.
Hlady-Rispal, M., & Jouison-Laffitte, E. (2014). Qualitative research methods and epistemological frameworks: A review of publication trends in entrepreneurship. *Journal of Small Business Management*, *52*(4), 594–614.
Hlady-Rispal, M., Fayolle, A., & Gartner, W. B. (2021). In search of creative qualitative methods to capture current entrepreneurship research challenges. *Journal of Small Business Management*, *59*(5), 887–912.
Hsu, D. K., Simmons, S. A., & Wieland, A. M. (2017). Designing entrepreneurship experiments: A review, typology, and research agenda. *Organizational Research Methods*, *20*(3), 379–412.
Huarng, K. H., Guaita-Martínez, J. M., & Yu, T. H. K. (2021). Challenges and opportunities of new research methods in innovation, entrepreneurship, and knowledge. *Journal of Business Research*, *134*(3), 101–103.
Javadian, G., Dobratz, C., Gupta, A., Gupta, V. K., & Martin, J. A. (2020). Qualitative research in entrepreneurship studies: A state-of-science. *The Journal of Entrepreneurship*, *29*(2), 223–258.

Jones, P., Apostolopoulos, N., Kakouris, A., Moon, C., Ratten, V., and Walmsley, A. (2021). Universities and entrepreneurship: Meeting the educational and social challenges. In P. Jones, N. Apostolopoulos, A. Kakouris, C. Moon, V. Ratten, and A. Walmsley (Eds.), *Universities and entrepreneurship: Meeting the educational and social challenges*, Contemporary Issues in Entrepreneurship Research, Volume 11 (pp. 1–10). Emerald.

Karatas-Ozkan, M., Anderson, A. R., Fayolle, A., Howells, J., & Condor, R. (2014). Understanding entrepreneurship: Challenging dominant perspectives and theorising entrepreneurship through new postpositivist epistemologies. *Journal of Small Business Management*, *52*(4), 589–593.

Kerr, J., & Coviello, N. (2019). Formation and constitution of effectual networks: A systematic review and synthesis. *International Journal of Management Reviews*, *21*(3), 370–397.

Klusmann, C. D., Spieth, P., & Klein, S. (2021). When opportunity knocks: How the individual opportunity nexus explains evaluations of new business models. *International Journal of Entrepreneurial Venturing*, *13*(4), 319–345.

Krueger, N. F., & Carsrud, A. L. (1993). Entrepreneurial intentions: Applying the theory of planned behaviour. *Entrepreneurship & Regional Development*, *5*(4), 315–330.

Kuratko, D. F., & Morris, M. H. (2018). Examining the future trajectory of entrepreneurship. *Journal of Small Business Management*, *56*(1), 11–23.

Lackéus, M. (2020). Collecting digital research data through social media platforms: Can "scientific social media" disrupt entrepreneurship research methods? In Gartner, W. B., & Teague, B. T. (Eds.) *Research handbook on entrepreneurial behavior, practice and process* (pp. 199–241). Edward Elgar Publishing.

Landström, H. (2020). The evolution of entrepreneurship as a scholarly field. *Foundations and Trends® in Entrepreneurship*, *16*(2), 65–243.

Landström, H., & Harirchi, G. (2019). "That's interesting!" in entrepreneurship research. *Journal of Small Business Management*, *57*, 507–529.

Laveren, E., Ben-Hafaïedh, C., Kurczewska, A., & Jiang, Y. D. (2021). An introduction to *Contextual Heterogeneity in Entrepreneurship Research*. In Laveren, E., Ben-Hafaïedh, C., Kurczewska, A., & Jiang, Y. D. (Eds.) *Contextual heterogeneity in entrepreneurship research* (pp. 1–14). Edward Elgar Publishing.

Lévesque, M., Obschonka, M., & Nambisan, S. (2020). Pursuing impactful entrepreneurship research using artificial intelligence. *Entrepreneurship Theory and Practice*, *46*(4), 803–832. https://doi.org/10.1177/1042258720927369.

Liguori, E. W., El Tarabishy, A., & Passerini, K. (2021). Publishing entrepreneurship research: Strategies for success distilled from a review of over 3,500 submissions. *Journal of Small Business Management*, *59*(1), 1–12.

Litt, B. (1973). Why entrepreneurs succeed. *Journal of General Management*, *1*(2), 77–93.

Martínez-González, J. A., Kobylinska, U., & Gutiérrez-Taño, D. (2021). Exploring personal and contextual variables of the global entrepreneurship monitor through the Rasch mathematical model. *Mathematics*, *9*(16), 1838.

Maula, M., & Stam, W. (2020). Enhancing rigor in quantitative entrepreneurship research. *Entrepreneurship Theory and Practice*, *44*(6), 1059–1090.

McDonald, S., Gan, B. C., Fraser, S. S., Oke, A., & Anderson, A. R. (2015). A review of research methods in entrepreneurship 1985–2013. *International Journal of Entrepreneurial Behavior & Research*, *21*(3), 291–315.

Newth, J. (2018). "Hands-on" vs "arm's length" entrepreneurship research: Using ethnography to contextualise social innovation. *International Journal of Entrepreneurial Behavior & Research, 24*(3), 683–696.
Nicolaou, N., Phan, P. H., & Stephan, U. (2021). The biological perspective in entrepreneurship research. *Entrepreneurship Theory and Practice, 45*(1), 3–17.
Obschonka, M., & Audretsch, D. B. (2020). Artificial intelligence and big data in entrepreneurship: A new era has begun. *Small Business Economics, 55*(3), 529–539.
O'Neill, M. P. (1977). An analysis of entrepreneurship in economic development: a synthesis of Schumpeter, Hagen, and McClelland. Doctoral dissertation. The University of Oklahoma.
Peneder, M. (2009). The meaning of entrepreneurship: A modular concept. *Journal of Industry, Competition and Trade, 9*(2), 77–99.
Rajasinghe, D., Aluthgama-Baduge, C., & Mulholland, G. (2021). Researching entrepreneurship: An approach to develop subjective understanding. *International Journal of Entrepreneurial Behavior & Research, 27*(4), 866–883.
Rauch, A. (2020). Opportunities and threats in reviewing entrepreneurship theory and practice. *Entrepreneurship Theory and Practice, 44*(5), 847–860.
Ribeiro-Soriano, D., & Zeng, J. (2018). Some issues in recent entrepreneurship approaches: Joining previous and current theories. *International Entrepreneurship and Management Journal, 14*(1), 1–4.
Salamzadeh, A., & Arbatani, T. R. (2020). Developing a framework for understanding how media entrepreneurs act: An actor-network perspective. In Williams, I. (Ed.) *Contemporary applications of actor network theory* (pp. 77–98). Palgrave Macmillan.
Saridakis, G., & Cowling, M. (2020). Introduction to the *Handbook of Quantitative Research Methods in Entrepreneurship*. In Saridakis, G., & Cowling, M. (Eds.) *Handbook of quantitative research methods in entrepreneurship* (pp. 1–3). Edward Elgar Publishing.
Sassmannshausen, S. P., & Volkmann, C. (2018). The scientometrics of social entrepreneurship and its establishment as an academic field. *Journal of Small Business Management, 56*(2), 251–273.
Schumpeter, J. A. (1947). The creative response in economic history. *The Journal of Economic History, 7*(2), 149–159.
Schwab, A., & Zhang, Z. (2019). A new methodological frontier in entrepreneurship research: Big data studies. *Entrepreneurship Theory and Practice, 43*(5) 843–854.
Shane, S., & Venkataraman, S. (2001). Entrepreneurship as a field of research: A response to Zahra and Dess, Singh, and Erikson. *Academy of Management Review, 26*(1), 13–16.
Shepherd, D. A. (2015). Party on! A call for entrepreneurship research that is more interactive, activity based, cognitively hot, compassionate, and prosocial. *Journal of Business Venturing, 30*(4), 489–507.
Smith, B. R., McMullen, J. S., & Cardon, M. S. (2021). Toward a theological turn in entrepreneurship: How religion could enable transformative research in our field. *Journal of Business Venturing, 36*(5), 106139.
Stevenson, R., Josefy, M., McMullen, J. S., & Shepherd, D. (2020). Organisational and management theorising using experiment-based entrepreneurship research: Covered terrain and new frontiers. *Academy of Management Annals, 14*(2), 759–796.
Suddaby, R., Bruton, G. D., & Si, S. X. (2015). Entrepreneurship through a qualitative lens: Insights on the construction and/or discovery of entrepreneurial opportunity. *Journal of Business Venturing, 30*(1), 1–10.

Tyagarajan, M. (1959). The development of the theory of entrepreneurship. *Indian Economic Review*, *4*(4), 135–150.
Urban, B. (2010). Entrepreneurship as a discipline and field of study. In Urban, B. (Ed.) *Frontiers in entrepreneurship* (pp. 33–62). Springer.
Van Burg, E., Cornelissen, J., Stam, W., & Jack, S. (2020). Advancing qualitative entrepreneurship research: Leveraging methodological plurality for achieving scholarly impact, *Entrepreneurship Theory and Practice*, *46*(1), 1–18. https://doi.org/10.1177/1042258720943051.
van Ewijk, A. R., Oikkonen, E., & Belghiti-Mahut, S. (2020). Linking methods to outcomes: A multi-course mixed-method study of the effects of active and passive pedagogy on entrepreneurial intentions. *The International Journal of Management Education*, *18*(3), 100420.
van Gelderen, M., Wiklund, J., & McMullen, J. S. (2021). Entrepreneurship in the future: A Delphi study of ETP and JBV editorial board members. *Entrepreneurship Theory and Practice*, *45*(5), 1239–1275. https://doi.org/10.1177/10422587211010503.
Wadhwani, R. D., Kirsch, D., Welter, F., Gartner, W. B., & Jones, G. G. (2020). Context, time, and change: Historical approaches to entrepreneurship research. *Strategic Entrepreneurship Journal*, *14*(1), 3–19.
Weigel, C., & Soost, C. (2020). How to study context in quantitative entrepreneurship research. In Welter, F., & Urbano, D. (Eds.), *How to Make your Doctoral Research Relevant: Insights and Strategies for the Modern Research Environment* (pp. 80–91). Edward Elgar Publishing.
Zahra, S. A. (2005). Entrepreneurship and disciplinary scholarship: Return to the fountainhead. In Alvarez, S., Agarwal, R., & Sorenson, O. (Eds.) *Handbook of entrepreneurship research* (pp. 253–268). Springer.
Zahra, S., & Dess, G. G. (2001). Entrepreneurship as a field of research: Encouraging dialogue and debate. *Academy of Management Review*, *26*(1), 8–10.
Zhang, S. X., Foo, M. D., & Vassolo, R. S. (2021). The ramifications of effectuation on biases in entrepreneurship: Evidence from a mixed-method approach. *Journal of Business Venturing Insights*, *15*, e00238.

7. Up-to-date challenges in entrepreneurship quantitative research: what we have accomplished, the challenges that remain, and the new challenges on the block

Saulo Dubard Barbosa

INTRODUCTION

Entrepreneurship research has grown immensely over the last 50 years. From just a marginal topic in other academic disciplines (mainly economics and management), entrepreneurship has become a legitimate field of research. Although a historical account is beyond the scope of this chapter,[1] it might be beneficial to consider a very short historical sketch of this development as I perceived it: (1) until the 1970s, entrepreneurship research was very incipient and most studies were conducted by scholars from other academic disciplines who viewed entrepreneurship as an interesting subject (or object) of study; (2) during the 1980s a community of scholars who saw themselves as entrepreneurship scholars started to emerge, with the first conferences organized by Babson College (starting in 1981) and the creation of the *Journal of Business Venturing* in 1985 as the first academic journal fully dedicated to entrepreneurship; (3) during the 1990s that community started to "grow children", that is, an important generation of scholars conducted doctoral research and defended their PhD dissertations in entrepreneurship, and the field started to grow in number of scholars, publications, and dedicated journals; (4) from 2000 on, such growth became exponential and the field progressively gained legitimacy by all metrics and standards.[2]

Albeit very imperfect, this historical sketch synthesizes the exponential growth of contemporary entrepreneurship research, a growth that really materialized over the last 30 years. This growth is remarkable because, although I am considering a 50-year period as a relevant temporal window to observe the emergence and development of the field, its roots can be traced back at least a few centuries, to the seminal works of Schumpeter, Knight, Hayek, and well before them to Richard Cantillon and Jean-Baptiste Say.

Most importantly, this exponential growth in entrepreneurship research exhibits a couple of remarkable characteristics. First, it came at the cost of fragmentation. Some very experienced scholars have already debated the pros and cons of such fragmentation around 20 years ago (Davidsson, 2003, 2004; Gartner, 2004) and their observations might still be relevant today, since the exponential growth of the last 20 years has contributed to further fragmentation. Second, this exponential growth in entrepreneurship research includes an exponential growth in empirical papers that has been accompanied by, and to some extent driven by, a development and sophistication of analytic methods, data collection procedures, and quantitative datasets.

This second characteristic of contemporary growing entrepreneurship research constitutes the focal background of the present chapter. Although early entrepreneurship research was very occupied with definitional issues and conceptual debates (Bruyat, 1993; Bruyat & Julien, 2000; Gartner, 1985, 1988; Katz & Gartner, 1988; Shane & Venkataraman, 2000), and some of these debates remain while others have emerged (Alvarez & Barney, 2013; Davidsson, 2015, 2017; Eckhardt & Shane, 2013; Ramoglou & Tsang, 2016; Shane, 2012; Venkataraman et al., 2012), the field of entrepreneurship has produced an increasing amount of empirical research over the last decades while our individual and collective ability to conduct empirical research in the field has increased. Such empirical development includes both qualitative and quantitative studies, as both gained in sophistication and rigor over the last few decades. In this chapter, I will focus on quantitative research in entrepreneurship as it presents its own specific set of opportunities and challenges. Specifically, quantitative research in entrepreneurship can benefit today from the accumulated development and sophistication of analytic methods, data collection procedures, research designs, and available databases. However, these advantages also bring with them a set of challenges and potential pitfalls. If these challenges and pitfalls are not clearly identified and addressed, quantitative research in entrepreneurship runs the risk of becoming irrelevant.

In what follows, I shall highlight: (1) the main challenges we have addressed as a field to be able to do more and better quantitative research, (2) the main challenges that remain, and (3) the relatively newer challenges that have emerged over the last few decades.

WHAT WE HAVE ACCOMPLISHED THUS FAR

Quantitative studies in entrepreneurship have grown not only in number but also in quality. This is visible in the articles published in the main entrepreneurship journals as well as in the fact that quantitative entrepreneurship studies can be found today in most top journals in management, economics, sociology, and psychology.

In the emergence phase of the field, quantitative studies were mostly descriptive in nature and often failed to meet the high standards of methodological rigor demanded in more established fields. One of the main challenges at the time was to find reliable and interesting data about entrepreneurial phenomena. The very nature of entrepreneurship contributed to this challenge, as entrepreneurship usually refers to something that does not yet fully exist and yet is in the process of becoming. Traditional databases generally document what is already there: established firms, small and big. But entrepreneurship scholars were most interested in organizational emergence, i.e., what happens before firms and organizations are established (Gartner, 1985; Katz & Gartner, 1988). They were also interested in opportunities, and especially in how individuals identify, evaluate, and exploit opportunities, but finding data on it was not easy (Shane & Venkataraman, 2000). Finally, entrepreneurship scholars were interested in value creation, but it is hard to observe it *ex ante* or in real time (Bruyat & Julien, 2000; Davidsson, 2003). Thus, the first empirical challenge entrepreneurship scholars faced was access to reliable, relevant, and interesting data.

Fortunately, this first challenge has been surmounted, both individually and collectively, by entrepreneurship scholars doing quantitative research. Access to data does not seem to be a problem anymore, and several factors contributed to solve this issue. As we shall see, the active role of entrepreneurship researchers was key in facing this challenge.

First, through several collective efforts, entrepreneurship-specific panels and datasets were built and are now publicly available, such as the Panel Study of Entrepreneurial Dynamics (PSED), the Global Entrepreneurship Monitor (GEM), and the Global University Entrepreneurial Spirit Students' Survey (GUESSS). The making and availability of these entrepreneurship-specific datasets contributed to increase our individual and collective ability to do quantitative research in entrepreneurship, yielding a large number of studies over the years and contributing to advance our knowledge about the entrepreneurial process, its antecedents, some of its consequences, as well as how a large set of individual and contextual variables might affect it.

Second, the availability of such entrepreneurship-specific datasets enabled scholars to link them to other existent datasets, which then multiplied the possibilities for investigating different research questions. For instance, scholars have combined data from GEM, OECD, the World Bank, and the IMF, to investigate whether total entrepreneurial activity influences GDP growth (Van Stel et al., 2005) and to study how public spending in active labor market programs impacts entrepreneurship and unemployment rates (Laffineur et al., 2017). Other scholars have combined data from the PSED and O*NET – a US database compiled by the Department of Labor's Occupational Information Network – to investigate the impact of financial, human, and cultural capital on entrepreneurial entry (Kim et al., 2006), to explore how previous employment experience affects the size of founding collaborations (Kim & Longest, 2014), and to study how different occupational characteristics affect entrepreneurs' beliefs and the effort they put in their nascent ventures (Laffineur et al., 2020).

Third, entrepreneurship scholars have also been able to exploit secondary data from existing datasets that are not specifically focusing on entrepreneurship but are still very useful to understand entrepreneurial dynamics. This is particularly the case of longitudinal datasets, such as the US National Longitudinal Survey of Youth, which allow for tracking individuals' professional careers over time and therefore study modes of entry into entrepreneurship (Raffiee & Jie, 2014) as well as different factors associated with entry and exit (Carroll & Mosakowski, 1987). Of particular interest are longitudinal matched employee-employer datasets, which have been used to study, for instance, how workplace characteristics affect entrepreneurial entry (Sørensen, 2007) as well as different types of entry, such as hybrid entrepreneurship (Folta et al., 2010).

Finally, entrepreneurship scholars have been very active in collecting data themselves, through multiple approaches including surveys with several waves and different modalities such as telephone interviews, onsite visits, and online questionnaires (e.g., De Cock et al., 2020; Delmar & Shane, 2003; Delmar & Wiklund, 2008; Li et al., 2022; Murnieks et al., 2020), large surveys including both self-reported and behavioural measures (e.g., Koudstaal et al., 2019), and experiments (e.g., Dubard Barbosa et al., 2019; Holm et al., 2013; Shepherd, 1999; Zunino et al., 2022), to mention three of the most widely used approaches. Often, such efforts to collect primary data were also combined with secondary data allowing the investigation of relationships between individual-level variables and organizational- and environmental-level factors ultimately affecting venture performance (e.g., Dencker & Gruber, 2015; Hmieleski & Baron, 2009).

Such efforts to collect primary data have also produced more interesting and relevant data thanks to scale development efforts and technological progress. Specifically, over the past decades quantitative research in entrepreneurship followed the theoretical advancements of the field and produced specific scale instruments to measure theoretical constructs that are particularly relevant to the field, such as effectuation (Chandler et al., 2011), opportunity evaluation (Scheaf et al., 2020), entrepreneurial passion (Cardon et al., 2013), entrepreneurs' social identity (Sieger et al., 2016), fear of failure (Cacciotti et al., 2020), and frugality (Michaelis et al., 2020). Moreover, measurement efforts have also taken advantage of the use of new technology, such as facial expression analysis (e.g., Jiang et al., 2019; Stroe et al., 2020) and functional magnetic resonance imaging (Shane et al., 2020).

These advancements in measurement have also been accompanied by advancements in research design and analysis. As the field matures, we see an increasing number of studies using experimental designs and longitudinal data which allow for better tests of causality. Simultaneously, statistical packages have become more sophisticated and computational capability to process data has dramatically increased over the last decades. As a result, scholars doing quantitative research in entrepreneurship are now better equipped than ever: we are literally able to analyse tons of data from everywhere, with a level of sophistication that was hard to imagine a couple of decades ago.

THE CHALLENGES THAT STILL REMAIN

The availability of interesting datasets and our augmented capacity to collect and analyse huge amounts of data may give the impression that doing quantitative research in entrepreneurship has become easy. Such an impression is actually very far from true. Although quantitative studies have grown both in quantity and quality, several challenges persist and still need to be addressed. Some of them even threaten the validity of inferences made by previous quantitative studies and will keep threatening the validity of future studies if they are not properly addressed. I highlight and discuss below some of the main challenges that remain for scholars engaged in doing quantitative research in entrepreneurship.

Entrepreneurship is Not Normal

One methodological and empirical challenge that remains with quantitative studies in entrepreneurship is that most studies assume a normal distribution of the data, yet we all know that entrepreneurship is not normal. There is indeed little evidence of a normal distribution in any fundamental aspect of entrepreneurship. For instance, entry into entrepreneurship is a relatively rare event. The GEM Global Report 2017/18 estimated that nascent entrepreneurship rates ranged from 1.8% to 21.2% of the adult population aged 18–64 years across 54 countries, with an average of 5.1% in Europe and 11.7% in Latin America and the Caribbean, the two continents with the lowest and highest rates, respectively (GEM, 2018).[3] Thus, although a significant number of individuals will enter entrepreneurship at some point in their lives (Reynolds & White, 1997; Thornton, 1999), at any point in time only a relatively small number of individuals enter entrepreneurship (generally much less than two out of 10).

Exit is also a relatively rare event, since even underperforming firms tend to delay exit as long as they can (Gimeno et al., 1997). The GEM 2021/2022 Global Report shows that, even during the COVID-19 pandemic, less than one in 10 adults exited a business in three-quarters of the participating economies (GEM, 2022). In none of the GEM-participating economies did exit rates reach a level of two adults in 10.

When it comes to performance-related indicators, normality seems to be an even more unrealistic assumption. Entrepreneurship tends to disproportionally attract individuals from the tails of the earnings and ability distributions, i.e., "stars and misfits" who most likely become opportunity and necessity entrepreneurs (Åstebro et al., 2011; Åstebro & Chen, 2014). In such a context, average returns might not be very informative.[4] Several scholars actually call for a distinction between self-employment and entrepreneurship, arguing that only the latter contributes to economic growth and that the institutions that foster productive entrepreneurship are very different from (and even contradict) the institutions fostering self-employment (e.g., Acs et al., 2016; Henrekson & Sanandaji, 2014; Sanandaji & Leeson, 2013).

The point is that high performance in entrepreneurship is a rare event (Åstebro, 2017), even a "black swan" (Taleb, 2007). Growth is rare, regardless of how it is measured (Delmar et al., 2003, 2022). A successful exit is even rarer as one can see from Table 7.1.

As one can see, in any given year the number of IPOs in the United States is extremely low compared to the number of new start-ups filling in an application form. The highest number of IPOs in 2021 was inflated by a significant rise in the number of special purpose acquisition companies (SPACs) who went public with the sole goal of raising capital to acquire other existing companies. Hence, the number of IPOs in 2021 is not a good measure of successful exits, it is probably reflecting the unsuccessful exits of existing companies that were acquired during and after the shock of the COVID-19 pandemic crisis. Even if we disregard the fact that IPOs are not always a good proxy for successful exits, how could one understand the drivers of a successful IPO from studying a cohort of new start-ups out of which most likely less than .008% will successfully exit?

Thus, availability of data (and even its abundance) does not mean that the phenomenon of interest is largely available or frequent, and even less that it follows a normal distribution. Entrepreneurship is in fact a land of the abnormal, where outliers are more likely to enter (the stars and misfits) and only a small fraction of them are likely to succeed. This represents a major challenge for quantitative research assuming a normal distribution to explain entrepreneurial phenomena. Maybe we should indeed care more about outliers and extreme cases, and less about averages, as suggested by some strategic organization scholars (Forgues, 2012; Starbuck, 2006).

Table 7.1 *Number of new start-ups and IPOs per year in the United States*

Year	Number of Business Applications[a]	Number of IPOs[b]	Ratio IPOs/New Start-ups (%)
2005	2 489 308	286	0.011
2006	2 631 025	220	0.008
2007	2 637 271	268	0.010
2008	2 561 283	62	0.002
2009	2 408 461	79	0.003
2010	2 476 207	190	0.008
2011	2 552 464	171	0.007
2012	2 552 182	157	0.006
2013	2 593 011	251	0.010
2014	2 692 094	304	0.011
2015	2 796 800	206	0.007
2016	2 948 578	133	0.005
2017	3 177 314	217	0.007
2018	3 480 911	255	0.007
2019	3 496 489	232	0.007
2020	4 345 133	480	0.011
2021	5 364 046	1035	0.019
2022	5 044 748	181	0.004
Average per year	3 124 851	*263*	*0.008*

Sources: [a] United States Census Bureau (https://www.census.gov/econ/bfs/data.html); [b] Stock Analysis (Statista 2023 – https://www-statista-com.em-lyon.idm.oclc.org/statistics/270290/number-of-ipos-in-the-us-since-1999/).

Entrepreneurship is a Broad Concept

There is a general consensus about entrepreneurship being best seen as a process (Shane, 2012). However, there is much less consensus on what this process is about. Entrepreneurial action can take many forms, from the emancipation of communities (Marti et al., 2013; Peredo & Chrisman, 2006; Rindova et al., 2009) to the exploitation of technological opportunities through new firms (Shane, 2001a, 2001b), from informal economic activity (Salvi et al., 2022) to the creation of local organizations aiming to alleviate suffering in the aftermath of massive disasters (Shepherd & Williams, 2014;

Williams & Shepherd, 2016), from building inclusive markets (Mair et al., 2012; Mair & Marti, 2009) to simply developing and commercializing a new app on Facebook (Fan et al., 2021). This huge diversity of phenomena under the umbrella of entrepreneurship certainly contributes to make it such a fascinating field of research, but this diversity also poses several challenges for scholars doing quantitative research.

First, there is an issue of measurement. What should we be measuring when we assess entrepreneurial phenomena? This question is not new, yet it still calls for a careful choice of measures vis-à-vis a clear definition of research question and research design. Several constructs that are keen to the field are context-dependent and task-specific. For instance, intentionality and self-efficacy are related to and measured against a specific behaviour and context (Ajzen, 2002; Ajzen & Fishbein, 2005; Bandura, 1997), entrepreneurial passion and entrepreneurial self-efficacy have their own task-specific dimensions with potentially differential effects on the entrepreneurial process (Cardon et al., 2013; Kickul et al., 2009), and so on. Therefore, it is of utmost importance to clearly define the focal unit of analysis and the appropriate measures, consistent with the research question and the research design.

Second, the diversity of entrepreneurial phenomena and the measurement issues it entails also pose a challenge to meta-analytic efforts. Scholars doing systematic reviews and in particular meta-analysis should pay careful attention to the specific metrics used in quantitative studies, as well as to the empirical setting and all details of the research design used in each study. The goal is to make sure that meta-analyses compare apples to apples, and not to oranges, otherwise conclusions might be misleading.

Finally, a related challenge concerns the generalization of valid causal inferences. Although the statistical reasoning involved in quantitative studies is generally based on a logic that enables testing and generalization of findings, entrepreneurial phenomena might be so idiosyncratic that any attempt to generalize findings from a single study, quantitative or qualitative, is subject to criticism. Above and beyond the basic criteria for assessing statistical conclusion validity, entrepreneurship researchers must pay careful attention to the different factors affecting internal validity, construct validity, and external validity, before moving to any kind of generalization. This is because generalization should not occur at the level of the results themselves, it should occur at the level of the causal inferences they allow one to make (Shadish et al., 2002). Since entrepreneurship is such a broad and vague concept, we need to be very careful when moving back and forth from observations and specific measures (or operationalizations of our constructs) to constructs, and from constructs to theories about entrepreneurship, either in an inductive or in a deductive approach.[5]

Entrepreneurship is Path Dependent

Entrepreneurship is an intricated process that is embedded in the life processes of the people who participate in it. Such a process is path dependent, i.e., each step down the process is linked to previous steps and happens under conditions shaped by earlier phases of the process. Founding conditions leave a blueprint in the strategy, structure, and business models of organizations (Boeker, 1989; Snihur & Zott, 2020). The very act of starting a new business is embedded in the life processes of the individuals who become entrepreneurs (Bernard & Dubard Barbosa, 2016) and their previous experiences affect the nascent business in multiple ways, including its performance and survival (Delmar & Shane, 2006; Dencker et al., 2009; Dencker & Gruber, 2015). Thus, appropriate research designs should take into account this path-dependent nature of the entrepreneurial process.

However, a great deal of quantitative research in entrepreneurship still falls short at doing so. Cross-sectional studies can be informative about specific research questions, but they say little to nothing about causality, process, and path-dependence. Experimental designs are much better for making causal inferences around specific research questions (Shadish et al., 2002), but they generally trade off external (or ecological) validity for internal validity (Grégoire et al., 2019) and, in so doing, often neglect participants' path-dependent life trajectories.

Longitudinal studies, which are naturally more fit for a process perspective, also face several methodological challenges that hinder their ability to make valid causal inferences about the entrepreneurial process. First, longitudinal data often suffers from both left- and right-censoring, i.e., observations cover a window of time, but we lack information about what happened before and after such a period. Moreover, during the period of observation new participants/firms might enter the dataset, whereas others might exit. Our ability to understand such dynamics will depend on the quality of measures available as well as on the frequency of repeated measurement, to mention two key factors. But even when these two key factors are satisfactory, our ability to make causal inferences is still hindered by selection bias in two main forms: self-selection bias and survival (or success) bias (Aldrich, 2001; Aldrich & Ruef, 2006; Delmar et al., 2022).

Self-selection bias occurs when participants self-select into a group or treatment, which generally happens with entrepreneurial decisions about entry and growth (and oftentimes exit as well). Delmar et al. (2022) point out that theories assuming that growth and exit are exogenously determined tend to be less concerned about self-selection bias, whereas theories that understand growth and exit as a strategic decision are more concerned about self-selection bias as a problem of endogeneity. Indeed, self-selection bias can be considered as a subdimension of the greater endogeneity bias (Clougherty et al., 2016), which has three main sources: measurement error, simultaneity, and omitted variables (Wooldridge, 2002). Measurement error occurs when measurement instruments do not perfectly capture the underlying constructs they are supposed to measure. Simultaneity occurs when an independent variable is jointly determined along with the dependent variable, i.e., cause and effect are simultaneously measured. And omitted-variable bias arises when a latent factor (usually not measured and not included in the analysis) both affects the dependent variable and is correlated with the independent variable(s) included in the analysis. These sources of endogeneity bias tend to bias the effect of regression estimators and make them correlate with the error term, hence violating the exogeneity assumption of ordinary least squares (OLS) that the error term should have an expected value of zero given any explanatory variable (Clougherty et al., 2016; Wooldridge, 2002, 2013). Unfortunately, measurement error, simultaneity, and omitted-variable bias are still very common in entrepreneurship research, even in studies using longitudinal datasets.

Self-selection bias can indeed be considered a specific variation of the omitted-variable bias issue, because self-selection might result from a latent factor that manifests in the error term and correlates both with the endogenous choice to take the treatment (or be part of a group) and the outcome variable (Antonakis et al., 2010). This is a salient issue when one analyses entry and performance in entrepreneurship: since those who enter entrepreneurship come disproportionally from the tails of the earnings and ability distributions (Åstebro et al., 2011; Åstebro & Chen, 2014), their performance in entrepreneurship is most likely affected by the same factors that pushed them to enter: the lack of ability and choice (for necessity entrepreneurs) or the aspiration for greater rewards (for opportunity entrepreneurs). In such a context, it seems unrealistic to assume that the error term has an expected value of zero given any explanatory variable. Most likely, self-selection into entrepreneurship and our imperfect ability to observe what drives it is leading to poor and biased estimates.

Another well-known form of selection bias is survival (or success) bias, which occurs when units of analysis do not survive until they reach treatment or when researchers, knowingly or unknowingly, select cases based on successful outcomes – such as survival (Aldrich & Ruef, 2006; Delmar et al., 2022). In both cases, the selection of units of analysis is not random. It is most likely affected by path dependence and omitted variables. As a result, treatment effects are confounded with unobserved factors and survival/success effects, jeopardizing one's ability to make causal inferences from the study.

Entrepreneurship is Not a Linear Smooth Process

Entrepreneurship is not a linear, continuous process that follows a regular rhythm. Anyone monitoring a cohort of start-ups in any given context for a relatively long period will most likely observe that: (1) each of them follows a specific, idiosyncratic trajectory; and (2) albeit idiosyncratic, all trajectories exhibit periods of apparent inactivity (during which very little happens) and periods of intense activity (during which a lot happens in a relatively short period of time), as well as tipping points (triggered by external shocks, transformative encounters, saturation of an untenable situation, and so on). This is relatively easy to observe at a small scale in a qualitative approach, such as in an ethnographic study (Dumont, 2023). However, the challenge for quantitative entrepreneurship research is to be able to do so on a large scale.

There are two dimensions to this challenge, and both relate to research design and measurement. First, the quality of available measures must match not only the constructs they are supposed to capture but also the complexity of the phenomenon under study. Second, measurement needs to be done repeatedly for a long period and the frequency of repeated measures must allow a fine-grained analysis of the dynamics involved in the entrepreneurial process. Neither of these conditions is met in most quantitative studies in entrepreneurship since measures are often imperfect and less frequent than would be ideal. Secondary longitudinal datasets generally provide archival data measured once a year, thereby masking intra-year variation and presenting a risk of retrospective/recall bias. Moreover, researchers generally use such datasets to test theories and explore questions that go well beyond the initial purposes for which such data were collected in the first place.

One option to attenuate this problem could be the adoption of experience sampling methodology (ESM) to collect primary data (Uy et al., 2010). ESM would help reducing the risk of retrospective bias and enhance the researcher's ability to identify and model nonlinear dynamics of the entrepreneurial process. Nevertheless, it could still present measurement issues due to the fact that measures in ESM must be kept to short forms and few items to ease participant burden and maximize response rates (Uy et al., 2010).

An additional issue, related to analysis, is that most quantitative studies in entrepreneurship use linear models to analyse data and only a few studies capture and explore nonlinear relationships. As we move forward towards research with greater internal and ecological validity, it is important that our spectrum of analytic models expand and include more analyses of nonlinear effects (which are likely to be more common in entrepreneurship than entrepreneurship research has reported thus far).

THE NEW CHALLENGES ON THE BLOCK

As we gain in analytic capacity and sophistication, we augment the potential of quantitative research in entrepreneurship to expand the frontiers of our collective knowledge. However, we also run the risks associated with the misuse of an increasingly sophisticated technical apparatus, in particular the risk of producing many studies that are practically irrelevant and theoretically misleading. Entrepreneurship scholars, and social scientists in general, must keep in mind that technical knowledge or know-how (*techne*) does not automatically generate scientific knowledge (*episteme*), and neither of them replace the Aristotelien notion of *phronesis*, i.e., discerned and practical wisdom relating to judgment calls about what is good and bad in terms of courses of action (Flyvbjerg, 2001). Similarly, greater access to data and augmented analytic capacity do not replace methodological rigor and reasoned choices about what to study, when, and how.

Considering the challenges highlighted in the previous section, it is paramount to realize that our increased capacity to access and analyse data enhances our ability to produce more research but does not automatically translate into better research. In what follows, I discuss two relatively newer broad sets of challenges for quantitative research in entrepreneurship, which need to be addressed in moving the field forward.

Quantity Does Not Necessarily Breed Quality (or Impact)

Although the availability of data and the sophistication of quantitative analytic methods offer a myriad of opportunities for entrepreneurship scholars to produce more interesting research and overcome past challenges, they might also contribute to the proliferation of studies that are neither theoretically sound nor practically relevant. Even worse, their combined effects might enhance the risk of producing misleading results. This might happen for multiple reasons.

First, the availability of databases with big samples (in some cases, whole populations) increases the odds of finding statistical significance for effects that are actually small in practice. This favors non-scientific data mining practices – such as data fishing. It also favors "salami slicing" to the extent that the statistical power of big samples allows researchers to test different parts of a model and still find statistical significance for the relationships that would be considered substantively marginal in light of the whole model. Most importantly, even in the absence of such practices, this increase in statistical power contributes to further fragmentation as scholars specializing in specific parts of the entrepreneurial "elephant" most likely find statistical significance for their variables of interest. Therefore, it is crucial that entrepreneurship researchers prioritize theoretical and practical relevance, as well as methodological rigor, when designing and conducting their studies. As Combs (2010) puts it: "let's not trade relevance and rigor for power." If statistical power comes at the expense of relevance and rigor, entrepreneurship research might become misleading or, at best, irrelevant.

Indeed, Uncle Ben's advice to Peter Parker that "with greater power comes greater responsibility" could also be applied to entrepreneurship scholars. To some extent as a reaction to this increased statistical power, entrepreneurship journals are starting to ask authors to report marginal effects and effect sizes more systematically, emphasizing substantive significance along with statistical significance. This is definitely a good practice that entrepreneurship scholars should embrace.

In the same token, researchers should not trade clarity, rigor, and relevance for analytic sophistication. Software development has facilitated the use of sophisticated statistical methods, but such analytic methods alone do not fulfill the needs of relevant research questions, rigorous research designs, and clear writing. The greater responsibility that comes with the greater analytic power researchers have begins with the practice of choosing the appropriate analytic method to treat the research question at hand and of being transparent about its limitations. Sophistication does not equal rigor. For instance, the use of a relatively sophisticated statistical method such as structural equations modeling per se does not overcome limitations related to multicollinearity and measurement error (Grewal et al., 2004), common method bias (Podsakoff et al., 2003), lack of control variables, and the fact that non-experimental cross-sectional data might provide correlational evidence but that is not enough for making causal inferences.

Thus, one of the main challenges for entrepreneurship researchers moving ahead is to use the statistical power of big samples and the sophistication of statistical methods wisely. In doing quantitative research, wisdom must be exercised at least in four main stages of the research process:

- In the choice of research question, letting it be guided by *both* practical relevance and theoretical interest.
- In establishing the research design, in a way that favors the making of causal inferences. This generally involves controlling by design (whenever possible) and measuring control variables (when control by design is not possible), as well as some degree of manipulation of explanatory variables or longitudinal observation.
- In data analysis, by choosing the appropriate analytic method in light of the research question, research design, and potential counterfactuals.
- In writing the research report or article in a clear manner, being transparent about all aspects of the research project, reporting findings as well as

non-findings, i.e., supported and unsupported hypotheses, and making even sophisticated studies as accessible as possible to the reader.

Making academic work (and academic writing) as relevant and as accessible as possible to the general public is a challenge in itself. Entrepreneurship scholars doing quantitative research must face this challenge, if we are to fulfill our social mission of generating scientific knowledge that informs and guides policy makers, entrepreneurs, educators, and students.

Gains and Losses are Not Symmetric

The previous set of challenges related to the general risk of quantitative research in entrepreneurship becoming further fragmented and practically irrelevant. Therefore, I outlined a few guidelines for using wisdom throughout the research process. I now turn to a different set of challenges that are more specific in nature and that I hope will occupy entrepreneurship researchers for the years to come. It can be summarized in the sentence: gains and losses are not symmetric.

We have known for a long time that gains and losses are asymmetrically perceived by all kinds of individuals. This is the very basis of prospect theory (Kahneman & Tversky, 1979) and it has been shown in many studies in different fields (Kahneman, 2003, 2011), generally with individuals exhibiting risk aversion in the domain of gains and risk seeking in the domain of losses (Rieger et al., 2015). I have myself found the same in my own experimental studies, both with students and with entrepreneurs (Dubard Barbosa, 2008; Dubard Barbosa et al., 2019).

However, studies at the firm level have shown a more complex picture (Wennberg et al., 2016). More recently, Delmar and colleagues argued that the causal mechanisms of new venture growth might not be the same as the causal mechanisms of venture contraction (Delmar et al., 2022). They argued that there is neither theoretical nor empirical reason to believe that expansion and contraction are symmetric, and advocated instead for asymmetric causality, "where causal mechanisms might not only have differential effects, but might also entail different pathways." (p. 5). They propose event magnitude modeling (EMM) as an approach that estimates separately the probability of an event (growth, exit, or contraction) and its magnitude. Using longitudinal firm-level data from new Swedish ventures, they found significant differences in the coefficients of profitability, firm age, and size, on the magnitude of hiring vs. the magnitude of firing, indicating different forms of asymmetries between expansion and contraction (Delmar et al., 2022). Indeed, their proposed EMM offers a promising approach to help researchers deal with this causal asymmetry as well as a couple of the challenges previously mentioned, such as the distributional properties of new ventures (and their non-normality) and selection bias.

But above and beyond adopting a new modeling approach, I suggest entrepreneurship scholars explore and expand on this insight that expansion and contraction, gains and losses in entrepreneurship, might have different causal mechanisms. Intuitively, we might all agree that success and failure have different roots. But what are the implications of such insight in terms of research design? What type of data and analysis do we need to be able to tell entrepreneurs which things they must get right (to succeed) and which things they should avoid (to not fail)? If success and failure have different explanatory mechanisms, we should be able to study them quantitatively and empirically. I believe this is a fascinating avenue for future research and a significant challenge for quantitative research in entrepreneurship, with EMM being an important first step in facing it.

CONCLUSION

This chapter attempted to offer an overview and a discussion of the main challenges facing quantitative research in entrepreneurship. After providing a brief sketch of the historical development of the field, I highlighted the main achievements to date and concentrated on the challenges that remain and on the relatively newer challenges that lie ahead. Identifying challenges is a challenging task. In so doing, I purposefully made the choice to offer my personal view in selecting what I think are the main challenges threatening the validity and the relevance of quantitative studies in entrepreneurship. This choice is clearly subject to criticism, yet I hope it offers an authentic perspective that entrepreneurship researchers will consider when conducting their own quantitative studies.

Science is constantly evolving in a dynamic, collective process. The challenges we face are also opportunities for further development and scientific evolution. As Popper (1959, p. 94) claimed:

> Science does not rest upon solid bedrock. The bold structure of its theories rises, as it were, above a swamp. It is like a building erected on piles. The piles are driven down from above into the swamp, but not down to any natural or "given" base; and if we stop driving the piles deeper, it is not because we have reached firm ground. We simply stop when we are satisfied that the piles are firm enough to carry the structure, at least for the time being.

Today entrepreneurship scholars are better equipped than ever to do quantitative research and expand the frontiers of our knowledge. But it is pointless to use such advanced equipment to just keep piling up studies. Considering the challenges discussed in this chapter might help researchers to drive their piles deeper and maybe even question the structure of entrepreneurship theories. Facing the fact that entrepreneurship is not normal, that it is indeed a broad concept and a non-linear, path-dependent process, is important to better design and conduct quantitative studies that will drive our piles deeper. Acknowledging that quantity does not always breed quality might help us attenuate the downside effects of fragmentation, increased statistical power, and sophistication of analytic methods. Finally, exploring the asymmetries between gains and losses offers an opportunity to further drive our piles deeper and question conventional knowledge through more refined quantitative research.

NOTES

1. For a deeper historical view of the field of entrepreneurship research, see the work of Hans Landström (Landström, 2014; Landström & Lohrke, 2010).
2. For instance, the Entrepreneurship Division is one of the largest divisions at the American Academy of Management.
3. The 2021 GUESSS Global Report shows a more positive figure among students, with an average of 28.4% of students declaring to be in the process of starting a new venture (Sieger et al., 2021).
4. They are not very reliable either: although official numbers suggest that most individuals often earn less in self-employment than in paid employment (Hamilton, 2000), there is a high probability of income underreporting by entrepreneurs (Åstebro & Chen, 2014).
5. Although most quantitative studies tend to adopt a deductive approach, it is important to realize that doing quantitative research involves inductive, deductive, and abductive reasoning, often iteratively.

REFERENCES

Acs, Z. J., Åstebro, T., Audretsch, D. B., & Robinson, D. T. (2016). Public policy to promote entrepreneurship: A call to arms. *Small Business Economics*, *47*(1), 35–51.

Ajzen, I. (2002). Perceived behavioural control, self-efficacy, locus of control, and the theory of planned behavior. *Journal of Applied Social Psychology*, *32*(4), 665–683.

Ajzen, I., & Fishbein, M. (2005). The influence of attitudes on behavior. In D. Albarracín, B. T. Johnson, & M. P. Zanna (Eds.), *The handbook of attitudes* (p. 173–221). Erlbaum.

Aldrich, H. E. (2001). Who wants to be an evolutionary theorist? Remarks on the occasion of the Year 2000 OMT Distinguished Scholarly Career Award presentation. *Journal of Management Inquiry*, *10*(2), 115–127. https:// doi .org/ 10 .1177/ 1056492601102004.

Aldrich, H. E., & Ruef, M. (2006). *Organizations evolving* (2nd ed.). SAGE Publications.

Alvarez, S. A., & Barney, J. B. (2013). Epistemology, opportunities, and entrepreneurship: Comments on Venkataraman et al. (2012) and Shane (2012). *Academy of Management Review*, *38*(1), 154–157.

Antonakis, J., Bendahan, S., Jacquart, P., & Lalive, R. (2010). On making causal claims: A review and recommendations. *Leadership Quarterly Yearly Review*, *21*(6), 1086–1120. https://doi.org/10.1016/j.leaqua.2010.10.010.

Åstebro, T. (2017). The private financial gains to entrepreneurship: Is it a good use of public money to encourage individuals to become entrepreneurs? *Small Business Economics*, *48*(2), 323–329.

Åstebro, T., & Chen, J. (2014). The entrepreneurial earnings puzzle: Mismeasurement or real? *Journal of Business Venturing*, *29*(1), 88–105. https://doi.org/10.1016/j.jbusvent.2013.04.003.

Åstebro, T., Chen, J., & Thompson, P. (2011). Stars and misfits: Self-employment and labor market frictions. *Management Science*, *57*(11), 1999–2017. https://doi.org/10.1287/mnsc.1110.1400.

Bandura, A. (1997). *Self-efficacy: The exercise of control*. Freeman & Co. Publishers.

Bernard, M.-J., & Dubard Barbosa, S. (2016). Resilience and entrepreneurship: A dynamic and biographical approach to the entrepreneurial act. *M@n@gement*, *19*(2), 89–123.

Boeker, W. (1989). Strategic change: The effects of founding and history. *Academy of Management Journal*, *32*(3), 489–515.

Bruyat, C. (1993). Création d'entreprise: Contributions épistémologiques et modélisation. Doctoral dissertation. Université de Grenoble II.

Bruyat, C., & Julien, P.-A. (2000). Defining the field of research in entrepreneurship. *Journal of Business Venturing*, *16*, 165–180.

Cacciotti, G., Hayton, J. C., Mitchell, J. R., & Allen, D. G. (2020). Entrepreneurial fear of failure: Scale development and validation. *Journal of Business Venturing*, *35*(5), 106041. https://doi.org/10.1016/j.jbusvent.2020.106041.

Cardon, M. S., Gregoire, D. A., Stevens, C. E., & Patel, P. C. (2013). Measuring entrepreneurial passion: Conceptual foundations and scale validation. *Journal of Business Venturing*, *28*(3), 373–396. https://doi.org/10.1016/j.jbusvent.2012.03.003.

Carroll, G. R., & Mosakowski, E. (1987). The career dynamics of self-employment. *Administrative Science Quarterly*, *32*(4), 570–589.

Chandler, G. N., DeTienne, D. R., McKelvie, A., & Mumford, T. V. (2011). Causation and effectuation processes: A validation study. *Journal of Business Venturing*, *26*(3), 375–390.

Clougherty, J. A., Duso, T., & Muck, J. (2016). Correcting for self-selection based endogeneity in management research: Review, recommendations and simulations. *Organizational Research Methods*, *19*(2), 286–347.

Combs, J. G. (2010). From the Editors: Big samples and small effects: Let's not trade relevance and rigor for power. *Academy of Management Journal*, *53*(1), 9–13.

Davidsson, P. (2003). The domain of entrepreneurship research: Some suggestions. In J. A. Katz & D. A. Shepherd (Eds.), *Advances in Entrepreneurship, Firm Emergence and Growth* (Vol. 6, pp. 315–372). Elsevier/JAI Press.

Davidsson, P. (2004). *Researching entrepreneurship*. Springer.

Davidsson, P. (2015). Entrepreneurial opportunities and the entrepreneurship nexus: A re-conceptualization. *Journal of Business Venturing*, *30*(5), 674–695.

Davidsson, P. (2017). Entrepreneurial opportunities as propensities: Do Ramoglou & Tsang move the field forward? *Journal of Business Venturing Insights*, *7*, 82–85. https://doi.org/10.1016/j.jbvi.2016.02.002.

De Cock, R., Denoo, L., & Clarysse, B. (2020). Surviving the emotional rollercoaster called entrepreneurship: The role of emotion regulation. *Journal of Business Venturing*, *35*(2), 105936.

Delmar, F., Davidsson, P., & Gartner, W. B. (2003). Arriving at the high-growth firm. *Journal of Business Venturing, 18*(2), 189–216.
Delmar, F., & Shane, S. (2003). Does business planning facilitate the development of new ventures? *Strategic Management Journal, 24*, 1165–1185.
Delmar, F., & Shane, S. (2006). Does experience matter? The effect of founding team experience on the survival and sales of newly founded ventures. *Strategic Organization, 4*(3), 215–247.
Delmar, F., Wallin, J., & Nofal, A. M. (2022). Modeling new-firm growth and survival with panel data using event magnitude regression. *Journal of Business Venturing, 37*(5), 106245. https://doi.org/10.1016/j.jbusvent.2022.106245.
Delmar, F., & Wiklund, J. (2008). The effect of small business managers' growth motivation on firm growth: A longitudinal study. *Entrepreneurship Theory and Practice, 32*(3), 437–457.
Dencker, J. C., & Gruber, M. (2015). The effects of opportunities and founder experience on new firm performance. *Strategic Management Journal, 36*, 1035–1052.
Dencker, J. C., Gruber, M., & Shah, S. K. (2009). Pre-entry knowledge, learning, and the survival of new firms. *Organization Science, 20*(3), 516–537.
Dubard Barbosa, S. (2008). La perception du risque dans la décision de création d'entreprise. Doctoral dissertation. Université Pierre Mendès France.
Dubard Barbosa, S., Fayolle, A., & Smith, B. R. (2019). Biased and overconfident, unbiased but going for it: How framing and anchoring affect the decision to start a new venture. *Journal of Business Venturing, 34*(3), 528–557. https://doi.org/10.1016/j.jbusvent.2018.12.006.
Dumont, G. (2023). Immersion in organizational ethnography: Four methodological requirements to immerse oneself in the field. *Organizational Research Methods, 26*(3), 441–458. https://doi.org/10.1177/10944281221075365.
Eckhardt, J. T., & Shane, S. (2013). Response to the commentaries: The individual–opportunity (IO) nexus integrates objective and subjective aspects of entrepreneurship. *Academy of Management Review, 38*(1), 160–163.
Fan, T., Schwab, A., & Geng, X. (2021). Habitual entrepreneurship in digital platform ecosystems: A time-contingent model of learning from prior software project experiences. *Journal of Business Venturing, 36*(5), 106140. https://doi.org/10.1016/j.jbusvent.2021.106140.
Flyvbjerg, B. (2001). *Making social science matter*. Cambridge University Press.
Folta, T. B., Delmar, F., & Wennberg, K. (2010). Hybrid entrepreneurship. *Management Science, 56*(2), 253–269.
Forgues, B. (2012). Sampling on the dependent variable is not always that bad: Quantitative case-control designs for strategic organization research. *Strategic Organization, 10*(3), 269–275. https://doi.org/10.1177/1476127012452820.
Gartner, W. B. (1985). A conceptual framework for describing the phenomenon of new venture creation. *Academy of Management Review, 10*(4), 696–706.
Gartner, W. B. (1988). "Who is an entrepreneur?" is the wrong question. *American Journal of Small Business, 12*(4), 11–32.
Gartner, W. B. (2004). Achieving "critical mess" in entrepreneurship scholarship. In J. A. Katz & D. A. Shepherd (Eds.), *Advances in entrepreneurship, firm emergence, and growth* (Vol. 7, pp. 199–216). JAI Press.
GEM (Global Entrepreneurship Monitor). (2018). *Global report 2017/18*. https://www.gemconsortium.org/file/open?fileId=50012.
GEM (Global Entrepreneurship Monitor). (2022). *Global report 2021/22: Opportunity amid disruption*. https://www.gemconsortium.org/file/open?fileId=50900.

Gimeno, J., Folta, T. B., Cooper, A. C., & Woo, C. Y. (1997). Survival of the fittest? Entrepreneurial human capital and the persistence of underperforming firms. *Administrative Science Quarterly*, *42*(4), 750–783.

Grégoire, D. A., Binder, J. K., & Rauch, A. (2019). Navigating the validity tradeoffs of entrepreneurship research experiments: A systematic review and best-practice suggestions. *Journal of Business Venturing*, *34*(2), 284–310. https://doi.org/10.1016/j.jbusvent.2018.10.002.

Grewal, R., Cote, J. A., & Baumgartner, H. (2004). Multicollinearity and measurement error in structural equation models: Implications for theory testing. *Marketing Science*, *23*(4), 519–529.

Hamilton, B. H. (2000). Does entrepreneurship pay? An empirical analysis of the returns to self-employment. *Journal of Political Economy*, *108*(3), 604–631. https://doi.org/10.1086/262131.

Henrekson, M., & Sanandaji, T. (2014). Small business activity does not measure entrepreneurship. *Proceedings of the National Academy of Sciences*, *111*(5), 1760–1765. https://doi.org/10.1073/pnas.1307204111.

Hmieleski, K. M., & Baron, R. A. (2009). Entrepreneurs' optimism and new venture performance: A social cognitive perspective. *Academy of Management Journal*, *52*(3), 473–488.

Holm, H. J., Opper, S., & Nee, V. (2013). Entrepreneurs under uncertainty: An economic experiment in China. *Management Science*, *59*(7), 1671–1687.

Jiang, L., Yin, D., & Liu, D. (2019). Can joy buy you money? The impact of the strength, duration, and phases of an entrepreneur's peak displayed joy on funding performance. *Academy of Management Journal*, *62*(6), 1848–1871. https://doi.org/10.5465/amj.2017.1423.

Kahneman, D. (2003). Maps of bounded rationality: Psychology for behavioral economics. *The American Economic Review*, *93*(5), 1449–1475.

Kahneman, D. (2011). *Thinking, fast and slow*. Farrar, Straus and Giroux.

Kahneman, D., & Tversky, A. (1979). Prospect theory: An analysis of decision under risk. *Econometrica*, *47*(2), 263–291.

Katz, J. A., & Gartner, W. B. (1988). Properties of emerging organizations. *Academy of Management Review*, *13*(3), 429–441.

Kickul, J., Gundry, L. K., Dubard Barbosa, S., & Whitcanack, L. (2009). Intuition versus analysis? Testing differential models of cognitive style on entrepreneurial self-efficacy and the new venture creation process. *Entrepreneurship Theory and Practice*, *33*(2), 439–453.

Kim, P. H., Aldrich, H. E., & Keister, L. A. (2006). Access (not) denied: The impact of financial, human, and cultural capital on entrepreneurial entry in the United States. *Small Business Economics*, *27*(1), 5–22.

Kim, P. H., & Longest, K. C. (2014). You can't leave your work behind: Employment experience and founding collaborations. *Journal of Business Venturing*, *29*(6), 785–806.

Koudstaal, M., Sloof, R., & Van Praag, M. (2019). Entrepreneurs: Intuitive or contemplative decision-makers? *Small Business Economics*, *53*, 901–920.

Laffineur, C., Dubard Barbosa, S., Fayolle, A., & Montmartin, B. (2020). The unshackled entrepreneur: Occupational determinants of entrepreneurial effort. *Journal of Business Venturing*, *35*(5), 105983. https://doi.org/10.1016/j.jbusvent.2019.105983.

Laffineur, C., Dubard Barbosa, S., Fayolle, A., & Nziali, E. (2017). The effects of active labor market programs on entrepreneurship and unemployment. *Small Business Economics*, *49*(4), 889–918. https://doi.org/10.1007/s11187-017-9857-7.

Landström, H. (2014). A history of entrepreneurship research. In Landström, H. (Ed.), *Handbook of research on entrepreneurship: What we know and what we need to know* (pp. 23–62). Edward Elgar Publishing. https://doi.org/10.4337/9780857936929.00008.

Landström, H., & Lohrke, F. (2010). *Historical foundations of entrepreneurship research*. Edward Elgar Publishing.

Li, H., Ozdemir, S. Z., & Heslin, P. A. (2022). Merely folklore? The role of a growth mindset in the taking and timing of entrepreneurial actions. *Entrepreneurship Theory and Practice*, *47*(6), 2077–2120.

Mair, J., & Marti, I. (2009). Entrepreneurship in and around institutional voids: A case study from Bangladesh. *Journal of Business Venturing*, *24*(5), 419–435.

Mair, J., Marti, I., & Ventresca, M. J. (2012). Building inclusive markets in rural Bangladesh: How intermediaries work institutional voids. *Academy of Management Journal*, *55*(4), 819–850. https://doi.org/10.5465/amj.2010.0627.

Marti, I., Courpasson, D., & Dubard Barbosa, S. (2013). "Living in the fishbowl": Generating an entrepreneurial culture in a local community in Argentina. *Journal of Business Venturing*, *28*(1), 10–29.

Michaelis, T. L., Carr, J. C., Scheaf, D. J., & Pollack, J. M. (2020). The frugal entrepreneur: A self-regulatory perspective of resourceful entrepreneurial behavior. *Journal of Business Venturing*, *35*(4), 105969. https://doi.org/10.1016/j.jbusvent.2019.105969.

Murnieks, C. Y., Arthurs, J. D., Cardon, M. S., Farah, N., Stornelli, J., & Michael Haynie, J. (2020). Close your eyes or open your mind: Effects of sleep and mindfulness exercises on entrepreneurs' exhaustion. *Journal of Business Venturing*, *35*(2), 105918. https://doi.org/10.1016/j.jbusvent.2018.12.004.

Peredo, A. M., & Chrisman, J. J. (2006). Toward a theory of community-based enterprise. *Academy of Management Review*, *31*(2), 309–328.

Podsakoff, P. M., MacKenzie, S. B., Lee, J.-Y., & Podsakoff, N. P. (2003). Common method biases in behavioral research: A critical review of the literature and recommended remedies. *Journal of Applied Psychology*, *88*(5), 879–903.

Popper, K. (1959). *The logic of scientific discovery* (2004 edn). Routledge.

Raffiee, J., & Jie, F. (2014). Should I quit my day job? A hybrid path to entrepreneurship. *Academy of Management Journal*, *57*(4), 936–963. https://doi.org/10.5465/amj.2012.0522.

Ramoglou, S., & Tsang, E. W. K. (2016). A realist perspective of entrepreneurship: Opportunities as propensities. *Academy of Management Review*, *41*(3), 410–434. https://doi.org/10.5465/amr.2014.0281.

Reynolds, P. D., & White, S. B. (1997). *The entrepreneurial process: Economic growth, men, women, and minorities*. Quorum Books.

Rieger, M. O., Wang, M., & Hens, T. (2015). Risk preferences around the world. *Management Science*, *61*(3), 637–648. https://doi.org/10.1287/mnsc.2013.1869.

Rindova, V., Barry, D., & Ketchen, D. J. (2009). Entrepreneuring as emancipation. *Academy of Management Review*, *34*(3), 477–491.

Salvi, E., Belz, F.-M., & Bacq, S. (2022). Informal entrepreneurship: An integrative review and future research agenda. *Entrepreneurship Theory and Practice*, *47*(2), 265–303. https://doi.org/10.1177/10422587221115365.

Sanandaji, T., & Leeson, P. T. (2013). Billionaires. *Industrial and Corporate Change*, *22*(1), 313–337. https://doi.org/10.1093/icc/dts052.

Scheaf, D. J., Loignon, A. C., Webb, J. W., Heggestad, E. D., & Wood, M. S. (2020). Measuring opportunity evaluation: Conceptual synthesis and scale development. *Journal of Business Venturing*, *35*(2), 105935.
Shadish, W. R., Cook, T. D., & Campbell, D. T. (2002). *Experimental and quasi-experimental designs for generalized causal inference*. Houghton Mifflin Company.
Shane, S. (2001a). Technological opportunities and new firm creation. *Management Science*, *47*(2), 205–220.
Shane, S. (2001b). Technology regimes and new firm formation. *Management Science*, *47*(9), 1173–1181.
Shane, S. (2012). Reflections on the 2010 AMR Decade Award: Delivering on the promise of entrepreneurship as a field of research. *Academy of Management Review*, *37*(1), 10–20.
Shane, S., Drover, W., Clingingsmith, D., & Cerf, M. (2020). Founder passion, neural engagement and informal investor interest in startup pitches: An fMRI study. *Journal of Business Venturing*, *35*(4), 105949. https://doi.org/10.1016/j.jbusvent.2019.105949.
Shane, S., & Venkataraman, S. (2000). The promise of entrepreneurship as a field of research. *Academy of Management Review*, *25*(1), 217–226.
Shepherd, D. A. (1999). Venture capitalists' assessment of new venture survival. *Management Science*, *45*(5), 621–632.
Shepherd, D. A., & Williams, T. A. (2014). Local venturing as compassion organizing in the aftermath of a natural disaster: The role of localness and community in reducing suffering. *Journal of Management Studies*, *51*(6), 952–994. https://doi.org/10.1111/joms.12084.
Sieger, P., Gruber, M., Fauchart, E., & Zellweger, T. (2016). Measuring the social identity of entrepreneurs: Scale development and international validation. *Journal of Business Venturing*, *31*(5), 542–572. https://doi.org/10.1016/j.jbusvent.2016.07.001.
Sieger, P., Raemy, L., Zellweger, T., Fueglistaller, U., & Hatak, I. (2021). *Global student entrepreneurship 2021: Insights from 58 countries*. KMU-HSG/IMU-U.
Snihur, Y., & Zott, C. (2020). The genesis and metamorphosis of novelty imprints: How business model innovation emerges in young ventures. *Academy of Management Journal*, *63*(2), 554–583. https://doi.org/10.5465/amj.2017.0706.
Sørensen, J. B. (2007). Bureaucracy and entrepreneurship: Workplace effects on entrepreneurial entry. *Administrative Science Quarterly*, *52*, 387–412.
Starbuck, W. H. (2006). *The production of knowledge: The challenges of social science research*. Oxford University Press.
Stroe, S., Sirén, C., Shepherd, D., & Wincent, J. (2020). The dualistic regulatory effect of passion on the relationship between fear of failure and negative affect: Insights from facial expression analysis. *Journal of Business Venturing*, *35*(4), 105948. https://doi.org/10.1016/j.jbusvent.2019.105948.
Taleb, N. N. (2007). *The black swan: The impact of the highly improbable*. Penguin Books.
Thornton, P. H. (1999). The sociology of entrepreneurship. *Annual Review of Sociology*, *25*, 19–46.
Uy, M. A., Foo, M.-D., & Aguinis, H. (2010). Using experience sampling methodology to advance entrepreneurship theory and research. *Organizational Research Methods*, *13*(1), 31–54. https://doi.org/10.1177/1094428109334977.

Van Stel, A., Carree, M., & Thurik, R. (2005). The effect of entrepreneurial activity on national economic growth. *Small Business Economics*, *24*, 311–321. https://doi.org/10.1007/s11187-005-1996-6.

Venkataraman, S., Sarasvathy, S. D., Dew, N., & Forster, W. R. (2012). Reflections on the 2012 AMR Decade Award: Whither the promise ? Moving forward with entrepreneurship as a science of the artificial. *Academy of Management Review*, *37*(1), 21–33. https://doi.org/10.5465/amr.2011.0079.

Wennberg, K., Delmar, F., & McKelvie, A. (2016). Variable risk preferences in new firm growth and survival. *Journal of Business Venturing*, *31*, 408–427.

Williams, T. A., & Shepherd, D. A. (2016). Building resilience or providing sustenance: Different paths of emergent ventures in the aftermath of the Haiti earthquake. *Academy of Management Journal*, *59*(6), 2069–2102. https://doi.org/10.5465/amj.2015.0682.

Wooldridge, J. M. (2002). *Econometric analysis of cross section and panel data*. MIT Press.

Wooldridge, J. M. (2013). *Introductory econometrics: A modern approach*. Thomson-South Western.

Zunino, D., Dushnitsky, G., & van Praag, M. (2022). How do investors evaluate past entrepreneurial failure? Unpacking failure due to lack of skill versus bad luck. *Academy of Management Journal*, *65*(4), 1083–1109. https://doi.org/10.5465/amj.2018.0579.

8. In search of creative qualitative methods to capture current entrepreneurship research challenges[1]

Martine Hlady-Rispal, Alain Fayolle and William B. Gartner

INTRODUCTION

The academic community recognizes that qualitative methodologies fundamentally contribute to the comprehension of intricate entrepreneurial contexts and processes (Welter, Baker and Wirsching 2019; Welter and Gartner 2016; Griffin 2007). They rely on tools to capture and analyze open, creative, flexible and contextualized data. They describe, decode, and question the meaning of facts, actions, decisions, and actors' representations that are currently taking place or that took place in the past (Hlady-Rispal and Jouison-Laffitte 2014). We argue that qualitative methodologies will continue to enhance knowledge on entrepreneurship because these tools are well adapted to the study of entrepreneurial processes that comprise loops, ruptures, enrichments, and rejections (Fayolle 2018; Bygrave 2007; Hindle 2007).

As advances in information technologies redesign economic and social conditions, the use of big data provides substantial and innovative approaches to observe entrepreneurial activities. Researchers engaged in elaborating qualitative designs for exploratory investigations now have the possibility of using quantitative exploratory studies (Schwab and Zhang 2019). Quantitative theory-testing methods develop theory and practice as well (Anderson, Wennberg and McMullen 2019). However, we posit that the knowledge developed from these methods, as prevalent tools, might be insufficient to explain, for example, why a particular context is unique and influences theorizing. As discussed in more detail below, by emphasizing qualitative research more intensively, entrepreneurship research can improve understanding on contexts, complexity, sense-making processes, and theory emergence as well as trigger relevant action.

The objective of this chapter, therefore, is to examine the overall body of qualitative methods used in the study of entrepreneurship phenomena, indicating the singular contribution of specific qualitative methods when appropriate. Concretely, it attempts to determine why and how qualitative methods contribute clearly and distinctively to the understanding of modern-day entrepreneurship. Other intentions of this work are to gauge the benefits of such studies for entrepreneurship research and to help entrepreneurship researchers become more familiar with methods that are more unusual. In addition, we aim to offer some guidance, through the presentation of qualitative data, with a view to enlighten significant entrepreneurship issues.

The remainder of this chapter is structured as follows. The first section qualifies the richness of qualitative methods in terms of core contributions to the study of contemporary entrepreneurship phenomena. The second section summarizes the five papers that comprise Volume 59, Number 5 of the *Journal of Small Business Management*. Despite their common focus on qualitative methods, the articles employ a wide range of empirical approaches and represent a diverse set of topics and epistemological postures. We conclude this chapter by encouraging researchers in entrepreneurship to reflect on a few principles with a view to enhancing significant entrepreneurship issues and increasing the likelihood of publication in quality journals such as *JSBM*.

QUALITATIVE METHODS ILLUMINATING CURRENT ENTREPRENEURSHIP CHALLENGES

Entrepreneurship is a multi-dimensional and a multi-disciplinary phenomenon (Fayolle, Landstrom, Gartner and Berglund 2016; Berglund and Johansson 2007). More than the capacity to set up new businesses, entrepreneurship is about a posture and a mindset that enables one to see opportunities, to take chances despite risk, to accept setbacks, to creatively gather and mobilize resources, and to have the persistence to beat the odds and turn an idea into reality (Kuratko and Morris 2018). Researching current entrepreneurship challenges calls for answers to questions on theorization, entrepreneurial contexts, actors and organizations. Do we need specific theories for the study of current entrepreneurship challenges? How can research deal with current challenges such as uberization, digitalization, neurosciences, pandemic crises or sustainable entrepreneurship? How can they reveal the entrepreneurs' idealized representations as regards society and innovative contexts; how can they unveil new ways of capturing aspects of modern entrepreneurial worlds? How can researchers follow entrepreneurial actors, organizations and environment in transformation? How can they capture the entrepreneur's new sense-making processes concerning responsibility and performance and establish the interdependence between the entrepreneur, their venture and their contemporary environment? How can research explain the role of personal and historical contingencies in the setting up of innovative starts-ups? Can they show the situated nature of modern entrepreneurial routines and praxes? Can they grasp temporal processes and their acceleration due to information sciences? One final question: can qualitative research contribute to answering these questions?

We know that qualitative methods are particularly valuable for extricating the complex overlapping mechanisms of social dynamics and resource interchange (Fayolle et al. 2016; Hlady-Rispal et al. 2016; Greenwood and Suddaby 2006). They are appropriate for understanding the full complexity and diversity of entrepreneurial contexts and processes (Welter, Baker and Wirsching 2019). They aim to understand the compound processes needed to interlink different implicated actors that cannot be easily quantified (Chalmers and Shaw 2017).

We also state that qualitative research is potent because qualitative methods are diverse. Each method has its main objective, focus and approach but can mix with other qualitative methods (or quantitative methods and then become a specific approach – Molina-Azorin 2012). Well-documented approaches such as case studies encompass a large array of possible objectives and often deploy a multi-method protocol. The method naturally lends itself to the analysis of any entrepreneurial issue as it aims to gain an in-depth understanding of how a system works (Yin 2003). Researchers choosing narratives, conversation analysis, autobiographies and interviews primarily examine the central role and perspective of specific actors as well as entrepreneurial emergence and enactment (Fletcher, 2007). Observations focus exclusively on individuals to study the daily behavior of entrepreneurs and their part in the creation and development of a venture (Volery, Mueller and von Siemens 2015), or more rarely explore a collective decision-making process (Maxwell, Jeffrey and Lévesque 2011). Rarely published, this method calls for the use of videos and visual mapping as analyzed in Ormiston and Thompson (2021; see also Chapter 11 in this volume) and Khelil's paper (2021). Ethnographies mostly focus on groups of entrepreneurs in relation to their firm and environment and may combine observation techniques and video recording (Cornelissen, Clarke and Cienki 2012). Methods such as auto-ethnographies or biographies also appear to be very promising in the future as more and more scholars will have either started their lives as entrepreneurs, or, as academics, will have undertaken some kind of entrepreneurial venture (Johannisson, 2020; Poldner, 2020; Hulsink and Rauch, 2021; Marks, 2021). Grounded theory mainly analyzes decision-making and growth within organizations as well as network construction or evolution. All papers in Vol. 59, No. 5 of the *JSBM* have a grounded approach but none strictly followed the methodological processes Glaser and Strauss (1967) first imagined. Finally, action research essentially takes place to examine learning processes within organizations as well as regional development involving knowledge transfer and collective learning. Few papers adopt this promising research strategy approach, often developed in books on education (Hlady-Rispal et al. 2016). Even though pragmatism characterizes several papers in this issue of the *JSBM*, none of the selected papers adopted an action research perspective.

As it is, the qualitative papers presented in the *JSBM* issue, along with other recent qualitative papers, revealed five main contributions in their examination of current entrepreneurial challenges. Table 8.1 summarizes their key inputs. For each of these contributions, we discuss the common as well as specific characteristics of the methods employed to study today's entrepreneurship phenomena around the main dimensions characterizing the multi-dimensionality of entrepreneurship: entrepreneurs, organizations, processes and environment (Gartner, 1985).

Understanding Context

Because qualitative studies that address entrepreneurial processes focus on the comprehension of the "how" and "why" aspects of a given phenomenon, understanding context is a unique strength as well as a powerful constraint (Dooley 2002). Qualitative papers published in entrepreneurship top journals such as *Journal of Business Venturing*, *Entrepreneurship Theory & Practice*, *Strategic Entrepreneurship Journal*, or *Entrepreneurship & Regional Development*, all share a will to contextualize.

Contextualization enables the researchers to show the situated nature of entrepreneurial routines and praxes (Chalmers and Shaw 2017). This contextualization can be an opportunity to study varieties and differences in entrepreneurship and is most evident in ethnographies, longitudinal studies and phenomenological studies (interviews or case studies). This family of methods involves long-term immersion and experiential participation by a researcher in a specific context (Cope 2011). It enables the examination of the relationships between entrepreneur, location and community in a vivid way. Rich depiction is inherent to the investigation. A detailed illustration is Bolzani, Marabello and Honig's (2020) examination of the multi-level processes of legitimacy in transnational social ventures. The authors describe how one member of the research team used her former experience of the place as an anthropologist consultant to establish contact with local people and how her understanding of the locality served the researchers' understanding of the interactions under study.

Contextualization also provides immediate interaction information. When the researchers are aiming to communicate the individuals' shared experiences within a particular context, they will be using "power quotes" to tell the story

Table 8.1 Overview of core contributions of qualitative methods in the study of today's entrepreneurship phenomena

Core contribution	Main qualitative methods	Main dimension	Key procedures
Understanding context	All qualitative methods, To a greater degree *Ethnography* *Phenomenological studies*	Environment Organizations Entrepreneurs Processes	• Studying time, spatial, social and institutional varieties and differences in entrepreneurship • Showing the situated nature of entrepreneurial routines and praxes • Studying immediate interaction information • Analyzing how entrepreneurs and their stakeholders deal with contextual constrictions as they arise and dispel over time
Dealing with complexity	*Longitudinal studies* *Multi-method approaches*	Processes Environment Organizations	• Studying entrepreneurship as a context-based and dynamic phenomenon • Apprehending the spatial, temporal, industry, social and institutional dimensions of entrepreneurship
Sense making	Longitudinal case studies Action research Case studies *Phenomenological* interviews Phenomenological case studies Grounded theory *Narratives* Life stories *Ethnographies (auto)*	Organizations Processes Entrepreneurs Environment Entrepreneurs Entrepreneurs Communities	• Grasping temporal processes • Following entrepreneurial actors, organizations and environment in transformation; studying them as "something in motion". Unveiling new ways of capturing some aspect of entrepreneurial worlds • Analyzing entrepreneurs' sense-making process. Establishing the interdependence between the entrepreneur, their venture and their environment • Revealing idealized representations • Explaining the role of personal and historical contingencies • Writing in order to make sense

Core contribution	Main qualitative methods	Main dimension	Key procedures
Socially constructed Theory	*Grounded Theory* *Conversation analysis* Auto-biographies Narratives Ethnographies Case studies Action research	Organizations Entrepreneurs Environment Processes	• Transforming data on a specific entrepreneurial process into a set of interpretations that have significance beyond the specific context under study • Studying the progressive construction between personal sense-making and the entrepreneurial actors' sense-giving • To extend concepts or expand a specific theory
Triggering action	*Action research* Observation Ethnographies Case studies	Environment Organizations Processes Entrepreneurs	• Improving the entrepreneurial actors' and researchers' practice and quality of their understanding • Managing change through collaboration • Getting involved in a process of continual reflection

from the interviewees' perspective and the communities in which they are implanted. In their paper on the occupational identity of entrepreneurs in rural Ghana, Shantz, Kistruck and Zietsma (2018) organized their nine-page findings around field data, using extensive quotes in tables and texts. Ethnography is a qualitative method claiming to get as close as possible to the social context (e.g., everyday life, chats and talks) with the researcher's lengthy immersion with the local population or community (Hammersley 1997). The objective is to produce in situ contextual knowledge seizing the actors' perceptions and practices.

Likewise, contextualization enables one to grasp how the different actors under study deal with time, spatial, social and institutional constrictions as they appear and dispel (Zahra and Wright 2011). Qualitative studies show the way entrepreneurs in interaction with their stakeholders enact and construct contexts (Baker and Welter 2017). Narratives and ethnographic approaches relate contextualization to text, language, and conversations. They "narrate contexts" (Gartner 2016). The exercise is time consuming. It requires registering detailed observations, substantial trial and error and a context-rich interpretive framework, which will consider the constant interplay between the actors and contexts under study. An interesting example is Bolzani et al.'s study (2020). The researchers followed a social venture's transnational entrepreneurs across Ghana and Italy through a multi-sited ethnography. In this way, they had the opportunity to study their world while recognizing that their local realities were from elsewhere and were influencing aspects of the overall interpretation itself.

Finally, we recognize the growing influence of historical perspectives and approaches to the study of entrepreneurship (Wadhwani et al. 2020; Wadhwani and Lubinski 2017; Wadhwani 2016; Wadhwani and Jones 2014). Historians are, inherently, focused on context, as a particular historical event occurs at a specific time and in a particular situation with specific individuals. Historians bring to the table a variety of methods and logics for engaging in research about the past, as well as different ways that historical evidence and insights are reported and conveyed (Kipping, Wadhwani and Bucheli 2014; Wadhwani and Decker 2017). Much can be learned from historians in regard to the rules of evidence for supporting facts that lead to insights into the past as well as how such evidence can be used to portray entrepreneurial processes over time and the impact of individual agency on situational constraints and vice-versa.

Dealing with Complexity

Mobilizing complexity sciences and theories to study entrepreneurship phenomena is not new. At the end of the 1980s, Bygrave (1989) already suggested looking at chaos and catastrophes paradigms/theories in the field of entrepreneurship. At the beginning of the 1990s, Bruyat (1993) in his doctoral dissertation used as a metaphor and in a qualitative way (visual representation) the theory of catastrophes to provide a comprehensive understanding of the entrepreneurial commitment within his conceptualization of the entrepreneurship as a research field and his modelization of the entrepreneurial process.[2] Bruyat (1993) and Bruyat and Julien (2001) claimed that the study of the entrepreneurial venture is one of the most complex in the social sciences while Lichtenstein (2011: 473) noticed that "The fields of entrepreneurship and complexity science are linked in a number of important ways. In particular, studies of entrepreneurship and complexity science are both focused on innovation, novelty and emergence: entrepreneurship scholars study the *emergence* of new organizations, while complexity science scholars study the dynamics of *emergence*". The concepts of emergence and entrepreneuring process are at the heart of entrepreneurship research as advocated by a number of scholars (see more particularly, Lichtenstein 2011, 2016; Gartner and Brush 2007; Gartner 1985, 1993; Steyaert 2007). These entrepreneurship researchers are in the same vein of thought as McKelvey (2004) who contributed to the growing attention of complexity in the field arguing notably that: "Complexity science focuses on order creation, hence is a better platform for a science of entrepreneurship" (p. 313).

At the research methods level, to study complex systems in the field, entrepreneurship scholars are highlighting the need for new, emergent and neglected research methods (Berger and Kuckertz 2016; Bruyat and Julien 2001). Berger and Kuckertz (2016) provide examples, illustrations and cases concerning the application of mixed-methods designs, computer simulation, thinking-aloud method, qualitative comparative analysis, and semantic analysis, to capture the essence of complexity in entrepreneurship research. Bruyat and Julien (2001) suggest borrowing methods and tools from other disciplines and fields, and to invent new methods. Most entrepreneurship researchers consider that qualitative research methods are appropriate to examine complexity-based issues in the field. Fuller, Warren and Argyle (2008) applied a longitudinal qualitative case study. Lichtenstein and McKelvey (2011) argue for longitudinal multi-method narrative while Lichtenstein (2011) demonstrate the usefulness of cross-level or multi-level qualitative studies. Selden and Fletcher (2015) adopted artifact emergence as a key unit of analysis and show, among other things, the importance of multi-contextual and multi-level explanations in a qualitative approach of the entrepreneurial journey complexity. However, until now and despite the recommendations from key scholars in the area of complexity/emergence of entrepreneurship, there are very few empirical qualitative studies based on longitudinal multi-method/level narratives that appear, from the best of our knowledge, as useful and powerful ways to address complexity research issues.

Sense Making

Sense making first concerns the intention to build understanding with the involved parties as the researcher attempts to develop a meaningful interpretation that seizes the nature of the entrepreneurial process under study. Sense making is therefore both "grounded in identity construction" and the "social" environment (Weick 1995). It involves auto-reflexivity for the researcher who needs to be aware of their frames of mind and interpretation schemes as well as the search for good intelligibility between the researchers and the interviewees since personal sense making strongly emanates from outsider sense giving (Smith 2018; Klag and Langley 2013). Sense making also has to do with making sense using conceptual frameworks or generating theory. Sense making qualifies either as a theory (Weick 1979) or a methodological approach (Gioia and Chittipeddi 1991). These include longitudinal case studies, phenomenological interviews, historical case studies, narratives, biographies, ethnographies, action research, observations, and grounded theory research.

Sense making can also be guided by the role of time perspective and time management on an entrepreneur, an organization, a specific culture or context (Lévesque and Stephan 2020). Researchers can consider duration through longitudinal studies as they examine the complex process of entrepreneurship over time. For example, in their six-year study of a social venture, André, Cho and Laine (2018) focused on how social performance measurement progressively elaborated made sense for the organizational members. The authors used a broad archival dataset of some 2500 documents gathered during the project and conducted 36 interviews in two stages. Researchers can also take a historical perspective of the sequencing of events that describe the synchronization of actions and events when they occur. Using a micro-historical method to analyze entrepreneurial networks, Hollow (2020) studied the lived experience, social and political circumstances of Isaac Holden, a 19th century British entrepreneur to make sense of his entrepreneurial network at that time. To extract the meaning of the entrepreneur's networking activities, Hollow analyzed the letters that Holden received and sent between 1826 and 1860 (581 individual letters sent by 206 persons or businesses over 33 years).

A third possibility to make sense while grasping temporal processes is when actors report on the past, present and future, and experience them as a continuity through narratives, life stories or phenomenological interviews. Based on entrepreneurs' perspectives, Cope's (2011) interpretive phenomenological study reflected on the causes and outcomes of failure, providing rich depiction of the entrepreneurs' experience. Other methods such as observation (Volery, Mueller and von Siemens 2015) or qualitative approaches using diaries studies and interviews (Kaandorp, van Burg and Karlsson 2020; Kaffka et al., 2021) capture time in order to explain how the entrepreneurial actors make sense of their actions as individuals or as teams. With discernment, Kaandorp et al. 2020 introduced the concept of network momentum as an essential, temporary sense-making device in networking processes that entrepreneurs adopt to encourage themselves, and other actors to participate in their networking process.

Following entrepreneurial actors, organizations and environment in transformation, studying these dimensions as something in action is part of a processual sense-making project (Hjorth, Holt and Steyaert 2015). Such was the aim of Bertschi-Michel, Kammerlander and Strike (2020) who used interviews, observation, meeting minutes and archival data to accompany one advisor and examine five family firm succession cases over four years, apprehending evolving emotions during the succession process. Understanding growth (its origins, modalities or impact), transmission (the dynamics of the succession process, the transgenerational value creation) and failure (its origins, its legitimation or its psychological processing) convey how sense qualitative studies reveal singularly. Analyzing entrepreneurs' sense making is a reflexivity exercise that qualitative researchers realize along with entrepreneurial actors during a legitimation process mainly using ethnographies. This methodological choice enables the researchers to adopt a loosely structured and flexible participant-observation posture, while they enter a specific organizational culture and observe the way the entrepreneurs interpret and legitimate their experience in relation with their organization and institutional environment (O'Connor 2002).

The use of sense-making analysis enables one to grasp how entrepreneurs convince stakeholders about the venture potential and what course of action needs to be taken as was the case with Kaandorp et al.'s study (2020). Sense making analysis recently examined entrepreneurial processes mainly through ethnographies, case studies or interviews. The processes involved sorrow and distress such as failure (Nummela, Saarenketo and Loane 2016) or tense psychological processes as diverse as conflicts between entrepreneurs and venture capitalists (Zou, Chen, Lam and Liu 2016), an organizational crisis (Doern 2016) or the endogenous construction of entrepreneurial contexts (Chalmers and Shaw 2017), etc. The studied tensions acted as breakdowns that enable a need for sense making for both entrepreneurial actors and researchers. In fact, the study of the tensions between the unexpected and the unanticipated along with the entrepreneurs' expectations and anticipations potentially delivers insightful analysis. A great number of qualitative papers explicitly quote sense making as a prior objective (Hlady-Rispal et al. 2016).

What is worth emphasizing is that even when the authors choose the case study method, their main way of collecting and analyzing data is through narratives. Other studies apply an exclusive narrative or life story method in their sense making approach (Yitshaki and Kropp 2016; Courpasson, Dany and Martí 2016). Narrative sense making provides rich insights and exemplifies the diversity of actors and their role in an intricate "story" (O'Connor 2002). The studies using the narrative method do not necessarily offer "heroic stories". They sometimes reveal potentially noxious idealized representations. Entrepreneurs search to legitimize or convey values while researchers try to stir insight, using writing as a tool to "knowing" (Weick 1995).

Socially Constructed Theory

Building theory is not a specific contribution of qualitative methods since quantitative studies constantly develop new theoretical ideas on entrepreneurial phenomena (Anderson, et al. 2019). It is more the way that qualitative methods develop theory that can be qualified as singular, since they enable socially constructed theory development. Socially constructed theory relies on the researchers and field actors' knowledge of reality, based on a specific historical, cultural, political, and social context that exists because of a relatively stable shared representation. Grounded theory, conversation analysis, (auto)-ethnographies, case studies, interviews, narratives, observations or action-research all indicate a focus on theory building. All are socially constructed, but each approach makes different contributions to theory building.

A first common goal is transforming data on a specific entrepreneurial phenomenon into a set of interpretations or propositions that have significance beyond the specific context under study. However, Grounded Theory is one of the more detailed approaches to achieve this goal. Grounded Theory's uniqueness resides in the fact that it is simultaneously a methodology (a theory-inducing initiative) and a method (procedures to collect and analyze data founded on sampling and theoretical saturation, while relying on specific data codification techniques). The approach was essentially generated by Glaser and Strauss (1967), amended by Glaser (1978), Strauss and Corbin (1994) and Langley (1999). As we see through the grounded theory studies published in entrepreneurship's top-journals, researchers elaborate their theory progressively via codification, which implies analyzing the data on a recurring basis in order to infer codes, categories and meta categories (Younger and Fisher 2020; Farny, Kibler, Hai and Landoni 2019). In their study of "new venture image formation in an emergent organizational category", Younger and Fisher (2020) combined Gioia, Corley and Hamilton's (2013) approach on inductive research with techniques from the "grounded theory" research strategy. They chose codes such as "sharing of models and ideas", "assessing performance" or "mentioning specific accelerators" and many others that were first-order concepts that gave meaning to the data, trying to stay as close as possible to their interviewees' language or written sources. Open-coding meant isolating incidents (words or texts related with organizational images), then qualifying their dimensions and properties. Subsequently, the authors clarified how they used axial codification to gather the 31 first-order codes to six sub-categories. In the final stage (selective codification), they studied the semantic relationships between the six sub-categories to generate the three concepts of emulation, experimentation and divergences. During the whole process, they used constant comparative analysis to relate and differentiate data over time and across sources. With this goal in mind, the researchers wrote analytic memos to rethink and reconsider their initial codifications. Once the three concepts were identified, Younger and Fisher compared the data to the literature to refine the delineations of the three concepts and their sub-categories.

Emphasizing entrepreneurship as a socially constructed phenomenon, many qualitative studies embrace an inductive and grounded approach. With a theorizing goal in mind, researchers conduct a meticulous investigation of events and circumstances over a certain period in order to study the progressive transformation of entrepreneurial actors' vision and actions, their organizations and contexts (e.g. Kaandorp et al. 2020; Dentoni, Pascucci, Poldner and Gartner 2018; André et al. 2018). These studies generate theory through a process of iteration from data to theory. Induction is indeed beneficial to creative research. In fact, induction often goes with abduction (Hlady-Rispal et al. 2016). Researchers intuitively move back and forth between data and theory. They are "interactive processors" (Fairfield and Charman 2019). In inductive qualitative research, inference is always temporary. Researchers never conclusively refute or confirm the emerging theories. They sometimes intuitively amend their theories in light of new ideas and new data, while refusing to deplete or lose previous information. During the data analysis stages, researchers enter into an on-going process of aggregating data, thematic coding and iterating between the data, emerging concepts and the literature (André et al. 2018). Throughout analysis and paper development, researchers may pursue interpretive legitimacy (or intelligibility) through the presentation of their data and analysis to entrepreneurial actors and other researchers interested in the investigation. The method enables verification and feedbacks on the quality of the data (Dentoni et al. 2018). The emergent theory is then the fruit of a collective representation.

A stimulating illustration of a collective theory construction is conversation analysis. Conversation analysis is a relatively new and promising method that focuses on the entrepreneurs' conversation in order to understand how and why social interactions might influence a given phenomenon such as its contribution to an emerging opportunity (Haines, 2023). The researcher observes the conversation in order to infer theory that stems from interactive contextual elements identified during a registered meeting or informal discussions between actors. The entrepreneurs might react to the explanation of the observed patterns and participate therefore in theory building.

Ethnographers also explain very precisely the progressive construction between the researchers' personal sense making and the entrepreneurial actor's sense giving. More than any other qualitative method, ethnography welcomes flexible and incomplete research designs as well as structured partiality in order to build theory (Marcus 2012). Ethnographers show who they are, the process they follow to develop knowledge and co-product reality with the field, and the way they compare empirical material with pre-existing concepts and theories. For example, Bolzani et al. (2020) narrated who was the main field researcher and her different postures (consultant, then researcher) towards the Ghanaian and Italian entrepreneurial and institutional actors she interrelated with, all along the two-year immersion in a transnational social venture. Quite precisely, the authors explained the reflexive ethnographic writing as well as the dual-researcher approach enabling outside researchers to complement the ethnographer's interpretation. They progressively showed how they elaborated a model of multi-level and multi-sited processes of legitimization in transnational social ventures.

Other research mobilizes, on the contrary, a specific theoretical framework in order to further develop theory or enlarge a specific concept within a particular context. As an example, Salmivaara and Kibler (2020) used Toulmin's rhetoric model to analyze how European Union policy rhetoric enunciates the significance of entrepreneurship for sustainable entrepreneurship. This is one of the main particularities of this approach: it develops ad hoc tools or frameworks that stem from the translation or extension of a theoretical model to solve a problem in situ (Hlady-Rispal et al. 2016).

Triggering Action

Qualitative methods are part of a sense-making process where "new ideas and possibilities become enacted, selected and legitimated until potential users come to accept them" (Steyaert 2009, p. 459). This is the case when the researchers participate in the daily lives of the entrepreneurs they observe during ethnographies, phenomenological case studies, observations or action-research. These approaches require sensitivity to what Steyaert (2009) calls "anomalies" to identify the potential needs for change and improvements in the entrepreneurs' behavior, in the organization itself or in the positioning of the organization within a specific context. Steyaert (2009, p. 461) interestingly explains that "what makes change possible, then, is that entrepreneurs hold on to these anomalies long enough for their meaning to become clear; they then reduce the given disharmony by changing the style in which it initially appeared". We observed in several qualitative papers how researchers and entrepreneurs collaborate in order to identify these anomalies and implement proper actions to promote the necessary changes. In those instances, the main goals are to improve the entrepreneurial actors' and researchers' practice and quality of their understanding on the one hand, managing change through collaboration on the other hand.

Interestingly, action research is the only method in which the identification of anomalies and problem solving are systematically the most important goals. Indeed, as a process itself, the first step of any action research study is to identify the problem to solve. It is a problem that the entrepreneurial participants have identified, and will formulate together with the researcher(s) collaborating in the problem-solving process. The planning phase enables the definition of the problem and corresponding research method. Action takes place in a second phase with the implementation of a pilot approach by a team made of researchers and entrepreneurial actors. During a third stage, observation occurs on the impact of the implemented action. The fourth stage is about developing revised action based on the observations. The cycle takes place in loops (at least two) and the final stage of the cycle is about solving the problem and co-producing theoretical knowledge in the perspective of co-learning and enacting action (Susman and Evered, 1978). In their paper, Santini, Marinelli, Boden, Cavicchi and Haegeman (2016) explored the entrepreneurial dynamics of a region through a participatory action-research. The authors engaged in the participatory action research and experience-based methods led by the Joint Research Centre and the Institute of Prospective Technological studies of the European Commission in the Greek region of Eastern Macedonia and Thrace. The action purpose was to accompany the enactment of a regional economic development program. The stated academic goal was to reduce the gap between researchers and entrepreneurial actors. In this case, researchers worked closely with institutional actors as well, in order to advance the effectiveness of policy-making.

Because qualitative papers focus on sense making, different research designs enable both researchers and entrepreneurial actors to get involved in a process of reflection, facilitating personal and organizational change. Observation is another too rarely published method. Volery, Mueller and von Siemens (2015), for example, mobilized the sociological method of structured observation to observe entrepreneurs' behaviors and skills that enable ambidexterity, i.e. the capacity to explore and exploit concurrently. The method combines the malleability of open observation with the consistency of researching types of structured data (Mintzberg, 2009). Capturing entrepreneurship in motion, Ormiston and Thompson (2021 and Chapter 11 in this volume) demonstrate that videos offer multimodality (eye gaze, gestures, atmosphere sensing) that also contribute to help entrepreneurs understand the "interactional, embodied, material, and emotional nature" of their own practice. Authenticity (educative, tactical or catalytic) is indeed an important quality criterium used by constructivist researchers to check if participants learnt from participating, if their investigations acted as an impetus to change things or if participants have been empowered to act (Hlady-Rispal and Jouison-Laffitte 2014).

An important point to recall is that practical implications are not exclusive to the action research method. They are a stated contribution in many qualitative papers (e.g. Värlander, Sölvell and Klyver 2020; Muñoz, Cacciotti and Cohen 2018; Shantz et al. 2018). An interesting example is Muñoz et al.'s (2018) research on the relationship between purpose and purposeful organizing in B-Corps. Their results show, for example, that sustainable entrepreneurs should not formalize purpose too soon during the organization formation process. The authors warn entrepreneurs not to seek B-Corp certification (and thus formalize purpose) before assessing the viability of the business model and receiving customers' acknowledgement. Early formalization via certification can generate restricted aptitude for adjusting the ventures' Business Model and distracts the entrepreneurs from their responsibility to achieve the purpose of having a replicable business model.

As an overall observation, we can say that the qualitative researchers' triggering action comes from their proximity with entrepreneurial actors. In this sense, we can posit that qualitative research in entrepreneurship is relevant (Wiklund, Wright and Zahra 2019). Qualitative researchers visit enterprises, associations or institutions. They interact and engage in informal and professional conversations with entrepreneurial actors. They also learn the field language and can use it to change the entrepreneurs' and their stakeholders' representations and convince them to take action as advised by Wiklund et al. (2019) or Santini et al. (2016). Researchers do not need to communicate about their complex methodologies or theorization. However, while searching to make sense of the collected data through face-to-face encounters with entrepreneurs and consultants, they achieve relevant research that changes impetus.

CONTRIBUTING ARTICLES IN THE SPECIAL ISSUE OF THE *JOURNAL OF SMALL BUSINESS MANAGEMENT*

JSBM is a multi-contextual journal, which publishes scholarly research articles in the fields of small business management and entrepreneurship. In compliance with the journal's objectives, we invited submissions from a wide diversity of researchers and promoted the call for papers through international networks. We received 24 submissions from authors or teams working in more than 30 different universities around the world and asked 11 of them to revise and resubmit their work. From these revisions, eight papers were accepted for publication, five for Vol. 59, No. 5 of the journal and three which were published later. Table 8.2 summarizes those five that were selected for this issue of the journal on creative qualitative methods to capture current entrepreneurship research challenges.

The authors in this issue of the *JSBM* contribute to the debates that could have taken place among entrepreneurship scholars interacting during a webinar on qualitative methods and epistemological postures. For example, Hulsink and Rauch (2021, pp. 913–945) investigate autobiographies' potential and limits through five possible analytical processes and this links to more relevant, contextual, and process-oriented research (Welter, Baker and Wirsching 2019, Welter and Gartner 2016; Griffin 2007). Likewise, Marks (2021, pp. 946–975) joins conversations on "what is not said or 'hidden' in the public narrative", revealing idealized postures and participating in the discussion on sense-making practices. For their part, Kaffka, Singaram, Kraaijenbrink and Groen (2021, pp. 1050–1080) link with discussions around sensebreaking-sensemaking iterations over time effect that are gaining attraction in top journals (e.g., Lévesque and Stephan 2020) and advance the conversation by expanding the opportunity co-construction literature. Ormiston and Thompson (2021, pp. 976–1011; see also Chapter 11 in this volume) examine the current ways in which video is being used in entrepreneurship research and this links to a deeper comprehension of entrepreneurial action that deals with complexity (McKelvey, 2004). Finally, by evaluating the potential of the visual graph-based method and the matrix-multiplication-based method, Khelil (2021, pp. 1012–1049) ties to both the causal contribution theory and precisely shows what these two methods offer to the field of entrepreneurial cognition that the currently used methods do not. The five papers written by authors working in Australia, UK, the Netherlands and France, illustrate the journal's international scope by founding their empirical work or empirical examples in a wide variety of contexts.

PATHWAYS TO INSIGHTFUL AND CREATIVE QUALITATIVE ENTREPRENEURSHIP RESEARCH

We outline four areas (exploring "entrepreneurial action" in action, embracing co-design and collective intelligence, revealing a constructive critical attitude, and joining a phenomenon-driven conversation) that may improve researchers' efforts to conceive insightful and creative qualitative research that attracts the attention of quality journals such as *JSBM*.

Exploring "Entrepreneurial Action" in Action

Insightful qualitative research aims at better comprehending "what actually occurs" in the setting being studied (Marks, 2021, pp. 946–975). Exploring entrepreneurial action in action takes place when the researchers meticulously

Table 8.2 Summary of the five papers accepted in this issue of the JSBM

Author(s)	Qualitative method(s) deployed	Research question(s)	Contribution to entrepreneurship theory	Contribution to research on qualitative methods
Hulsink & Rauch	Auto-biographies	Which studies shift the research paradigms toward more relevant, contextual, and process-oriented research?	Developing a life course theory of entrepreneurship. Providing agent-inspired evidence as it is contextualized and indicating what works for whom and under what circumstances	Showing how to conduct and analyze scientific auto-biographies through five different approaches, while taking into account their limitations
Marks	Auto-ethnography	How is "inspiring and empowering" female entrepreneurial success performed in the role model narrative? What is not said or "hidden" in the public narrative? What might explain the occlusions or divergences between public and unspoken narratives?	Theorizing a performative paradox in role-model narratives	Challenging the ontological foundations of "true-to-life" accounts. Identifying and naming a number of discursive practices in the construction of one such story
Kaffka, Singaram, Kraaijenbrink & Groen	Longitudinal analysis of weekly diary reports	How sensebreaking-sensemaking iterations over time effect changes to the shared cognition between entrepreneurs and their stakeholders while driving opportunity development?	Expanding the opportunity co-construction literature	Demonstrating that sensebreaking aids novel sensemaking

Author(s)	Qualitative method(s) deployed	Research question(s)	Contribution to entrepreneurship theory	Contribution to research on qualitative methods
Ormiston & Thompson	Video methods	What are the current ways in which video is being used in entrepreneurship research? To what extent is video data utilized in research designs? What are the potentials of video methods to further our understanding of entrepreneurial action?	Extending insights on interaction theory, entrepreneurial practice theory, emotional theory, and discussions on socio-materiality	Examining three main ways of using video-based methods, each with benefits, limitations and future opportunities
Khelil	Visual graph-based method & matrix-multiplication-based method	How do the underlying methodological principles differ between the visual graph method that uses Decision Explorer and the matrix-multiplication method? How can these two methods of causal mapping better complement each other to obtain a deeper understanding of entrepreneurs' cognitions? What do these methods offer to the field of entrepreneurial cognition that the currently used methods do not offer?	Enlarging the causal contribution theory	Providing step-by-step guidance to empower scholars who either choose between these two methods or seek to use these methods in a complementary manner

notice the actions, meanings, atmosphere, background details and interactions which embrace the multiple dimensions of entrepreneurial activities. Such observations, when combined with discussions, interviews, and the examination of written, filmed or photographed material, make it possible to produce discerning interpretations (theories) of "contextualized" entrepreneurial actions (Johannisson, 2020; Welter et al. 2019; Watson 2013). One of the most powerful tools to capture modern-day challenges as they happen are video research methods. Ormiston and Thompson (2021, pp. 976–1011; see also Chapter 11 in this volume) differentiate videography of naturally occurring activities, entrepreneurs' archival videos and video during field entrepreneurs and researchers' interactions. Their insightful research agenda shows how the integration of visual data on interaction, embodiment, emotions and materiality shape entrepreneurial action in "motion" and can boost novel theoretical contributions. Moreover, video conferences during the pandemic have become unexceptional and may suggest new in situ ways to examine social interactions without as much interference into the entrepreneurs' everyday activities (Howard, 2020).

Besides videography, each qualitative method may prove relevant depending on the researchers' actions attuned to a specific context. With participant observation, the researchers aim to understand a phenomenon from the inside and capture certain mechanisms that are difficult to decipher from an external point of view. With observant participation, the researchers intensify their involvement since they become fully-fledged members of the research field (Tillmar 2020). Being emotionally and cognitively very close to the field members creates a greater level of acceptation on their part (Simonÿ et al. 2018). With autobiographies, the entrepreneur benefits from a complete access to the field and its stakeholders. The researcher-entrepreneur can exchange with the field members, reflect, confirm or deny facts and feelings, validate data or not, and continue to collect a wealth of "confidential" information (Hulsink and Rauch, 2021, pp. 913–945). The research can better explain the entrepreneurial interactions through time, the entrepreneur's choices that contribute to their understanding of the reasons for their decisions. When exploring the divergences between an idealized representation of entrepreneurial activity and its more authentic version, it challenges the foundations of "true-to-life" accounts (Gartner 2007), even though the researcher remains aware of and needs to reflect on their own cognitive, emotional and behavioral biases (Marks, 2021, pp. 946–975).

Embracing Co-design and Collective Intelligence

The web culture constitutes one of the most challenging modern-day realities for enterprises, researchers, teachers, institutions and communities. Since the pandemic, the necessity to adopt and learn its mechanics and codes in a certain number of processes and activities in everyday life highly accelerated to ensure continuity in a large field related to, but not limited to, entrepreneurship and education. From an academic perspective, the Web culture produces big data that may seem to threaten qualitative research since it allows quantitative exploratory studies that were exclusively developed by qualitative protocols a few years ago (Schwab and Zhang 2019). Now, qualitative researchers' strength and privilege is their proximity and close contact with the actors in the field. The Web culture and pandemic may induce physical distancing from the field (less immersion possible, less face-to-face interviews, less time to give to researchers, etc.). However, we argue that the Web culture and even the pandemic may prove to be a fantastic opportunity for qualitative researchers. First, because the Web culture intensifies the contribution of knowledge, the ideas, the research and teamwork in the creative development processes (Buffardi 2020). The Web culture is characterized by new tools, by open-source processes and by the exploitation of the enormous amount of data available today. This exploitation of big data will have repercussions in various research fields and necessitates a transdisciplinary approach, as offered by co-design and collective intelligence. Second, because this exceptional and unique global phenomenon, associated with the consequential rise of the amount of data available, may well be the dawn of a complete redefinition of the scopes and criteria of methodologies and methods, be they quantitative or qualitative.

We also realize that Web culture principles match the qualitative researchers' posture and skills. Openness dynamics, connectivity and collaboration depict the Web culture (Giovannella 2020). It invites researchers to develop an adequate set of individual, socio-relational and management skills that modern firms are seeking. Qualitative researchers are often partners with the firms they investigate and develop problem setting, problem solving, as well as other human skills in order to co-construct knowledge that will inform action and that will encourage them to enlarge their own interests and projects as entrepreneurs (Watson 2013). Among the skills sought by entrepreneurial ventures are critical analysis, team work and the ability to define goals (problem setting), creativity and resource management skills (problem solving), flexibility, trustworthiness and communication skills (additional human skills) (Giovannella 2020). Qualitative researchers, while producing knowledge, need to develop the same skills in order to converse with entrepreneurs and give value to their participation, creativity, and innovation together with the field actors. In a co-design/collective intelligence approach, the researchers will contemplate the needs for multiple expertise and external knowledge that complement their own, but will also generate something more valuable than the simple sum of their added value. That process implies identifying and looking for specific profiles to reach the designated goal. Facing complex data, qualitative researchers may need to adopt a more systematic co-design approach, to ensure the correct collected data mining as well as its correct examination and interpretation. Researchers also need to observe how entrepreneurs interact with them and/or interact with other stakeholders or modify their vision and behaviors in time. Such methods as conversation analysis or causal cognitive mapping contribute to this goal. In order to offer knowledge that helps entrepreneurs to "cope with the world" (Mounce 1997, p. 177), the main objective is to achieve practical as well as scientific relevance.

Revealing a Constructive Critical Attitude

Thanks to the diffusion of web culture, "the hacker ethic" (Himanen 2001) diffuses values of sharing, participation, collaboration to a wider community of users, thus greatly influencing society. The connected construction of ideas, products and services is anchored to the vision of companies committed to creating sustainable, social, cultural and economic opportunities. For "hacker" entrepreneurs and researchers, it is about contributing to the community, the environment and identifying solutions that respond to the challenges of change. Among qualitative researchers, we can establish a kind of parallel with critical constructivists who also acknowledge the importance of values and ethical concerns in science and promote the ideas of building communities of solidarity and challenging assumptions about politics, culture, psychology, human potential and economics to favor research practices embedded in integrity and truth (Bayne, 2009). Since they affirm the social and political nature of all knowledge (in particular scientific knowledge) production, justification and ownership, critical constructionists value the creation and development of critical research communities (Bentley, 2003).

Critical constructivism is a well-established school of thought in education sciences while it is just in its infancy in the field of entrepreneurship. It would refer to entrepreneurship a theoretical stance related to developing a set of attitudes and disposition about knowledge understood as contingent and value-laden from a cultural, social and political point of view in research. In other words, revealing a critical constructivist attitude would allow, especially through multi-methodological, multi-theoretical and multidisciplinary approaches and lenses, the incorporation of social, cultural, economic, political and cognitive dynamics in examining entrepreneurship research issues. For instance, critical constructivism tends to be used in qualitative entrepreneurship research focusing on bricolage (see, for example, the Special Issue in *Entrepreneurship & Regional Development*, on "Social entrepreneurship and 'Bricolage': Taking stock and looking ahead", 2018, *30*(3–4)) and in a collective work in entrepreneurship, education aiming at challenging taken-for-granted assumptions and opening new perspectives in the field (Loi et al., 2021).

Joining a Phenomenon-driven Conversation

A central trait of insightful qualitative research that navigates the publication process is that this research captures current entrepreneurship research challenges. Insightful qualitative research also offers a well-argued link to entrepreneurial phenomena that are of profound interest to researchers conversing in the targeted journal or offer an insightful perspective on a new entrepreneurial phenomenon. Creative problem solving through viewpoint examination and prospective thinking on new venture ideas (Kier and McMullen 2018), research on innovative contexts created by digitalization (Gay and Szostak 2019) or the need for sustainable environment (Wiklund et al. 2019), research on temporal processes (Kaandorp et al. 2020, Kaffka et al. 2021, pp. 1050–1080) etc., all call for creative methodologies and techniques. As discussed in this chapter, qualitative research serves as a palette of methods and tools that empirically seizes the phenomenon in a way other methods cannot. Qualitative researchers need to explain their collection and analytical procedures precisely, since the methods they deploy are often creative because they need to adapt to each singular context, its constraints and opportunities. However, at the same time, the aim is always to make a valuable contribution to theory, practice, and/or pedagogy.

If researchers answer a call for papers dedicated to methods (such as in the *JSBM* Special Issue), the focus will be on the method itself in close connection with a specific research field. For example, Khelil (2021, pp. 1012–1049) aims to aid researchers in dealing with the methodological difficulties of causal cognitive mapping, the final objective being enriching research on sense-making processes and entrepreneurial cognition. Kaffka et al. (2021, pp. 1050–1080) extend the literature on social exchanges during opportunity development while contributing to qualitative methods through the implementation of longitudinal analysis based on the diary method. Otherwise, we invite qualitative researchers who wish to publish in top journals to study the link between paradigms and research designs in order to develop socially constructed theory (Hlady-Rispal and Jouison-Laffitte 2014). There is always a need to develop theory from past research with a coherent methodology. Qualitative methods serve the discovery of new insights of the phenomenon under study and follow a teleological perspective.

CONCLUSION

Opportunities for qualitative methodologies have never been so real. They show the situated nature of entrepreneurial routines and praxes, they deal with complexity, they engage in sensemaking, develop socially constructed theory as they trigger action and help entrepreneurs flourish in the modern world. Given these core contributions, with this chapter, we wanted to provide a setting for underlining methods that exemplify creative practices in qualitative research. While many qualitative methods and co-design protocols were not included in this chapter, we tried to characterize several of them, aware that many still need to be envisioned and co-constructed. We therefore conclude by encouraging entrepreneurship researchers to continue to adopt and develop qualitative methods in future research to tackle complex and innovative research questions helping the community, society and entrepreneurs to cope with modern complexities and trials.

NOTES

1. This chapter has been adapted with slight revisions from an article (the Special Issue editorial) published in the *Journal of Small Business Management* (Hlady-Rispal, M., Fayolle, A., & Gartner, W. B. (2021). In search of creative qualitative methods to capture current entrepreneurship research challenges. *Journal of Small Business Management*, *59*(5), 887–912, © Informa UK Limited, trading as Taylor & Francis Group). Reprinted by permission of Taylor & Francis Ltd, https://www.tandfonline.com/.
2. See also Fayolle (2007) and Fayolle, Basso and Tornokoski (2011) for a presentation/discussion in English of the Bruyat's model of entrepreneurial process and commitment.

REFERENCES

Anderson, B. S., Wennberg, K., & McMullen, J. S. (2019). Enhancing quantitative theory-testing entrepreneurship research. *Journal of Business Venturing*, *34*(5), 105928.

André, K., Cho, C. H., & Laine, M. (2018). Reference points for measuring social performance: Case study of a social business venture. *Journal of Business Venturing*, *33*(5), 660–678.

Baker, T., & Welter, F. (2017). Come on out of the ghetto, please! – Building the future of entrepreneurship research. *International Journal of Entrepreneurial Behavior & Research*, *23*(2), 170–184.

Bayne, G.U. (2009). Joe L. Kincheloe: Embracing criticality in science education. *Critical Studies of Science Education*, *4*, 559–567.

Bentley, M. L. (2003). Critical consciousness through a critical constructivist pedagogy. Paper presented at the Annual Meeting of the American Educational Studies Association Mexico City, Mexico, October.

Berger, E. S. C., & Kuckertz, A. (Eds.) (2016). *Complexity in entrepreneurship, innovation and technology research: Applications of emergent and neglected methods*. Cham: Springer International Publishing Switzerland. DOI 10.1007/978-3-319-27108-8_1.

Berglund, K., & Johansson, A. W. (2007). Entrepreneurship, discourses and conscientization in processes of regional development. *Entrepreneurship and Regional Development, 19*(6), 499–525.

Bertschi-Michel, A., Kammerlander, N., & Strike, V. M. (2020). Unearthing and alleviating emotions in family business successions. *Entrepreneurship Theory and Practice, 44*(1), 81–108.

Bolzani, D., Marabello, S., & Honig, B. (2020). Exploring the multi-level processes of legitimacy in transnational social enterprises. *Journal of Business Venturing, 35*(3), 105941.

Bruyat, C. (1993). Création d'entreprise: Contribution épistémologique et modélisation. Dissertation for the doctor's degree in business administration. University Pierre Mendes France, Grenoble, France.

Bruyat, C., & Julien, P. A. (2001). Defining the field of research in entrepreneurship. *Journal of Business Venturing, 16*, 165–180.

Buffardi, A. (2020). Digital making and entrepreneurship: Imagine the future. In Mealha, Ó., Rehm, M., & Rebedea, T. (Eds.), *Ludic, Co-design and Tools Supporting Smart Learning Ecosystems and Smart Education* (pp. 155–163). Singapore: Springer.

Bygrave, W. D. (1989). The entrepreneurship paradigm (II): Chaos and catastrophes among quantum jumps. *Entrepreneurship Theory and Practice, 14*(2), 7–30.

Bygrave, W. D. (2007). The entrepreneurship paradigm (I) revisited. In Neergaard, H., & Ulhøi, J. P. (Eds.), *Handbook of qualitative research methods in entrepreneurship* (pp. 17–48). Cheltenham, UK and Northampton, MA, USA: Edward Elgar Publishing.

Chalmers, D. M., & Shaw, E. (2017). The endogenous construction of entrepreneurial contexts: A practice-based perspective. *International Small Business Journal, 35*(1), 19–39.

Cope, J. (2011). Entrepreneurial learning from failure: An interpretative phenomenological analysis. *Journal of Business Venturing, 26*(6), 604–623.

Cornelissen, J. P., Clarke, J. S., & Cienki, A. (2012). Sensegiving in entrepreneurial contexts: The use of metaphors in speech and gesture to gain and sustain support for novel business ventures. *International Small Business Journal, 30*(3), 213–241.

Courpasson, D., Dany, F., & Martí, I. (2016). Organizational entrepreneurship as active resistance: A struggle against outsourcing. *Entrepreneurship Theory and Practice, 40*(1), 131–160.

Dentoni, D., Pascucci, S., Poldner, K., & Gartner, W. B. (2018). Learning "who we are" by doing: Processes of co-constructing prosocial identities in community-based enterprises. *Journal of Business Venturing, 33*(5), 603–622.

Doern, R. (2016). Entrepreneurship and crisis management: The experiences of small businesses during the London 2011 riots. *International Small Business Journal, 34*(3), 276–302.

Dooley, L. M. (2002). Case study research and theory building. *Advances in Developing Human Resources, 4*(3), 335–354.

Fairfield, T., & Charman, A. (2019). A dialogue with the data: The Bayesian foundations of iterative research in qualitative social science. *Perspectives on Politics, 17*(1), 154–167.

Farny, S., Kibler, E., Hai, S., & Landoni, P. (2019). Volunteer retention in prosocial venturing: The role of emotional connectivity. *Entrepreneurship Theory and Practice*, *43*(6), 1094–1123.
Fayolle, A. (2007). *Entrepreneurship and new value creation: The dynamic of entrepreneurial process*, Cambridge: Cambridge University Press.
Fayolle, A. (2018). Personal views on the future of entrepreneurship education. In Fayolle, A. (Ed.), *A research agenda for entrepreneurship education* (pp. 127–138). Cheltenham, UK and Northampton, MA, USA: Edward Elgar Publishing.
Fayolle, A., Basso, O., Tornikoski, E. (2011). Entrepreneurial commitment and new venture creation: a conceptual exploration. In Hindle, K., & Klyver, K. (Eds.), *Handbook of research on new venture creation* (pp. 160–182). Cheltenham, UK and Northampton, MA, USA: Edward Elgar Publishing.
Fayolle, A., Landstrom, H., Gartner, W. B., & Berglund, K. (2016). The institutionalization of entrepreneurship: Questioning the status quo and re-gaining hope for entrepreneurship research. *Entrepreneurship & Regional Development*, *28*(7–8), 477–486.
Fletcher, D. (2007). "Toy Story": The narrative world of entrepreneurship and the creation of interpretive communities. *Journal of Business Venturing*, *22*(5), 649–672.
Fuller, T., Warren, L., & Argyle, P. (2008). Sustaining entrepreneurial business: A complexity perspective on processes that produce emergent practice. *International Entrepreneurship and Management Journal*, *4*, 1–17. https://doi.org/10.1007/s11365-007-0047-y.
Gartner, W. B. (1985). A conceptual framework for describing the phenomenon of new venture creation. *Academy of Management Review*, *10*(4), 696–706.
Gartner, W. B. (1993). Words lead to deeds: Towards an organizational emergence vocabulary. *Journal of Business Venturing*, *8*, 231–239.
Gartner, W. B. (2007). Entrepreneurial narrative and a science of the imagination. *Journal of Business Venturing*, *22*(5), 613–627.
Gartner, W. B. (2016). *Entrepreneurship as organizing: Selected papers of William B. Gartner*. Cheltenham, UK and Northampton, MA, USA: Edward Elgar Publishing.
Gartner, W. B., & Brush, C. (2007). Entrepreneurship as organizing: Emergence, newness and transformation. In Rice, T. H. M. (Ed.), *Praeger perspectives on entrepreneurship* (Vol. 3, pp. 1–20). Westport, CT: Praeger Publishers.
Gay, C., & Szostak, B. L. (2019). *Innovation and creativity in SMEs: Challenges, evolutions and prospects*. Hoboken, NJ: John Wiley & Sons.
Gioia, D. A., & Chittipeddi, K. (1991). Sensemaking and sensegiving in strategic change initiation. *Strategic Management Journal*, *12*(6), 433–448.
Gioia, D. A., Corley, K. G., & Hamilton, A. L. (2013). Seeking qualitative rigor in inductive research: Notes on the Gioia methodology. *Organizational Research Methods*, *16*(1), 15–31.
Giovannella, C. (2020). An analysis of alternation schemes to increase student employability and the smartness of secondary schools. In Mealha, Ó., Rehm, M., & Rebedea, T. (Eds.), *Ludic, Co-design and tools supporting smart learning ecosystems and smart education* (pp. 39–51). Singapore: Springer.
Glaser, A. L., & Strauss B. G. (1967). *The discovery of grounded theory: Strategies for qualitative research*. London: Weidenfeld & Nicolson.
Glaser B. G. (1978). *Theoretical sensitivity*. Mill Valley, CA: The Sociology Press.
Greenwood, R., & Suddaby, R. (2006). Institutional entrepreneurship in mature fields: The big five accounting firms. *Academy of Management Journal*, *49*(1), 27–48.

Griffin, M. A. (2007). Specifying organizational contexts: systematic links between contexts and processes in organizational behavior. *Journal of Organizational Behavior, 28* (7), 859–863.

Haines, H. (2023). The room where it happened: Conversation analysis of entrepreneur meetups. *Journal of Small Business Management, 61*(6), 2418–2439.

Hammersley, M. (1997). Qualitative data archiving: some reflections on its prospects and problems. *Sociology, 31*(1), 131–142.

Himanen, P. (2001). *The information society and the welfare state: The Finnish model.* Oxford: Oxford University Press.

Hindle, K. (2007). Teaching entrepreneurship at university: From the wrong building to the right philosophy. In Fayolle, A. (Ed.), *Handbook of research in entrepreneurship education, Volume 1* (pp. 104–126). Cheltenham, UK and Northampton, MA, USA: Edward Elgar Publishing.

Hjorth, D., Holt, R., & Steyaert, C. (2015). Entrepreneurship and process studies. *International Small Business Journal, 33*(6), 599–611.

Hlady-Rispal, M., & Jouison-Laffitte, E. (2014). Qualitative research methods and epistemological frameworks: A review of publication trends in entrepreneurship. *Journal of Small Business Management, 52*(4), 594–614.

Hlady-Rispal, M., Randerson, K., Jouison-Laffitte, E., & Zolin, R. (2016). Entrepreneurship research: What can we learn from qualitative methods? In Taneja, S. (Ed.), *Academy of Management Proceedings* (Vol. 2016, No. 1, p. 12898). Briarcliff Manor, NY: Academy of Management.

Hollow, M. (2020). Historicizing entrepreneurial networks. *Strategic Entrepreneurship Journal, 14*(1), 66–88.

Howard, E. S. (2020). *Entrepreneurial collaboration: A narrative research study exploring multi-party collaboration practices of Fulbright entrepreneurs in STEM fields*. Northeastern University.

Hulsink, W. & Rauch, A. (2021). About the lives and times of extraordinary entrepreneurs: The methodological contribution of autobiographies to the life course theory of entrepreneurship. *Journal of Small Business Management, 59*(5), 913–945.

Janssen, F., Fayolle, A., & Wuilaume, A. (2018). Social entrepreneurship and "bricolage": Taking stock and looking ahead. *Entrepreneurship and Regional Development, 30*(3–4), 450–470.

Johannisson, B. (2020). Searching for the roots of entrepreneuring as practice: Introducing the enactive approach. In Gartner, W. B., & Teague, B. T. (Eds.), *Research handbook on entrepreneurial behavior, practice and process* (pp. 138–167). Cheltenham, UK and Northampton, MA, USA: Edward Elgar Publishing.

Kaandorp, M., Van Burg, E., & Karlsson, T. (2020). Initial networking processes of student entrepreneurs: The role of action and evaluation. *Entrepreneurship Theory and Practice, 44*(3), 527–556.

Kaffka, G. A., Singaram, R., Kraaijenbrink, J, & Groen, A. J. (2021). "Yes and …, but wait …, heck no!": A socially situated cognitive approach towards understanding how startup entrepreneurs process critical feedback. *Journal of Small Business Management, 59*(5), 1050–1080.

Khelil, N. (2021). Causal cognitive mapping in the entrepreneurial cognition field: A comparison of two alternative methods. *Journal of Small Business Management, 59*(5), 1012–1049.

Kier, A. S., & McMullen, J. S. (2018). Entrepreneurial imaginativeness in new venture ideation. *Academy of Management Journal, 61*(6), 2265–2295.

Kipping, M., Wadhwani, R. D., & Bucheli, M. (2014). Analyzing and interpreting historical sources: A basic methodology. In Bucheli, M., & Wadhwani, R. D. (Eds.), *Organizations in time: History, theory, methods* (pp. 305–329). Oxford: Oxford University Press.
Klag, M., & Langley, A. (2013). Approaching the conceptual leap in qualitative research. *International Journal of Management Reviews, 15*(2), 149–166.
Kuratko, D. F., & Morris, M. H. (2018). Examining the future trajectory of entrepreneurship. *Journal of Small Business Management, 56*(1), 11–23.
Langley, A. (1999). Strategies for theorizing from process data. *Academy of Management Review, 24*(4), 691–710.
Lévesque, M., & Stephan, U. (2020). It's time we talk about time in entrepreneurship. *Entrepreneurship Theory and Practice, 44*(2), 163–184.
Lichtenstein, B. (2011). Complexity science: Contributions to the field of entrepreneurship. In Allen, P., Maguire, S., & McKelvey, B. (Eds.), *Sage handbook of complexity and management* (pp. 473–494). London: Sage Publications.
Lichtenstein, B. (2016). Emergence and emergents in entrepreneurship: Complexity science insights into new venture creation. *Entrepreneurship Research Journal, 6*(1), 43–52.
Lichtenstein, B., & McKelvey, B. (2011). Four types of emergence: A typology of complexity and its implications for a science of management. *International Journal of Complexity in Leadership and Management, 1*(4), 330–378.
Loi, M., Fayolle, A., Refai, D., Higgins, D., Haloub, R., Salusse, M. A. Y., Lamy, E., Verzat, C., van Gelderen, M., Riot, E., & Cavaretta, F. (2021). Entrepreneurship education at the crossroads: Challenging taken-for-granted assumptions and opening new perspectives. *Journal of Management Inquiry, 31*(2), 123–134.
Marcus, G. E. (2012). Multi-sited ethnography: Five or six things I know about it now. In Coleman, S., & Von Hellerman, P. (Eds.), *Multi-sited ethnography* (pp. 24–40). New York: Routledge.
Marks, S. (2021). Performing and unperforming entrepreneurial success: Confessions of a female role model. *Journal of Small Business Management, 59*(5), 946–975.
Maxwell, A. L., Jeffrey, S. A., & Lévesque, M. (2011). Business angel early stage decision making. *Journal of Business Venturing, 26*(2), 212–225.
McKelvey, B. (2004). Toward a complexity science of entrepreneurship. *Journal of Business Venturing, 19*(3), 313–341.
Mintzberg, H. (2009). *Managing*. Oakland, CA: Berrett-Koehler Publishers.
Molina-Azorin, J. F. (2012). Mixed methods research in strategic management: Impact and applications. *Organizational Research Methods, 15*(1), 33–56.
Mounce, H. O. (1997). *The two pragmatisms*. London: Routledge.
Muñoz, P., Cacciotti, G., & Cohen, B. (2018). The double-edged sword of purpose-driven behavior in sustainable venturing. *Journal of Business Venturing, 33*(2), 149–178.
Nummela, N., Saarenketo, S., & Loane, S. (2016). The dynamics of failure in international new ventures: A case study of Finnish and Irish software companies. *International Small Business Journal, 34*(1), 51–69.
O'Connor, E. (2002). Storied business: Typology, intertextuality, and traffic in entrepreneurial narrative. *International Journal of Business Communication, 39*(1), 36–54.
Ormiston, J., & Thompson, N.A. (2021). Viewing entrepreneurship 'in motion': exploring current uses and future possibilities of video-based entrepreneurship research. *Journal of Small Business Management, 59*(5), 976–1011.

Poldner, K. (2020). Performing affirmation: Autoethnography as an activist approach to entrepreneurship. In Gartner, W. B., & Teague, B. T. (Eds.), *Research handbook on entrepreneurial behavior, practice and process* (pp. 102–137). Cheltenham, UK and Northampton, MA, USA: Edward Elgar Publishing.

Salmivaara, V., & Kibler, E. (2020). "Rhetoric mix" of argumentations: How policy rhetoric conveys meaning of entrepreneurship for sustainable development. *Entrepreneurship Theory and Practice*, *44*(4), 700–732.

Santini, C., Marinelli, E., Boden, M., Cavicchi, A., & Haegeman, K. (2016). Reducing the distance between thinkers and doers in the entrepreneurial discovery process: An exploratory study. *Journal of Business Research*, *69*(5), 1840–1844.

Schwab, A., & Zhang, Z. (2019). A new methodological frontier in entrepreneurship research: big data studies. *Entrepreneurship Theory and Practice*, *43*(5) 843–854.

Selden, P., & Fletcher, D. (2015). The entrepreneurial journey as an emergent hierarchical system of artifact-creating processes. *Journal of Business Venturing*, *30*, 603–615, https://doi:10.1016/j.jbusvent.2014.09.002.

Shantz, A. S., Kistruck, G., & Zietsma, C. (2018). The opportunity not taken: The occupational identity of entrepreneurs in contexts of poverty. *Journal of Business Venturing*, *33*(4), 416–437.

Simonÿ, C., Specht, K., Andersen, I. C., Johansen, K. K., Nielsen, C., & Agerskov, H. (2018). A Ricoeur-inspired approach to interpret participant observations and interviews. *Global Qualitative Nursing Research*, *5*, https:// doi .org/ 10 .1177/ 2333393618807395.

Smith, R. (2018). Reading liminal and temporal dimensionality in the Baxter family "public narrative". *International Small Business Journal*, *36*(1), 41–59.

Steyaert, C. (2007). "Entrepreneuring" as a conceptual attractor? A review of process theories in 20 years of entrepreneurship studies. *Entrepreneurship and Regional Development*, *19*, 453–477.

Steyaert, C. (2009). Enacting urban ethnographies of artistic interventions in the entrepreneurial city. In Beyes, T., Deuflhard, A., & Krempl, S.-T. (Eds.), *ParCITYpate: Artistic interventions and urban space* (pp. 382–465). Sulgen: Niggli.

Strauss, A., & Corbin, J. (1994). Grounded theory methodology. In Denzin, N. K., & Lincoln, Y. S. (Eds.), *Handbook of qualitative research* (pp. 273–285). Thousand Oaks, CA: SAGE.

Susman, G. I., & Evered, R. D. (1978). An assessment of the scientific merits of action research. *Administrative Science Quarterly*, *23*(4), 582–603.

Tillmar, M. (2020). Practicing participant observations: Capturing entrepreneurial practices. In Gartner, W. B., & Teague, B. T. (Eds.), *Research handbook on entrepreneurial behavior, practice and process* (pp. 168–181). Cheltenham, UK and Northampton, MA, USA: Edward Elgar Publishing.

Värlander, S. W., Sölvell, I., & Klyver, K. (2020). Entrepreneurship as a vocational choice in contested entrepreneurship communities: The role of entrepreneurs' justification strategies. *Journal of Business Venturing*, *35*(3), 106006.

Volery, T., Mueller, S., & von Siemens, B. (2015). Entrepreneur ambidexterity: A study of entrepreneur behaviours and competencies in growth-oriented small and medium-sized enterprises. *International Small Business Journal*, *33*(2), 109–129.

Wadhwani, R. D. (2016). Entrepreneurship in historical context: Using history to develop theory and understand process. In Welter, F., & Gartner, W. B. (Eds.), *A research agenda for entrepreneurship and context* (pp. 134–145). Cheltenham, UK and Northampton, MA, USA: Edward Elgar Publishing.

Wadhwani, R. D., & Decker, S. (2017). Clio's toolkit: The practice of historical methods in organization studies. In Mir, R., & Jain, S. (Eds.), *The Routledge companion to qualitative research in organization studies* (pp. 113–127). Abingdon, UK: Routledge.
Wadhwani, R. D., & Jones, G. (2014). Schumpeter's plea: Historical reasoning in entrepreneurship theory and research. In Bucheli, M., & Wadhwani, R. D. (Eds.), *Organizations in time: History, theory, methods* (pp. 192–216). Oxford: Oxford University Press.
Wadhwani, R. D., Kirsch, D., Welter, F., Gartner, W. B., & Jones, G. G. (2020). Context, time, and change: Historical approaches to entrepreneurship research. *Strategic Entrepreneurship Journal*, *14*(1), 3–19.
Wadhwani, R. D., & Lubinski, C. (2017). Reinventing entrepreneurial history. *Business History Review*, *91*(4), 767–799.
Watson, T. J. (2013). Entrepreneurial action and the Euro-American social science tradition: Pragmatism, realism and looking beyond "the entrepreneur". *Entrepreneurship and Regional Development*, *25*(1–2), 16–33.
Weick, K. E. (1979). Cognitive processes in organizations. *Research in organizational behavior*, *1*(1), 41–74.
Weick, K. E. (1995). *Sensemaking in organizations* (Vol. 3). London: Sage Publications.
Welter, F., Baker, T., & Wirsching, K. (2019). Three waves and counting: the rising tide of contextualization in entrepreneurship research. *Small Business Economics*, *52*(2), 319–330.
Welter, F., & Gartner, W. B. (Eds.) (2016). *A research agenda for entrepreneurship and context*. Cheltenham, UK and Northampton, MA, USA: Edward Elgar Publishing.
Wiklund, J., Wright, M., & Zahra, S. A. (2019). Conquering relevance: Entrepreneurship research's grand challenge. *Entrepreneurship Theory and Practice*, *43*(3) 419–436.
Yin, R. K. (2003). Designing case studies. *Qualitative Research Methods*, *5*(14), 359–386.
Yitshaki, R., & Kropp, F. (2016). Entrepreneurial passions and identities in different contexts: A comparison between high-tech and social entrepreneurs. *Entrepreneurship & Regional Development*, *28*(3–4), 206–233.
Younger, S., & Fisher, G. (2020). The exemplar enigma: New venture image formation in an emergent organizational category. *Journal of Business Venturing*, *35*(1), 105897.
Zahra, S. A., & Wright, M. (2011). Entrepreneurship's next act. *Academy of Management Perspectives*, *25*(4), 67–83.
Zou, H., Chen, X., Lam, L. W. R., & Liu, X. (2016). Psychological capital and conflict management in the entrepreneur–venture capitalist relationship in China: The entrepreneur perspective. *International Small Business Journal*, *34*(4), 446–467.

Qualitative methods – understanding the "why" and "how" of entrepreneurship: a review of "In search of creative qualitative methods to capture current entrepreneurship research challenges"

R. Duncan M. Pelly

The chapter "In search of creative qualitative methods to capture current entrepreneurship research challenges" is more germane than ever to addressing big questions in entrepreneurship research. Not only does this chapter highlight the importance of qualitative methods in the age of artificial intelligence, post-COVID-19, and the movement to online work, it also underscores the diversity of qualitative methods and their applications in the face of these new challenges. The fact that this work was the opener for a special issue in the *Journal of Small Business Management*, a journal dedicated to frequently overlooked methodologies, provides legitimacy for the methods cited in the 2021 special issue. Moreover, the chapter paves the way for other writers to craft their own approaches because of three salient points that will be emphasized in this review. First of all, qualitative research should highlight "what actually occurs" by reviewing context. Second, gaining a deeper understanding of entrepreneurship can be achieved through co-creation. Lastly, interdisciplinarity of entrepreneurship and entrepreneurship research coalesce.

Context is of utmost importance to entrepreneurship research from the perspective of the authors. The big questions surrounding routines and praxes are frequently overlooked since many quantitative methods take a snapshot in time, but fail to provide the meaning between data points (Pelly and Fayolle, 2020). This issue in social sciences is not new – Weber's interpretative sociology bemoaned this as the erklaeren (describing) versus verstehen (understanding) debate (Weber, 2001). Context is seen as critical because it provides in situ knowledge that reveals linkages otherwise overlooked. This may include "power quotes" and narrations with respect to paths not taken, or sensemaking – both of which can provide clarity in complex phenomena.

A recurring theme in this chapter is the co-construction of knowledge with academics and practitioners, which the authors refer to as "the hacker ethic", and "co-design". Co-construction offers a compelling avenue to answering the big questions of entrepreneurship – it encourages researchers to gain proximity to the field and become part of the processes they are exploring (Newth, 2018). By joining the entrepreneurial struggle, researchers not only contribute to the processes they are studying (if they so choose), they can also gain a profound understanding of the context and temporality, thus providing enhanced sensemaking for readers and researchers alike. Scholars who have such proximity to their field are able to answer the most important inquiries in entrepreneurship because field experiences and lived experiences become intertwined (Tillmar, 2020).

The authors maintain that entrepreneurship benefits from tremendous intellectual diversity. This diversity stems from the fact that entrepreneurship is identified as a mindset or a posture that allows the agent to enact opportunities (Hindle, 2007). This intellectual flexibility enables entrepreneurship researchers to attack big questions, identified in the chapter as including uberization, digitalization, neurosciences, pandemics, and sustainability. As such, it would be a non sequitur to utilize methods that stem from one basic discipline, math, to explain this diversity of problems. Furthermore, mathematical abstraction obfuscates context and the in-depth system workings that the writers seek to understand through qualitative methods (Bygrave, 2007).

One of the more profound points contained within the chapter was that qualitative methods serve as a prelude to the discovery of new insights of the phenomenon under study and follow a teleological perspective. The authors are correct in their assessment that the majority of quantitative (and sometimes qualitative) research follows Aristotle's auxiliary three causes: formal, efficient, and material. They stress that dominant methods are insufficient to explain context, complexity, sensemaking, and the "spark" that lights entrepreneurial action. Of equal importance in support of their advocacy of qualitative methods as a means to promote teleology is the implication that the research *itself* provides teleology for the reader. In other words, the focus on the "Why" and "How" provides an avenue for readers to fill in the blanks during their own entrepreneurial journeys. This approach to analyzing data means that our research and findings can do more than simply be cited in the halls of academia; it is an opportunity to make the world a better place by including readers in the sensemaking process.

REFERENCES

Bygrave, W. D. (2007). The entrepreneurship paradigm (I) revisited. In Neergaard, H., & Ulhøi, J. P. (Eds.), *Handbook of qualitative research methods in entrepre-*

neurship (pp. 17–48). Cheltenham, UK and Northampton, MA, USA: Edward Elgar Publishing.

Hindle, K. (2007). Teaching entrepreneurship at university: From the wrong building to the right philosophy. In Fayolle, A. (Ed.), *Handbook of research in entrepreneurship education, Volume 1* (pp. 104–126). Cheltenham, UK and Northampton, MA, USA: Edward Elgar Publishing.

Newth, J. (2018). "Hands-on" vs "arm's length" entrepreneurship research: Using ethnography to contextualize social innovation. *International Journal of Entrepreneurial Behavior & Research, 24*(3), 683–696.

Pelly, R. D. M., & Fayolle, A. (2020). Ethnography's answer to the plus zone challenge of entrepreneurship. In Gartner, W. B., & Teague, B. T. (Eds.), *Research handbook on entrepreneurial behavior, practice and process* (pp. 82–101). Cheltenham, UK and Northampton, MA, USA: Edward Elgar Publishing.

Tillmar, M. (2020). Practicing participant observations: Capturing entrepreneurial practices. In Gartner, W. B., & Teague, B. T. (Eds.), *Research handbook on entrepreneurial behavior, practice and process* (pp. 168–181). Cheltenham, UK and Northampton, MA, USA: Edward Elgar Publishing.

Weber, M. (2001) [1930]. *The Protestant ethic and the spirit of capitalism.* New York: Routledge.

9. Why a systematic literature review is a powerful tool for gaining insights into entrepreneurship: application to entrepreneurial teams in the venture creation process

Sara Maryami and Michela Loi

INTRODUCTION

In the dynamic field of entrepreneurship, continuous and comprehensive research is vital to improve our understanding of crucial phenomena that have significant implications for economic and societal development (Kraus et al., 2020). Over the past decade, a significant body of research papers has been dedicated to improving the entrepreneurship field's quality of literature reviews (e.g., Champenois et al., 2020; Galvão et al., 2018; Godonoga and Sporn, 2023; Motta and Galina, 2023; Pittaway et al., 2014; Sirelkhatim and Gangi, 2015). Among the various research methodologies available, systematic literature reviews (SLRs) play a pivotal role in providing a comprehensive and structured approach to reviewing existing literature on a specific topic that can be valuable in understanding the current state of research, identifying gaps or areas for improvement in methodology, and guiding future research efforts (Tranfield et al., 2003).

A multitude of scholars have drafted recommendations to support researchers in advancing the practice of SLR in various fields such as business research and management (e.g., Snyder, 2019; Tranfield et al., 2003). Despite the valuable contribution of previous guidelines to the literature review, in this chapter, we intend to contribute to the literature by combining the main steps to conduct SLR while presenting a case in practice. Therefore, this chapter focuses on a fast-growing field of research: the study of entrepreneurial teams (ETs). Although previous guidelines and recommendations may have covered established topics, this study is at the forefront of offering a systematic review of a relatively new and dynamic area of investigation. Our SLR specifically narrows its focus on the concept of ETs in the venture creation stage, an aspect that has not been extensively studied despite its significant relevance in the overall entrepreneurial process. The venture creation involves various activities that set the groundwork for the new venture, including legal and operational aspects, establishing the company's vision and culture, building credibility, gathering business intelligence, networking, and validating the market potential (Gruber, 2002). Focusing on this stage, we can thoroughly examine and synthesize the existing literature on this critical phase of entrepreneurship.

In the following sections, first, we elucidate the key steps in conducting the SLR, emphasizing their importance and providing guidance to researchers. These steps typically include formulating a research question, establishing inclusion and exclusion criteria, conducting a thorough literature search, screening and selecting relevant studies, assessing their quality, extracting, synthesizing data, and presenting a comprehensive overview of the findings. Subsequently, we will present a specific SLR on ETs as an illustrative example. By providing a step-by-step guide and a practical example of conducting an SLR on ETs, researchers will gain valuable insights into systematic searching, analysis, and synthesis of existing literature on their topic of interest.

Furthermore, we will address the inherent limitations of using an SLR as a standalone approach. These limitations may include potential biases in the available literature, such as publication and language biases, as well as the exclusion of unpublished or gray literature. To complement the SLR approach, we will discuss alternative or complementary methodologies that researchers can consider. These alternatives may include conducting primary research studies to gather firsthand data, utilizing other review methods like scoping reviews or narrative reviews or integrating quantitative research methods to gain deeper insights into specific aspects of the research question. Such practical recommendations to conduct the SLR will empower researchers to conduct more robust and insightful investigations in the field of entrepreneurship and beyond, enhancing the overall quality and impact of their research endeavors.

SYSTEMATIC LITERATURE REVIEW

Kraus et al. (2020) define SLRs as "a review of an existing body of literature that follows a transparent and reproducible methodology in searching, assessing its quality and synthesizing it, with a high level of objectivity" (Kraus et al., 2020, p. 106). In academic fields such as medical and health sciences, SLRs were initially developed (Tranfield et al., 2003). In recent times, SLRs have become a preferred approach for conducting comprehensive literature reviews in management and entrepreneurship studies (Calabrò et al., 2019; Kraus et al., 2020; Liñán and Fayolle, 2015; Nabi et al., 2017; Pittaway and Cope, 2007).

In business sciences, an SLR is a rigorous and structured approach to synthesizing existing research evidence about a specific research question or topic (Snyder, 2019; Sirelkhatim and Gangi, 2015).

While traditional literature reviews have been used to tackle the main problem by summarizing existing research, the SLR follows a structured and systematic framework to guide researchers on how to proceed step by step in the review process (Schuhmacher and Thieu, 2022). By employing these standardized procedures, SLRs help to ensure transparency and mitigate the impact of individual biases that may influence the outcomes of a literature review (Davis et al., 2014; Fisch and Block, 2018; Kraus et al., 2020).

Moreover, in some cases, researchers employ statistical techniques such as meta-analysis to integrate and analyze the results from studies included in a systematic review (Snyder, 2019). Paul and Barari (2022, p. 1099) define meta-analysis as "a research method for systematically combining and synthesizing findings from multiple quantitative studies in a research domain." Meta-analysis is commonly used in various scientific disciplines, including medicine, psychology, education, and entrepreneurship (Gurevitch et al., 2018; Martin et al., 2013; Martínez-Gregorio et al., 2021; Schermuly et al., 2022). Therefore, meta-analyses serve as a valuable tool for addressing open research questions (Eden, 2002), a tool for theory testing in research (Shaw and Ertug, 2017), and extending existing theories (Guzzo et al., 1987). Instead of relying on the findings of a single study, a meta-analysis combines the results from various primary studies to draw more robust conclusions (Rauch and Frese, 2006).

The Value and Applications of SLRs in Entrepreneurship Research

Applying SLRs has become increasingly prominent in entrepreneurship research due to their potential to provide valuable insights into various aspects of a research field (Cao and Shi, 2021; Champenois et al., 2020; Pittaway et al., 2014). In this section, we delve into the value and applications of SLRs, shedding light on their contributions to methodology and their impact on advancing our understanding of entrepreneurship. It is essential to note that SLRs themselves can vary in scope and quality depending on the authors' research purpose. Through an examination of the search context, objectives, and research questions of the SLRs that have been conducted in the field of entrepreneurship, we have observed variations in their scopes. Table 9.1 provides a synthesis of these scopes, and below, we present examples to illustrate the potential diversity of areas that researchers may explore when conducting SLRs in the entrepreneurship field.

Table 9.1 *Summary of systematic literature reviews based on scope*

Classification	Example	Research Question(s)	Main Findings
Best Practices	Sirelkhatim and Gangi (2015)	What are the common and recommended practices in curriculum content and teaching methods for entrepreneurship education at the tertiary level? and how do they correlate with practices recommended by the entrepreneurial learning field of research?	• Provides a comprehensive overview of best practices in curricular content and teaching methods for entrepreneurship education at the tertiary level. Identifies the most effective approaches and methods recommended in the field.
Research Gaps	Nabi et al. (2017)	What is the impact of entrepreneurship education in higher education?	• Highlights the need for more longitudinal research to understand the long-term effects of entrepreneurship education. • Calls for studies exploring contextual factors, pedagogical approaches, and the influence of entrepreneurship education beyond the individual level. • Identifies a research agenda for future studies in this area.
	Banha et al. (2022)	What is the intersection between entrepreneurship education and public policies, and what are the gaps in understanding the decision-making process?	• Reveals a gap in understanding the decision-making process of implementing entrepreneurship education programs (EEPs). • Highlights the need for comprehensive studies that consider public policies and the respective policy-making processes.

Classification	Example	Research Question(s)	Main Findings
Narrowing the Scope	Fox et al. (2018)	What is the role and impact of serious games, specifically computer simulations, in entrepreneurship education?	• Provides a detailed insight into the use and impact of serious games, particularly computer simulations, as a pedagogical tool in entrepreneurship education. • Expands knowledge of the educational practices involving serious games in entrepreneurship.
	Blenker et al. (2014)	What are the methods used in entrepreneurship education research, and what are their strengths and limitations?	• Offers an integrative framework for understanding the strengths and limitations of various research methodologies in teaching entrepreneurship. • Reviews and categorizes the methods applied in entrepreneurship education research.

Searching for best practices

By systematically analyzing a large body of literature, SLRs may assist in pinpointing best practices in a particular field or area of research (Kraus et al., 2020). These practices are considered to be the most reliable and beneficial for addressing the research questions or achieving the desired outcomes, making them particularly valuable for practitioners and decision-makers seeking evidence-based guidance (Champenois et al., 2020). For instance, an SLR of curricula contents and teaching methods by Sirelkhatim and Gangi (2015) provides a comprehensive overview of the common and recommended practices in terms of curriculum content and teaching methods that have proven to be effective in achieving positive outcomes for entrepreneurship education. In this context, "best practices" refers to the most effective and successful approaches or methods that have been identified and recommended in the field of teaching entrepreneurship at the tertiary level (university or college level).

Identifying research gaps

Furthermore, researchers apply SLRs to identify research gaps in the existing literature (Kraus et al., 2020). Specifically, SLRs allow researchers to examine previous studies' limitations and unanswered questions, helping them to identify and discuss areas that require further investigation (Xi et al., 2015). This approach guides future research efforts and helps researchers to focus on areas that have not yet been adequately explored (Liñán and Fayolle, 2015; Santos and Neumeyer, 2021). For example, Nabi et al. (2017) conducted an SLR to explore the impact of entrepreneurship education in higher education and provide a research agenda for future studies in this area. Drawing insights from their SLR, the authors emphasize the need for more longitudinal research to understand the long-term effects of entrepreneurship education on students' entrepreneurial outcomes. They also call for studies that explore the role of contextual factors, pedagogical approaches, and the influence of entrepreneurship education beyond the individual level. Similarly, Banha et al.'s (2022) SLR on the intersection between entrepreneurship education and public policies reveals a gap in the holistic understanding of the decision-making process involved in implementing entrepreneurship education programs in compulsory schooling. Their SLR focuses on a lack of work that considers public policies and the respective policy-making processes, hindering a comprehensive understanding of decision-making in this context.

Narrowing the scope of research

Moreover, implementing the SLR allows researchers to narrow the scope of research within a field (Hausberg and Korreck, 2020). For example, Fox et al. (2018) expanded knowledge of educational practices in entrepreneurship by focusing on serious games, particularly computer simulations. Their SLR provides a closer and more detailed insight into this specific pedagogical tool than more extensive reviews on entrepreneurship education in general. Another example that we can mention is the SLR of Blenker et al. (2014) which offers an integrative framework for methods used in entrepreneurship education. They applied an SLR to review and categorize the research methods that were applied in entrepreneurship education research. By narrowing the focus on the strengths and limitations of methodology in entrepreneurship education, their work enhances a deeper understanding of the challenges and trends in teaching entrepreneurship.

As is evident from the examples discussed above, the scope of SLRs varies significantly. It is important to note that these scopes are not necessarily mutually exclusive and can be mixed. In other words, an SLR may include multiple objectives and research questions simultaneously, providing a comprehensive analysis of a particular field or area of study.

CONDUCTING AN SLR: STEPS AND METHODOLOGICAL CONSIDERATIONS FOR COMPREHENSIVE RESEARCH SYNTHESIS

In this section, we will present our SLR applied to ETs by illustrating step-by-step the procedure followed and the findings obtained to understand the team inputs and processes implicated in the venture creation phase.

Undoubtedly, teams and human capital are necessary for any organization to grow. One of the key characteristics of competent human capital strengths is the ability to work as part of a team (Omri and Boujelbene, 2015). ETs play a critical role in the success and growth of entrepreneurial ventures (Lazar et al., 2020). Therefore, the competitiveness of new ventures is greatly affected by the fact that a large number of entrepreneurs continue their entrepreneurial journey with another partner on a team rather than as a lone entrepreneur (Lim and Busenitz, 2020). In entrepreneurship, teams are a combination of two or more individuals who establish a business (Kamm et al., 1990) with a common goal that can be achieved only through relevant alliances of individual entrepreneurial activities (Cooney, 2005). Therefore, research on ETs has become one of the most significant research topics in entrepreneurship (Lazar et al., 2020).

In recent years, research on the role of teams in the entrepreneurial process has been on the rise (De Mol et al., 2015; Klotz et al., 2014; Lazar et al., 2020; Maryami et al., 2023). Numerous empirical studies have shown that ETs play a critical role in the success of a venture, access to resources, and business growth (Santos and Neumeyer, 2021). Simultaneously, there exists a group of studies that have applied systematic literature reviews (SLRs) to examine the concept of teams in entrepreneurship (Das et al., 2021; De Mol et al., 2015; Klotz et al., 2014). Implementing an SLR provides an opportunity for researchers to comprehensively review and synthesize the existing literature on ETs (De Mol et al., 2015). Thereby, this process facilitates the uncovering of gaps, specifying emerging trends and theoretical perspectives that may shape an entrepreneurship research's future direction. Moreover, the ETs perform within a more inclusive ecosystem that comprises institutions, policymakers, and stakeholders. The SLR on ETs has the potential to shed light on the importance and function of team formation, collaboration, and performance. Providing precious information on how ETs form, collaborate, and perform in various contexts might help the diverse players in the ecosystem in designing and implementing initiatives, programs, and policies that foster ET and entrepreneurial effectiveness.

Despite the existing SLRs on the role of ETs, there is still a need to refine perspectives and gain a more focused understanding of ETs research within specific entrepreneurial phases (Bolzani et al., 2019). The current literature has raised questions about interconnected team mechanisms linking team characteristics to important outcomes in the early stages of entrepreneurship (Chen et al., 2017; Santos and Neumeyer, 2021). This points to the need for further research in this area to better understand the link between team inputs, mechanisms, and outcomes in the entrepreneurial process (Bolzani et al., 2019; Newman et al., 2018). The reason behind such a focus relies on the acknowledgment that the early stage of entrepreneurship is a crucial time for startups and teams, as it often determines their future success or failure (Kaulio, 2003; Lazar et al., 2020).

Furthermore, by narrowing the investigation of existing knowledge to the early phase of entrepreneurship and emphasizing the role of ETs, we can provide a clear research direction for scholars interested in studying this specific aspect of entrepreneurship. Additionally, this focused approach provides an opportunity to identify common themes and trends in the literature that may be useful to enhance our understanding of key factors in team formation, composition, and dynamics that can influence entrepreneurial outcomes and success (Khitous et al., 2020; Pret and Cogan, 2019). Accordingly, this knowledge could theoretically and practically enrich the broader field of entrepreneurship research.

Proceeding with an SLR: An Overview of the Role of Entrepreneurial Teams in the Venture Creation Phase

Proceeding with an SLR involves several steps to ensure a comprehensive and structured analysis of existing research on a specific topic. This overview will delve into the step-by-step process that researchers have undertaken to design this specific kind of literature review. Following standardized steps for conducting an SLR ensures that researchers remain focused and more on track during the process, thereby reducing the chances of missing relevant studies or making mistakes during data extraction and analysis (Kraus et al., 2020; Moher et al., 2015). In planning and conducting a systematic review, it is critical to address key questions at each stage to ensure the rigor and relevance of the review. As pointed out by Snyder (2019), a comprehensive set of questions such as: (i) designing the review, (ii) conducting the review, (iii) analyzing, and (iv) writing up the reports can guide researchers in planning, conducting, analyzing, and writing an effective review report (Snyder, 2019).

To demonstrate the significance of conducting an SLR in entrepreneurship, particularly focusing on the team context, we will present their own SLR as an example. The purpose of this example is to demonstrate ETs' antecedents and processes in the specific phase of venture creation. Table 9.2 displays the main steps that we applied to conduct our SLR.

Formulating the research question

To conduct the SLR, the first step is to define the research question to articulate clearly the objective of the review (Snyder, 2019; Thomé et al., 2016). In the formulation of the research question, it is essential to conduct some preliminary exploration of the existing literature (Xiao and Watson, 2019). This can involve conducting initial searches, reviewing relevant articles, and researching gaps in the field. This exploration will help us to identify potential research questions and refine our focus (Massaro et al., 2016). By clearly defining this research question, we can maintain coherence and alignment with the stated objective of the review. For this purpose, researchers recommend

Table 9.2 Steps for conducting a systematic literature review

Steps	Description
Formulating the Research Question	Clearly defining the research question or objective of the review.
Defining keywords	Create effective search queries.
Identifying Relevant Databases and Sources	Identify relevant databases, sources, and search terms to systematically search for relevant studies.
Developing Inclusion and Exclusion Criteria	Include the selected studies that meet the eligibility criteria for further analysis.
Screening and Selecting Studies	Screen the retrieved studies based on predefined inclusion and exclusion criteria.
Data Extraction Processes	Extract relevant data from the included studies using a predefined data extraction form.
Analyze and Synthesize Studies	Analyze and synthesize the extracted data to identify patterns, themes, or relationships.

starting with a literature search of potential databases that encompass most of the literature that is relevant to your research topic and research question (Kraus et al., 2020). At this stage, researchers need to assess whether the literature review is necessary concerning the general field of research and whether it makes a substantial, practical, or theoretical contribution (Snyder, 2019).

In our SLR on ETs and venture creation, we began by conducting a literature review on the topic of ETs in entrepreneurship to obtain an initial overview of existing research, theories, and concepts related to the role of ETs. This process helped us to identify gaps and areas that require further investigation leading us to identify the following research questions: "What are the main team antecedents influencing the venture creation phase in entrepreneurship?" and "What are the key team processes that contribute to creating the venture?"

Defining keywords

Defining the keyword stream for an SLR involves determining the relevant keywords and search terms that will be used to search for studies related to the research question (Torraco, 2005). To determine the proper keywords for an SLR, one way would be to review relevant literature within the field to identify the common terminology and keywords used by other researchers (Donthu et al., 2021). In addition, it is important to note the consistent appearance of keywords in studies that are aligned with the research question (Thomé et al., 2016). Subsequently, through a brainstorming session among the author's team and experts, the authors get an overview of both general terms and specific keywords that are closely related to their research question (Rao et al., 2023).

To conduct the present SLR, based on the study objectives, and following previous works in the context of ETs (Bolzani et al., 2019), a set of relevant keywords was selected for this SLR. Furthermore, to search keywords we used Boolean operators (e.g., AND, OR, NOT) to create effective search queries. In our search, the following keywords were used as criteria for inclusion: Team AND ((("pre-organi$ation*") or ("pre organi$ation") or ("firm* creation") or ("firm* formation") or ("compan* creation") or ("compan* formation") or ("business creation") or ("business formation") or ("business launch*") or ("organi$ation* creation") or ("organi$ation* formation") or ("preorgani$ation*") or ("pre-organi$ation*") or ("companfound") or ("business found*") or ("organi$ation* prefounding") or ("firm* found*") or ("ventur* creation") or ("ventur* formation") or ("ventur* found*") or ("ventur* Fund*") or ("ventur* emergence") or ("ventur* Performance") or ("ventur* Capital"))).

Identifying relevant databases and sources

The third step includes choosing the appropriate databases, which will help ensure a comprehensive search of the articles dealing with the researched topic (Thomé et al., 2016). This typically involves searching electronic databases, such as, for instance, ScienceDirect, SpringerLink, PubMed, Scopus, JSTOR, or Web of Science.

In our SLR, the keywords search was performed in the Web of Science (WoS) database to retrieve journal articles. According to previous studies (Moher et al. 2015; Rethlefsen et al. 2021), WoS provides access to interdisciplinary papers and offers bibliometric tools for rationalizing the literature in a research field (Mongeon and Paul-Hus, 2016). The WoS database is well-accepted among researchers because of its wide scope of literature on entrepreneurship and business (Luor et al., 2014). We searched for articles related to the team in venture creation phases, which were published between the years 1985–2020 to consider all the periods in which the concept of team in entrepreneurship has become a recognized discipline (Landström, 2020). The initial search for the document's title, abstract, and keywords yielded 545 journal articles. These initial primary keywords were ample to cover the largest possible number of articles in the first search and to produce a significant number of articles, despite many being less relevant to the present study.

Developing inclusion and exclusion criteria

To ensure the appropriate selection of studies, researchers need to establish predefined inclusion and exclusion criteria (Tranfield et al., 2003). These criteria typically consider aspects such as study methodology, document type, field of study, intervention or exposure, outcome measures, and language of publication. Determining these inclusion and exclusion criteria allows researchers to critically assess the quality and relevancy of each study (Fisch and Block, 2018). By applying these criteria, the researchers may effectively assess the eligibility of studies, ensuring that only appropriate and relevant studies are included in the SLR (Snyder, 2019).

In the following step, in this SLR, the screening process was conducted by applying inclusion and exclusion criteria to eliminate duplicate or irrelevant articles. Regarding our research questions and the aim of this study, we applied various inclusion criteria, including specific domain or field of study, document type, years, source type, language, and access type, to identify eligible articles. This led to the exclusion of book chapters, thesis, brief reports, and non-English papers. Using a single language, such as English, in scientific publications promotes consistency and facilitates the exchange of knowledge (Morrison et al., 2012). As a result, researchers usually target English-language journals to achieve a wider audience and gain more significant visibility for their work. A total of 115 out of 554 articles were initially identified as meeting the above inclusion criteria.

Moreover, to ensure access to relevant information related to the subject of study, we focused on articles published in top-ranked journals, as determined by the Association of Business Schools (ABS) in 2018. The ABS publishes an annual journal guide, a reference tool that provides information on the quality and reputation of business journals. This guide is widely used by researchers and academics in the field of business and management to identify the most reputable and influential journals in which to publish their research (Muñoz and Cohen, 2018). We excluded papers that were not rated at least 3 stars, which indicates that they publish original and well-executed research, or 4 stars, which denotes that they publish the most original and best-executed research; 4* stars are examples of excellence in the guide (Mingers and Willmott, 2013). This resulted in a range of top-tier journals that are widely recognized and respected in the academic community and are considered reputable sources of new knowledge and insights in the field (Harvey et al. 2010). In this step, we excluded 27 articles that were not on the ABS list. Overall, 88 articles matched the inclusion criteria that are relevant to the question of this systematic review.

Screening and selecting the studies

After identifying relevant articles through a database keyword search, it is time to screen the retrieved articles according to predefined inclusion and exclusion criteria (Snyder, 2019). Typically, researchers begin by searching the list of keywords in the database. After having the list of the initial results, the researchers apply the inclusion and exclusion criteria to the search results to identify potentially relevant studies. This process usually starts with screening titles and abstracts and then proceeds to full-text screening for those articles that meet the initial criteria.

After the initial screening, we have to carefully examine the full texts of potentially relevant studies. In the specific case of our study, we assessed the eligibility of each study by reading the entire article to assess whether the study methodology, data collection methods, analysis techniques, and results apply to the research question and contribute valuable insights. In our SLR, we excluded those articles that did not directly investigate or speculate on the team factors that can influence the team and entrepreneurial outcomes during the venture creation phase (e.g., Domurath et al., 2020), and those focusing on the role of teams for the later phases of entrepreneurship (e.g., Loane et al., 2014; Mathisen and Rasmussen, 2019). At last, we examined the full text of 88 articles to achieve the final sample for review. Overall, 36 articles matched the inclusion criteria relevant to this SLR's aim for further analysis.

Typically, researchers use approved protocols (e.g., Farrell et al., 2022; Liu et al., 2021; Senali et al., 2022) such as the Preferred Reporting Items for Systematic Reviews and Meta-Analyses (PRISMA) (Moher et al., 2009), which provides standard guidelines for implementing and reporting systematic reviews. Specifically, the PRISMA guidelines are a set of recommendations on the conduct and reporting of systematic reviews, which were developed to improve the transparency and quality of systematic reviews and to summarize and synthesize the existing evidence on a particular research question (Moher et al., 2015). In addition to the PRISMA guideline, the PRISMA flow diagram is highly recommended as it serves as a visual representation summarizing the count of records identified, included, and excluded, along with the corresponding reasons for exclusion at each stage of the review process (Page et al., 2021). The process of screening and selection of studies are displayed in Figure 9.1, which represents a summarizing diagram usually adapted to provide a visual representation of the process and flow of conducting an SLR.

Data extraction processes

After selecting relevant studies based on inclusion and exclusion criteria, the researchers apply the data extraction process that involves the systematic extraction and recording of relevant information from each selected study (Snyder, 2019). During the data extraction process, specific data or variables needed to answer the research question or objectives are collected from the studies (Kraus et al., 2020). These data may vary depending on the nature of the review and the information to be extracted. To facilitate this process, the authors use a standardized data recording form and guidance notes. This form contains all the necessary information for the synthesis of the papers such as general information about the paper (e.g., title, authors, publication year), research methods, theory, and main results.

In this step, we extracted the key data elements that address our study's research question and objective. For the current SLR, we created a form with Excel to capture relevant information across all selected studies. This form includes specific data elements such as: (A) study characteristics (e.g., Author's name, Publication year, Title, Journal/Source, Aim of the study, Theory); (B) Study design and methodology (e.g., Qualitative, quantitative, or Mixed method); and (C) Results and Key Findings (e.g., Summary of Findings, Statistical Significance, Limitations, and Implications). In Table 9.3, we provide an example of the data extraction form that we used in our SLR. As displayed in Table 9.3, regarding the specific objective and research question in our study, we also seek to examine the team input and process focus on the selected papers. For this purpose, we included two additional columns within our analysis that are specifically devoted to exploring aspects of team inputs and processes.

Analyze and synthesize studies

After deciding on the final sample, it is important to consider how to analyze and synthesize the results of the included studies. The synthesis of the literature review depends on the question and objectives of the reviewed articles (Tranfield et al., 2003). Data synthesis is a crucial step in SLRs, in which the

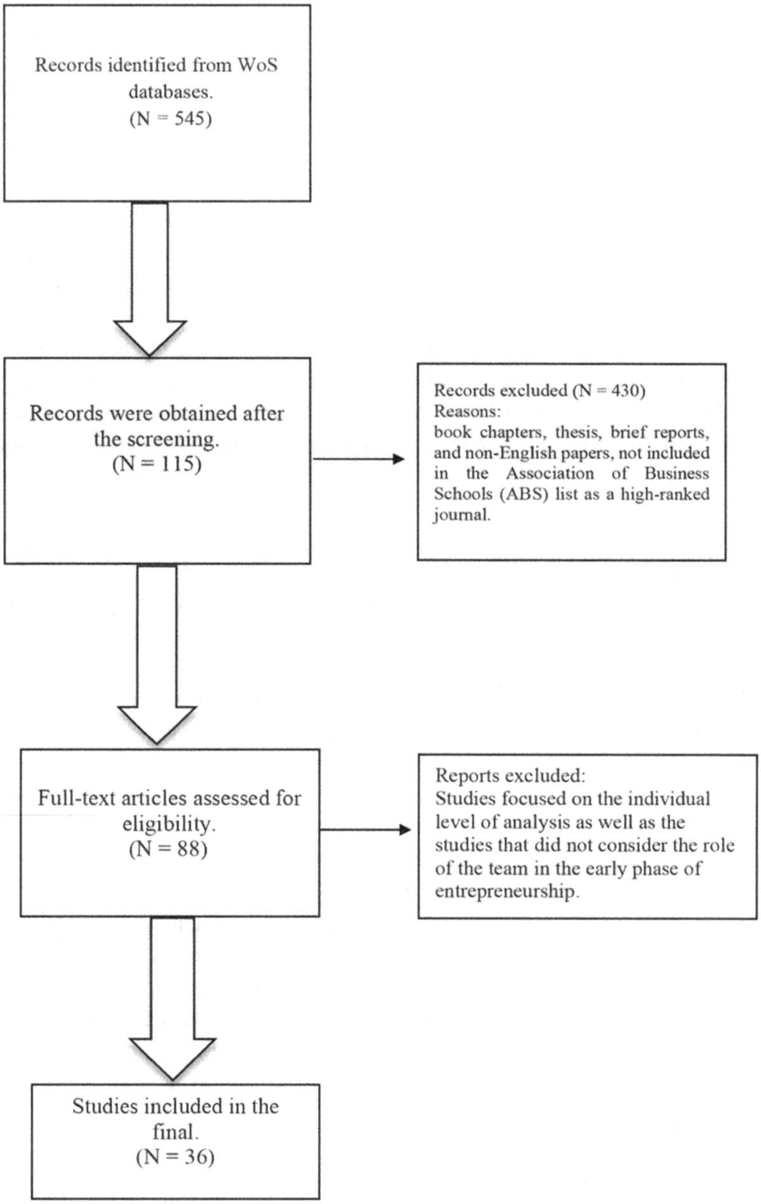

Source: Authors' own.

Figure 9.1 *The flow of information through systematic review*

Table 9.3 *Data extraction form*

Study ID	Author(s)	Publication Year	Title	Journal/ Source	Aim of the Study	Theory	Study Design and Methodology	Key Findings	Team input	Team process

results of selected studies are analyzed and integrated to derive meaningful insights and draw conclusions (Kraus et al., 2020). Data synthesis involves organizing, categorizing, and summarizing the extracted data to identify patterns, trends, relationships, or overarching themes within the literature. Finally, we have started to analyze and synthesize the studies by critically evaluating the selected papers and integrating their findings to derive meaningful insights. Regarding the aim of this SLR, we applied thematic analysis that involves identifying and organizing themes or categories based on recurring concepts, ideas, or patterns found in the literature (Braun and Clarke, 2006; Liñán and Fayolle, 2015; Tranfield et al., 2003).

Interpretation and discussion

In SLRs, the primary focus is to identify common themes, patterns, relationships, or gaps in the literature and provide a comprehensive understanding of the research area. Meantime, the SLR provides us with summary statistics or characteristics of the included studies such as the number of studies retrieved, their publication years, geographic distribution, research designs employed, or other relevant studies characteristics.

In our SLR, we summarized the descriptive results as part of the analysis. By extracting and summarizing this information, the current SLR on ETs provides an overview of the publication trends, key team variables explored (team inputs and processes), relevant papers, journals, and research methodologies used in the field of ETs in the venture creation phase of entrepreneurship. After reporting the initial information related to the included studies, we have provided the analysis and synthesis of the results.

For the current SLR, we designed a thematic analysis to identify and analyze themes within the identified studies related to ETs. This thematic analysis is based on the Input-Process-Output (IPO) model which provides a structured framework for analyzing and categorizing data (Zhang et al., 2021). Thematic analysis based on this model allows for a comprehensive examination of various aspects of a phenomenon, including its inputs, processes, and outputs. The IPO is used in various fields, including systems theory, management, engineering, and psychology, to understand and analyze complex systems and processes (Borrego et al., 2014; Chang and Chien, 2012; Carbone et al., 2022; Fan et al., 2022). Moreover, this model has been applied in studies exploring the role of teams in the context of entrepreneurship to gain a comprehensive understanding of their functioning and outcomes (Antoni and Hertel, 2009; Bolzani et al., 2019; Zhang et al., 2021). The model is based on the idea that any system can be broken down into three main components: the "Inputs" sections represent the resources, factors, or variables that are fed into the system at the beginning, the "Process" sections include activities, operations, transformations, or actions that occur within the system, "Outputs" include the results or products that are generated as a result of the system's processes (Ilgen et al., 2005; Bolzani et al., 2019).

To conduct a thematic analysis, we first extract relevant information and findings from the included studies, focusing on the ETs inputs and processes in the venture creation phase. Then, we used a thematic synthesis approach to systematically group and categorize the extracted data into themes and sub-themes. In our case, we divided the papers into two distinct groups based on their emphasis on team input and team process. The main theme identified in the SLR on team input is team composition, with sub-themes including diversity, human capital, and previous experience. By applying the thematic analysis approach to the findings of the SLR, we provide a comprehensive understanding of the inputs and processes that influence team performance and venture outcomes during the venture creation phase. Table 9.4 presents the list of papers that explored team inputs in this phase. Table 9.5 reports the main identified themes comprised of team networking, team cognition, and team conflict. Thus, by using the IPO model, we can systematically organize data into meaningful themes related to inputs, processes, and outputs. Such organizing approaches provide a clear understanding of the different components and their interrelationships. As demonstrated in Figure 9.2, the IPO model serves as a visual tool to summarize our findings coherently.

DISCUSSION

The SLRs encompass a comprehensive and systematized search procedure to identify all relevant studies on the topic (Xiao and Watson, 2019). Since SLRs follow transparent and systematic guidelines which include well-defined criteria for paper selection, data extraction, and quality assessment, this stringent process ensures the authors that they would reach the relevant studies while minimizing bias (Williams et al., 2021). In addition, SLRs serve a crucial role in assessing the breadth and depth of the available evidence, enabling researchers to identify gaps in knowledge and provide a narrative synthesis of the findings (Snyder, 2019). This qualitative approach is particularly suitable when the aim is to explore a broad research question or provide an overview of the existing literature without conducting quantitative pooling of data (Donthu et al., 2021).

Conducting SLR is particularly beneficial when the scope of the review is specific, as it enables a focused and thorough examination of the literature (Snyder, 2019). Since our study focuses on the role of teams in the venture creation process, an SLR allows us to comprehensively summarize and synthesize the existing literature on this specific research topic. In our case, the SLR approach ensures that a wide range of studies exploring different aspects

Table 9.4 Selected papers on team inputs in venture creation phase

Main theme		
Team composition	Method	Journal
Hmieleski and Sheppard (2019)	Quantitative	*Journal of Management*
Hoogendoorn (2013)	Quantitative	*Management Science*
Jin et al. (2017)	Qualitative	*Entrepreneurship Theory and Practice*
Vanaelst et al. (2006)	Qualitative	*Entrepreneurship Theory and Practice*
Ben-Hafaïedh, Micozzi, and Pattitoni (2018)	Qualitative	*The Journal of Technology Transfer*
Knockaert and Vanacker (2013)	Quantitative	*Small Business Economics*
Hechavarria et al. (2019)	Qualitative	*Journal of Small Business Management*
Kaiser and Müller (2015)	Quantitative	*Small Business Economics*
De Jong, Song, and Song (2013)	Quantitative	*Journal of Management*
Zhao, Song, and Storm (2013)	Quantitative	*Entrepreneurship Theory and Practice*
Sine, Mitsuhashi, and Kirsch (2006)	Quantitative	*Academy of Management Journal*
Steffens, Terjesen, and Davidsson (2012)	Quantitative	*Small Business Economics*
Muñoz-Bullon, Sanchez-Bueno, and Vos-Saz (2015)	Quantitative	*Entrepreneurship and Regional Development*
Zheng (2012)	Quantitative	*Journal of Business Venturing*
Pérez-Calero, Larrañeta, and Wright (2019)	Quantitative	*Corporate Governance: An International Review*
Shrader and Siegel (2007)	Quantitative	*Entrepreneurship Theory and Practice*
Boeker and Wiltbank (2005)	Quantitative	*Organization Science*
Haeussler, Hennicke, and Mueller (2019)	Quantitative	*Strategic Entrepreneurship Journal*
Samuelsson and Davidsson (2009)	Quantitative	*Small Business Economics*

Table 9.5 *Selected papers on team processes in the venture creation phase*

Main themes		Method	Journal
	Grandi and Grimaldi (2003)	Qualitative	*Small Business Economics*
	Brannon, Wiklund, and Haynie (2013)	Quantitative	*Entrepreneurship Theory and Practice*
Networking	Hasan and Koning (2019)	Quantitative	*Strategic Management Journal*
	Lundqvist (2014)	Qualitative	*Technovation*
	Shaw, Wilson, and Pret (2017)	Qualitative	*International Small Business Journal*
	Watson, Ponthieu, and Critelli (1995)	Quantitative	*Journal of Business Venturing*
	Aldrich and Kim (2007)	Qualitative	*Strategic Entrepreneurship Journal*
	Brinckmann and Hoegl (2011)	Quantitative	*Entrepreneurship Journal*
	Clarysse and Moray (2004)	Qualitative	*Journal of Business Venturing*
	Visintin and Pittino (2014)	Quantitative	*Technovation*
	Breugst, Patzelt, and Rathgeber (2015)	Qualitative	*Journal of Business Venturing*
	Huang, Souitaris, and Barsade (2019)	Quantitative	*Strategic Management Journal*
Team cognition	Ensley et al. (2006)	Quantitative	*The Leadership Quarterly*
	Hmieleski, Cole, and Baron (2012)	Quantitative	*Journal of Management*
	Wang, Zhou, and Lan (2019)	Quantitative	*Industrial Management and Data Systems*
Team conflict	Ensley and Pearce (2001)	Quantitative	*Journal of Organizational Behavior*
	Breugst and Shepherd (2017)	Quantitative	*Entrepreneurship Theory and Practice*

of team concepts in entrepreneurship are included, reducing the risk of missing important literature.

Furthermore, our study directly responds to Bolzani et al.'s (2019) call to investigate trade-offs between different characteristics of ETs during the seed

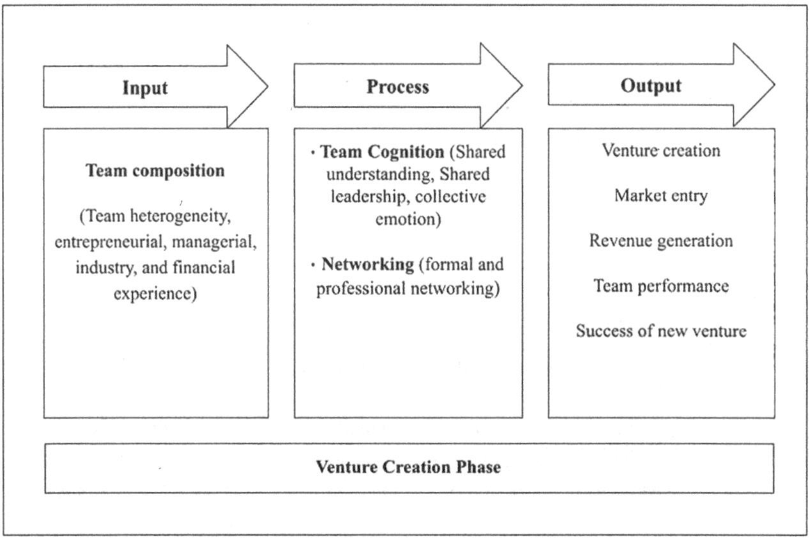

Source: Authors' own.

Figure 9.2 Conceptual Input-Process-Output (IPO) model

and start-up stages and answers the question "What characteristics do ETs need during different stages of the business?" In response to this call, we conducted an SLR specifically focused on the processes and characteristics of the team during the start-up phase of the business. Specifically, conducting SLRs facilitates the process of synthesis of the findings in the existing literature on a research topic (Donthu et al., 2021). In the current SLR, by using this method we highlight areas that require further investigation and contribute to the existing knowledge base on the role of a team in entrepreneurship. For example, through this SLR we address the gap related to the team composition in the team literature. Current literature on team composition focuses mainly on individuals' abilities and job-related skills rather than on team members' psychological and emotional aspects (Soleimani and Stauffer 2024). As a result, studies on ETs have not extensively explored the psychological and emotional factors that can impact ET performance and business outcomes (Xiao et al., 2020). Therefore, we suggest that further research is needed to understand how collective emotions and psychological dimensions can foster entrepreneurial behaviors during different phases of the entrepreneurship life cycle and how they influence venture and team outcomes.

Moreover, by systematically reviewing the ET literature, the results provide evidence-based insights and recommendations regarding the role of a team in a particular phase of entrepreneurship. Specifically, through thematic analysis of the studies and utilizing the IPO model for identifying and categorizing team inputs and processes, we gain a deeper comprehension of the key team inputs during various phases of the entrepreneurial life cycle and their potential influence on the team selection process. These findings can inform entrepreneurs, policymakers, and researchers about the importance of team dynamics and how it impacts entrepreneurial success. Such insights can guide the development of effective team-building strategies, training programs, and policy interventions.

Limitations of the SLR

Despite the potential advantages of SLR, this methodology has limitations that researchers need to be aware of. Here are some common limitations associated with SLRs.

First, in terms of the databases that are selected for SLR, there is a possibility of missing relevant studies that are indexed in other databases. For this reason, the researchers suggest considering the use of multiple data sources instead of a single source (Cui et al., 2020). Relying on one data source will increase the likelihood of missing relevant studies that either use diverse terminology or are classified differently in other databases. Importantly, using multiple data sources decreases the bias of database selection and increases the likelihood of capturing a more diverse range of relevant studies (Jeong and Yoo, 2022).

Second, the process of selecting papers for inclusion in the SLR can be subjective, and if not conducted carefully, it can introduce bias in the results. Defining appropriate inclusion and exclusion criteria helps the researchers to select relevant studies that are most relevant to their research question (Fisch and Block, 2018). However, improper inclusion and exclusion criteria have the potential to achieve comprehensive coverage of relevant papers in databases (Jahan et al., 2016). Similarly, the inclusion of broader data would provide a more comprehensive exploration of the subject and facilitate a better understanding of perspectives in both academic and practical settings (Jeong and Yoo, 2022). For example, in our SLR, book chapters and dissertations were excluded during the screening process. This criterion narrows the scope of the review and potentially omits relevant information that could be found in these excluded sources.

Third, the researchers sometimes define a specific period for selecting the papers in their inclusion and exclusion criteria. By excluding studies published before the specified timeframe, the review may lack a comprehensive understanding of the development and evolution of the topic (Snyder, 2019). In our study, for instance, we designated 1985 as the starting point for paper selection, as it denoted the beginning of substantial interest in the role of teams within the field of entrepreneurship (Landström, 2020).

Fourth, the use of English-language papers is prevalent in various research contexts, particularly in the fields of management and entrepreneurship (e.g., Shiferaw et al., 2023; Watts and Robertson, 2011). Although English has become the dominant language for the international dissemination of research, excluding non-English-language work raises the likelihood of potential language bias and limitations (Demir et al., 2020; Faling et al., 2019; Shabbir et al., 2022).

Fifth, in the screening phase of the SLR search, researchers restrict their keyword searches to specific journals (e.g., McDonald et al., 2015). Focusing exclusively on particular journals may neglect insights and research conducted outside these specific journals such as Academic Journal Guide/ABS, and Australian Business Deans Council (Kumar et al., 2022; Mio et al., 2020), limiting the comprehensiveness of the study. Since these journals represent a portion of the literature, they do not encompass the entirety of research conducted in the field.

Furthermore, in many cases, researchers utilize meta-analysis as a complementary tool to an SLR to synthesize empirical evidence from quantitative studies (Shaw and Ertug, 2017; Zupic and Čater, 2015). Additionally, meta-analysis helps the researchers to uncover relationships between variables, testing hypotheses especially when a sufficient number of homogeneous studies are available (Brandstätter, 2011; Donthu et al., 2021). For instance, Howard and Boudreaux (2024) conducted an SLR and meta-analysis to explore the relationship between personality traits and entrepreneurship. Similarly, Pennetta et al. (2023) applied SLR and meta-analysis to classify and interlink entrepreneurial skills such as abilities, skills, and competencies, which were inconsistently used in the field of entrepreneurship. Whereas SLRs provide a narrative summary and identify themes in the literature, a meta-analysis adds a quantitative dimension, offers statistical evidence, and combines the results of multiple studies to derive overall conclusions and estimate effect sizes (Paul and Barari, 2022).

Therefore, the choice between these methods or a mix of them depends on various factors, including the specific research objectives, the scope of the review, the availability of homogeneous studies, and the desired level of quantitative or qualitative analysis required to address the research questions effectively (Donthu et al., 2021; Paul and Barari, 2022; Snyder, 2019).

CONCLUSION

Throughout this chapter, we have emphasized the importance of using SLR as a scientific method for researchers in the field of entrepreneurship. Therefore, by presenting an SLR as an example, we planned to provide a practical guide on following the standard steps in this methodology to obtain valuable results that respond to the identified research questions. Indeed, there are many more prospects for systematic techniques than outlined here. However, we intended to show the value and benefits of using the SLR methodology in reviewing and synthesizing the existing literature on entrepreneurship.

REFERENCES

Aldrich, H. E., and Kim, P. H. (2007), 'Small worlds, infinite possibilities? How social networks affect entrepreneurial team formation and search', *Strategic Entrepreneurship Journal*, **1** (1–2), 147–165.

Antoni, C., and Hertel, G. (2009), 'Team processes, their antecedents, and consequences: Implications for different types of teamwork', *European Journal of Work and Organizational Psychology*, **18** (3), 253–266.

Banha, F., Coelho, L. S., and Flores, A. (2022), 'Entrepreneurship education: A systematic literature review and identification of an existing gap in the field', *Education Sciences*, **12** (5), 336.

Ben-Hafaïedh, C., Micozzi, A., and Pattitoni, P. (2018), 'Academic spin-offs' entrepreneurial teams and performance: A subgroups approach', *The Journal of Technology Transfer*, **43** (3), 714–733.

Blenker, P., Elmholdt, S. T., Frederiksen, S. H., Korsgaard, S., and Wagner, K. (2014), 'Methods in entrepreneurship education research: A review and integrative framework', *Education + Training*, **56**(8/9), 697–715.

Boeker, W., and Wiltbank, R. (2005), 'New venture evolution and managerial capabilities', *Organization Science*, **16** (2), 123–133.

Bolzani, D., Fini, R., Napolitano, S., and Toschi, L. (2019), 'Entrepreneurial teams: An input process-outcome framework', *Foundations and Trends® in Entrepreneurship*, **15** (2), 56–258.

Borrego, M., Foster, M. J., and Froyd, J. E. (2014), 'Systematic literature reviews in engineering education and other developing interdisciplinary fields', *Journal of Engineering Education*, **103** (1), 45–76.

Brandstätter, H. (2011), 'Personality aspects of entrepreneurship: A look at five meta-analyses', *Personality and Individual Differences*, **51** (3), 222–230.

Brannon, D. L., Wiklund, J., and Haynie, J. M. (2013), 'The varying effects of family relationships in entrepreneurial teams', *Entrepreneurship Theory and Practice*, **37** (1), 107–132.

Braun, V., and Clarke, V. (2006), 'Using thematic analysis in psychology', *Qualitative Research in Psychology*, **3** (2), 77–101.

Breugst, N., and Shepherd, D. A. (2017), 'If you fight with me, I'll get mad! A social model of entrepreneurial effect', *Entrepreneurship Theory and Practice*, **41** (3), 379–418.

Breugst, N., Patzelt, H., and Rathgeber, P. (2015), How should we divide the pie? Equity distribution and its impact on entrepreneurial teams', *Journal of Business Venturing*, **30** (1), 66–94.

Brinckmann, J., and Hoegl, M. (2011), 'Effects of initial teamwork capability and initial relational capability on the development of new technology-based firms', *Strategic Entrepreneurship Journal*, **5** (1), 37–57.

Calabrò, A., Vecchiarini, M., Gast, J., Campopiano, G., De Massis, A., and Kraus, S. (2019), 'Innovation in family firms: A systematic literature review and guidance for future research', *International Journal of Management Reviews*, **21** (3), 317–355.

Cao, Z., and Shi, X. (2021), 'A systematic literature review of entrepreneurial ecosystems in advanced and emerging economies', *Small Business Economics*, **57**, 75–110.

Carbone, E., Cirillo, A., Saggese, S., and Sarto, F. (2022), 'IPO in family business: A systematic review and directions for future research', *Journal of Family Business Strategy*, **13** (1), 100433.

Chang, H. H., and Chien, G. C. (2012), 'Input-process-output of hotel training in Taiwan', *Asia Pacific Journal of Tourism Research*, **17** (3), 246–260.

Champenois, C., Lefebvre, V., and Ronteau, S. (2020), 'Entrepreneurship as practice: A systematic literature review of a nascent field', *Entrepreneurship and Regional Development*, **32** (3–4), 281–312.

Chen, M. H., Chang, Y. Y., and Chang, Y. C. (2017), 'The trinity of entrepreneurial team dynamics: cognition, conflicts, and cohesion', *International Journal of Entrepreneurial Behaviour and Research*, **23** (6), 934–951.

Clarysse, B., and Moray, N. (2004), 'A process study of entrepreneurial team formation: The case of a research-based spin-off', *Journal of Business Venturing*, **19** (1), 55–79.

Cooney, T. M. (2005), 'What is an entrepreneurial team?', *International Small Business Journal*, **23** (3), 226–235.

Cui, Y., Kara, S., and Chan, K. C. (2020), 'Manufacturing big data ecosystem: A systematic literature review', *Robotics and Computer-Integrated Manufacturing*, **62**, 101861.

Das, W., Das, S., and Chattopadhyay, M. (2021), 'The emergence of the entrepreneurial team as a research field – way forward', *Journal of Small Business and Enterprise Development*, **28** (6), 831–855.

Davis, J., Mengersen, K., Bennett, S., and Mazerolle, L. (2014), 'Viewing systematic reviews and meta-analysis in social research through different lenses', *SpringerPlus*, **3**, 1–9.

De Jong, A., Song, M., and Song, L. Z. (2013), 'How lead founder personality affects new venture performance: The mediating role of team conflict', *Journal of Management*, **39** (7), 1825–1854.

De Mol, E., Khapova, S. N., and Elfring, T. (2015), 'Entrepreneurial team cognition: A review', *International Journal of Management Reviews*, **17** (2), 232–255.

Demir, C., Werner, A., Kraus, S., and Jones, P. (2020), 'Hybrid entrepreneurship: A systematic literature review', *Journal of Small Business and Entrepreneurship*, **34** (1), 29–52.

Domurath, A., Coviello, N., Patzelt, H., and Ganal, B. (2020), 'New venture adaptation in international markets: A goal orientation theory perspective', *Journal of World Business*, **55** (1), 101019.

Donthu, N., Kumar, S., Mukherjee, D., Pandey, N., and Lim, W. M. (2021), 'How to conduct a bibliometric analysis: An overview and guidelines', *Journal of Business Research*, **133**, 285–296.

Eden, D. (2002), 'From the editors: Replication, meta-analysis, scientific progress, and AMJ's publication policy', *Academy of Management Journal*, **45** (5), 841–846.

Ensley, M. D., Hmieleski, K. M., and Pearce, C. L. (2006), 'The importance of vertical and shared leadership within new venture top management teams: Implications for the performance of startups', *The Leadership Quarterly*, **17** (3), 217–231.

Ensley, M., and Pearce, C. (2001), 'Shared cognition in top management teams: Implications for new venture performance', *Journal of Organizational Behavior*, **22** (2), 145–160.

Faling, M., Biesbroek, R., Karlsson-Vinkhuyzen, S., and Termeer, K. (2019), 'Policy entrepreneurship across boundaries: A systematic literature review', *Journal of Public Policy*, **39** (2), 393–422.

Fan, Z., Sun, H., Wang, L., Zhu, M., and Peng, T. (2022), 'Team idiosyncratic deals and team breakthrough innovation: Based on the perspective of the input-process-output model', *Frontiers in Psychology*, **13**, 974569.

Farrell, A., Mapanga, W., Chitha, N., Ashton, J., and Joffe, M. (2022), 'Characteristics, enablers and barriers affecting entrepreneurial behavior for academics in low-and middle-income countries: A scoping review', *Development Southern Africa*, **39** (4), 589–603.

Fisch, C., and Block, J. (2018), 'Six tips for your (systematic) literature review in business and management research', *Management Review Quarterly*, **68**, 103–106.

Fox, J., Pittaway, L., and Uzuegbunam, I. (2018), 'Simulations in entrepreneurship education: Serious games and learning through play', *Entrepreneurship Education and Pedagogy*, **1** (1), 61–89.

Galvão, A., Ferreira, J. J., and Marques, C. (2018), 'Entrepreneurship education and training as facilitators of regional development: A systematic literature review', *Journal of Small Business and Enterprise Development*, **25** (1), 17–40.

Godonoga, A., and Sporn, B. (2023), 'The conceptualisation of socially responsible universities in higher education research: A systematic literature review', *Studies in Higher Education*, **48** (3), 445–459.

Grandi, A., and Grimaldi, R. (2003), 'Exploring the networking characteristics of new venture founding teams: A study of Italian academic spin-off', *Small Business Economics*, **21** (4), 329–341.

Gruber, M. (2002). 'Transformation as a challenge: New ventures on their way to viable entities'. In Füglistaller, U., Pleitner, H., Volery, T., and Weber, W. (eds.), *Radical change in the world: Will SMEs soar or crash?*, St Gallen: University of St. Gallen, pp. 193–201.

Gurevitch, J., Koricheva, J., Nakagawa, S., and Stewart, G. (2018), 'Meta-analysis and the science of research synthesis', *Nature*, **555** (7695), 175–182.

Guzzo, R. A., Jackson, S. E., and Katzell, R. A. (1987), 'Meta-analysis analysis', *Research in Organizational Behavior*, **9** (1), 407–442.

Haeussler, C., Hennicke, M., and Mueller, E. (2019), 'Founder–inventors and their investors: Spurring firm survival and growth', *Strategic Entrepreneurship Journal*, **13** (3), 288–325.

Harvey, C., Kelly, A., Morris, H., and Rowlinson, M. (2010), 'The Association of Business Schools', *Academic Journal Quality Guide*, **4**, 1–15.

Hasan, S., and Koning, R. (2019), 'Prior ties and the limits of peer effects on startup team performance', *Strategic Management Journal*, **40** (9), 1394–1416.

Hausberg, J. P., and Korreck, S. (2020), 'Business incubators and accelerators: A co-citation analysis-based, systematic literature review', *The Journal of Technology Transfer*, **45**, 151–176.

Hechavarria, D., Bullough, A., Brush, C., and Edelman, L. (2019), 'High-growth women's entrepreneurship: Fueling social and economic development', *Journal of Small Business Management*, **57** (1), 5–13.

Hmieleski, K. M., Cole, M. S., and Baron, R. A. (2012), 'Shared authentic leadership and new venture performance', *Journal of Management*, **38** (5), 1476–1499.

Hmieleski, K. M., and Sheppard, L. D. (2019), 'The yin and yang of entrepreneurship: Gender differences in the importance of communal and agentic characteristics for entrepreneurs' subjective well-being and performance', *Journal of Business Venturing*, **34** (4), 709–730.

Hoogendoorn, S., Oosterbeek, H., and Van Praag, M. (2013), 'The impact of gender diversity on the performance of business teams: Evidence from a field experiment', *Management Science*, **59** (7), 1514–1528.

Howard, M. C., and Boudreaux, M. (2024), 'A systematic literature review and meta-analysis of entrepreneurial personality', *Entrepreneurship Research Journal*, **14**(1), 283–312.

Huang, T. Y., Souitaris, V., and Barsade, S. G. (2019), 'Which matters more? Group fear versus hope in entrepreneurial escalation of commitment', *Strategic Management Journal*, **40** (11), 1852.

Huber, L. R., Sloof, R., Van Praag, M., and Parker, S. C. (2020), 'Diverse cognitive skills and team performance: A field experiment based on an entrepreneurship education program', *Journal of Economic Behavior and Organization*, **177**, 569–588.

Ilgen, D. R., Hollenbeck, J. R., Johnson, M., and Jundt, D. (2005), 'Teams in organizations: From input-process-output models to IMOI models', *Annual Review of Psychology*, **56**, 517–543.

Jahan, N., Naveed, S., Zeshan, M., and Tahir, M. A. (2016), 'How to conduct a systematic review: A narrative literature review', *Cureus*, **8** (11), e864.

Jeong, E., and Yoo, H. (2022), 'A systematic literature review of women in social entrepreneurship', *Service Business*, **16** (4), 935–970.

Jin, L., Madison, K., Kraiczy, N. D., Kellermanns, F. W., Crook, T. R., and Xi, J. (2017), 'Entrepreneurial team composition characteristics and new venture performance: A meta-analysis', *Entrepreneurship Theory and Practice*, **41** (5), 743–771.

Kaiser, U., and Müller, B. (2015), 'Skill heterogeneity in startups and its development over time', *Small Business Economics*, **45** (4), 787–804.

Kamm, J. B., Shuman, J. C., Seeger, J. A., and Nurick, A. J. (1990), 'Entrepreneurial teams in new venture creation: A research agenda', *Entrepreneurship Theory and Practice*, **14** (4), 7–17.

Kaulio, M. A. (2003), 'Initial conditions or process of development? Critical incidents in the early stages of new ventures', *R&D Management*, **33** (2), 165–175.

Khitous, F., Strozzi, F., Urbinati, A., and Alberti, F. (2020), 'A systematic literature network analysis of existing themes and emerging research trends in circular economy', *Sustainability*, **12** (4), 1633.

Klotz, A. C., Hmieleski, K. M., Bradley, B. H., and Busenitz, L. W. (2014), 'New venture teams: A review of the literature and roadmap for future research', *Journal of Management*, **40** (1), 226–255.

Knockaert, M., and Vanacker, T. (2013), 'The association between venture capitalists' selection and value-adding behavior: Evidence from early-stage high-tech venture capitalists', *Small Business Economics*, **40**, 493–509.

Kraus, S., Breier, M., and Dasí-Rodríguez, S. (2020), 'The art of crafting a systematic literature review in entrepreneurship research', *International Entrepreneurship and Management Journal*, **16**, 1023–1042.

Kumar, S., Sahoo, S., Lim, W. M., and Dana, L. P. (2022), 'Religion as a social shaping force in entrepreneurship and business: Insights from a technology-empowered systematic literature review', *Technological Forecasting and Social Change*, **175**, 121393.

Landström, H. (2020), 'The evolution of entrepreneurship as a scholarly field', *Foundations and Trends® in Entrepreneurship*, **16** (2), 65–243.

Lazar, M., Miron-Spektor, E., Agarwal, R., Erez, M., Goldfarb, B., and Chen, G. (2020), 'Entrepreneurial team formation', *Academy of Management Annals*, **14** (1), 29–59.

Lim, J. Y. K., and Busenitz, L. W. (2020), 'Evolving human capital of entrepreneurs in an equity crowdfunding era', *Journal of Small Business Management*, **58**(1), 106–129.

Liñán, F., and Fayolle, A. (2015), 'A systematic literature review on entrepreneurial intentions: Citation, thematic analyses, and research agenda', *International Entrepreneurship and Management Journal*, **11**, 907–933.

Liu, D., Zhu, T., Huang, X., Wang, M., and Huang, M. (2021), 'Narcissism and entrepreneurship: a systematic review and an agenda for future research', *Frontiers in Psychology*, **12**, 657681.

Loane, S., Bell, J., and Cunningham, I. (2014), 'Entrepreneurial founding team exits in rapidly internationalizing SMEs: A double edged sword', *International Business Review*, **23** (2), 468–477.

Lundqvist, M. A. (2014), 'The importance of surrogate entrepreneurship for incubated Swedish technology ventures', *Technovation*, **34** (2), 93–100.

Luor, T., Lu, H. P., Yu, H., and Chang, K. (2014), 'Trends in and contributions to entrepreneurship research: a broad review of literature from 1996 to June 2012', *Scientometrics*, **99** (2), 353–369.

Martínez-Gregorio, S., Badenes-Ribera, L., and Oliver, A. (2021), 'Effect of entrepreneurship education on entrepreneurship intention and related outcomes in educational contexts: A meta-analysis', *The International Journal of Management Education*, **19**(3), 100545.

Massaro, M., Dumay, J. and Guthrie, J. (2016), 'On the shoulders of giants: undertaking a structured literature review in accounting', *Accounting, Auditing and Accountability Journal*, **29** (5), 767–801.

Mathisen, M. T., and Rasmussen, E. (2019), 'The development, growth, and performance of university spin-offs: A critical review', *The Journal of Technology Transfer*, **44** (6), 1891–1938.

Mariani, M. M., Al-Sultan, K., and De Massis, A. (2023), 'Corporate social responsibility in family firms: A systematic literature review', *Journal of Small Business Management*, **61** (3), 1192–1246.

Martin, B. C., McNally, J. J., and Kay, M. J. (2013), 'Examining the formation of human capital in entrepreneurship: A meta-analysis of entrepreneurship education outcomes', *Journal of Business Venturing*, **28** (2), 211–224.

Maryami, S., Loi, M., Martinez, M., and Di Guardo, M. C. (2023), 'On the role of team passion in inventing, founding and developing: What happens in the early stages of entrepreneurship?', *Journal of Small Business and Enterprise Development*, **30**(4), 692–713.

McDonald, S., Gan, B. C., Fraser, S. S., Oke, A., and Anderson, A. R. (2015), 'A review of research methods in entrepreneurship 1985–2013', *International Journal of Entrepreneurial Behavior and Research*, **21** (3), 291–315.

Mingers, J., and Willmott, H. (2013), 'Taylorizing business school research: On the "one best way" performative effects of journal ranking list', *Human Relations*, **66** (8), 1051–1073.

Mio, C., Panfilo, S., and Blundo, B. (2020), 'Sustainable development goals and the strategic role of business: A systematic literature review', *Business Strategy and the Environment*, **29** (8), 3220–3245.

Moher, D., Shamseer, L., Clarke, M., Ghersi, D., Liberati, A., Petticrew, M., ... and Stewart, L. A. (2015), 'Preferred reporting items for systematic review and meta-analysis protocols (PRISMA-P) 2015 statement', *Systematic Reviews*, **4** (1), 1–9.

Moher, D., Liberati, A., Tetzlaff, J., Altman, D. G., and PRISMA Group (2009), 'Preferred reporting items for systematic reviews and meta-analyses: The PRISMA statement, *Annals of Internal Medicine*, **151** (4), 264–269.

Mongeon, P., and Paul-Hus, A. (2016), 'The journal coverage of Web of Science and Scopus: A comparative analysis', *Scientometrics*, **106**, 213–228.

Morrison, A., Polisena, J., Husereau, D., Moulton, K., Clark, M., Fiander, M., ... and Rabb, D. (2012), 'The effect of English-language restriction on systematic review-based meta-analyses: A systematic review of empirical studies', *International Journal of Technology Assessment in Health Care*, **28** (2), 138–144.

Motta, V. F., and Galina, S. V. R. (2023), 'Experiential learning in entrepreneurship education: A systematic literature review', *Teaching and Teacher Education*, **121**, 103919.

Muñoz, P., and Cohen, B. (2018), 'Sustainable entrepreneurship research: Taking stock and looking ahead', *Business Strategy and the Environment*, **27** (3), 300–322.

Muñoz-Bullon, F., Sanchez-Bueno, M. J., and Vos-Saz, A. (2015), 'Startup team contributions and new firm creation: The role of founding team experience', *Entrepreneurship and Regional Development*, **27** (1–2), 80–105.

Nabi, G., Liñán, F., Fayolle, A., Krueger, N., and Walmsley, A. (2017), 'The impact of entrepreneurship education in higher education: A systematic review and research agenda', *Academy of Management Learning and Education*, **16** (2), 277–299.

Newman, A., Herman, H. M., Schwarz, G., and Nielsen, I. (2018), 'The effects of employees' creative self-efficacy on innovative behavior: The role of entrepreneurial leadership', *Journal of Business Research*, **89**, 1–9.

Omri, A., and Boujelbene, Y. (2015), 'Entrepreneurial team: How human and social capital influence entrepreneurial opportunity identification and mobilization of external resources', *Journal of Entrepreneurship, Management and Innovation*, **11**(3), 25–42.

Page, M. J., McKenzie, J. E., Bossuyt, P. M., Boutron, I., Hoffmann, T. C., Mulrow, C. D., ... and Moher, D. (2021), 'The PRISMA 2020 statement: An updated guideline for reporting systematic reviews', *International Journal of Surgery*, **88**, 105906.

Patrício, L., and Franco, M. (2022), 'A systematic literature review about team diversity and team performance: Future lines of investigation', *Administrative Sciences*, **12** (1), 31.

Paul, J., and Barari, M. (2022), 'Meta-analysis and traditional systematic literature reviews: What, why, when, where, and how?', *Psychology and Marketing*, **39** (6), 1099–1115.

Pennetta, S., Anglani, F. and Mathews, S. (2023), 'Navigating through entrepreneurial skills, competencies and capabilities: A systematic literature review and the development of the entrepreneurial ability model', *Journal of Entrepreneurship in Emerging Economies*, **16** (4). https://doi.org/10.1108/JEEE-09-2022-0257.

Pérez-Calero, L., Larrañeta, B., and Wright, M. (2019), 'Initial public offering valuation and prior shared experience in the boardroom of threshold ventures: A study of industry effects', *Corporate Governance: An International Review*, **27** (5), 322–340.

Pittaway, L., Holt, R., and Broad, J. (2014), 'Synthesising knowledge in entrepreneurship research–the role of systematic literature'. In Chell, E., and Karatas-Ozkan, M. (eds.), *Handbook of research on small business and entrepreneurship*, Cheltenham, UK and Northampton, MA, USA: Edward Elgar Publishing, pp. 83–105.

Pittaway, L., and Cope, J. (2007), 'Entrepreneurship education: A systematic review of the evidence', *International Small Business Journal*, **25** (5), 479–510.

Pret, T., and Cogan, A. (2019), 'Artisan entrepreneurship: A systematic literature review and research agenda', *International Journal of Entrepreneurial Behavior and Research*, **25** (4), 592–614.

Rao, P., Kumar, S., Chavan, M., and Lim, W. M. (2023), 'A systematic literature review on SME financing: Trends and future directions', *Journal of Small Business Management*, **61** (3), 1247–1277.

Rauch, A., and Frese, M. (2006), 'Meta-analysis as a tool for developing entrepreneurship research and theory.' In Wiklund, J., Dimov, D., Katz, J. A., and Shepherd, D. A. (eds.), *Entrepreneurship: Frameworks and empirical investigations from forthcoming leaders of European research* (Advances in Entrepreneurship, Firm Emergence and Growth, Vol. 9), Bingley, UK: Emerald Group Publishing Limited, pp. 29–51.

Rethlefsen, M. L., Kirtley, S., Waffenschmidt, S., Ayala, A. P., Moher, D., Page, M. J., and Koffel, J. B. (2021), 'PRISMA-S: An extension to the PRISMA statement for reporting literature searches in systematic reviews', *Systematic Reviews*, **10** (1), 1–19.

Samuelsson, M., and Davidsson, P. (2009), 'Does venture opportunity variation matter? Investigating systematic process differences between innovative and imitative new ventures', *Small Business Economics*, **33** (2), 229–255.

Santos, S. C., and Neumeyer, X. (2021), 'Culture and gender in entrepreneurial teams: The effect on team processes and outcomes', *Small Business Economics*, **58**, 1035–1050.

Schermuly, C. C., Creon, L., Gerlach, P., Graßmann, C., and Koch, J. (2022), 'Leadership styles and psychological empowerment: A meta-analysis', *Journal of Leadership and Organizational Studies*, **29** (1), 73–95.

Schuhmacher, M. C., and Thieu, H. T. (2022), 'The role of students, educators, and educational institutes in entrepreneurship education: A systematic literature review and directions for future research', *Entrepreneurship Education and Pedagogy*, **5** (3), 279–319.

Senali, M. G., Iranmanesh, M., Ghobakhloo, M., Gengatharen, D., Tseng, M. L., and Nilsashi, M. (2022), 'Flipped classroom in business and entrepreneurship education: A systematic review and future research agenda', *The International Journal of Management Education*, **20** (1), 100614.

Shabbir, M. S., Batool, F., and Mahmood, A. (2022), 'Trends in entrepreneurship education: A systematic literature review', *Higher Education, Skills and Work-based Learning*, **12** (6), 1040–1056.

Shaw, E., Wilson, J., and Pret, T. (2017), 'The process of embedding a small firm in its industrial context', *International Small Business Journal*, **35** (3), 219–243.

Shaw, J. D., and Ertug, G. (2017), 'The suitability of simulations and meta-analyses for submissions to academy of management journal', *Academy of Management Journal*, **60**(6), 2045–2049.

Shiferaw, R. M., Birbirsa, Z. A., and Werke, S. Z. (2023), 'Entrepreneurial leadership, learning organization and organizational culture relationship: A systematic literature

review', *Journal of Innovation and Entrepreneurship*, **12** (1), 38. https://doi.org/10.1186/s13731-023-00305-z.
Shrader, R., and Siegel, D. S. (2007), 'Assessing the relationship between human capital and firm performance: Evidence from technology-based new ventures', *Entrepreneurship Theory and Practice*, **31** (6), 893–908.
Sine, W. D., Mitsuhashi, H., and Kirsch, D. A. (2006), 'Revisiting Burns and Stalker: Formal structure and new venture performance in emerging economic sectors', *Academy of Management Journal*, **49** (1), 121–132.
Sirelkhatim, F., and Gangi, Y. (2015), 'Entrepreneurship education: A systematic literature review of curricula contents and teaching methods', *Cogent Business and Management*, **2** (1), 1052034.
Snyder, H. (2019), 'Literature review as a research methodology: An overview and guidelines', *Journal of Business Research*, **104**, 333–339.
Soleimani, L., and Stauffer, R. (2024), 'New venture teams and acquisition: Team composition matters', *Journal of Small Business Management*, **62**(2), 1030–1057.
Steffens, P., Terjesen, S., and Davidsson, P. (2012), 'Birds of a feather get lost together: New venture team composition and performance', *Small Business Economics*, **39** (3), 727–743.
Thomé, A. M. T., Scavarda, L. F., and Scavarda, A. J. (2016), 'Conducting systematic literature review in operations management', *Production Planning and Control*, **27** (5), 408–420.
Torraco, R. J. (2005), 'Writing integrative literature reviews: Guidelines and examples', *Human Resource Development Review*, **4** (3), 356–367.
Tranfield, D., Denyer, D., and Smart, P. (2003), 'Towards a methodology for developing evidence-informed management knowledge by means of systematic review', *British Journal of Management*, **14** (3), 207–222.
Vanaelst, I., Clarysse, B., Wright, M., Lockett, A., Moray, N., and S'Jegers, R. (2006), 'Entrepreneurial team development in academic spinouts: An examination of team heterogeneity', *Entrepreneurship Theory and Practice*, **30** (2), 249–271.
Visintin, F., and Pittino, D. (2014), 'Founding team composition and early performance of university-based spin-off companies', *Technovation*, **34** (1), 31–43.
Wang, G., Li, X., Zhou, J., and Lan, S. (2020), 'The influence of entrepreneurial team's cognitive adaptability on its risk decision making', *Industrial Management and Data Systems*, **120** (2), 329–349.
Watson, W. E., Ponthieu, L. D., and Critelli, J. W. (1995), 'Team interpersonal process effectiveness in venture partnerships and its connection to perceived success', *Journal of Business Venturing*, **10** (5), 393–411.
Watts, J., and Robertson, N. (2011), 'Burnout in university teaching staff: A systematic literature review', *Educational Research*, **53** (1), 33–50.
Williams Jr, R. I., Clark, L. A., Clark, W. R., and Raffo, D. M. (2021), 'Re-examining systematic literature review in management research: Additional benefits and execution protocols', *European Management Journal*, **39** (4), 521–533.
Xi, J., Kraus, S., Filser, M., and Kellermanns, F. W. (2015), 'Mapping the field of family business research: Past trends and future directions', *International Entrepreneurship and Management Journal*, **11**(1), 113–132.
Xiao, Y., Dowejko, M. K., Au, K., and Hsu, A. J. (2020), '"Jack-of-all-trades" with passion: Keener to pursue startup in a team?', *Journal of Small Business Management*, **58** (4), 806–833.
Xiao, Y., and Watson, M. (2019), 'Guidance on conducting a systematic literature review', *Journal of Planning Education and Research*, **39** (1), 93–112.

Zhang, Z., Zhu, L., Chen, G., Shang, L., Zhao, Q., and Ren, F. (2021), 'How entrepreneurial team heterogeneity impacts decision-making performance? An input-process-output approach', *Chinese Management Studies*, **16** (5), 965–992.

Zhao, Y. L., Song, M., and Storm, G. L. (2013), 'Founding team capabilities and new venture performance: The mediating role of strategic positional advantages', *Entrepreneurship Theory and Practice*, **37** (4), 789–814.

Zheng, Y. (2012), 'Unlocking founding team prior shared experience: A transactive memory system perspective', *Journal of Business Venturing*, **27** (5), 577–591.

Zupic, I., and Čater, T. (2015), 'Bibliometric methods in management and organization', *Organizational Research Methods*, **18** (3), 429–472.

10. Combining coherence and effectiveness in an entrepreneurship doctoral article-based dissertation

Sandrine Le Pontois and Stéphane Foliard

INTRODUCTION

The doctoral pathway is a process that starts with an initial exchange between the student and a potential supervisor about a research project (in this case, entrepreneurship). It ends when the doctoral thesis (a product) has been defended before an academic jury. Developing a doctorate is part of the formation of academic identities (Dowling et al., 2012) and includes a wide range of institutionalising actions (Yazdani & Shokooh, 2018). These are embedded in a pathway comprising several rites of passage that transform the doctoral student into a researcher, a doctor (Hodgson, 2020) and then an Assistant/Associate/Full professor. The cleverly ironic title of the article '"It's a PhD, not a Nobel Prize": how experienced examiners assess research theses' (Mullins & Kiley, 2002) sums up the difficulty of assessing the academic quality of doctoral work. It is no longer simply a matter of training a research novice to produce a relevant thesis that is critically engaged in the academic conversation, well-constructed and coherent, theoretically and methodologically sound, original, creative and elegant. Inscribed in a highly competitive international context, the doctoral process now often requires the production of early publications in scientific journals dedicated to entrepreneurship, with an ever-higher level of demand.

Initially, the PhD by publication was designed to enable practitioners who were already published[1] to gain high-level academic recognition (Butt, 2013). In a context of ever-accelerating academic productivism and strong competition, it quickly became a rational way to respond to both the pressure to publish and the canons of academic employability. A subject of study for just over two decades, the article-based thesis[2] is now a hot topic in the academic world, almost monopolistically among researchers in the educational sciences, even though there is still no real national or international consensus on what a PhD by publication is (Niven & Grant, 2012) and what it should include (Jackson, 2013) depending on the discipline. However, the training of PhDs in entrepreneurship is an issue that deserves to be addressed by the players in the field.[3] This question concerns the formation of professional identity and the professionalism of Entrepreneurship PhDs and supervisors.

Preceding the very function of the PhD to train responsible scholars (Lin & Cranton, 2005), should the sole choice of thesis format prevail (Frick, 2019) over the PhD project? Since the 1990s, the number of single-authored papers has been steadily decreasing in favour of the rise of co-authored papers (Hagen, 2010), and the determination of authorship credit in published dissertation is becoming a real issue in the training of PhD students.[4] At the same time, the number of PhDs by publication has steadily increased in the entrepreneurship research field. Finally, it is only very recently that critical approaches via feedback are proposed around the doctoral experience in entrepreneurship and more broadly in management sciences (e.g. Germain et al., 2020; Gaillard et al., 2023).

The purpose of this chapter is to give the PhD candidate in Entrepreneurship the insights and practical keys to combine coherence and effectiveness in entrepreneurship doctoral article-based dissertation. To do so, we draw on both an integrative literature review[5] and our own experience. We first propose elements of explanation for the rise of this format by analysing the contextual elements of the massification of scientific production in parallel with the standardisation and professionalisation of the doctoral path. Faced with the issues and challenges raised for PhD students, supervisors and research laboratories, we present the reasons why the article-based dissertation may constitute a methodological response that satisfies the current expectations of the academic world in entrepreneurship, without prejudging that it is of better quality than the monograph format. On the basis of this study, practical guidelines both for doctoral candidates intending to submit article-based dissertation and for supervisors and examiners are provided to support their reflection and decision making regarding the choice of format. Finally, we present a canva proposal (ABPhD^2 canva) to combine coherence and effectiveness in entrepreneurship doctoral article-based dissertation.

UNDERSTANDING THE RISE OF THE ARTICLE-BASED DISSERTATION: MASSIFICATION OF SCIENTIFIC PRODUCTION, STANDARDISATION AND PROFESSIONALISATION OF THE DOCTORAL PATH

Since the 1990s, academic work has been standardised (Vähämäki et al., 2021) in order to better compare different practices within a competitive and productivist global culture (Knights & Clarke, 2014; Kallio et al., 2016; Deuchar, 2008; Kihn & Näsi, 2017). This process of neoliberalisation of higher education supported by the introduction of new public management techniques at universities (Shore & Wright, 2000) has been widely studied (Cannizzo, 2018; Sutton, 2017). It has impacted on the educational objective: from developing PhD students' capacity for thought and inquiry towards preparing them for employment and for employability, e.g. to act entrepreneurially (Holdsworth, 2018) in an academic world of performance measures and benchmarking (Cannizzo, 2018).

The hypercompetitive culture of research (Coriat, 2019) and academic productivism led in fact to increased competition, both at individual (PhD candidates, supervisors and researchers) and institutional (higher education institutions) levels. The relationship to time is changing[6] in a context of constant acceleration (Rosa, 2010), following the model of performance management practices. Thus, the neoliberal university invites researchers to adopt individualistic approaches to scholarship and a performance culture (Dowling et al., 2012). The doctoral experience is then impacted, with the duration of completion now being much shorter (three years) with the parallel pressure to publish (Frick, 2019) inscribed in a productivist culture (Sharmini et al., 2015) oriented towards employability. Depending on the country, the relationship to the article-based dissertation varies between two extremes: either it is seen as a norm or it is seen by dissertation committees as a 'quick-fix' solution or an 'easy-way-out' to the qualification (Niven & Grant, 2012).

This productivism leads to the search for short-term tangible outcomes (high ranked journals) at the expense of long-term sustainable academic work. For example, US accounting research has been increasingly criticised for its lack of innovation and progress by training PhD students with a focus on standard journal content, methods and research topics (Pelger & Grottke, 2015). Curiosity and intellectual interest in reading and participating in academic conversation can be sacrificed for a streamlined and technical approach to using knowledge to produce research articles, with journal rankings as a benchmark for successful research. Yet the most innovative research is rarely produced in A-ranked journals. It is only after following a path of institutionalisation that the innovative contribution produced can be disseminated in these journals. In any case, inspired by a format model derived from the hard sciences, which are well versed in journal rankings, the article-based dissertation has gradually found its way into the humanities, particularly in management sciences and entrepreneurship.

Ultimately, the article-based dissertation seems like a win-win format (Frick, 2019) for PhD students, supervisors (Laurance et al., 2013 in Pretorius), peers and the whole scientific community. Indeed, it seems to respond to the constraints of time (papers seen as so many short projects during the doctoral course), productivity (producing to publish) and quality assurance of articles (thanks to the peer/double blind-reviewing system) with a view to employability in the academic field.[7] In 2015, 83% of the 50 participating educational institutions (UKCGE study) allowed PhD by publication or equivalent (Christianson et al., 2015).

MAJOR ISSUES AND CHALLENGES OF THE DOCTORAL PATHWAY FOR DOCTORAL STUDENTS, SUPERVISORS AND RESEARCH LABORATORIES IN A COMPETITIVE INTERNATIONAL CONTEXT

Entering a doctoral research pathway is therefore the PhD candidate's first step in elaborating and developing their professionality as an academic. Academic practice is the vehicle for moving from the periphery to the centre of professionality (Rae, 2017), i.e. from being a PhD student/candidate in entrepreneurship to being a PhD in entrepreneurship/assistant-associate professor or consultant in business. It is this shared peer practice that opens the doors to the research ecosystem and its explicit and implicit practices, codes and norms. PhD students develop their identity as young researchers by learning how research is conducted and how its conduct informs the activities of the research community (Löfström & Pyhältö, 2021). The creation of the researcher identity in the PhD student is supported by peers, colleagues in the professional environment and supervision (Mawson & Abbott, 2017). Three main areas constitute this academic practice: researchers' actions (reading, collecting data, (re)writing, publishing, presenting at conferences, evaluating, ...), their level of socialisation including their ability to integrate research communities, and their motivations to produce research by claiming a specific professional identity (Le Pontois, forthcoming publication). Thus, the professional identities of PhD students, supervisors and peers are interdependent as they evolve in the same communities. Entering the communities is the result of the legitimisation process: obtaining the PhD is the first step of this recognition, which is itself supported by the ability to publish.

The doctoral thesis is thus the entry point to academic practice from two major angles: academic writing (a central activity in higher education) and varied and iterative contingent learning cycles (de Lange & Wittek, 2014). However, the quality of doctoral work is measured by its contribution to knowledge and its originality (Gilbert, 2009; Lee, 2010). The aim for the doctoral student is to take part in academic practice through internalisation (acquisition of knowledge) and externalisation (participation in a practice), to use Vygotsky's model (1978). Writing may be perceived as identity formation (de Lange & Wittek, 2014) through the lenses of a study skills approach or an academic socialisation approach.

Several issues then emerge for the PhD candidate. First of all, the *main* challenge for the PhD candidate concerning their research production is to learn. Learning to collect and analyse data, learning to use methods consistent with the epistemological positioning of their research, learning to articulate and explain their results clearly in an academic conversation and learning to take into account the suggestions of reviewers to improve their research work, all this through the iterative experience of reading/writing/presenting. All of this is part of the necessary consideration of time, maturation and the influence of feedback on the thinking and writing experience (de Lange & Wittek, 2014). Furthermore, they have to project themselves into several types of professionalism (academic/corporate researcher) and reflect on a strategy to support the desired professional trajectory. If the chosen path is the academic one, the PhD candidate must ensure their potential to meet the standards of academic practices (see above) including networking. Other issues then emerge: their ability to read and write English (academia lingua) as a pass to establish credibility as an international researcher; their eligibility for research grants (fellowships) which often assess candidates on the basis of their previous publication capacity (impact and productivity) (Coriat, 2019); the choice to write a monograph or an article-based dissertation with intrinsic temporal issues that impact the writing itself, the degree of ownership of one's own writing (more or less individual or collective process) as well as the identity of the academic author (Burgess & Ivanič, 2010). The challenge here is for the PhD candidate to try to adjust as well as possible (or to limit the mismatch) between the temporality of the doctoral course – which is generally three years – and the temporality of writing: the monograph requires a long writing time versus the article-based thesis which is based on different 'mini-projects' with mix-methods, to be coordinated with the central question of the thesis (or study). In both cases, doctoral time is seen 'as circular', including a continuous series of time negotiations (Araújo, 2005).

Supervisors face other challenges. Choosing to supervise a PhD student requires having validated the fit between the PhD student's research project and the supervisor's own expertise, having assessed the candidate's learning, writing and perseverance skills, their ability to integrate into research communities and finally both being clear regarding the envisaged post-thesis professional project, i.e. the employability objective. Supervising an article-based dissertation or a monograph requires different support and a different relationship to the written production of the PhD student (see below). The supervisor's ability to meet these challenges conditions their legitimacy among peers (Le Pontois et al., forthcoming publication).

For the institution, via the research laboratories, the main issues are the quality of the doctoral training provided (success/dropout rate, professional insertion rate – professional or academic), the funding of this training and the ability to hire competent supervisors to accompany the PhD student to recognised publications in ranked journals.

REASONS WHY THE ARTICLE-BASED THESIS IS A 'GOOD' ANSWER TO THESE ISSUES AND CHALLENGES

Recurrently, two formats of doctoral thesis (de Lange & Wittek, 2014), also called 'dissertation book' (Fridlund, 2010), are presented as diverging: the 'monograph' format, also referred to as the 'traditional dissertation', and the 'paper/article-based thesis' format (see definitions in Table 10.1).

While the contours and processes of the monograph seem fairly clear in the minds of researchers and their communities, this is less the case for the paper/article-based thesis format. What are we actually talking about? In fact, the expressions 'paper-based thesis' and 'article-based thesis' cover different formal realities, more or less explicitly specified by other expressions (Table 10.2). This first semantic field thus refers to the intrinsic material of the thesis, the articles and chapters. A second semantic category is linked to the notion of publication ('PhD by publication', 'PhD dissertation book', 'dissertation

Table 10.1 Definitions: the 'PhD by publication' versus the 'monograph'

'The article-based dissertation' or 'the PhD by publication' (modern dissertation)	'in which a dissertation comprises a number of stand-alone "publishable" papers, along with introductory and concluding overviews' (Dowling et al., 2012: 293) '… consists of an unspecified number of stand-alone published or 'publishable' papers' (Robins & Kanowski, 2008) 'Articles suitable for publication and bounded together with an introduction chapter and integrated discussion chapter' (Baggs, 2011 in Lewis et al, 2021) '… consists of a number of published peer-reviewed academic papers or equivalents […] accompanied by an over-arching text [which] summarizes the contributions of the publications to knowledge in the field' (Peacock, 2017)
'The monograph' (traditional dissertation)	'A genre, in both form and content: including introduction, literature review, description of methods and procedures used, presentation of results, discussion of the meaning of the results, in an original research written as a unified and coherent work' (Duke & Beck, 1999) 'A comprehensive and extensive book with a theoretical part (introduction, concepts, literature review and theoretical framework) and an empirical part (design, data collection and analysis, results, discussion, conclusion/ implication, references)' (Fridlund, 2010)

Table 10.2 Semantic fields around the expression 'paper/article-based thesis' (16 articles in the corpus)

Semantic categories	Expressions	Authors of the corpus studied
1. Articles and chapters as thesis material	'paper-based thesis' 'article-based thesis'	Pretorius, 2016 De Lange, 2010 Lewis, 2020
2. Articles and chapters as publication material	'article-based dissertation' 'PhD by publication' 'Publication-based thesis' 'PhD dissertation book' 'publishing during the PhD' 'PhD by published works/ papers' 'dissertation book based on articles'	Lewis, 2020 Dowling, 2012 Frick, 2019 Jackson, 2013 O'Keeffe, 2019 Peacock, 2017 Robins & Kanowski, 2008 Sharmini, 2014 Horta, 2015 Fridlund, 2010 Peacock, 2017 Fridlund, 2010
3. Articles and chapters as *serial elements constituting an object*	'compilation thesis' 'compilation dissertation' 'dissertation book based on articles'	Fridlund, 2010
4. Articles and chapters as *characteristics of an innovative thesis format* in the humanities and social sciences	'modern thesis' 'alternative format'	Hagen, 2010 Duke & Beck, 1999
5. *Taxonomy proposal*	'PhD *by* publication' (in the sense of 'by means of') 'PhD *through* publication' 'PhD *with* publication' (alongside a main thesis) 'PhD *along* publication' (publication/project)	Niven, 2012

book based on article', 'publishing during the PhD', 'PhD by published works/ papers'). The third category evokes the idea of compilation: 'compilation thesis', 'compilation dissertation'. The fourth semantic category refers to the recent and innovative nature of the format employed by the use of the expression 'modern thesis'. Finally, Niven & Grant (2012) question the lack of rigour of the term, which does not cover the reality of the steps and processes used by the doctoral student to construct a thesis that includes scientific articles published during the doctoral path. They propose (category 5), following the example of Biggs evoking the forms of Entrepreneurship Education, names reflecting the approaches and writing projects of students enrolled in a doctoral path: 'PhD *by* publication', 'PhD *through* publication', 'PhD *with* publication' and 'PhD *along* publication'.

There are therefore as many formats of paper-based PhD dissertation as there are names, referring to the objective pursued by the PhD candidate. The first category refers to publications as a support for the thesis defended in the PhD dissertation. This thesis becomes a new contribution to the academic conversation. The second and third categories refer to publications as material that will be aggregated and presented in a more or less coherent way within a single work. These first three semantic categories present the format as a strategic choice of opportunity to publish. The fourth category notes the novelty of this format in the 2000s, a format that is institutionalised or in the process of being institutionalised in the field of entrepreneurship today. The fifth and final category proposes a unifying taxonomy of article-based dissertation names, taking up the previous categories.

What then are the decisive factors to take into account when choosing between the monograph and the article-based dissertation when pursuing a doctoral path in entrepreneurship? Curiously, this does not really seem to be a topic discussed in the entrepreneurship methodological literature. If the current standard of three years to complete a PhD and the possibility in several countries[8] to change the format along the way seem to encourage PhD students and their supervisors to turn to the article-based dissertation format, it is worth looking at the scientific literature on paper-based writing. Since very few articles on the subject are available in management sciences and even fewer in entrepreneurship, we have opened our scope to the educational sciences, which study the whole range of doctoral courses. We selected 17 articles dealing with the subject ('paper-based writing') to examine the pros and cons of the choice of the 'paper-based writing' format, the authors of these articles sometimes comparing it to the monograph. We then aggregated the data collected thematically (Table 10.3).

This literature review identifies six key factors that may underlie the choice of PhD dissertation format:

- *Academic culture:* performance culture is associated with paper-based writing while craft culture is linked to the monograph. It is the amount of time available for each of the two projects and their volume that condition this vision (a set of 'mini'-projects that can be published versus a 'large work' that gives rise to a 'voice');
- *Networking:* the paper-based writing format induces more collaboration and interaction to learn about writing than the monograph format:

Table 10.3 *What does educational science research on paper-based approach tell us about 'Paper-based writing' versus 'monograph'?*

Implications for	Paper-based writing	Monograph writing
Academic culture	Performance culture (Dowling et al., 2012) → publishing during doctoral studies	Craft culture: long-term work of shaping (Dowling et al., 2012) → possibility of publishing during the doctoral course or after obtaining the doctoral degree
Levels involved (micro, meso, macro)	By publishing, three levels may be involved: micro level (individual), meso level (local academic network -university), macro level (international network, institutions, policies) (Horta & Santos, 2015)	Monograph involves two levels: micro and meso (conferences may involve the third one)
Pedagogy	Necessity of a pedagogy that supports the publication of doctoral work (Paré, 2010 in Frick, 2019)	
Peer roles	Assessment Project-based work (Dowling et al., 2012)	Supervision (Dowling et al., 2012)
Supervisor roles	Potential visible and literal co-author who mediates reviewer comments (Kamler, 2010 in Frick, 2019) Formative (Frick, 2019) assessment (Dowling et al., 2012) Project-based work (Dowling et al., 2012)	Invisible second author (Paré, 2010 in Frick, 2019)
Characteristics of the supervisor–PhD student relationship	Focus on writing work supported by mentoring for publication Thesis writing is collaborative with support from the broader scholarly community (supervisors, editors, reviewers, colleagues, peers) (Dowling et al., 2012)	Identical, if the doctoral student submits proposals for articles to conferences

Implications for	Paper-based writing	Monograph writing
PhD student's motivations	Develop the requisite skills for an academic career (expertise in academic writing/experience in publishing process) and publication record (Dowling et al., 2012)	Leading your own project with your own voice (de Lange & Wittek, 2014) Finding your own voice (Dowling et al., 2012)
Creativity *vs* Crafting	Fosters creativity and interdisciplinarity (Dowling et al., 2012) → developing a writer's identity and self-discipline (Dowling et al., 2012)	Encourages a craft-based approach
Topic fit and thesis mode/genre	Mix-methods Mini-projects (Dowling et al., 2012) or multiple project format (Jackson, 2013) The 'multiple project format' allows for a closer relationship with practice (Davies & Rolfe, 2009 in Jackson, 2013)	
Conceptual framing	Different papers with different conceptual frames and different contributions → overarching argument = PhD thesis (stand-alone papers → able to be woven together into a thesis) (Dowling et al., 2012)	One conceptual framing
Methodology and data	Opportunities for PhD students to take different angles on their data: different articles and different methodological approaches (Duke & Beck, 1999)	Need for a central methodological focus included in un explicit template framing a single research study (substantial and coherent plan) (Duke & Beck, 1999)
Doctoral temporalities	New rhythm Meeting journals' requirements may be time-consuming -lengthy timeframe (Robins & Kanowski, 2008) Writing and data collection may occur simultaneously, applied on different parallel paper projects (Dowling et al., 2012; Robins & Kanowski, 2008) Desirable to produce one article per year (Fridlund, 2010)	Conventional rhythm Year 1: setting up topic and contextual framework Year 2: data collection Year 3: writing (Dowling et al., 2012)

Implications for	Paper-based writing	Monograph writing
Publication	Progressive publication as a necessity: adopt a very productive writing Uncertainty of the reviewing process, flexibility is essential (Dowling et al., 2012) The long evaluation process means that it is not always possible to publish before the end of the doctoral process (Bluntz, in Germain et al., 2020)	Few monograph publications; often reworked in depth (Duke & Beck, 1999) and over a long period of time (Fridlund, 2010) before being read.
Dealing with emotions, stress and learning during assessment	Significant exposure to critical academic conversation generating feelings of uncertainty and anxiety (articulation of current conversation/data/theory within a coherent framework) (Dowling et al., 2012) A destabilizing and uncomfortable journey (Peacock, 2017) Publication-related anxiety from lengthy review processes aggravated by rejections or major revision (Jackson, 2013) Co-authoring is a way to manage anxiety around uncertainty (Dowling et al., 2012) as PhD by publication offers possibilities for collegial collaboration (Jackson, 2013)	Much less training in integrating academic conversation (done through lectures) Authoring as an individual Monograph implies a risk of isolation (Jackson, 2013)
Degree of involvement in communities, academic culture, frameworks and standards	Paper-based enables becoming a member of the community (engagement with supervisor, peers, …) (Dowling et al., 2012)	
Impact of the doctoral thesis process on the development of academic skills	Development of KSA:* disciplinary knowledge, research skills, project management skills, leadership, communication and networking skills, teaching skills, team working skills (Mowbray & Halse, 2010 in Horta) Planning and writing skills are challenged when creating a coherent narrative both close to the publication and easy to read for the audience (Peacock, 2017) Instill professional work practices and foster academic development (Robins & Kanowski, 2008)	Developing an academic voice (Dowling et al., 2012)

Implications for	Paper-based writing	Monograph writing
Impact of the doctoral process on the thesis defence	The components of the thesis (articles and chapters) have already been peer-reviewed: a priori confidence in the quality of the work produced (Dowling et al., 2012; Fridlund, 2010)	Discovery of an academic voice by the jury (Dowling et al., 2012) More common not to pass when doing a monograph (Sandstedt et al., 2005 in Fridlund 2010)
Impact of the thesis on the audience	Written often in English (Fridlund, 2010) Larger audience than the thesis defence committee because of publications (Duke & Beck, 1999)	Written often in the native language (Fridlund, 2010) Limited readership of the traditional dissertation (PhD student's committee, friends, family, colleagues) Need for recrafting the dissertation into publishable forms (Duke & Beck, 1999)
Impact of format on early career	Puts the student/researcher 'on the scientific map' very early/easier to get fundings (Fridlund, 2010) Publishing during the PhD journey induces greater research production and productivity, greater numbers of yearly citations during the career and positive effects on employability – including networking (Horta & Santos, 2015; O'Keeffe, 2019) More likely to be successful in all scholarly facets (pedagogy, research) (Sutherland et al., 2013 in Frick 2019)	

Note: * KSA is the acronym for Knowledge Skills Attitude.

co-authoring, reviews, responses to reviewers. It allows for rapid integration into the community, international if the articles are written in English;
- *Topic fit and conceptual/methodological framing:* the multiple project format inherent in paper-based writing allows one to stay as close as possible to academic practice (publishing) but increases the risk of incoherence in the final essay, which is much less present in the monograph. It is necessary to foresee a phase of writing an overarching argument to reconcile different approaches;
- *Relationship to time:* the multiple project format requires the PhD student to be able to move from one writing project to another, and therefore from one writing phase to another (writing for submission, responding to reviewers, finalising the manuscript before publication, etc.) and from one team to another. The monograph remains the expression of a voice and allows for more creativity;
- *Relationship to stress:* the high exposure to critical academic conversation can generate feelings of uncertainty and anxiety: what if at the end of the three years of the doctoral career not enough papers have been published or accepted? The monograph is written and can be submitted for defence without prior publication;
- *Academic recognition over time:* the components of the thesis (articles and chapters) have already been peer-reviewed in the paper-based writing format (a priori confidence in the quality of the work produced which enhances perceived employability). The monograph is discovered in its entirety by the community only from the defence.

Ultimately, it is the nature of the research project, the student's interests (topic, methodology, ...) and the timelines associated with the doctoral work project that invite a choice of format by themselves. Whatever format is chosen, the PhD student can use it creatively (O'Keeffe, 2019) by being the entrepreneur of their doctoral journey (Bluntz; Muhlerin, in Germain et al., 2020). They are accountable for their learning and its depth (Sharmini et al., 2015). In particular, the PhD candidate is invited to reflect on their relationship with stress and their ability to manage it before choosing the article-based thesis format in a context where the pressure of publication and time pressure are aggravating factors requiring, for example, certain personality requirements: time management skills, strong writing capabilities, understanding of the current literature (Jackson, 2013).

To address all the issues and challenges formulated above, the PhD by/with publication seems to be an efficient vector.[9] During the defence, the publications constitute an outcome that is easy to evaluate for the supervision team and the members of the thesis jury, both quantitatively (number of articles and chapters) and qualitatively (journal ranking, blind peer-reviewing, entry into an ongoing academic dialogue through collective writing). Co-authored publications guarantee the PhD student's ability to work in a team, to integrate a network and to identify role models, to enter into the academic conversation by responding to reviewers before publication. They guarantee the supervisor's competence to guide and accompany the PhD student from the periphery to the centre of the targeted academic professionalism. Finally, they include the name of the institution that will be able to count these publications. Compared to writing a monograph, writing an article-based dissertation thus constitutes an opportunity to experience the reality of publication processes and to contribute to the frontiers of academic research. However, one major limitation is that developing one's own voice as an academic may be more difficult than in a monograph.

KEY ISSUES, GUIDELINES AND CANVA PROPOSAL (ABPHD^2 CANVA) TO COMBINE COHERENCE AND EFFECTIVENESS IN ENTREPRENEURSHIP DOCTORAL ARTICLE-BASED DISSERTATION

The paper-based dissertation approach has advantages but also risks that need to be taken into account. Writing different papers around the same research object can lead to conceptual, theoretical or methodological inconsistencies between papers written in different contexts and time frames (Niven & Grant, 2012; Sharmini et al., 2015). Maintaining coherence is one of the very purposes of the process. As we have seen, there are several elements to consider before embarking on a PhD by publication: the PhD student's competence at juggling multiple projects/frames, capacity to write (and rewrite, and 'let go'), coping skills to face criticisms from peers, the potential to become a publishing academic (Dowling et al., 2012), and the capacity to establish boundaries around the relevant literatures (Robins & Kanowski, 2008). A major challenge concerns the impact of the evaluation of the articles and chapters submitted during the doctoral journey and the temporality in which these evaluations are carried out; the evaluation processes and the different journal pipelines imply potential changes of direction on the focus and contributions of the written output that iteratively impact the internal economy of the PhD project and may threaten its realisation in case of rejected articles (de Lange & Wittek, 2014). It is therefore important at the end of the PhD process to clearly dissociate two distinct activities: 'doing research' (work reported in articles) and 'reporting on a PhD process' (the PhD study).

In order to contextualise how to combine coherence and effectiveness in entrepreneurship doctoral article-based dissertation, we propose to immerse you in a singular doctoral path (Box 10.1).

BOX 10.1 PAPER-BASED PHD DISSERTATION: PERSONAL VIEWS ON A DOCTORAL JOURNEY (LE PONTOIS, 2020)

When I started my doctoral journey in the middle of my professional career in 2016, I was both full of enthusiasm and apprehension. On the advice of my supervisor, I embarked on the paper-based PhD dissertation process with the common goal of publishing part of the papers in English and the other in French. My initial subject was student entrepreneurial teams and I immediately adopted a qualitative research approach. In my first year, I had the opportunity to collaborate with fellow researchers at my university to submit a first article in a collective work and then with my supervisor's network for a second paper in a French ranked journal. By the middle of my second year, I had co-authored four papers (conceptual and empirical) and had two papers under review. These were all initiated by my supervisor, whom I consider a great gate opener. But despite the enthusiasm and success of the publications, this was the start of a long period of doubt. Although I was enjoying working on very different research projects, I was having real difficulty imagining how I would be able to fit them together at the end of the day. During a presentation of my doctoral work in front of other PhD students and researchers, I was firmly questioned: *What is the conceptual framework of your thesis? What is your epistemological posture?* For the next two years, feelings of confusion, discomfiture, incomprehension and discouragement, even flabbergasting (in the sense of not being able to act anymore) arose in the face of my inability to articulate a research production of all different articles (empirical/theoretical, different objects) within a study (the dissertation) on various objects of entrepreneurship education. In parallel with the production of other articles, I first looked for guidance in the textbooks accompanying the writing of a thesis in management sciences. I then identified the need to adopt an encompassing epistemological positioning to ensure the coherence of the whole of my research work produced by unit of articles. The major difficulty was that although I had thought through the epistemological positioning, methodology and conceptual framework of each of my co-authored papers, they were all very different. I was not then able to carry out the epistemological reflection that is consubstantial (Martinet, 1990) to the elaboration of the research *design* that allows the researcher to build a coherent and dense scientific discourse. In retrospect, it seems to me that this is only possible when the researcher is a researcher and not an apprentice researcher, as is the case for any doctoral student, especially when the thesis project is built through articles in an abductive approach. Indeed, the novice researcher is expected to be able to include, in the same movement, several scientific productions (which may come from different epistemological positions) in a single epistemological current, which is the foundation of the research carried out over several years. The institutional demand for a precise epistemological positioning at the beginning and during the course of the thesis by articles does not necessarily seem to be fruitful in my case. This is not to say that one should not ask oneself the question of the said positioning, nor that it is not possible to decide on it a priori, because asking oneself the question of the positioning remains obviously fundamental (Dumez, 2011). In this case, it is during the various stages of learning about research that the doctoral student's positioning and approach – sometimes intuitive and dictated by the choices of action – builds *ex post* an anchorage in a clearly defined epistemological current. Dumez (2013: 29) specifies that 'epistemological considerations are concrete questions that must be confronted throughout the research process, from its beginnings to its conclusion, in a reflexive mode'. Five months before I submitted my PhD dissertation, I had not written a line of what I then called my 'Frankensteinian PhD thesis'. I was paralysed. To comply with the classical canons of a thesis, writing an introduction and a conclusion would have been enough, as my doctoral work was already recognised by the community because it was published. But this possibility did not suit me intellectually in the sense that I absolutely wanted to solve this problem of lack of coherence between the articles. It was then that, less than six months before my defence, I immersed myself with great pleasure in the literature on epistemology and research methodology. After having rather easily positioned my research in pragmatic constructivism, I felt a lightning strike when I discovered the Hlady-Rispal model entitled 'From empirical data to theory. A helical representation of process' (2002: 178). It was then that I realised that I had conducted a dialogical qualitative study (Le Pontois, 2020: 96) in which my articles responded to each other. Instead of applying this model to a specific piece of research resulting in an article, I applied it to my entire research process, i.e. my study, in a retrospective manner. This led me to propose a new original contribution resulting from the perspective of my articles through a meta-reflexive practice. I have chosen to adopt an integrative approach that goes beyond the simple compilation of articles framed by an introduction and a conclusion. Finally, I chose to write a 150-page dissertation defending a thesis (new contribution composed of a model) including a state of the art of my research object, the setting of research objectives (including the design and epistemological positioning), the presentation of the stakes of my research object accompanied by the presentation of the articles as well as the new contribution, and then a conclusion on the scientificity of the research work by articles and the synthesis of the contributions. This ability to integrate my scientific work into a broader epistemological, methodological and philosophical reflection than the standard requirements has been rewarded by the French-speaking scientific community (obtaining two thesis prizes awarded by international French-speaking learned societies). Beyond this recognition, what has marked me the most is to have felt this flow of being on the edge of the limits of knowledge.

Ensuring the coherence and effectiveness of an article-based dissertation relies on weaving a robust research model (design) involving either a prospective or retrospective approach. The PhD candidate who embarked on the paper-based dissertation adventure was offered two possibilities of formal formats: the 'PhD *by* publication/research papers' (prospective) and the 'PhD *with* publications' (retrospective).

On the one hand, the 'PhD *by* publication' makes it possible to write a book comprising a general introduction, followed by a presentation of the conceptual framework and epistemological positioning of the thesis, to then integrate the various articles produced as chapters, taking care to give the reader access to understanding the links between the articles, and to finish by writing an integrated discussion chapter. This chapter preceding the conclusion can be written in four steps (Lewis et al., 2021): (1) outlining the integrated discussion chapter (summary of the overall purpose of the dissertation, main findings, main point of discussion, strengths and limitations of the dissertation, practical, managerial, methodological and theoretical implications, conclusion), (2) mapping individual article's findings (discussion points of each articles, overarching points, disciplinary implications), (3) drafting the main integrated discussion point (identifying supporting or refuting arguments from the individual articles), and finally (4) writing the integrated discussion chapter. It should be noted that a good integrated discussion can be published as such as an article. This is the format most commonly followed by doctoral students and most often follows a forward-looking approach (Peacock, 2017) in that the publications are planned – form, topic, temporality. For example, it is common to construct a thesis in entrepreneurship in three articles, the first conceptual (literature review), the second empirical (qualitative exploratory) and the third quantitative to validate the hypotheses identified earlier.

On the other hand, the 'PhD *with* publication' is an emerging format that allows for a monograph to be written about the entire doctoral research process and for published articles or articles under review to be placed in an appendix (e.g. with appended publications). The doctoral student then dissociates his articles (body of work) from his study (PhD thesis). This approach requires a clear dissociation between the epistemological positioning and the theoretical/conceptual framework of each article (which may be different from one to the other) and the epistemological positioning and theoretical framework of the whole doctoral research or study. This involves the doctoral student entering into an integrative process of constructing an overarching meta-inference (or meta-narrative/over-arching narrative) which requires an alternative epistemological positioning (Niven & Grant, 2012; Peacock, 2017). This format is epistemologically and ontologically different from classical formats. The challenge is then to construct a posteriori its retrospective design by re-contextualising papers within the setting of the doctoral study. The question of the connectiveness of the papers becomes central. This connectivity can for example be found at the theoretical and conceptual level, in common literature reviews or in the elaboration of a new original contribution based on the contributions of the different articles put in perspective (deeper findings). The abductive approach is then often the most appropriate and leads to a reflexive practice on the part of the doctoral student (deconstruction and reconfiguration) to crystallise the methodology underpinning the research (Peacock, 2017). In a sense, the doctoral student adopts the entrepreneurial approaches of bricolage and effectuation. This format follows a retrospective approach. It is this second format that was finally adopted by the PhD candidate (Box 10.1). To summarise, it is necessary to understand the explicit and implicit expectations of evaluators of doctoral theses in general and in entrepreneurship in particular.[10]

The overall aim of this chapter is to provide some insights and guidance to build a successful article-based PhD thesis in entrepreneurship. On the basis of this research, we recommend some guidelines both for PhD candidates and supervisors to ensure the necessary links between the research object, epistemological positioning, research methodology, knowledge of the literature and the dissertation format.

Guidelines for doctoral students intending to submit a paper-based PhD dissertation: a PhD candidate should:

(a) Be aware of the different article-based PhD dissertation formats and their specificities (notably in relation to time and stress). Discuss/negotiate them with their supervisor, before and during the doctoral journey, as the context may lead to a modification of the initial choices.
(b) Clarify the research approach adopted: prospective (the study design is pre-defined before starting work on the first article) or retrospective (a research object is examined in a multi-angulated way through several articles, with a study design carried out a posteriori). Whatever the approach chosen, be attentive to the alignment between the different publication projects (thematic and/or methodological and/or procedural).

(c) Dissociate the epistemological positioning of each article from the epistemological positioning of the study (doctoral journey).
(d) Specify for each of the articles whether it is published or under evaluation, in which journal, indicate the form of intellectual contribution of each of the authors in case of co-authorship (in particular that of the PhD candidate) and at which stages of the article the author contributed and in what way: editorial, methodological, conceptual, … .
(e) Give an account in the thesis of a professional development trajectory and produce a quality scientific object in the field of entrepreneurship. Ensure that you demonstrate a sufficiently wide range of academic skills to be recognised as a fully-fledged researcher at the end of the course.
(f) Structure the final document (PhD dissertation) in such a way as to present the research process in a coherent manner, with particular attention to bridging sections between chapters that are published (prospective dissertation).
(g) Present in conclusion the scientificity of the research work by articles, the synthesis of the theoretical, methodological and managerial contributions of the articles, the practical implications for the management sciences and the field of entrepreneurship, and to conclude with the limits of the study and the avenues for future research.

Guidelines for supervisors coaching doctoral students intending to submit a paper-based PhD dissertation: a supervisor should:

(a) Present the different PhD dissertation formats (monograph vs. article-based PhD dissertation) and their specificities (notably in relation to time and stress. Discuss/negotiate them with your PhD student, before and during the doctoral journey, and explain that the context may lead to modifying the initial choices;[11]
(b) Ensure the PhD student's ability to quickly integrate academic practices: learn quickly to read, write and rewrite articles (concepts, method, data, overall coherence) and to integrate into an academic community and research teams.
(c) Mediate between the reviewers and the PhD student during the evaluation phases; accompany the acculturation to academic practice by adopting a 'gate opener' behaviour; know how to welcome moments of doubt.
(d) Bring to the attention of the PhD student the extended set of criteria for assessing article-based PhD dissertation in Entrepreneurship.
(e) Explain to the PhD candidate the different levels of defense issues.

In order to support students' reflective thinking throughout their doctoral studies, we are proposing an evolving tool to put the research design of the

PhD dissertation on the table. The Article-Based PhD Dissertation Canva (for Management Sciences) or ABPhD^2 Canva (license Creative Commons CC-BY-NC-ND) is an artefact made up of different boxes grouped into six areas: components of the PhD thesis (book) as the result of the doctoral path; ABPhD thesis format; key KSA learned and professional trajectory (professional development); articles/chapters design (1/2) : types and epistemological positioning; articles/chapters design (2/2) : research question, theory, data; articles' findings. This canva is designed to allow the doctoral project to evolve. The doctoral journey takes time and it is not uncommon to change course, to branch off, to go backwards in order to find one's way. Each box contains one or more questions linked to key research concepts and issues to guide the doctoral student in their thinking and in drafting and writing the PhD dissertation. As the format of the book means that the ABPhD^2 Canva cannot be viewed clearly (the canva has to be printed in 42x49.4 cm format/A3 or better, A2), the authors are offering it as a free download on the Open Science portal HAL.[12]

AVENUES FOR REFLECTION

Our intention in this chapter is not to advocate for the paper-based PhD, nor to provide an analysis of its benefits and costs. But it is important to underline the rise over the last three decades of the fabrication of the *homo academicus neoliberalis*, shaped as a subject who has to commit to '*publish or perish*', albeit with the help and support of peers, supervisors, reviewers, … . The rationality of the market has transformed higher education from a public social good to a personal investment in the individual future where the young researcher marks their network, their papers for ranking and their own employability (Brown, 2015). Choosing to write a PhD dissertation *by/with* publication can be an eminently rational, calculated and entrepreneurial decision, guided by performativity, in the context of a neoliberalised higher education measuring the academic performance (O'Keeffe, 2019). But it is also to choose the option to 'play the game' and enter into the challenging and exciting competition to publish with the following benefits for the PhD student, the discipline and the institution: entry into the academic community, generation of new knowledge promoting understanding in the discipline, and increased research productivity within institutions (Peacock, 2017).

Indeed, the growing and now exclusive use of the census and the measurement of scientific publication of authors to measure their impact can raise questions about choices guided more by the famous '*publish or perish*' than by innovation, the quality of research that requires a long time and chosen collaborations. At the same time, PhD students and early career researchers are confronted with the challenges and detrimental effects of the current academic system (Coriat, 2019). While the academic career of doctoral students remains satisfactory for a majority of them, the overall level of satisfaction (including mental health) has been declining for several decades[13] (Bleasdale, 2019).

Doctoral training provides useful qualifications for many careers outside academia (Coriat, 2019) so why focus almost exclusively on publication, which ultimately concerns only doctoral students wishing to work in higher education? It seems necessary to look again at the very nature of the PhD, its purpose, the interest of the student and the ethics underlying the choice of a dissertation format before even determining its form (Frick, 2019). What research excellence do we want? Should our research be limited to the goal of publication to support one's career or can it (also) pursue a greater purpose? Research should remain a place of emancipation, a 'liminal space rather than a solely institutional space' (Germain & Taskin, 2017) where critical thinking (evaluation, analysis by the doctoral student of their own work) allows emancipation within the framework of scientifically robust and excellent research. It is less the format than the time we can devote to our research, doctoral and academic, that will make the difference.

NOTES

1. Professional doctorate (in arts, health, management, ...).
2. The term 'article-based PhD dissertation' is broader than 'PhD by publication'. We invite the reader to go to the second section of this chapter to find their way through the semantic jungle surrounding this object.
3. The idea for this article came about after one of the authors, an entrepreneurial researcher, defended her thesis and obtained an associate professorship: it is the article she wished she had read when she was struggling to complete what she then called her 'Frankensteinian article-based PhD dissertation'.
4. It is easily observable in universities that the regulation underlying the submission of an article-based thesis varies regularly (number of articles, number of articles published or under revision, number of articles in authorship and co-authorship, formal format, ...).
5. The integrative literature review (Torraco, 2005; 2016; Elsbach & van Knippenberg, 2020; Snyder, 2019) makes it possible to investigate in a robust manner themes that are little or not dealt with in the literature of the field under study by borrowing from other fields (in this case, mainly the educational sciences).
6. In France, for example, there was the format of the state thesis, which took seasoned researchers an average of ten years to write.
7. In 2023 (France), the Fondation Nationale pour l'Enseignement de la Gestion (FNEGE) had already shown that 75% of PhDs in management sciences chose an academic career. Over the last 10 years, the number of theses written in English has more than doubled and these are mainly

article-based dissertations, which shows the impact of the internationalisation of the doctoral research process.

8. Depending on the country, organisational cultural dimensions reinforce this choice (e.g. pools of doctoral students involved in research projects born before their arrival versus more artisanal and creative research for the PhD student).
9. This is not to say that a monograph presented at the end of a doctoral course including participation in several conferences followed, later, by publications, is not a vector that can meet the same expectations and requirements of the academic community.
10. For example, the identity of a doctoral thesis in entrepreneurship can be recognised if at least two of the following conditions are met in the doctoral research work (Paturel, 2004 : 49): 'presence in the title of the term "entrepreneurship" or a word in the same family or a word related to entrepreneurship ("entrepreneurship", "entrepreneur", "business creation", "business takeover", "intrapreneurship", "spin-off", "start-up", etc.); title with very common words in entrepreneurship ("craft", "TPE", "PE", etc.); research supervisor recognised in the field we are interested in; jury composed for the most part of colleagues with a reputation specialising in the discipline or interested in it for one reason or another' (translated from French by the authors).
11. One of our colleagues had initially planned to present an article-based dissertation. Due to the long evaluation and revision time of some of the submitted articles, she was forced to finally produce a monograph a few months before the end of her doctoral course, which was awarded two thesis prizes (Gabay-Mariani, 2020).
12. ABPhD^2 Canva, Article-Based PhD Dissertation Canva: 1) with explanatory notes: https://hal.science/hal-04401588; 2) to be filled in: https://hal.science/hal-04401584.
13. '722 PhD supervisors (45%) said they had noticed increasing cases of mental health issues among PhD students.'

REFERENCES

Alvesson, M., & Sandberg, J. (2011). Generating research questions through problematization. *Academy of Management Review*, *36*(2), 247–271.

Araújo, E. R. (2005). Understanding the PhD as a phase in time. *Time & Society*, *14*(2–3), 191–211.

Bergh, D. D., Boyd, B. K., Byron, K., Gove, S., & Ketchen Jr, D. J. (2022). What constitutes a methodological contribution? *Journal of Management*, *48*(7), 1835–1848.

Bleasdale, B. (2019). Researchers pay the cost of research. *Nature Materials*, *18*(8), 772–772.

Brown, W. (2015). *Undoing the demos: Neoliberalism's stealth revolution*. Cambridge, MA: MIT Press.

Burgess, A., & Ivanič, R. (2010). Writing and being written: Issues of identity across timescales. *Written Communication*, *27*(2), 228–255.

Butt, M. (2013). One I made earlier: On the PhD by publication. *TEXT*, *17*(Special 22), 1–14.

Cannizzo, F. (2018). Tactical evaluations: Everyday neoliberalism in academia. *Journal of Sociology*, *54*(1), 77–91.

Christianson, B., Elliott, M., & Massey, B. (2015). The role of publications and other artefacts in submissions for the UK PhD. UK Council for Graduate Education.

Coriat, A. M. (2019). PhD merit needs to be defined by more than just publications. *Nature Human Behaviour*, *3*(10), 1007–1007.

de Lange, T., & Wittek, L. (2014). Divergent paths to parallel ends: Two routes to the doctoral dissertation. *Special Edition of the Journal of School Public Relations*, *35*(3), 383–401.

Deuchar, R. (2008). Facilitator, director or critical friend? Contradiction and congruence in doctoral supervision styles. *Teaching in Higher Education*, *13*(4), 489–500.

Dowling, R., Gorman-Murray, A., Power, E., & Luzia, K. (2012). Critical reflections on doctoral research and supervision in human geography: The 'PhD by publication'. *Journal of Geography in Higher Education*, *36*(2), 293–305.

Dumez, H. (2011). Eléments pour une épistémologie de la recherche qualitative en gestion (2). *Le Libellio d'Aegis*, *7*(1), 39–52.

Dumez, H. (2013). Qu'est-ce que la recherche qualitative? Problèmes épistémologiques, méthodologiques et de théorisation. *Gérer et comprendre*, (2), 29–42.

Elsbach, K. D., & van Knippenberg, D. (2020). Creating high-impact literature reviews: An argument for 'integrative reviews'. *Journal of Management Studies*, *57*(6), 1277–1289.

Frick, L. (2019). PhD by publication: Panacea or paralysis? *Africa Education Review*, *16*(5), 47–59.

Fridlund, B. (2010). The dissertation book: Should it be a monograph or a compilation thesis? *European Journal of Cardiovascular Nursing*, *9*(3), 144–145.

Gabay-Mariani, L. (2020). Le processus entrepreneurial à l'épreuve de l'engagement: contributions théoriques et méthodologiques à l'analyse de l'engagement des entrepreneurs naissants: une application au contexte de l'entrepreneuriat étudiant. [The entrepreneurial process put to the test of commitment: theoretical and methodological contribution on nascent entrepreneurs' commitment: an empirical application to student-entrepreneurs]. (Doctoral dissertation, Université Grenoble Alpes).

Gaillard, H., Cloarec, J., Senn, J., & Grandazzi, A. (2023). *L'expérience de la thèse en management: Regards croisés de jeunes docteurs*. Éditions EMS.

Germain, O., Wang, P. Y., Delisle, J ., Moulaï, K., Bluntz, C., Dahlman, S., Friis Christensen, J., Burø, T., Mulherin, T., Taylor, H. (2020). Living the PhD journey: Unplugged session. *M@n@gement*, *23*(1), 102–141.

Germain, O., & Taskin, L. (2017). Être formé pour et … par la recherche 1. *Revue internationale PME*, *30*(2), 7–16.

Gilbert, R. (2009). The doctorate as curriculum: A perspective on goals and outcomes of doctoral education. In Boud, D., & Lee, A. (Eds.), *Changing practices of doctoral education*, (pp. 54–68). Routledge.

Hagen, N. (2010). Deconstructing doctoral dissertations: How many papers does it take to make a PhD? *Scientometrics*, *85*(2), 567–579.

Hlady-Rispal, M. (2002). *La méthode des cas: Application à la recherche en gestion*. De Boeck.

Hodgson, D. (2020). Helping doctoral students understand PhD thesis examination expectations: A framework and a tool for supervision. *Active Learning in Higher Education*, *21*(1), 51–63.

Holdsworth, C. (2018). Generic distinctiveness and the entrepreneurial self: A case study of English Higher Education. *Journal of Youth Studies, 21*(9), 1216–1231.
Hulley, S. B., Cummings, S. R., Browner, W. S., Grady, D. G., Newman, T. B. (2007). Conceiving the research question. In *Designing Clinical Research*, 3rd ed. (pp. 17–26). Lippincott Williams & Wilkins.
Jackson, D. (2013). Completing a PhD by publication: A review of Australian policy and implications for practice. *Higher Education Research & Development, 32*(3), 355–368.
Kallio, K. M., Kallio, T. J., Tienari, J., & Hyvönen, T. (2016). Ethos at stake: Performance management and academic work in universities. *Human Relations, 69*(3), 685–709.
Kihn, L. A., & Näsi, S. (2017). Emerging diversity in management accounting research: The case of Finnish doctoral dissertations, 1945–2015. *Journal of Accounting & Organizational Change, 13*(1), 131–160.
Knights, D., & Clarke, C. A. (2014). It's a bittersweet symphony, this life: Fragile academic selves and insecure identities at work. *Organization Studies, 35*(3), 335–357.
Laurance, W. F., Useche, C., Laurance, S. G., & Bradshaw, C. J. A. (2013). Predicting publication success for biologists. *Bioscience, 63*(10), 817–823.
Le Pontois, S. (2020). L'impact de l'éducation en entrepreneuriat au prisme de son évaluation: Pour une approche multidimensionnelle de l'efficacité de l'éducation en entrepreneuriat. [A critical approach to impact studies in entrepreneurship education: A multidimensional approach to assess the effectiveness of entrepreneurship education]. (Doctoral dissertation, Université Grenoble Alpes). https://theses.hal.science/tel-03275765/.
Lee, A. (2010). When the article is the dissertation: Pedagogies for a PhD by publication. In Aitchison, C., Kamler, B., & Lee, A. (Eds.), *Publishing pedagogies for the doctorate and beyond* (pp. 12–29). London: Routledge.
Lewis, K. B., Graham, I. D., Boland, L., & Stacey, D. (2021). Writing a compelling integrated discussion: A guide for integrated discussions in article-based theses and dissertations. *International Journal of Nursing Education Scholarship, 18*(1). https://doi.org/10.1515/ijnes-2020-0057.
Lin, L., & Cranton, P. (2005). From scholarship student to responsible scholar: A transformative process. *Teaching in Higher Education, 10*(4), 447–459.
Löfström, E., & Pyhältö, K. (2021). How research on ethics in doctoral supervision can inform doctoral education policy. In Lee, A., & Bongaardt, R. (Eds.), *The Future of Doctoral Research* (pp. 295–306). Routledge.
Martinet, A. C. (1990) (ed.). *Épistémologie et sciences de gestion*. Economica.
Mawson, K., & Abbott, I. (2017). Supervising the professional doctoral student: Less process and progress, more peripheral participation and personal identity. *Management in Education, 31*(4), 187–193.
Mullins, G., & Kiley, M. (2002). 'It's a PhD, not a Nobel Prize': How experienced examiners assess research theses. *Studies in Higher Education, 27*(4), 369–386.
Niven, P., & Grant, C. (2012). PhDs by publications: an 'easy way out'? *Teaching in Higher Education, 17*(1), 105–111.
O'Keeffe, P. (2019). PhD by publication: Innovative approach to social science research, or operationalisation of the doctoral student … or both? *Higher Education Research & Development, 39*(2), 288–301.
Paturel, R. (2004). Les choix méthodologiques de la recherche doctorale française en entrepreneuriat. *Revue de l'Entrepreneuriat, 3*(1), 47–65.

Peacock, S. (2017). The PhD by publication. *International Journal of Doctoral Studies, 12*, 123–134.
Pelger, C., & Grottke, M. (2015). What about the future of the academy? Some remarks on the looming colonisation of doctoral education. *Critical Perspectives on Accounting, 26*, 117–129.
Rae, D. (2017). Entrepreneurial learning: Peripherality and connectedness. *International Journal of Entrepreneurial Behavior & Research, 23*(3), 486–503.
Robins, L., & Kanowski, P. (2008). PhD by publication: A student's perspective. *Journal of Research Practice, 4*(2), M3.
Rosa, H. (Ed.). (2010). *High-speed society: Social acceleration, power, and modernity*. Penn State Press.
Sharmini, S., Spronken-Smith, R., Golding, C., & Harland, T. (2015). Assessing the doctoral thesis when it includes published work. *Assessment & Evaluation in Higher Education, 40*(1), 89–102.
Shore, C., & Wright, S. (2000). Coercive accountability: The new audit culture and its impact on anthropology. In Strathern, M. (Ed.), *Audit cultures: Anthropological studies in accountability, ethics and the academy*, (pp. 57–89). Routledge.
Snyder, H. (2019). Literature review as a research methodology: An overview and guidelines. *Journal of Business Research, 104*, 333–339.
Sutton, P. (2017). Lost souls? The demoralization of academic labour in the measured university. *Higher Education Research & Development, 36*(3), 625–636.
Torraco, R. J. (2016). Writing integrative literature reviews: Using the past and present to explore the future. *Human Resource Development Review, 15*(4), 404–428.
Torraco, R. J. (2005). Writing integrative literature reviews: Guidelines and examples. *Human Resource Development Review, 4*(3), 356–367.
Vähämäki, M., Saru, E., & Palmunen, L. M. (2021). Doctoral supervision as an academic practice and leader–member relationship: A critical approach to relationship dynamics. *The International Journal of Management Education, 19*(3), 100510.
Vygotsky, L. S. (1978). *Mind in society: Development of higher psychological processes*. Harvard University Press.
Yazdani, S., & Shokooh, F. (2018). Defining doctorateness: A concept analysis. *International Journal of Doctoral Studies, 13*, 31–48.

PART III

Examining new models and methodologies in entrepreneurship education

11. Viewing entrepreneurship 'in motion': exploring current uses and future possibilities of video research methods in entrepreneurship research[1]

Jarrod Ormiston and Neil A. Thompson

INTRODUCTION

In order for the field of entrepreneurship research to stay relevant, there is a need to move towards more transformational research and novelty in theorizing and methods (Shepherd, 2015). Entrepreneurial action is now widely viewed as a future-oriented, interactive, material, emotional, non-linear and contextual process under conditions of uncertainty (Hindle, 2004; Karatas-Ozkan et al., 2014; Neergaard & Ulhøi, 2007; Suddaby et al., 2015). However, a number of scholars have pointed out that dominant methods, such as surveys, interviews, experiments and secondary data, provide only limited insight into entrepreneurial action as it happens (Dana & Dana, 2007; Zahra & Wright, 2011). There have been growing calls to further entrepreneurship research by observing (and participating with) entrepreneurial practitioners 'in action' within their social, economic and environmental contexts (Chalmers & Shaw, 2017; Hjorth et al., 2015; Sklaveniti & Steyaert, 2019; Thompson et al., 2020). This demands an expansion of the methodological tools used to observe and examine overlooked aspects of entrepreneurial action (Hindle, 2004; Berglund, 2007; Shepherd & Suddaby, 2017). In this article, we argue that video-based methods provide a powerful yet accessible way for researchers to observe and theorize the contextual, interactional, material and emotional aspects of entrepreneurial action (Christianson, 2018).

Over the past few years, a growing number of entrepreneurship scholars have adopted various video research methods in their research designs. Broadly speaking, video research methods incorporate the collection, creation or curation of video clips, drawing on positivist or interpretivist methodologies. Clarke (2011) and Thompson and Illes (2020), for example, demonstrate that video-based methods enable researchers to observe and abductively theorize the embodied (such as use of non-verbal communication) and relational (such as conversational turn-taking) aspects of entrepreneurial learning and persuasion. On the other hand, video-based methods also provide researchers novel sources of archival and crowdfunding data to understand entrepreneurial outcomes and have even been used in deductive experimental studies. For example, Shane et al. (2019) examine the effect of founder passion on the decision making of informal investors by using videos to elicit responses by treatment and control groups of informal investors, which are subsequently measured by both surveys and fMRI technology. Given these important recent developments, it is clear that many new opportunities have emerged for using video-based methods in entrepreneurship research.

While video research methods have gained a foothold in entrepreneurship studies, there are currently no articles that provide an overview or clearly delineate the value of video research methods for addressing novel entrepreneurship research topics. This has led to little dialogue among entrepreneurship researchers about the value and procedures of video research methods, which is particularly important given the unique challenges of entrepreneurship as a research context. Indeed, designing and implementing video methods in research designs is far from trivial because of the uncertainty, heterogeneity, and disequilibrium in entrepreneurial phenomena, as well as the practical research skills necessary to shoot, handle and analyse video data. Many entrepreneurship researchers, editors and reviewers alike may be unfamiliar with the use of video methods in research designs, and conventional journal formats often create challenges for displaying video data (Christianson, 2018; Le Baron et al., 2018). A lack of reflexive examination means the methodological differences underpinning the use of video data remain unclear, which limits awareness of the full possibilities of video research methods in the field. Consequently, we ask 'what are the current ways in which video is being used in entrepreneurship research, to what extent is video data utilized in research designs, and what are the potentials of video methods to further our understanding of entrepreneurial action?'

We address this question by taking stock of video research methods in entrepreneurship articles published in leading journals. We systematically review 142 empirical entrepreneurship research articles in 41 prominent management, organization and entrepreneurship journals that use video methods in their research design. A thematic analysis reveals three main video research methods in empirical entrepreneurship articles: (i) videography of entrepreneurship 'in the wild' (such as pitching and other naturally occurring practices); (ii) video content analysis of entrepreneur generated videos (such as crowdfunding and archival videos); and (iii) video elicitation in 'manufactured' contexts (such as interviews and focus groups, and experiments and interventions). We find a steady rise in entrepreneurship research using video research methods (24 articles from 2010–2014 to 102 from 2015–present), driven by the increasing use of video content analysis of crowdfunding and archival videos. Delving deeper into each method, we unpack the different methodologies (inductive/deductive), key exemplars (extensive use of video data), benefits and limitations. Building on this review, we then develop a research agenda for video-based research to further entrepreneurship scholarship by providing a novel insight into the interactional, embodied, emotional and material aspects of entrepreneurial action.

This article contributes to entrepreneurship research in two main ways. First, we bring coherence to and appraise existing entrepreneurship research that uses video research methods in empirical studies for the first time. Our literature analysis reveals that researchers have leaned heavily on video elicitation and video content analysis in experimental and case study research, but in many of these studies, video data takes a secondary role in analyses. Moreover, we establish that few scholars venture into the enormous possibilities of using videography to observe naturally occurring practices of entrepreneurship as they happen in context. Second, we develop a research agenda that explains how the unique audio, visual and timing affordances of video can be further utilized to systematically analyse the interactional, embodied, emotional and material aspects of entrepreneurial action (Christianson, 2018). We thus specifically address growing calls for new qualitative research methods that can further entrepreneurship research by discussing the ways in which video uniquely renders visible the practices of entrepreneurship for further analysis, whilst taking into account their embeddedness in various social, economic and environmental contexts (Karatas-Ozkan et al., 2014).

SETTING THE SCENE – THE VALUE OF VIDEO FOR ENTREPRENEURSHIP RESEARCH

Entrepreneurship research has traditionally been founded upon aims to develop explanatory theories based on the measurement, isolation and relation among variables and constructs (Hjorth et al., 2015). The field of entrepreneurship has therefore been dominated by methodological approaches, such as surveys, experiments and secondary data, that search for and measure stable relationships between concepts, in attempts to discover the generic and distinct features of entrepreneurial action (Dana & Dana, 2007; Moroz & Hindle, 2012; Zahra & Wright, 2011). A growing number of scholars alternatively argue that entrepreneurial action is fundamentally future-oriented, relational, emotional, embodied, non-linear and contextual, and conducted under conditions of uncertainty (Hindle, 2004; Karatas-Ozkan et al., 2014; Neergaard & Ulhøi, 2007; Suddaby et al., 2015). This perspective encourages an empirical focus on the interactive, embodied, emotional and material aspects of entrepreneurial action (Barinaga, 2017; Johannisson, 2011; Tatli et al., 2014).

To understand these aspects, scholars have increasingly turned their attention to 'episodes of situated social interaction' (Campbell, 2019; Chalmers & Shaw, 2017) to address questions of how and why entrepreneurial practitioners accomplish mundane – though significant – practices, such as pitching, networking, resourcing (Drakopoulou Dodd et al., 2018; Keating et al., 2013; McKeever et al., 2014; Thompson et al., 2020). This has led researchers to focus on the ways in which entrepreneurs use their bodies in interaction (Clarke & Cornelissen, 2011), and how emotions arise and may influence interactional outcomes (Cardon et al., 2017). Moreover, recent studies argue that entrepreneurs pursue their aims using objects, artefacts and technologies (Holt, 2008; Korsgaard, 2011), thus materiality is not a background element, but the very means through which entrepreneurs collaborate and conduct their practical activities. As a consequence, more researchers are turning towards novel qualitative methods that can observe the lived experience of entrepreneurial action and, more specifically, their interactional, embodied, emotional and material properties as they occur in real-time (Hindle, 2004; Karatas-Ozkan et al., 2014; Neergaard & Ulhøi, 2007; Suddaby et al., 2015).

There are a number of methodological challenges to this form of entrepreneurship research. One main challenge is that entrepreneurs themselves are often not fully aware of the interactional, affective, embodied and material aspects of unfolding entrepreneurial action as they happen, thus surveys and interviews have natural limits in producing new insights. Similarly, entrepreneurship occurring in real-time often happens too quickly to capture using ethnographic notetaking, which limits later analysis. Finally, research on entrepreneurial practices *in situ* often depends on the researcher's memory from field experiences, which may reduce the reliability of findings by limiting the sharing of observations and, at worst, enabling *post hoc* interpretations that are not faithful to the situation. To advance research on entrepreneurial action, new methods are needed that enable researchers to carefully reveal and examine the variety of entrepreneurial practices, their constitutive properties, and how they are enacted to organize new ventures under conditions of uncertainty.

To address these challenges, video research methods have a number of distinct advantages for entrepreneurship research. First, video recordings provide a permanent record of events and interactions (LeBaron et al., 2018), whilst rendering the fast pace of entrepreneurship amenable for repeat analysis by researchers (Gylfe et al., 2016). This improves trustworthiness of findings by reducing reliance on the memory and post hoc interpretations by both entrepreneurs and researchers (Smets et al., 2014). When combined with other qualitative methods such as observation, interviews or archival data, video-based methods provide a powerful alternative view of entrepreneurial activity that can confirm, complement or contrast with what entrepreneurs say they do, or what the researchers themselves can see (Gylfe et al., 2016). Second, shooting, collecting, storing and analysing video has never been more accessible, affordable, reliable and rigorous, which empowers users to produce more frequent and encompassing videos from different vantage points than possible in previous decades (Christianson, 2018). Spurred on by significant cost reductions, advances in video recording technology and video analytical software (LeBaron et al., 2018), a growing number of scholars have leveraged videos in order to render visible entrepreneurial activity in ways not possible using other methods. Finally, numerous software packages, such as V-Note, Transana and Dedoose, have been developed to assist researchers in the careful analysis of videos. This software enables researchers to edit raw video footage, share video fragments via cloud storage platforms, slow down video play, transcribe interactions and talk *in situ* and analyse video fragments using multi-coder features (Brugman & Kita, 1995; Christianson, 2018; Koch & Zumbach, 2002; LeBaron et al., 2018). Accordingly, these unique features allow scholars an ability to study the dynamics of entrepreneurial action that is sensitive to interaction, embodiment, emotion and materiality – theoretical concepts that remain fundamental to the future of entrepreneurship studies (Chalmers & Shaw, 2017; Christianson, 2018; Zundel et al., 2018).

Despite these benefits, video research methods are varied, which can make it difficult for interested researchers to grasp its value and possibilities. For example, scholars have increasingly acquired video data produced by entrepreneurs for crowdfunding campaigns. At its most reductive, this can be reflected in simple binary coding of whether a video is present or not, which is then used as a predictive factor for campaign success. Contrastingly, videography has been used by ethnographers to observe the minutiae of naturally occurring practices among entrepreneurs and stakeholders, using multimodal analyses (verbal and non-verbal forms of communication) to inductively find 'thick description' explanations (Clarke, 2011; Thompson & Illes, 2020). Scholars have also used video elicitation using paid actors to implement treatment effects in experimental studies with the aim of testing hypotheses (Shane et al., 2019). These examples point to different methodological underpinnings that guide researchers (i.e., positivism and interpretivism), which adds a layer of complexity to understanding the uses of video research methods. What is more, entrepreneurial phenomena can be difficult to capture using video methods as entrepreneurship is an uncertain enterprise, is empirically very diverse, and often takes place in private spaces. The challenges and varieties of uses of video research methods, hence, are diverse in their assumptions, limitations and benefits. In the remainder of this study, we aim to bring coherence to the uses of video research methods for entrepreneurship scholars, and to highlight further possibilities.

METHODS: REVIEWING RESEARCH USING VIDEO METHODS IN ENTREPRENEURSHIP

Our review focuses on research in leading international journals that publish entrepreneurship studies and use video methods in their research designs. The methodology for our review is guided by Christianson's (2018) review of video-based research in the organization and management literature. To begin, we identified the top-tier journals using the *Academic Journal Guide* maintained by the Chartered Association of Business Schools (ABS), which is recognized by entrepreneurship scholars as a quality list of rankings (Fayolle & Wright, 2014). We focused on the leading journals (ranked 3, 4 and 4*) in the fields of 'Entrepreneurship and small business management', 'Innovation', 'General management' and 'Organization studies'. This resulted in a group of 41 journals that represented entrepreneurship specific journals as well as broader management and organization studies journals. We excluded five journals as they do not publish empirical studies (e.g. *Academy of Management Annals*, *International Journal of Management Reviews*).

To discover relevant video-based entrepreneurship studies, we searched for the word *video** in entrepreneurship specific journals, and *video* AND entrepreneur** in general management and organization journals, that appear anywhere in the full text. This led to an initial list of 1,598 articles identified. To narrow our focus, we manually reviewed the articles and only included articles that were empirical, and that used video recordings as part of their methodology. We included studies where video was used to generate other data (e.g. using video as stimulus for an experiment), as well as where videos are themselves subject to analysis. These criteria resulted in 142 articles being included in our review. Table 11.1 provides an overview of the articles included from each journal. It shows the number of hits in the initial *video* (AND *entrepreneur)* search and the number of articles that met the inclusion criteria for review, both as an absolute number and classified by analysis type (e.g., qualitative, mixed methods, quantitative).

We utilized thematic analysis (Boyatzis, 1998; Braun & Clarke 2006) to examine the current video methods used in entrepreneurship research. In the first round of analysis we read each article and coded the articles for basic information about the research question, phenomena of interest, theoretical lens, overarching research methodology (e.g. grounded theory, ethnography, case study, comparative statistical analysis), and sources of data other than video (e.g. interviews, ethnographic field notes, surveys, documents, archival). We also coded how researchers were using videos in their method-

Table 11.1 *Articles by journal and analysis type*

Journal	Articles with video*(AND entrepreneur*) in full text	Articles with video used in research design	Quality	Mixed Methods	Quantity
Journal of Business Venturing	93	25	8	4	13
Entrepreneurship Theory and Practice	84	16	4	4	8
Academy of Management Journal	75	12	6	1	5
Entrepreneurship and Regional Development	45	12	12	–	–
Journal of Business Research	79	9	7	–	2
Research Policy	91	9	6	2	1
Journal of Small Business Management	37	7	3	2	2
Journal of Management Studies	55	6	5	1	–
Organization Studies	89	6	6	–	–
International Small Business Journal	40	5	5	–	–
Journal of Business Ethics	113	5	5	–	–
Small Business Economics	60	5	1	1	3
Strategic Entrepreneurship Journal	37	5	4	–	1
Organization Science	97	4	2	1	1
R and D Management	58	4	3	–	1
Academy of Management Perspectives	81	3	3	–	–
British Journal of Management	18	2	2	–	–

Journal	Articles with video*(AND entrepreneur*) in full text	Articles with video used in research design	Quality	Mixed Methods	Quantity
Business and Society	19	1	1	–	–
California Management Review	101	1	1	–	–
European Management Review	9	1	1	–	–
Family Business Review	11	1	1	–	–
Group and Organization Management	15	1	–	–	1
Journal of Management Inquiry	17	1	1	–	–
Organization	42	1	1	–	–
Total	1366	142	88	16	38

Table 11.2 Articles by video research method and year range

Type/year range	Pre-2005	2005–2009	2010–2014	2015–2019	Total
1. Videography – pitching	–	0	3	10	13
2. Videography – other	–	1	4	9	14
3. Video content analysis – crowdfunding	–	0	1	24	25
4. Video content analysis – archival video	3	5	13	41	62
5. Video elicitation – interviews	1	3	1	9	14
6. Video elicitation – experiments and interventions	1	1	2	9	13
Other	–	1	–	–	1
Total	5	11	24	102	142

ology: description of videos; nature of video; videographer (e.g. researcher, participant or third party generated); form of data (e.g., verbatim transcript, conversation analysis (CA) transcript, direct from video, multimodal); data analysis (e.g., gestalt, coding, count); and focus of video analysis (e.g., verbal, nonverbal, emotional, interactional, sociomaterial).

In the second round of analysis, we compared the use of video methods in the research designs of these articles and clustered them into six broader themes (naturally occurring pitching practice, naturally occurring other practices, crowdfunding, archival data, video interviews, and experiments and interventions), which we then organized into three main categories (videography of entrepreneurship 'in the wild', video content analysis of entrepreneur generated videos, and video elicitation in manufactured contexts). Table 11.2 shows the spread of articles across the six sub-categories over time.

In the final round of analysis, we re-read the articles within each of the six sub-categories and identified the common themes in terms of phenomena, types of data and focus of analysis. As part of this round we coded articles on whether video data was a necessary element that drove the interpretation of entrepreneurial phenomena. We examined whether video data was a necessary element in the development of the findings. Specifically, we coded each study to understand how the unique timing, visual and audio affordances of video brought decisive information that would not have been possible with any other method. For example, some studies use video recorded interviews, but subsequently converted them into verbal transcripts, thereby losing the timing and visual affordances of video. Similarly, many video content analysis studies included videos as archival documents, yet there is little evidence that video data informed the analysis. Through this process we identified exemplar studies for each form of video method and highlighted the potential of video research to shed new light on entrepreneurship phenomena in the findings section.

FINDINGS: THREE VIDEO RESEARCH METHODS IN ENTREPRENEURSHIP RESEARCH

Our review reveals three main video research methods currently used in entrepreneurship research: (i) videography of entrepreneurship 'in the wild' (such as live pitching and other naturally occurring practices); (ii) video content analysis of entrepreneur-generated videos (such as crowdfunding and archival videos); and (iii) video elicitation in manufactured contexts (such as interviews, focus groups, and experiments and interventions). Table 11.3 provides an overview of these three types of video studies categorized into six sub-types.

As highlighted in Figure 11.1, there has been a rapid rise in entrepreneurship research utilizing video methods in recent years. Prior to 2010, only 16 studies of entrepreneurship had involved videos in their methodology. These early studies mainly relied on reviewing archival company produced videos in case analysis (e.g. Bradbury & Clair, 1999) or creating video-taped interviews or focus groups with entrepreneurs (e.g. Buttner, 2001; Hienerth, 2006). In terms of analysis, most of this early video-based research focused on either on converting video to verbatim transcripts (thus losing visual elements) (e.g. Buttner, 2001; Hienerth, 2006) or reviewing videos as part of a broader interpretive analysis of case (e.g. Berger et al., 2004).

The first half of the last decade saw a steady rise in entrepreneurship research using video research methods (24 articles from 2010–2014), driven mainly by the increasing use of videos as a form of archival data in single or multiple case study analysis. This time period also saw the first use of videography in entrepreneurship research, with efforts to observe entrepreneurial practice 'in the wild' in order to study everyday practices enacted by entrepreneurs and various stakeholders (e.g. Clarke, 2011; Cornelissen et al., 2012). It has only been in the past five years however that video research methods has really expanded in entrepreneurship studies, driven by the accessibility and affordability of quality video recording equipment. We found that 102 articles in leading entrepreneurship, management and organization journals were published in this timeframe, with 90 of these (63% of total video articles) published in just the past three years (2017–2019). One explanation of this dramatic rise can be explained by the surge in crowdfunding research, follow-

Table 11.3 *Overview of types of video research methods*

Type	Data	Phenomena	Exemplar studies	Limitations	Possibilities
Videography of entrepreneurship 'in the Wild'					
1. Entrepreneurial pitching	Pitching competitions Q&A with judges	Gender inequalities Verbal, non-verbal, socio-material, temporal, emotional cues	Wheadon & Duval-Couetil (2019) Katila et al. (2019) Chalmers & Shaw (2017)	Investment is sole purpose of pitching Heavily produced and edited videos	Varied interactions Broader institutional practices surrounding pitching Material elements
2. Other practices	Everyday practices of entrepreneurship	Interaction organization between entrepreneurs and other stakeholders; Impression management; Gestures, Metaphors	Clarke (2011) Cornelissen et al. (2012)	Decontextualizing across cases Entrepreneurs' behaviour, rather than interactional	Holistic inclusion of interaction, bodily conduct, materiality and talk during the Accomplishment of various entrepreneurship practices
Video content analysis of entrepreneur generated videos					
3. Crowdfunding videos	Crowdfunding campaign videos (e.g. Kickstarter, Indiegogo)	Determinants of crowdfunding success	Jiang et al. (2019) Kaminski & Hopp (2019 Parhankangas & Renko (2017)	Reliance on count data Deductive theory testing Underappreciating the crowd Stripping videos of context	Role of object artefacts Emotions in crowdfunding Interactions with the crowd

Type	Data	Phenomena	Exemplar studies	Limitations	Possibilities
4. Archival videos	Promotional and informational Second-hand interviews Television news stories Documentaries Presentations	Social entrepreneurship Innovation Family business issues Business model development	Dodd (2014) Yu et al. (2013)	Objective insight into complex processes Decontextualization of the original purpose of videos	Contextually situated meanings of videos Visibility in findings sections
Elicitation videos in 'manufactured' contexts					
5. Interviews and focus groups	Individual interviews Paired interviews Focus groups	Sociomateriality Power structures Co-creating knowledge	Poldner et al. (2019) Haberman & Danes (2007) Henry et al. (2018)	Reduction to verbatim transcripts	Understanding relationality and power structures Situating the researcher Tone, expression and gestures Entrepreneurs in context (body/artefacts)
6. Experiments and interventions	Professional actors Television clips Entrepreneur generated videos	Investor decision making and biases Entrepreneurial passion	Shane et al. (2019) Ashman et al. (2018)	Positivist manipulations and decontextualization	Engage online entrepreneurial communities Stimulate qualitative insights from entrepreneurs

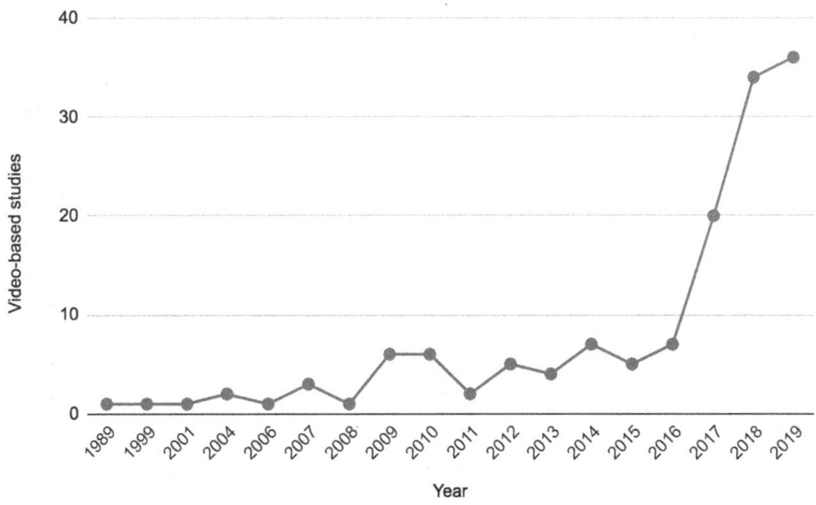

Figure 11.1 Video-based studies by year

ing the publication of the seminal paper by Mollick in 2014. The accessibility of crowdfunding data and its clear performance outcomes has been a boon for positivist video content analysis in entrepreneurship research. Nevertheless, we find that the majority of these studies use a simple binary measure if a video exists or not, in order to predict crowdfunding outcomes, which utilizes very little information from the video data itself.

The majority of entrepreneurship studies using video methods utilized qualitative analysis, with less than a third of studies using solely quantitative analysis. The growing research on crowdfunding was the only domain in which qualitative analysis has not been used, as all 28 studies published to date relied on quantitative analysis. The most common form of video research method was the use of video content analysis of archival videos (44%). These predominantly qualitative studies utilized company generated videos as part of the secondary documents in conducting case study research. However, a closer look at articles using videos as archival data raises doubts about the extent to which these videos were truly part of the research design. Whilst some studies show clear linkages to how the archival videos were core to the findings and analysis (e.g. Yu et al., 2013), many studies only make passing reference to the archival videos in the methodology, which leaves the reader uncertain to what degree the videos formed part of the overall understanding of the case. We now delve into each of the three main video research methods.

Videography of Entrepreneurship 'in the Wild'

A small number of researchers are pioneering the use of videography for viewing real-time, naturally occurring entrepreneurial phenomena. By 'real-time' and 'natural', we mean that researchers shoot or collect video recordings of entrepreneurs and stakeholders as they go about their daily work, with limited researcher intervention. The majority of these videos have focused on entrepreneurial pitching, with only a few studies venturing into more everyday entrepreneurial action and interaction (which we return to in the research agenda).

Videography of entrepreneurial pitching

Videography on pitching emphasizes the benefits of focusing in real-time on the subtle actions and interactions enacted by entrepreneurs and investors throughout the pitching process (Pollack et al., 2012). Early videography on pitching relied heavily on (sometimes edited) footage from popular entrepreneurship reality television programmes 'Shark Tank' and 'Dragons' Den' (e.g. Maxwell et al., 2011; Maxwell & Lévesque, 2014; Pollack et al., 2012). Whilst most of these studies focus on the televised pitch and interactions with judges, some studies utilized novel elements of the program to better understand the practices of pitching such as the back stories of the participants and interviews with investors (Wheadon & Duval-Couetil 2019). More recent studies have accessed insights from the expanding world of entrepreneurship pitching competitions at the global and local levels, while other studies made use of videos of interactions with investors in Q&A sessions (Cardon et al., 2017; Chalmers & Shaw, 2017; Kanze et al., 2018) and feedback sessions with mentors prior to the pitch (van Werven et al., 2019).

Most videographic studies of pitching focus on coding direct from video to capture the textual, audio and visual elements. Mixed methods coding was the most common analysis approach either through: (i) fine grained qualitative coding frame is used to produce quantitative insights was the most common form of analysis (Maxwell et al., 2011; Maxwell and Lévesque, 2014; Wheadon & Duval-Couetil, 2019), or (ii) inductive coding of pitching followed by experiment to understand causality (Chen et al., 2009; Clarke et al., 2018). Other studies utilized computer-aided analysis through the use of basket of words techniques on transcripts (Kanze et al., 2018) or the use of machine learning algorithms to detect emotional displays in facial expressions in videos (Stroe et al., 2019). More interpretive oriented studies engaged in qualitative analytic traditions such as narrative analysis to understand rhetoric (van Werven et al., 2019); ethnographic field notes to capture material and affective experiences (Katila et al., 2019); or conversation analysis (Chalmers & Shaw, 2017).

Exemplary studies

One influential stream of videographic pitching research focuses on rhetoric, narratives and emotional displays used by entrepreneurs to legitimize their ventures. Katila et al. (2019) exemplify a fine-grained videographic approach by engaging in a more gestalt analysis of the verbal, non-verbal, material, temporal, spatial, and relational, and bodily elements of pitching. The authors' analysis reveals the cues utilized by the eventual winner to convey openness, trustworthiness and confidence to the judges. Katila et al. (2019) thus show the value of combining video with ethnographic field notes, as the video recordings of pitches allowed the authors to revisit and re-examine the embodied performances of the entrepreneurial pitching in greater detail than was captured through initial observations. Similarly, Wheadon and Duval-Couetil (2019) tap into the rich emotional, interactional and socio-material elements of videography to reveal how the content and social interactions displayed in the Shark Tank programs to create, reinforce or challenge gender inequalities. Finally, Chalmers and Shaw (2017) illustrate the potential of fine-grained conversation analysis of videos focusing upon the verbal, non-verbal (e.g. facial expressions, nodding), socio-material, temporal, and emotional dimensions entrepreneur-investor interactions.

Limitations

It is common for pitching research to view the relationship between entrepreneurs and investor(s) based upon little more than a financial exchange – a relationship that is easily quantified for purposes of objective study. However, Teague et al. (2020) point out that there may be a variety of forms of pitching practices that are useful in different circumstances, such as gaining feedback or practicing non-verbal communication techniques. Another limitation of current videographic research on pitching is the use of heavily produced and edited videos that moves more towards the realm of video content analysis (which we discuss next). As noted by Wheadon and Duval-Couetil (2019) and Maxwell et al. (2011), reality television shows such as Shark Tank selectively emphasize or downplay certain features to portray entrepreneurs and investors in ways that align with their narrative and stories. Some researchers have taken steps to limit this issue by analysing unedited pitching footage (e.g., Maxwell et al., 2011; Maxwell & Lévesque, 2014) or contacting the producers of the show and the entrepreneur to verify the 'authenticity' of the pitches and interaction portrayed on the show (Pollack et al., 2012). Nevertheless, these videos are primarily for entertainment purposes, which results in potentially artificial interactions between entrepreneurs and investors in front of an audience, as investors may be emphasizing certain behaviours in the knowledge they are being assessed by a televised public.

Videography of other entrepreneurship practices

Just as video-based research on pitching emphasizes real-time behaviour, scholars have begun to use videography to understand a broader scope of entrepreneurship practices whilst keeping focus on the subtle actions and interactions enacted by entrepreneurs and (possible) stakeholders. Many of these studies default towards adopting a positivist methodology of qualitative inquiry, which aims to theorize stable explanations across cases amenable to further quantitative inquiry. For example, Preller et al. (2018) videotaped naturally occurring team strategy meetings to investigate how entrepreneurial visions held by members of founding teams impact the future development of entrepreneurial opportunities. Others adopt interpretivist methodologies that remain contextually rich (Clarke, 2011; Cornelissen et al., 2012; Thompson & Illes, 2020). A main strength of these studies are often a combination of verbal, non-verbal (tone, gestures, facial expressions), relational (interactions among employees, customers and financiers) and material objects (visual symbols, artefacts). By combining these elements, the authors aim to connect the bodily, material and discursive components of entrepreneurial practices. These studies often supplement video with other forms of qualitative data, such as observation notes, interviews and archival data.

Exemplary studies

The work by Clarke (2011) and Cornelissen et al. (2012) exemplifies the potential of videography for understanding the real-time unfolding of practices of entrepreneurship. In Clarke's (2011) study, the author asks how entrepreneurs justify and legitimize their new ventures to acquire necessary resources for venture growth. Rather than interview or survey entrepreneurs and stakeholders separately, the author made videos of three entrepreneurs as they interacted with various stakeholders in real time. The study has vastly deepened our understanding of resourcing practice and impression management by offering recorded material that includes real-time entrepreneurial language, gestures and visual tools and symbols used to develop, discuss and establish legitimacy. In particular, a close analysis of the videos reveals the ways in which entrepreneurs 'set the scene', embody their professional identity, and regulate their emotions when engaging in resourcing practice. Similar to Clarke (2011), Cornelissen et al. (2012) explored how entrepreneurs gain support and traction for novel venture ideas by shadowing and shooting video of the interactions of two entrepreneurs over the course of one month. An analysis of the video corpus shows how gestures and metaphors are utilized alongside speech to emphasize the agency of the entrepreneur, their control of the venture, and argue for the predictability of an uncertain future. The authors also utilized unstructured interviews with the entrepreneurs in order to gain the entrepreneurs' reflection on specific recorded incidents.

Limitations

Despite the gains being made with using videography to understand real-time entrepreneurial action, there are a number of limitations of current research. Often studies emphasize verbal language (i.e., verbal transcripts), and subsequently code and combine coding patterns of verbal talk across data of multiple cases to generate theory. However, developing codes and organizing them across cases may remove much of the contextual richness available in natural conversation, while downplaying the temporal, embodied, emotional, material nature of the interactions. Studies that remain contextually rich also nevertheless remain entrepreneur-centred. In these studies, the authors observe naturally occurring practices, but the analytical focus remains on theorizing entrepreneurial behaviour (talk, gestures, use of visuals). Hence, while data captures interactions among entrepreneurial practitioners (entrepreneurs, investors, suppliers, employees), theorizing reflects the researchers' *a priori* assumptions and interests of the entrepreneur's behaviour. While observable interactions in real-time evidences the importance and connectedness of the body, materials and discursive elements, aiming to create generalizable theories may downplay the variability of these interactions in the real world. A final limitation is that current research using videography of naturally occurring practices often presumes that the resulting videos represent objective data upon which new theory can be constructed. This fails to appreciate that the nuances and varieties of practices, as well as the researchers' presence and decisions about what and how to film that are vital to the production of the data in the first place.

Video Content Analysis of Entrepreneur-generated Videos

Our review shows that the most common method is conduct video content analysis that collects and analyses videos generated by entrepreneurs themselves. Crowdfunding videos are publicly available and have provided a novel source for the growth of quantitative video content analysis, whilst qualitative studies have included videos generated by enterprises for promotional and informational purposes as part of their case study archives.

Crowdfunding videos

To date, researchers have utilized video content analysis of crowdfunding videos to gain insight to campaign success using exclusively quantitative methods. Hence, video content analysis on crowdfunding draws on a positivist methodology in an attempt to create objectivity and predict the outcomes of crowdfunding campaigns. Crowdfunding research is thus exclusively quantitative, with a heavily reliance on count data (e.g. video/no video, number of videos, video length). Even those studies which engage with videos in more depth still attempt to reduce the video to a score out of five based on certain characteristics, such as 'video quality' or 'passion displayed' that can be linked to success. The focus on quantitative research can be explained by the allure of large-Ns (e.g. Thies et al.'s 2019 study of 56,000 Kickstarter campaigns) and the accessibility of dependent variables of success such as 'funds raised', 'goals reached' and 'numbers of contributors'. This quantitative treatment is compounded by the seminal study on crowdfunding by Mollick (2014), which found that the mere presence of a video can influence campaign success. Building on this study, the majority of crowdfunding studies (13/25) incorporate the binary variable of whether video was present as part of the crowdfunding campaign as a control or independent variable to analyse determinants of success. As a result, over half of the video content analysis-based studies on crowdfunding reduce the complexity of crowdfunding campaign videos to a 'yes' or 'no'.

Only nine of the studies made use of meaningful elements of crowdfunding videos, such as: (i) coding direct from video to understand quality through questions such as 'This video was well done' and 'This video is high quality' assessed in a likert scale (Chan et al., 2019; Scheaf et al., 2018; Younkin & Kuppuswamy, 2019); (ii) converting videos to verbatim transcripts and using word counts and basket of words approaches to understand persuasion and rhetoric (Anglin et al., 2018; Kaminski & Hopp, 2019; Parhankangas & Renko, 2017); (iii) coding directly from videos to understand displays of entrepreneurial passion using Chen et al.'s (2009) passion scale (Chan et al., 2019; Oo et al., 2019); and (iv) utilizing machine learning algorithms to identify specific elements in video such as objects (Kaminski & Hopp, 2019) or facial expressions (Jiang et al., 2019). While the focus of video-based crowdfunding research has been on quantitatively examining determinants of success, these studies provide a grounding for more interpretative inquiry.

Exemplary studies

Exemplary studies using video content analysis of crowdfunding videos have explored how displays of positive emotions such as passion and joy are linked to campaign success (Chan et al., 2019; Oo et al., 2019). Jiang et al.'s (2019) recent study makes use of automated facial expression analysis technology, FaceReader, to understand the role of joy displayed by entrepreneurs at the beginning and ending of crowdfunding pitches. Kaminski and Hopp (2019) explore how language and visual cues (e.g. objects, images, artefacts) influence campaign outcomes by using the Google Cloud Video Intelligence API. Analysis of over 900,000 objects from just over 20,000 campaigns reveals that illustrations or sketches of products have a negative impact on campaign success as investors may be more interested in finished products or prototypes than depictions and plans. Finally, Parhankangas and Renko (2017) use basket of word analysis on verbatim transcripts to argue that social campaigns are more successful when they use language that is more understandable and relatable to the crowd. Throughout these exemplary studies, the authors support insights from the audio and visual elements from crowdfunding videos with text from campaign descriptions.

Limitations

Video content analysis on crowdfunding has some clear limitations. First, most studies reduce videos to count data, which, while gaining in generalizability, loses the potential richness of videos and fails to elaborate the role of video in legitimizing the venture or persuading the investor. As such, video data plays a relatively subordinate role in analyses and findings. This research may also under-appreciate the role of the 'crowd' in crowdfunding by ignoring the relational and interactional nature of crowdfunding (videos), such as their sharing/commenting on social media. Finally, whilst studies of crowdfunding videos using machine learning show promise for analysing the wealth of data available, they tend to strip videos of their context through analytical procedures, which may create contextual voids and reduce practical applicability in the pursuit of quantitative predictions.

Archival videos

The second use of video content analysis is collecting and analysing of archival videos. Researchers who draw on archival videos overwhelmingly use positivist methodologies in order to view this source of data is an objective historical account of events, decisions or actions over the course of the research timeframe. For example, Yu et al. (2013) argue that China Central Television provides accurate and unbiased stories of Chinese rural entrepreneurs, which can be used to qualitatively build new theory. Archival videos are predominantly used in qualitative case studies and remain the most common form of method using videos in entrepreneurship research overall. The content of archival videos ranges broadly from promotional and informational videos, to second-hand interviews, television news stories, documentaries, presentations by managers and entrepreneurs, and recorded histories of product development. All of these archival videos are produced either by the focal organizations, or a third-party, and may vary in their manufactured/natural dimensions (e.g., television story versus a recorded conversation). Archival videos are mostly used in combination with other qualitative information (e.g., observations and interviews, archival documents and images) to generate insights into single or multiple case studies. Overall, content analysis of archival videos is seen as a way to gain insight into the development trajectory of a case and develop theoretical concepts.

Exemplary studies

One exemplary case using content analysis of archival videos in a single case design is that of Dodd (2014). In this study, the author explores entrepreneurial notions of place, power and practice in creative entrepreneurship through a longitudinal single case analysis of the punk rock band Rancid. The author combines 64 archival videos (including, second-hand video interviews, 'webisodes' and music videos) with a wide range of other data sources including albums, reviews, commentaries and web sources. Investigating the qualitative data through content coding, the author distils Rancid's entrepreneurial story as a cyclical, non-linear journey from periphery to centre, and back again. Another exemplary study is that of Yu et al. (2013) who use a multiple case study design. The authors use 91 television news stories, each about one case, produced by China Central Television to understand how Chinese rural entrepreneurs navigate their institutional environment. Using qualitative content coding, the authors investigate the links between institutional elements (i.e., regulative, normative, and cognitive components) and the strategic behaviours of the entrepreneurs as they are represented in the news stories.

Limitations

Studies using content analysis of archival videos have a number of limitations. First and foremost, a closer investigation into the precise role an archival video played in analyses reveals that many studies remain unclear how the video informed findings. Findings sections of these studies sometimes indicate a quote of a practitioner taken from an archival video, but many studies do not. As such, archival video often plays a subordinate role to other qualitative data, such as primary interview. Second, by co-opting archival videos for research purposes and arguing they provide objective insight into complex processes by which entrepreneurs generally achieve their aims, researchers might be downplaying the impact of decontextualization. For example, many archival videos are created for situational and practical reasons by entrepreneurs: the videos are themselves products of situationally relevant practitioner meanings, interests and goals. Thus, using them as objective data for cross-case content analysis may remove the reasons for which the videos were created in the first place. Alternatively, Abdelnour and Branzei (2010) adopt an interpretivist methodology and explore the development of fuel-efficient stoves in Darfur to theorize how subsistence markets are socially constructed in post-conflict settings. In this study, videos are conceived not as objective data but as a core element of discursive strategies by development organizations operating in post-conflict settings.

Video Elicitation in Manufactured Contexts

Our review found that a number of researchers use video elicitation methods in manufactured contexts in order to generate other qualitative or quantitative data that can be used for further analysis. By 'manufactured contexts', we mean that the researchers (and sometimes third parties) have taken a number of steps to control and construct the context in which videos are created.

Interviews and focus groups

The simplest form of video elicitation involves video-recorded interviews and focus groups. Entrepreneurship studies using video interviews and focus groups are exclusively qualitative, with the videos generally accompanied with observations and document analysis. Despite the explicit mention of video recording in the methods section of these papers, the authors tend to reduce these video interviews to verbatim transcripts in their analysis, rendering them equivalent to audio-recorded interviews. The methodological stance underpinning verbatim transcripts is often positivism, which views the statements by entrepreneurs in video recorded interviews or focus groups as objective data, which can be used in cross-case analysis for generating theory. However, a few studies have adopted interpretivism and have taken advantage of audio-visual and interactional elements to illustrate the potential of individual and group video interviews in explaining entrepreneurial phenomena.

Exemplary studies

Poldner et al.'s (2019) study of sustainable entrepreneurship in the fashion industry exposes the potential of using video interviews to examine socio-materiality and the bodily nature of entrepreneurial endeavour. The authors use video interviews with designer entrepreneurs in their own studios to analyse the combination of verbal talk, gestures, visual materials and objects, which reveals how the body and material come together in the performance of sustainable entrepreneurship. The authors make use of multiple sources of qualitative data to support insights from the video interviews including participant observation, photos, attended catwalk shows, collected brochures and purchased artifacts. Additionally, Haberman and Danes (2007) illustrate how video-recorded group interviews can reveal power structures in entrepreneurial teams. They record video interviews with father-son and father-daughter dyads in family businesses who are in the process of transferring management control. The analysis of the videos focuses on the ways in which power structures, hierarchy and gender roles are enacted through verbal and non-verbal actions in intergenerational relationships. Finally, Henry et al.'s (2018) study of Māori entrepreneurship in the mainstream screen industry demonstrates how video interviews can assist in the co-creation of knowledge with the community. The authors co-create a video documentary and investigate the tone of voice and facial expressions whilst empowering and advancing Māori entrepreneurship. This exemplar reflects how the production of video interviews can be a tool to conduct research alongside and for communities, aligning with calls for participatory and emancipatory inquiry in entrepreneurship (Gough et al., 2014).

Limitations

Current research using video-recorded interviews is often limited by the reduction of videos to verbatim transcripts. While reducing interviews to verbatim transcripts is necessary from a positivist standpoint, it may lose the potential richness of video interviews by failing to exploit the insights offered by tone and facial expression, body language and gestures, and other material elements that influence entrepreneurial lived experience. Rendering video recorded interviews and focus groups to text may obscure the insights that could be garnered from analysing interactions and group dynamics between those in the videos. As highlighted by Poldner et al. (2019), the overreliance on talk and text, and the prioritization of verbal accounts, dismisses how 'video and other visual methods offer an aesthetic avenue to knowledge creation beyond the textual, rational evidence' (p. 222). In this current treatment, the use of video recorded interviews often does not take full advantage of multimodal elements that uncover the everyday practices of entrepreneurship, relying instead on how entrepreneurs describe their world.

Experiments and interventions

The second way in which scholars use video elicitation methods is through experimental and interventionist research designs. The purpose of videos in these studies is to elicit various responses from research participants (entrepreneurs, investors, students or 'the crowd') in order to generate other qualitative or quantitative data. Hence, video is commonly seen as a 'stimulus' to generate survey or qualitative data, rather than being the subject of analysis itself. Scholars that use video elicitation to generate quantitative data begin from a positivist methodology and thus strive to eliminate contextual aspects of a phenomenon to focus subjects' impressions on a single behaviour. For example, Shane et al. (2019) commissioned the production of videos that include only one person in the frame, the paid actor, who pitches a short-scripted idea. The use of manufactured context videos has recently gained traction in experimental studies, which includes: scholars using entrepreneur generated video, or videotaping hired professional actors to enact various forms of behaviour. These videos are then used to stimulate the participant to generate another dataset, such as completion of a survey, which is analysed quantitatively.

Exemplary studies

One exemplary study of using video to elicit responses combines manufactured context videos, surveys and fMRI technology. Shane et al. (2019) examine the effect of founder passion on the decision making of informal investors by testing hypotheses formulated from entrepreneurial passion and neural engagement theories. To do so, the authors recruit ten actors and had them deliver two scripted pitches each in front of a camera: once with high passion and once with low passion. Next, the authors asked 19 randomly assigned informal investors to view the entrepreneur pitch videos while undergoing fMRI scanning. Subsequently, the participants were asked to complete a short survey that reported interest in investing in the ventures.

Only one study using videos to elicit responses begins with an interpretative methodology to generate qualitative data. In their innovative study, Ashman et al. (2018) engaged with young YouTubers striving to become 'autopreneurs' (a portmanteau of the terms 'autobiographical' and 'entrepreneur') by participating in 'vlogging' – the practices of creating, uploading and commenting upon YouTube videos. Their analyses of participatory observation notes, combined with interviews, reveal the ways in which neoliberal ideologies shape and govern how these young entrepreneurs think and act. Ashman et al. (2018) hence aim to produce knowledge through technology-enabled interaction with participants on their own terms.

Limitations

In Shane et al.'s (2019) article, the brain images of informal investors that result from watching the manufactured videos are assumed to be driven from only the actors' behaviour in the video and not confounded by the manipulated and decontextualized nature of the videos, the reliability of fMRI technology, nor the research participants' unusual immediate environment (i.e. being in an fMRI machine watching entrepreneurship videos). Hence, studies that adopt a positivist methodology and use elicitation videos to generate quantitative data are possibly limited in their applicability to real world settings, where contextual information, pre-existing relations, norms, situational cues and differing interpretations of information also shape entrepreneurial outcomes. On the other hand, using videos to participate in entrepreneurship communities may have the limitation of shaping entrepreneurial behaviour that the researchers wish to study, which, at an extreme, may lead to self-fulfilling research findings.

A RESEARCH AGENDA FOR VIDEO-BASED ENTREPRENEURSHIP RESEARCH

Our literature review demonstrates that researchers have utilized three video research methods – videography, video content analysis and video elicitation – to yield a greater understanding of entrepreneurial phenomena. Nevertheless, video data often takes a subordinate role to other forms of qualitative and quantitative data, and only a limited number of studies fully utilize video's unique affordances. In particular, the field has scarcely used videography of real-time, naturally occurring entrepreneurship practices, despite its unique ability to render them visible for analysis.

In this section, we develop a research agenda for video-based entrepreneurship studies that capitalizes on the unique audio, visual and timing affordances of video by building upon the exemplary studies from the systematic review. We draw inspiration from traditions of video-based research in management, organization and strategy research (Christianson, 2018; Gylfe et al., 2016; LeBaron et al., 2018) and the broader fields of research on anthropology, sociology and psychology (Erickson, 2011; Knoblauch et al., 2008; Reavey, 2012). The research agenda overall highlights how video-based entrepreneurship research provides unparalleled insight into the interactional, embodied, emotional and material aspects of entrepreneurial action – theoretical concepts that remain fundamental to the future of entrepreneurship studies.

Table 11.4 provides a summary of the possible research directions to understand the relational, embodied, material and emotional aspects of entrepreneurial action. Whilst we have separated these elements in this review, one of the main benefits of video-based research is the ability to observe the combination of verbal, non-verbal (tone, gestures, facial expressions), interactional (founders, employees, customers and financiers) and material objects (visual symbols, artefacts). Future research can, therefore, use video data to explore the combinations of interactional, bodily, emotional and material components that shape entrepreneurial action.

Viewing the Interactional Aspects of Entrepreneurial Action

A growing number of entrepreneurship scholars argue that most, if not all, aspects of entrepreneurship happens in and through interaction with others (Chalmers & Shaw, 2017). In particular, these scholars aim to unpack interaction sequences related to entrepreneurship by revealing the underlying, and often tacit, ways in which entrepreneurial actors (entrepreneurs, investors, clients, etc.) orient to and respond to immediately prior actions *in situ* (Campbell, 2019).

Table 11.4 A research agenda for video in entrepreneurship research

Theoretical Focus	Videography of entrepreneurship 'in the Wild' (Pitching & other practices)	Video content analysis of entrepreneur generated videos (Crowdfunding & archival videos)	Elicitation videos in 'manufactured' contexts (Interview, focus groups & experiments)	Research Questions
Interaction	Varieties of interaction sequences among entrepreneurs, audiences, and investors before, after and during pitches Interaction sequences among entrepreneurs and other stakeholders in various naturalistic settings	Interaction dynamics between the entrepreneur and the crowd and how these are revealed in video updates Enactment and maintenance of gender stereotypes enacted in crowdfunding communities.	Power relations, gender roles and group dynamics in investor-entrepreneur relationships or entrepreneurial teams.	How do entrepreneurs build support and legitimate ideas in interaction with investors, customers and community? How, why and when do entrepreneurs interact with their crowd in crowdfunding campaigns? How are power relations and gender roles enacted in investor-entrepreneur relationships?
Embodiment	Gestures, gaze and body position in pitching Analysing gestures, gaze and body position within interaction sequences in various naturalistic settings	Facial expression, body language and gestures in crowdfunding pitches	Embodied aspects of everyday entrepreneurial work in context Participatory documentaries to examine culturally embedded, inarticulate, and embodied aspects of entrepreneurial action	How do bodily gestures, gaze and position matter for interactional outcomes? How do entrepreneurs consciously and unconsciously utilize bodies to gain support for their ventures? How do entrepreneurs physically orient themselves to accomplish their everyday work?

Theoretical Focus	Videography of entrepreneurship 'in the Wild' (Pitching & other practices)	Video content analysis of entrepreneur generated videos (Crowdfunding & archival videos)	Elicitation videos in 'manufactured' contexts (Interview, focus groups & experiments)	Research Questions
Emotion	Verbal, vocal, facial and bodily emotional displays in pitching and other setting	Verbal, vocal, facial and bodily emotional displays in crowdfunding Shared emotions between entrepreneurs and crowd	Emotional tone, expression and gestures in interviews and focus groups	How and why do entrepreneurs use emotions to gain support for their ventures? How do collective emotions emerge along the entrepreneurial journey? How do entrepreneurs create emotional contagion amongst other stakeholders?
Materiality	Material elements of pitching such as pitch decks, demos, clothing, uniforms and sets Everyday objects and artefacts related to entrepreneurial practice	Objects and artefacts, such as images and prototypes, in crowdfunding	The material context in which the interviews take place	When, where, how and why material objects, settings and technologies are used in real-time to accomplish entrepreneurship practices? How do material objects and artefacts become relevant in entrepreneurial interactions? How and why are material objects and artefacts being used before, during and after pitches?

One of video's key strengths is observational access to the fast-paced interactional sequences practitioners actually undertake (Hindmarsh & Llewellyn, 2018; Jarrett & Liu, 2018). Researchers analysing video data can carefully reveal the variety of forms of particular interactional sequences and practitioner methods that give an orderliness to social situations and accomplish tasks and aims (Vesa & Vaara, 2014). Hence, rather than turn to individual introspection, video data draws analytical attention to interactions that underscore entrepreneurial phenomena, such as decision making, creativity and design (Campbell, 2019). For example, videography enables researchers to understand the (variety of) interaction sequences among entrepreneurs, audiences, judges and investors that occur before, after and during pitches in certain contexts. This would help answer questions as to how entrepreneurs build support and legitimate ideas in interaction. Research could also explore a broader range of venture-making practices than currently considered. For example, researchers can use videography to reveal and explain the common venture-making practice of 'selling' (Matthews et al., 2018), which incorporates customer agency into interactional processes of opportunity identification, refinement, and exploitation.

Possibilities also exist to explore entrepreneurial interaction through video content analysis and video elicitation. Within crowdfunding research, video content analysis can augment positivist research on the predictors of campaign success by qualitatively appreciating the varieties of interactions and practices enacted and conveyed through crowdfunding videos. These may include unpacking identity work, sensemaking, and gender stereotypes produced through interactions between the entrepreneur and the crowd using real-time video updates and social media comments. Furthermore, following Haberman and Danes (2007), video elicitation can be used to combine group and individual interviews to explore how power structures, gender roles and group dynamics matter in different contexts such as investor-entrepreneur relationships or entrepreneurial teams.

Viewing the Embodied Aspects of Entrepreneurial Action

In recent years, interest in embodiment (and embodied cognition) has grown given findings that bodies (gestures, facial expressions, and positions) and bodily experience influence entrepreneurial action (Clarke et al., 2021). As such, new gains will be made by understanding of the ways in which entrepreneurial practitioners (consciously and unconsciously) use and respond with their bodies when pursuing their aims (Clarke et al., 2018; Cornelissen et al., 2012).

Video provides a powerful means through which researchers can explore embodied lived experience of entrepreneurship. Videography of naturally occurring practices have a natural strength in revealing the importance of bodily gestures, gaze and position for interactional outcomes, such as acquiring resources and legitimacy or establishing partnership (Clarke, 2011; Cornelissen et al., 2012). In the realm of pitching, researchers could pay greater attention to the embodied performances of entrepreneurs to answer questions of how various gestures and body language matter in their conversations with investors and audiences. Video content analysis of crowdfunding videos could pay greater attention to the bodily performances used to secure funding, while, building on Poldner et al. (2019), future video elicitation research could use on-site video interviewing to understand the embodied aspects of everyday entrepreneurial work. Following Slutskaya et al. (2018), future research could also collaborate with entrepreneurs to create participatory video ethnographic documentaries. These videos could subsequently be shown to the same practitioners in order for them to generate qualitative insights into the culturally embedded, inarticulate, and embodied aspects of entrepreneurial action.

Viewing the Emotional Aspects of Entrepreneurial Action

Entrepreneurship scholarship has acknowledged that entrepreneurship is an emotional journey (Baron, 2008; Cardon et al., 2012; Shepherd, 2015), yet scholars have traditionally drawn on survey, interview and experimental data to shed light on entrepreneurial emotions. Recently, a number of researchers have called for further understanding of the situational and contextual occurrences of emotional displays, in order to better theorize how they come to matter for interactional outcomes.

Video-based methods render episodic expressions of emotions as they happen in context and interaction (Liu & Maitlis, 2014). Hence, they provide an opportunity for scholars to understand the situations and contexts in which emotions arise, how they influence interactional outcomes and to challenge the notion of decontextualized emotional displays, emotions as separate processes or as private events (Cardon et al., 2017). Future research could build on recent work that utilizes videography to explore how emotional displays involved in tone, gestures, and facial expressions influence interactions with various stakeholders (Clarke et al., 2018; Jiang et al., 2019; Stroe et al., 2019). On the other hand, future video content analysis studies could explore how various enactments of emotions in crowdfunding campaigns shape emotional contagion between entrepreneurs and their crowd. Finally, video elicitation studies using video interviews also have the potential to gain insights into emotional experiences of passion or failure by analysing audio-visual elements that better appreciate tone, expression and gestures.

Viewing the Material Aspects of Entrepreneurial Action

Future video-based entrepreneurship research is uniquely positioned to enhance our understanding of the ways 'matter matters' for entrepreneurial practice (Hindmarsh & Llewellyn, 2018). As entrepreneurs pursue their aims, they interact with, manipulate and deploy objects, artefacts and technologies (Holt, 2008; Korsgaard, 2011). Livestock, tractors, phones, desks, computers, software etc. are not background elements or abstract resources of entrepreneurship, but are the very means of conducting entrepreneurship (Jones & Holt, 2008; Morgan-Thomas, 2016; Thompson & Byrne, 2019). Current research mostly overlooks or downplays when, where, how and why material objects, settings and technologies are used in real-time to accomplish entrepreneurship practices.

Video methods enables researchers to observe and study the role of material objects, settings and technologies by focusing analytical attention on the conduct of practitioners toward some (but not all) material features of the settings they inhabit. Videography can assist in focusing analytical attention on 'matter as a members' concern', unlocking insight into how and why practitioners manipulate and deploy objects, artefacts and technologies during the performance of a particular entrepreneurship practice (Hindmarsh & Llewellyn, 2018; Holt, 2008; Korsgaard, 2011). As such, video-based methods are critical as they allow researchers to establish the 'procedural consequentiality' of when, where, how and why some object, artefact or technology can be seen to have determinate consequences for the way in which a practice unfolds (Schegloff, 2007).

Future research could utilize videography of the naturally occurring practices related to 'idea generation' to focus on how objects and artefacts, such as Post-It notes, canvases, and whiteboards, become relevant within moments of entrepreneurial actions. In the context of pitching, research could also use videography to explore the role of material elements in conveying meaning, such as pitch decks, demos, and sets, as well as the practices that were used to create them. By attending to materiality in real-time observations of pitching and other practices, researchers have the opportunity to explore the development and varied role of artefacts throughout the entrepreneurial journey.

Studies utilizing video content analysis could also provide access to the material nature of entrepreneurial action. For example, focusing on the material elements of crowdfunding videos provides a fruitful research avenue. Building on the work of Kaminski and Hopp (2019), future qualitative research using crowdfunding videos could also explore the ways in which entrepreneurs engage with objects, artefacts, images, prototypes in their pitches in order to legitimize their ideas and persuade funders. Future video elicitation studies using interviews could also pay greater attention to the material contexts in which the interviews take place. Following Poldner et al. (2019), video recorded interviews of entrepreneurs at their workplace can shift attention to the role of artefacts and place in understanding entrepreneurial action.

Illustrative example

We provide a brief illustrative example to visualize and ground the research agenda. The illustrative example video excerpt in Table 11.5 is taken from a larger corpus of videographic data collected by the authors. The context of the excerpt is a startup weekend event in which a team made up of two entrepreneurs and two student participants are co-developing initial ideas for a business model. Table 11.6 provides an analysis of this short excerpt (1 minute, 12 seconds) to illustrate the potential of video data to deepen insights into each section of the research agenda.

DISCUSSION AND CONCLUSION

While the use of video methods has seen rapid growth in the past few years, we have lacked an overview of its various types, the extent of their integration into research designs, and their future potential for the understanding of entrepreneurial action. This study contributes to calls for more creative qualitative research methods by conducting a systematic review that identifies three main ways of using video-based methods, each with benefits, limitations and future opportunities. Building on these findings, we further contribute by developing a research agenda by arguing that the unique affordances of video allow researchers (and practitioners) unparalleled access to the interactive, embodied, emotional and material aspects of entrepreneurship action.

Our research agenda shows that video-based research enables us to view entrepreneurship from a new angle, which can drive novel theoretical contributions. Video-based research on interaction can extend insights on power relations (Goss et al., 2011), social capital (Anderson et al., 2007) and the interactional nature of resource mobilization (Tatli et al., 2014). Video-based research on embodiment can add depth to the bodily nature of entrepreneurial practice (Thompson et al., 2020), and highlight the entanglement of body and mind in entrepreneurial practice (Merleau-Ponty, 2004). Using video to understand entrepreneurial emotion can help theorize their collective nature as enacted in entrepreneurs (Zietsma et al., 2019) and the diversity of cues (e.g. verbal, vocal, facial, bodily) that entrepreneurs use in emotional work (Planalp, 1996). Finally, using video can help expand conversations on how materiality shapes entrepreneurial action, bringing entrepreneurship research into closer contact with discussions on sociomateriality in studies of management and organizations (Katila et al., 2019; Symon & Whiting, 2019).

Table 11.5 *Excerpt of videographic data from a startup weekend event (Student participants 1 and 2; Entrepreneurs 1 and 2)*

Line	Participant (P1/P2) Entrepreneur (E1/E2)		P1 P2 E1 E2
1		(P2, E1, E2 read 'lean startup canvas' box 'value proposition'; P1 folds direction paper.) (1.0)	 *Figure 11.2 Video Still 1: Two entrepreneurs interacting with two students*
2	P2	Something you mentioned … um … (P2 turns and points to P1)	 *Figure 11.3 Video Still 2: Two entrepreneurs interacting with two students*

Line	Participant (P1/P2) Entrepreneur (E1/E2)		P1 P2 E1 E2
3	P1	(reading paper, nods head)	
4	E1	yeah (glances at P1) (1.0)	
5	E2	he mentioned it like 5 minutes ago (smiles at P2)	
6	P1	Who? (looking up from reading paper)	
7	E2	(laughs) he mentioned it 5 minutes ago (addressing P2, points towards P1)	
8	P2	oh yeah, it was the … (P1–P4 all smile)	
9	P1	Yeah … I think that's an important aspect and that's why it attracted me, you know, to join you guys (E1 and E2 nod)	

Figure 11.4 Video Still 3: Two entrepreneurs interacting with two students

Line	Participant (P1/P2) Entrepreneur (E1/E2)		P1 P2 E1 E2
10	E2	We can repeat ourselves, about the inclusion of disabled people (draws attention to the canvas) … to … (gestures with open left hand looking at P1)	 *Figure 11.5 Video Still 4: Two entrepreneurs interacting with two students*
11	P1	yes but it's not only about hearing the referee or ... able to uh play uh better football (gestures with pen in circle)	 *Figure 11.6 Video Still 5: Two entrepreneurs interacting with two students*

Line	Participant (P1/P2) Entrepreneur (E1/E2)		P1	P2	E1	E2
12	E2	yeah I'm just saying that … it's not like				
13	P1	= it's not by itself				
14	E2	yeah it's not only … but also about playing the game so it kinda of fulfills two purposes at once (gestures with two fingers towards P1)				

Figure 11.7 Video Still 6: Two entrepreneurs interacting with two students

Line	Participant (P1/P2) Entrepreneur (E1/E2)		P1 P2 E1 E2
15	P1	> but that's already on the game perspective <, I mean it broader like for me if I couldn't play football during my whole life I would be a totally different person like sports is like feeling part of the team (gestures with both hands as if opening curtains)	 *Figure 11.8 Video Still 7: Two entrepreneurs interacting with two students*
16	P1	It's more than only hearing the whistle of the referee. when you feeling included to the team therefore the quality of life you are living (E1 and E2 nodding)	 *Figure 11.9 Video Still 8: Two entrepreneurs interacting with two students*

Table 11.6 *Analysis of illustrative example*

Theoretical Focus	Insights from exemplar
Interaction	The illustrative example allows us to observe 'who begins' as an immediate concern that needs to be interactionally organized. For instance, after reading from the 'lean startup canvas' (line 1), P2 invites P1 to begin the discussion by recalling that he had previously mentioned an idea (Line 2). P1, however, does not take up the invitation to begin, but rather nods his head and remains silent (Line 3). This prompts E1 and E2 to invite P1 again to begin the discussion (Line 4–8). P1 finally realizes that they would like him to start, but instead of doing so, he begins by reaffirming his interest (student participants had a choice between six entrepreneurial teams) (Line 9). Finally, on Line 10, E2 redirects everyone's attention back to the task at hand. P1 interjects 'yes but it's not' to begin a negotiation of the currently stated value proposition (Line 11). E2 reiterates to P1 that his view of the value proposition contains two sources of value (Line 14). However, P1 responds quickly again with a 'but', and develops a longer explanation that the value is more broadly about 'quality of life', with E1 and E2 nodding (Line 15 and 16). In these lines, we can see how the video data allows us to observe the fast-paced nature of an interaction in which practitioners solve the problem of 'who begins', and the language used to negotiate their ideas.
Embodiment	The illustrative example provides a few instances of how gestures come to matter for interactional outcomes. First, on line 2, line 7 and line 10, we observe a pointing gesture, which is involved in invitations to begin the discussion. Moreover, we see that gestures by E2 and P1 matter during their negotiation of the value proposition. On lines 15 and 16, P1 uses a two-handed gesture to communicate an 'opening up' (as if opening curtains), which is suggestive of his proposal to broaden the possible value proposition. Similarly, E2 uses a two-fingered hand gesture on line 14 to communicate to P1 that he views the value proposition as having dual objectives. These gestures (not to mention facial expressions and bodily position), while slight, are an important element of how the team recognizes and organizes 'who begins' and how they negotiate their ideas in real-time. As such, we gain a glimpse into the embodied aspects of entrepreneurial interaction made visible by the video data.

Theoretical Focus	Insights from exemplar
Emotion	The illustrative example provides a few suggestive instances of expressions of emotions and how they might shape entrepreneurial action. On Line 7, E2 gives a small laugh as he realizes that P1 has not picked up on prior invitations by P2 and E1 to begin, which suggests discomfort that the team is still out of sync. Importantly, P1 observes E2's emotion of discomfort, and he immediately states his affiliation with the entrepreneurs' idea, which could suggest that E2's emotional expression prompted P1's response in this way. Moreover, on lines 15 and 16, P1 uses gestures and facial expressions, as already mentioned, to explain his view that the value proposition should be considered more broadly, which suggests that P1 conveys an excited emotion aimed at convincing the entrepreneurs to follow his perspective. Accordingly, video data helps render episodic expressions of emotions visible as they happen in context and interaction, allowing future research to better theorize their causes and effects.
Materiality	The exemplar provides a glimpse into how the physical 'lean canvas' comes to matter in the team's interaction. On Line 1, the 'lean canvas' is printed on a large sheet of paper that allows them to read the text simultaneously (as opposed to individual pages or digitally on computer screens). Moreover, we see the 'lean canvas' object being referred to directly on Line 10 by E2, when he points to the value proposition box as he addresses P1. In this instance, E2's pointing to the object is not suggesting that P1 inspect and read the text immediately, but he rather uses the object to draw P1's attention to the team's invitations for him to begin the discussion on 'value proposition'. In this way, we get a glimpse into how material objects can be used in interaction to guide the conduct of practitioners.

Our findings also highlight the complementarity between video data and other qualitative data such as observation, interviews and archival documents. Video methods can be utilized to deepen the insights garnered through observation and ethnographic field notes by allowing researchers to revisit particular insights or observe incidents from different perspectives. Similar to traditional ethnographic data, video can complement interview-based studies by giving insights into real-time entrepreneurial practice. Other forms of qualitative data can enhance the insights from video-based studies. Interviews with entrepreneurs about specific video-recorded incidents can assist in the process of interpretation. Similarly, archival data such as documents or artefacts can confirm or contradict interpretations of video-recorded action. To take advantage of this complementarity, video methods should be added to the suite of qualitative researchers' methods.

Despite the potential offered by video-based research, entrepreneurship research should also consider the practical constraints and limitations of video-based methods. Video-based research creates numerous practical challenges in terms of privacy, access, timing, and the investment of time and resources in developing a mastery of video storage and analysis tools. Similar to other forms of observational research, video-based studies also face limitations related to volume of data generated, whether practitioners act 'naturally' when being filmed, and the positioning of the observer (and their equipment) (Heath & Hindmarsh, 2002; Heath et al., 2010). As Zundel et al. (2018) emphasize, 'epistemologically, video research not only documents but intervenes' (p. 388). Few entrepreneurship scholars take a critical perspective on why videos are produced in the first place, thus there is room for more reflexivity of appreciating the context and performative nature of videos themselves. Finally, entrepreneurship scholars will need to clarify why video data made a difference to a theoretical understanding of a phenomenon. Following LeBaron et al. (2018) 'simply showing that nonverbal communication is also part of group interactions, without furthering understanding about how groups interact, is not sufficient for a (theoretical) contribution' (p. 255). Researchers hoping to enter the world of video-based research should weigh these practical constraints and limitations against the potential benefits of accessing the interactive, embodied, emotional and material nature of entrepreneurial action.

NOTE

1. We would like to thank Ella Hafermalz for her detailed and insightful comments on this manuscript. We would also like to thank our co-authors on our own ongoing practice-based entrepreneurship studies for thinking through the value and possibilities of video-based research with us. This chapter comes from an article originally published in the *Journal of Small Business*

Management, in a special issue on qualitative methods in entrepreneurship research: Ormiston, J., & Thompson, N. (2021). Viewing entrepreneurship 'in motion': Exploring current uses and future possibilities of video-based entrepreneurship research, *Journal of Small Business Management*, 59, 5, 976–1011, DOI: 10.1080/00472778.2020.1866184, © Informa UK Limited, trading as Taylor & Francis Group. Reprinted by permission of Taylor & Francis Ltd, https://www.tandfonline.com/.

REFERENCES

Abdelnour, S., & Branzei, O. (2010). Fuel-efficient stoves for Darfur: The social construction of subsistence marketplaces in post-conflict settings. *Journal of Business Research*, *63*(6), 617–629.

Anderson, A., Park, J., & Jack, S. (2007). Entrepreneurial social capital: Conceptualizing social capital in new high-tech firms. *International Small Business Journal*, *25*(3), 245–272.

Anglin, A. H., Short, J. C., Drover, W., Stevenson, R. M., McKenny, A. F., & Allison, T. H. (2018). The power of positivity? The influence of positive psychological capital language on crowdfunding performance. *Journal of Business Venturing*, *33*(4), 470–492.

Anglin, A. H., Wolfe, M. T., Short, J. C., McKenny, A. F., & Pidduck, R. J. (2018). Narcissistic rhetoric and crowdfunding performance: A social role theory perspective. *Journal of Business Venturing*, *33*(6), 780–812.

Ashman, R., Patterson, A., & Brown, S. (2018). 'Don't forget to like, share and subscribe': Digital autopreneurs in a neoliberal world. *Journal of Business Research*, *92*, 474–483.

Barinaga, E. (2017). Tinkering with space: The organizational practices of a nascent social venture. *Organization Studies*, *38*(7), 937–958.

Baron, R. A. (2008). The role of affect in the entrepreneurial process. *Academy of Management Review*, *33*(2), 328–340.

Berger, I. E., Cunningham, P. H., & Drumwright, M. E. (2004). Social alliances: company/nonprofit collaboration. *California Management Review*, *47*(1), 58–90.

Berglund, H. (2007). Researching entrepreneurship as lived experience. In Ulhoi, J., & Neergaard, H. (Eds.), *Handbook of qualitative research methods in entrepreneurship* (pp. 75–93). Edward Elgar Publishing.

Boyatzis, R. E. (1998). *Transforming qualitative information: Thematic analysis and code development*. Sage.

Bradbury, H., & Clair, J. A. (1999). Promoting sustainable organizations with Sweden's Natural Step. *Academy of Management Perspectives*, *13*(4), 63–74.

Braun, V., & Clarke, V. (2006). Using thematic analysis in psychology. *Qualitative Research in Psychology*, *3*(2), 77–101.

Brugman, H., & Kita, S. (1995). Impact of digital video technology on transcription: A case of spontaneous gesture transcription. *Kodikas*, *18*(1–3), 95–112.

Buttner, E. H. (2001). Examining female entrepreneurs' management style: An application of a relational frame. *Journal of Business Ethics*, *29*(3), 253–269.

Campbell, B. (2019). *Practice theory in action: Empirical studies of interaction in innovation and entrepreneurship*. Taylor & Francis.

Cardon, M. S., Foo, M.-D., Shepherd, D., & Wiklund, J. (2012). Exploring the heart: Entrepreneurial emotion is a hot topic. *Entrepreneurship Theory and Practice*, *36*(1), 1–10.

Cardon, M. S., Mitteness, C., & Sudek, R. (2017). Motivational cues and angel investing: Interactions among enthusiasm, preparedness, and commitment. *Entrepreneurship Theory and Practice*, *41*(6), 1057–1085.

Chalmers, D. M., & Shaw, E. (2017). The endogenous construction of entrepreneurial contexts: A practice-based perspective. *International Small Business Journal*, *35*(1), 19–39.

Chan, C. S. R., Parhankangas, A., Sahaym, A., & Oo, P. (2019). Bellwether and the herd? Unpacking the u-shaped relationship between prior funding and subsequent contributions in reward-based crowdfunding. *Journal of Business Venturing*, *35*(2), 105934.

Chen, X.-P., Yao, X., & Kotha, S. (2009). Entrepreneur passion and preparedness in business plan presentations: A persuasion analysis of venture capitalists' funding decisions. *Academy of Management Journal*, *52*(1), 199–214.

Christianson, M. K. (2018). Mapping the terrain: The use of video-based research in top-tier organizational journals. *Organizational Research Methods*, *21*(2), 261–287.

Clarke, J. (2011). Revitalizing entrepreneurship: How visual symbols are used in entrepreneurial performances. *Journal of Management Studies*, *48*(6), 1365–1391.

Clarke, J., & Cornelissen, J. (2011). Language, communication, and socially situated cognition in entrepreneurship. *Academy of Management Review*, *36*(4), 776–778.

Clarke, J. S., Cornelissen, J. P., & Healey, M. P. (2018). Actions speak louder than words: How figurative language and gesturing in entrepreneurial pitches influences investment judgments. *Academy of Management Journal*, *62*(2), 335–360.

Clarke, J. S., Llewellyn, N., Cornelissen, J., & Viney, R. (2021). Gesture analysis and organizational research: The development and application of a protocol for naturalistic settings. *Organizational Research Methods*, *24*(1), 140–171.

Cornelissen, J. P., Clarke, J. S., & Cienki, A. (2012). Sensegiving in entrepreneurial contexts: The use of metaphors in speech and gesture to gain and sustain support for novel business ventures. *International Small Business Journal*, *30*(3), 213–241.

Dana, L. P., & Dana, T. E. (2007). Collective Entrepreneurship in a Mennonite Community in Paraguay. *Latin American Business Review*, *8*(4), 82–96.

Dodd, S. L. D. (2014). Roots radical: Place, power and practice in punk entrepreneurship. *Entrepreneurship & Regional Development*, *26*(1–2), 165–205.

Drakopoulou Dodd, S., Wilson, J., Bhaird, C. M., & Bisignano, A. P. (2018). Habitus emerging: The development of hybrid logics and collaborative business models in the Irish craft beer sector. *International Small Business Journal: Researching Entrepreneurship*, *36*(6), 637–661.

Erickson, F. (2011). Uses of video in social research: A brief history. *International Journal of Social Research Methodology*, *14*(3), 179–189.

Fayolle, A., & Wright, M. (2014). *How to get published in the best entrepreneurship journals: A guide to steer your academic career*. Edward Elgar Publishing.

Goss, D., Jones, R., Betta, M., & Latham, J. (2011). Power as practice: A micro-sociological analysis of the dynamics of emancipatory entrepreneurship. *Organization Studies*, *32*(2), 211–229.

Gough, K. V., Langevang, T., & Namatovu, R. (2014). Researching entrepreneurship in low-income settlements: The strengths and challenges of participatory methods. *Environment and Urbanization*, *26*(1), 297–311.

Gylfe, P., Franck, H., Lebaron, C., & Mantere, S. (2016). Video methods in strategy research: Focusing on embodied cognition. *Strategic Management Journal, 37*(1), 133–148.

Haberman, H., & Danes, S. M. (2007). Father-daughter and father-son family business management transfer comparison: Family FIRO model application. *Family Business Review, 20*(2), 163–184.

Heath, C., & Hindmarsh, J. (2002). Analysing interaction: Video, ethnography and situated conduct. In May, T. (Ed.), *Qualitative research in practice* (pp. 99–121). Sage.

Heath, C., Hindmarsh, J., & Luff, P. (2010). *Video in qualitative research: Analysing social interaction in everyday life*. Sage.

Henry, E. Y., Dana, L.-P., & Murphy, P. J. (2018). Telling their own stories: Māori entrepreneurship in the mainstream screen industry. *Entrepreneurship & Regional Development, 30*(1–2), 118–145.

Hienerth, C. (2006). The commercialization of user innovations: The development of the rodeo kayak industry. *R&D Management, 36*(3), 273–294.

Hindle, K. (2004). Choosing qualitative methods for entrepreneurial cognition research: A canonical development approach. *Entrepreneurship Theory and Practice, 28*(6), 575–607.

Hindmarsh, J., & Heath, C. (2007). Video-based studies of work practice. *Sociology Compass, 1*(1), 156–173.

Hindmarsh, J., & Llewellyn, N. (2018). Video in sociomaterial investigations: A solution to the problem of relevance for organizational research. *Organizational Research Methods, 21*(2), 412–437.

Hjorth, D., Holt, R., & Steyaert, C. (2015). Entrepreneurship and process studies. *International Small Business Journal, 33*(6), 599–611.

Holt, R. (2008). Using activity theory to understand entrepreneurial opportunity. *Mind, Culture, and Activity, 15*(1), 52–70.

Jarrett, M., & Liu, F. (2018). 'Zooming with': A participatory approach to the use of video ethnography in organizational studies. *Organizational Research Methods, 21*(2), 366–385.

Jiang, L., Yin, D., & Liu, D. (2019). Can joy buy you money? The impact of the strength, duration, and phases of an entrepreneur's peak displayed joy on funding performance. *Academy of Management Journal, 62*(6), 1848–1871.

Johannisson, B. (2011). Towards a practice theory of entrepreneuring, *Small Business Economics, 36*(2), 135–150.

Jones, O., & Holt, R. (2008). The creation and evolution of new business ventures: An activity theory perspective, *Journal of Small Business and Enterprise Development, 15*(1), 51–73.

Kaminski, J. C., & Hopp, C. (2019). Predicting outcomes in crowdfunding campaigns with textual, visual, and linguistic signals. *Small Business Economics, 55*, 627–649.

Kanze, D., Huang, L., Conley, M. A., & Higgins, E. T. (2018). We ask men to win and women not to lose: Closing the gender gap in startup funding. *Academy of Management Journal, 61*(2), 586–614.

Karatas-Ozkan, M., Anderson, A. R., Fayolle, A., Howells, J., & Condor, R. (2014). Understanding entrepreneurship: Challenging dominant perspectives and theorizing entrepreneurship through new postpositivist epistemologies, *Journal of Small Business Management, 52*(4), 589–593.

Katila, S., Laine, P.-M., & Parkkari, P. (2019). Sociomateriality and affect in institutional work: Constructing the identity of start-up entrepreneurs. *Journal of Management Inquiry, 28*(3), 381–394.

Keating, A., Geiger, S., & McLoughlin, D. (2013). Riding the practice waves: Social resourcing practices during new venture development. *Entrepreneurship: Theory and Practice*, *38*(5), 1–29.

Knoblauch, H., Baer, A., Laurier, E., Petschke, S., & Schnettler, B. (2008). Visual analysis: New developments in the interpretative analysis of video and photography. *Forum: Qualitative Social Research*, *9*(3), https://doi.org/10.17169/fqs-9.3.1170.

Koch, S. C., & Zumbach, J. (2002, May). The use of video analysis software in behavior observation research: Interaction patterns in task-oriented small groups. *Forum Qualitative Sozialforschung/Forum: Qualitative Social Research*, *3*(2). https://doi.org/10.17169/fqs-3.2.857.

Korsgaard, S. (2011). Entrepreneurship as translation: Understanding entrepreneurial opportunities through actor-network theory. *Entrepreneurship & Regional Development*, *23*(7–8), 661–680.

LeBaron, C., Jarzabkowski, P., Pratt, M. G., & Fetzer, G. (2018). An introduction to video methods in organizational research. *Organizational Research Methods*, *21*(2), 239–260.

Liu, F., & Maitlis, S. (2014). Emotional dynamics and strategizing processes: A study of strategic conversations in top team meetings. *Journal of Management Studies*, *51*(2), 202–234.

Matthews, R. S., Chalmers, D. M., & Fraser, S. S. (2018). The intersection of entrepreneurship and selling: An interdisciplinary review, framework, and future research agenda. *Journal of Business Venturing*, *33*(6), 691–719.

Maxwell, A. L., & Lévesque, M. (2014). Trustworthiness: A critical ingredient for entrepreneurs seeking investors. *Entrepreneurship Theory and Practice*, *38*(5), 1057–1080.

Maxwell, A. L., Jeffrey, S. A., & Lévesque, M. (2011). Business angel early stage decision making. *Journal of Business Venturing*, *26*(2), 212–225.

McKeever, E., Anderson, A., & Jack, S. (2014). Entrepreneurship and mutuality: Social capital in processes and practices, *Entrepreneurship and Regional Development*, *26*(5–6), 453–477.

Merleau-Ponty, M. (2004). *Maurice Merleau-Ponty: Basic writings*. Psychology Press.

Mollick, E. (2014). The dynamics of crowdfunding: An exploratory study. *Journal of Business Venturing*, *29*(1), 1–16.

Mondada, L. (2006). Video recording as the reflexive preservation and configuration of phenomenal features for analysis. *Video Analysis*, 51–68.

Morgan-Thomas, A. (2016). Rethinking technology in the SME context: Affordances, practices and ICTs, *International Small Business Journal*, *34*(8), 1122–1136.

Moroz, P. W., & Hindle, K. (2012). Entrepreneurship as a process: Toward harmonizing multiple perspectives. *Entrepreneurship Theory and Practice*, *36*(4), 781–818.

Neergaard, H., & Ulhøi, J. P. (2007). *Handbook of qualitative research methods in entrepreneurship*. Edward Elgar Publishing.

Oo, P. P., Allison, T. H., Sahaym, A., & Juasrikul, S. (2019). User entrepreneurs' multiple identities and crowdfunding performance: Effects through product innovativeness, perceived passion, and need similarity. *Journal of Business Venturing*, *34*(5), 105895.

Parhankangas, A., & Renko, M. (2017). Linguistic style and crowdfunding success among social and commercial entrepreneurs. *Journal of Business Venturing*, *32*(2), 215–236.

Planalp, S. (1996). Communicating emotion in everyday life: Cues, channels, and processes. In Anderson, P. A., & Guerrero, L. K. (Eds.), *Handbook of communication and emotion* (pp. 29–48). Academic Press.

Poldner, K., Branzei, O., & Steyaert, C. (2019). Fashioning ethical subjectivity: The embodied ethics of entrepreneurial self-formation. *Organization*, *26*(2), 151–174.

Pollack, J. M., Rutherford, M. W., & Nagy, B. G. (2012). Preparedness and cognitive legitimacy as antecedents of new venture funding in televised business pitches. *Entrepreneurship Theory and Practice*, *36*(5), 915–939.

Preller, R., Patzelt, H., & Breugst, N. (2018). Entrepreneurial visions in founding teams: Conceptualization, emergence, and effects on opportunity development. *Journal of Business Venturing*, *35*(2), 105914.

Reavey, P. (2012). *Visual methods in psychology: Using and interpreting images in qualitative research.* Routledge.

Scheaf, D. J., Davis, B. C., Webb, J. W., Coombs, J. E., Borns, J., & Holloway, G. (2018). Signals' flexibility and interaction with visual cues: Insights from crowdfunding. *Journal of Business Venturing*, *33*(6), 720–741.

Schegloff, E. A. (2007). *Sequence organization in interaction: A primer in conversation analysis* (Vol. 1). Cambridge University Press.

Shane, S., Drover, W., Clingingsmith, D., & Cerf, M. (2019). Founder passion, neural engagement and informal investor interest in startup pitches: An fMRI study. *Journal of Business* Venturing, *35*(4), 105949.

Shepherd, D. A. (2015). Party on! A call for entrepreneurship research that is more interactive, activity based, cognitively hot, compassionate, and prosocial. *Journal of Business Venturing*, *30*(4), 489–507.

Shepherd, D. A., & Suddaby, R. (2017). Theory building: A review and integration. *Journal of Management*, *43*(1), 59–86.

Sklaveniti, C., & Steyaert, C. (2019). Reflecting with Pierre Bourdieu: Towards a reflexive outlook for practice-based studies of entrepreneurship. *Entrepreneurship & Regional Development*, *32*(4), 1–21.

Slutskaya, N., Game, A. M., & Simpson, R. C. (2018). Better together: Examining the role of collaborative ethnographic documentary in organizational research. *Organizational Research Methods*, *21*(2), 341–365.

Smets, M., Burke, G., Jarzabkowski, P., & Spee, P. (2014). Charting new territory for organizational ethnography: Insights from a team-based video ethnography. *Journal of Organizational Ethnography*, *3*(1), 10–26.

Stroe, S., Sirén, C., Shepherd, D., & Wincent, J. (2019). The dualistic regulatory effect of passion on the relationship between fear of failure and negative affect: Insights from facial expression analysis. *Journal of Business Venturing*, *35*(4), 105978.

Suddaby, R., Bruton, G. D., & Si, S. X. (2015). Entrepreneurship through a qualitative lens: Insights on the construction and/or discovery of entrepreneurial opportunity. *Journal of Business Venturing*, *30*(1), 1–10.

Symon, G., & Whiting, R. (2019). The sociomaterial negotiation of social entrepreneurs' meaningful work. *Journal of Management Studies*, *56*(3), 655–684.

Tatli, A., Vassilopoulou, J., Özbilgin, M., Forson, C., & Slutskaya, N. (2014). A Bourdieuan relational perspective for entrepreneurship research. *Journal of Small Business Management*, *52*(4), 615–632.

Teague, B., Gorton, M. D., & Liu, Y. (2020). Different pitches for different stages of entrepreneurial development: The practice of pitching to business angels. *Entrepreneurship & Regional Development*, *32*(3–4), 334–352.

Thies, F., Huber, A., Bock, C., Benlian, A., & Kraus, S. (2019). Following the crowd: Does crowdfunding affect venture capitalists' selection of entrepreneurial ventures? *Journal of Small Business Management*, *57*(4), 1378–1398.

Thompson, N. A., & Byrne, O. (2019). Advancing entrepreneurship as practice: Previous developments and future possibilities. In Gartner, W. B., & Teague, B. T. (Eds.), *Research handbook on entrepreneurial: Behavior, practice, process and action*. Edward Elgar Publishing.

Thompson, N. A., & Illes, E. (2020). Entrepreneurial learning as practice: A video-ethnographic analysis. *International Journal of Entrepreneurial Behavior & Research*, *27*(3), 579–599.

Thompson, N. A., Verduyn, K., & Gartner, W. B. (2020). Entrepreneurship-as-practice: Grounding contemporary theories of practice into entrepreneurship studies. *Entrepreneurship and Regional Development*, *32*(3–4), 247–256.

van Werven, R., Bouwmeester, O., & Cornelissen, J. P. (2019). Pitching a business idea to investors: How new venture founders use micro-level rhetoric to achieve narrative plausibility and resonance. *International Small Business Journal*, *37*(3), 193–214.

Vesa, M., & Vaara, E. (2014). Strategic ethnography 2.0: Four methods for advancing strategy process and practice research. *Strategic Organization*, *12*(4), 288–298.

Wheadon, M., & Duval-Couetil, N. (2019). The gendering of entrepreneurship on reality television. *Journal of Small Business Management*, *57*(4), 1676–1697.

Younkin, P., & Kuppuswamy, V. (2019). Discounted: The effect of founder race on the price of new products. *Journal of Business Venturing*, *34*(2), 389–412.

Yu, J., Zhou, J. X., Wang, Y., & Xi, Y. (2013). Rural entrepreneurship in an emerging economy: Reading institutional perspectives from entrepreneur stories. *Journal of Small Business Management*, *51*(2), 183–195.

Zahra, S. A., & Wright, M. (2011). Entrepreneurship's next act. *Academy of Management Perspectives*, *25*(4), 67–83.

Zietsma, C., Toubiana, M., Voronov, M., & Roberts, A. (2019). *Emotions in organization theory*. Cambridge University Press.

Zundel, M., MacIntosh, R., & Mackay, D. (2018). The utility of video diaries for organizational research. *Organizational Research Methods*, *21*(2), 386–411.

Moving to a digital world of entrepreneurship research: a review of "Viewing entrepreneurship 'in motion': exploring current uses and future possibilities of video research methods in entrepreneurship research"

R. Duncan M. Pelly

"Click!" "Thumbs Up!" "Subscribe!" "Cough, Cough!" "Quarantine!" There may be no better words to articulate why this chapter 'Viewing, entrepreneurship "in motion": exploring current uses and future possibilities of video methods in entrepreneurship research' addresses some of the pivotal questions in entrepreneurship and in research of the post-COVID era. The authors performed a systematic literature review which analyzes the current state of research with respect to video analysis, and provides an opportunity to capitalize upon an increasingly important data source. This review highlights three key elements that underscore videography's importance in reposting new questions in entrepreneurship research. First, videos allow for a *témoignage* of entrepreneurship in a way that would be unachievable with more conventional methods. Second, the use of video has increasingly become the norm for entrepreneurial practice; thus, a methodology to capture this new reality is requisite. Third, this article furnishes an avenue for video research that paves the way for scholars.

Translation studies provide a useful metaphor for videos as empirical data in entrepreneurship research. Linguistic translation rarely captures the complete sensemaking among languages (Dobrzyńska, 1995; Hong and Rossi, 2021). In fact, the osmosis of words is at best a facsimile and at worst a distorted mirror image. By the same token, this chapter underscores that via translation, a loss of meaning occurs with conventionally used methods. The authors proclaim that surveys, interviews, experiments, and secondary data fall short in understanding entrepreneurial phenomena. This shortcoming stems directly from imprecise translations. Entrepreneurship transpires in five dimensions – three of which depict place (Hjorth, 2005), the fourth portrays time (Friedman, 1990), and the fifth is evinced as sensemaking (Hick, 2013). As entrepreneurial activities materialize, the researcher is forced to record activities within all five dimensions and transpose it into a data format occupying two dimensions at best, with the remaining three dimensions lost in translation. Using rich video data allows for a more accurate translation because it captures all five dimensions. Translation still occurs between the researcher and the setting, but it does not lose all of the dimensionality of the occurrence. Contextual components, including the environment and materiality, are captured in video, as are paralinguistic codes such as body language, tone, and conversational storytelling.

Moreover, in the post-COVID, webcam, and smart phone world, video is omnipresent, particularly with respect to entrepreneurial behaviors (Morales et al, 2021). The authors identify several entrepreneurship activities revolving around videos: pitching, zoom videos, deliberately recorded and/or produced media, and scenarios recorded for archival purposes. This dialogue acknowledges, in scholarly conversation, the importance of this type of data and its legitimacy. Less than a decade ago reviewers were disputing the validity of video data in both public and private forums. This review critiques exemplar articles that utilize various types of video media and highlights the limitations of each, paving the way for follow-on researchers to formulate their own methods sections.

After summarizing the current state of video research and the merits of using video, the authors propose a pathway for future research. They describe ways in which the five dimensions are captured using video data, thus forming a crucial foundation for follow-on studies that use this increasingly present data source. Videos allow the researcher (and the reader if video data are publicly available) to not only witness entrepreneurial exploits, but also to "be there". The use of video data provides a democratizing effect for research and offers opportunities for readers and research subjects to more fully participate in academic conversations.

REFERENCES

Dobrzyńska, T. (1995). Translating metaphor: Problems of meaning. *Journal of Pragmatics*, *24*(6), 595–604.

Friedman, W. (1990). *About time: Inventing the fourth dimension*. The MIT Press.

Hick, J. (2013). *The fifth dimension: An exploration of the spiritual realm*. Simon and Schuster.

Hjorth, D. (2005). Organizational entrepreneurship: With de Certeau on creating heterotopias (or spaces for play). *Journal of Management Inquiry*, *14*(4), 386–398.

Hong, W., & Rossi, C. (2021). The cognitive turn in metaphor translation studies: A critical overview. *Journal of Translation Studies*, *5*(2), 83–115.

Morales, A., Calvo, S., Martínez, J. M. G., & Martín, J. M. M. (2021). Hybrid forms of business: Understanding the development of indigenous social entrepreneurship practices. *Journal of Business Research, 124*, 212–222.

12. Playful learning as a pedagogical method in entrepreneurship education

Kati Suomi and Katriina Heljakka

INTRODUCTION

Several studies have reported on the usefulness of learning by doing, or experiential pedagogies, in entrepreneurship education (Fayolle, 2018). In short, experiential learning is considered a workable method to teach entrepreneurial thinking and behavior (e.g., Franzén, Heljakka & Nieminen, 2020). It may be augmented with tools and techniques that students find meaningful and at best, offer insights and memorable experiences that help them solve problems and overcome creative challenges in their future careers. One approach to learning focuses on playfulness throughout life. This pedagogy is most traditionally associated with young learners. For example, a recent study (Khan, Oad & Aslam, 2021) highlighted the essential relationship in early childhood education between play strategy and entrepreneurship competencies – play as a method is one of the strategies that improve social behaviors, such as collaboration, exploration, projects, problem-solving, decision-making, and innovation. Further, "Playful learning is a pedagogical methodology where it is sought that children are active, engaged, socially competent, and can have materials that are fun and meaningful to them" (Hassinger-Das et al., 2017; cf. in Manzano-León et al., 2021). As illustrated in this chapter, playful learning holds promise even for learners in higher education, such as young adults involved in university pedagogics.

For all ages, "play-sourced motivation is a major dynamic, within the developing brain, that produces learning" (Dearybury & Jones, 2020, xvii). Thus, play is important to learning throughout our lifetime (Whitton, 2018), and has been used to model a signature pedagogy of playful learning in higher education (Nørgård, Toft-Nielsen, & Whitton, 2017). Playfulness, a mindset that is a precondition to the activity of play, is, in fact a vital attribute for an effective teacher (Dearybury & Jones, 2020). It is important for the contemporary educator to understand and value the intrinsic lack of seriousness that comes with play, what Whitton and Moseley (2019) believe is actually the basis for its learning potential.

This chapter investigates the potential of playful approaches in teaching and learning in higher education, with a particular interest in entrepreneurship education and young adult learners. How might playful learning as a pedagogical method support the development of students' entrepreneurship competencies? We address this question by providing examples of ways in which playful learning might be implemented through playful approaches and three major components of invitations to play – atmosphere, physical space, and materials.

We take a broad view of entrepreneurship education, and refer to entrepreneurship as "when you act upon opportunities and ideas and transform them into value for others. The value that is created can be financial, cultural, or social". It is also acknowledged that value creation can occur in the private, public, and third sectors (Vestergaard, Moberg & Jørgensen, 2012, 11; see also Lackéus, 2018). The literature on entrepreneurship education has increasingly called for new ways of teaching and learning entrepreneurship, to enhance entrepreneurial awareness and mindset (e.g., Robinson et al., 2016). Accordingly, this chapter introduces student-centered learning design and tools for playful learning to build a culture that exposes students to entrepreneurial competencies (see also Stenholm et al., 2021).

The learning experiments described here were conducted at the Faculty of Humanities and School of Economics at a Finnish university located in a university consortium. The latter course was organized in the subject of entrepreneurship, but the use of the playful learning approach and the Comicubes learning tool introduced in this chapter is not limited to that subject alone, as it may be used in enhancing entrepreneurial competencies within non-entrepreneurship or non-business subjects, as well (see also Penaluna & Penaluna, 2021). Finally, the chapter discusses and evaluates the usefulness of the tool as a part of playful approaches in entrepreneurship education in the context of higher education, and in enhancing entrepreneurship competencies presented in EntreComp: The Entrepreneurship Competence Framework (Bacigalupo et al., 2016).

THE ROLE OF PLAY IN ADULT LIFE AND EDUCATION

Traditionally, play is understood as a particular type of leisure activity (Giddens, 1964). However, as Whitton and Moseley (2019, 178) observed, play is not a single activity but a wide spectrum of activities, which is "infinite in its variety". Moreover, as Dearybury and Jones (2020) correctly noted, play is not just an early childhood concept. Play belongs to all age groups.

Essentially, "play is a human right" (Play and Playground Encyclopedia, 2019).

While playfulness as a predisposition to play is often conceptualized as a mindset, play is itself defined as activities that are: (1) self-chosen and self-directed, (2) intrinsically motivated, (3) guided by rules, and (4) imaginative and conducted in an active, alert, but relatively non-stressed frame of mind (Gray, 2015, 125). The key here is that play is a voluntary activity that cannot be forced and, hence, is sparked by personal and individual motivation. Play may spur from spontaneous engagement with the environment, or other (human) players, regardless of their age, even with other species such as domestic animals. Despite its fleeting nature, rules are created in play while playing, and it is through rule-making that play becomes a social process guided by interaction between players. Play can be set in motion through *invitations to play*, which may be designed and facilitated within education.

Play in the Lives of Adults

Play in adulthood is still little understood and in the worst case stigmatized (Guitard, Ferland & Dutil, 2005). Adult play has usually been disguised as entertainment, recreational sports, leisure and tourism (Sutton-Smith, 2008; Henricks, 2015), hobbying, or collecting (Rogan, 1998), in order to camouflage it or avoid the associated stigma (Heljakka, Harviainen & Suominen, 2018). During the first two decennia of the 21st century, however, play has gained a more visible position in adult life. That is, adults not only relax in the name of play, but also perform playfully in the contexts of life-long and life-wide learning and work, as part of the everyday practices in institutions and organizations. Typically, adult play in the organizational realm is situated in the playful and creative use and design of space (Heljakka & Blomberg, 2022). Again, what has changed in the facilitation of play behavior among mature individuals is that play has entered the realm of work and adult education, specifically through processes of gamification (Huotari & Hamari, 2017), and more generally playification (Scott, 2012).

Intentional Playification

Games and play are interrelated constructs (Whitton & Moseley, 2019). Open-ended play turns its attention to the creative areas of play, as opposed to often structured, goal-oriented games designed to have specific outcomes, such as reaching a pre-determined aim. Following Whitton (2018), we propose shifting the focus from the use of games to a wider range of playful approaches. In doing so, our case studies demonstrate deliberate and intentional playification of learning through more open-ended and creative outcomes, than the pre-determined goals addressed in many games. Scott (2012) defines playification as follows:

> Playification is using engaging play-based interaction in situation and non-play contexts to make a product, service, activity, or application more engaging, enjoyable, and motivational. Playification is a method used to imbue an activity, task, or artifact with a psychological, emotional, social, or physical reward and then evaluate the levels of extrinsic and intrinsic motivational forces. (Scott, 2012)

In the context of education, playification is often the deliberate choice of the actor responsible for the design of learning, usually the teacher. With play taking many forms (Hughes, 2002), the playification of education may be achieved in many ways. This chapter proposes some ideas on how to enrich entrepreneurship education through playification.

Play in Education

According to Whitton and Moseley (2019), play in the context of learning is a philosophy of learning. Classrooms need playful experiences because the benefit of play is its capacity to enhance the flexibility and agility of thinking, but it also caters to developing social skills, emotional intelligence, and resolution ability (Jenson, 2005).

Individuals who are curious about the possibilities of play in education often find value in its ability to stimulate creativity and imagination (Lieberman, 1977), and support problem-solving. Dearybury and Jones (2020) described creativity as an idea in motion that is built up through components of a playful mindset – awareness, intentionality, and process. Again, (safe) failure, managing risk, building resilience, and developing true creativity and innovation attained in play (Whitton & Moseley, 2019), are all familiar concepts to any practicing entrepreneur and could be experimented with through playful approaches in entrepreneurship education.

Nørgård et al. (2017) highlighted the relationship between the surface structures of playful learning, the deep structures and the activities of play, and the implicit structure and the philosophy of playfulness. In our research, the surface structures of playful learning entail object play with physical artefacts (blocks/cubes through the Comicubes tool), the deep structures of a playful learning task given to students, and the implicit structure entails following the philosophy of adult play(fulness). In this chapter, the preconditions for achieving a successful playful learning experience are conceived to be composed of three elements – enabling the right atmosphere, making room for movement, and inviting play through appropriate materials. Each of these will be further elaborated in due course.

THE EFFECT OF PLAY IN SETTING A WELCOMING CLASS ENVIRONMENT

Whitton and Moseley (2019, 16) assured us that play cannot be "imposed but it can be encouraged and facilitated. We as educators, can create safe spaces and trusting communities where playfulness can thrive". Setting up a welcoming class environment for learners of any age requires the involvement of playful education professionals, who are open-minded and have a tolerance for the ambiguity and "amphibolous" nature of play (Spariosu, 1989), meaning its flexibility, which is often manifest in creative experiments. Hjorth (2005) described spaces for play and invention as heterotopias – "radically other spaces". Applied in education, these open up the possibility of new avenues for experimental teaching and playful learning. As suggested in the following, enabling play and playful learning pedagogy requires the facilitation of atmosphere, physical movement, and creatively engaging materials.

Allowing Atmosphere

Playful learning emphasizes a positive learning environment, as researchers have highlighted how the right climate for encouraging creativity is one where the students can feel they can take risks and feel free to ask "what would happen if?" without being ridiculed (Biggs & Tang, 2007, 147). Knight and Wood (2005) found that even a moderate shift towards more interactive and cooperative learning in class can result in significantly higher student learning gains than those achieved using a standard lecture format. At the same time, it is relevant to consider how informal activities bring about unanticipated learning in infinite ways (Biggs & Tang 2007, 186). We believe these informal activities can be accomplished as playful approaches and invitations to play. Novel ideas are born when the time, space and opportunity for play are provided (Dearybury & Jones, 2020). First, in order for play to take place, a playful environment filled with potential for learning needs to be set up. This entails a physically safe and mentally supportive space that is judgment-free, as well as inclusive.

Making Room for Movement

What is the first prerequisite for playful learning to happen, besides the pedagogical mindset? Biggs and Tang (2007, 17) noted how teaching rooms and media are specifically designed for one-way delivery, not interactive in-class work in a more informal setting (Knight & Wood, 2005).

In line with Hjorth's (2005) idea of combining the concept of heterotopia with organizational creativity, the connections between space and movement become relevant. We believe these ideas have value for learning, too.

Silverman has stated how play and play-oriented movements improve cognition (Silverman, 1993). Interactive group work with material tools demands, besides the freedom to fail, a reconfiguration of physical space, supported by playful elements and tools that are modular and can be moved around, if needed (see e.g., Heljakka & Blomberg, 2022): Movement, a crucial component of embodied cognition (Dearybury & Jones, 2020), requires making room for play.

Playful learning is often collaborative learning, and, groups stimulate creativity (Burke 2011, 87–88). The earlier literature illustrates how supplementing lectures with group work helps students feel engaged and, subsequently, learn more (Payne et al., 2004, c.f. in Burke 2011, 93). Working in groups accentuates the need to make room for movement. In reminiscing on her teaching, Steinert related that "I do not believe that I have ever conducted a small-group teaching session without moving the furniture around!" (Steinert 1996, 204)

Inviting Play through Materials

"Playful does not necessarily mean unstructured", asserted Cable (2019, 63). A great deal of play in the 21st century involves the consumption of various designed and structured play materials and activities, such as games, toys, and playful environments. Whitton and Moseley (2019) proposed that play can be invited through these kinds of signifiers or artefacts. For example, when we handle objects physically, manipulating them as we think, it can often help us think through things in a different way. This action recognizes that we think with our bodies (especially our hands), as well as our mind (Walsh 2019, 81–82). Therefore, it is important to include objects of various shapes, scale and size in playful learning, which require the learners to stand up and move about in the classroom. The benefits of such an approach have been demonstrated in the prior research. In a study conducted by Franzén et al. (2020), academic professionals as participants demonstrated how a playful approach, including the use of large-scale physical materials (cardboard cubes), can facilitate improvisation, collaboration, creativity, physical movement, and collective problem-solving – activities considered beneficial to the mental flexibility considered crucial to successful entrepreneurial individuals.

The two case studies presented in this chapter employ a physical prototyping tool and workshop method – the *Comicubes* (Heljakka, 2014). The tool, once assembled, is similar to a popular plaything, namely blocks, which have been with us for a long time, and alongside construction sets endure in open-ended play and learning opportunities (Hewitt, 2001). Blocks provide endless opportunities for both "toying" and constructing in spatial play. Similarly, they offer possibilities for object play of various kinds; they may be rotated and inspected from many angles, promoting multisensorial play. Moreover, cardboard cubes as a variation on blocks offer a pleasant surface to touch and can be drawn on and colored as a tool for creative play, unlike another type of block familiar from many studies exploring the playful engagement of children, namely LEGO. There are endless possibilities for ways in which to present information on the cube, including the use of images, words, numbers, and combinations thereof; and, if necessary, even a hybrid, technologically enhanced information layer. As previously described, the inviting, play(ful) qualities of the cardboard cubes present a simple, customizable interface and a never-ending potential for enhancement with different elements (both material and digital) (Heljakka & Ihamäki, 2016).

Playful Learning Pedagogy

Ihamäki and Heljakka (2020) noted that play is one of the strongest drivers of human behavior, and can be considered a constituent of almost every aspect of creative work. Again, Hjorth described entrepreneurship "as a form of social creativity, as a tactical art of creating space for play and/or invention within an established order, to actualize new practices." (Hjorth 2005, 387).

Playful learning pedagogy supports the philosophy of learning in unconventional and, therefore, creative ways. Besides the freedom to fail (to try out, experiment, and test), it asks for student engagement and for them to take responsibility for their own learning (self-directed learning).

It has been discovered that students learn substantially more from active inquiry-based activities and problem solving than from listening to lectures (Beichner & Saul, 2003; Hake, 1998, c.f. in Knight & Wood, 2005). Building on these ideas, it is easy to see how the emphasis in playful learning has to be placed on the learning more than the teaching. "Playful learning follows the constructivism approach, seeking that students be active participants in their learning process, and tries to offer them surmountable challenges to learn while being intrinsically motivated." (Whitton, 2018; cf. in Manzano-León, 2021). Playful learning often strives to allow students to work collaboratively with problem-based learning (Biggs & Tang, 2007, 149). Playful learning strategies, such as educational gamification, game-based learning, and escape rooms are increasingly being incorporated into the university education system (Manzano-León et al., 2021). "Expert teaching includes mastery over a variety of teaching techniques, but unless learning takes place, they are irrelevant", noted Biggs and Tang (2007, 19). For this reason, it is also crucial that students become intrinsically motivated to participate in play activities guided by playful learning pedagogies.

Play and Self-determination

According to the self-determination theory, motivation is based on three innate psychological needs: competence, relatedness, and autonomy. When these are satisfied, it leads to greater self-motivation (Ryan & Deci, 2000). It is acknowledged by developmentalists that children are from birth active, curious and playful, even without specific rewards (e.g., Harter, 1978; see also Ryan and Deci, 2000). Truly, intrinsic motivation reflects the positive potential of human nature. The concept of intrinsic motivation refers to a natural inclination towards assimilation, mastery, spontaneous interest, and exploration. These are essential to cognitive and social development, and function as a source of enjoyment and vitality throughout life. Although humans are blessed with a multitude of intrinsic motivational tendencies, the maintenance and enhancement of this inherent tendency necessitates supportive conditions (Ryan & Deci, 2000). Intrinsic motivation is important also for learning as a student becomes engaged and enjoys studying, and may reach a state of flow, leading to better learning outcomes (e.g., Csikszentmihalyi & Nakamura, 2014). Since play is acknowledged to be intrinsically motivated (Gray, 2015), and includes aspects such as exploration (Sutton-Smith, 1986; Hughes 2002) and fantasy (Jones, 2008), employing playful approaches in pedagogics can be considered to have the potential to support student engagement and learning outcomes also in higher education.

Play and Effectuation

Sarasvathy's (2001) well-known example, "Curry in a Hurry", demonstrates the difference between two logics of decision-making, causation and effectuation: "Causation processes take a particular effect as given and focus on selecting between means to create that effect. Effectuation processes take a set of means as given and focus on selecting between possible effects that can be created with that set of means." (Sarasvathy, 2001, 245). In the effectuation processes, we see a linkage to playfulness related to both social environments, as well as self-contained playfulness in the mind of an entrepreneur.

The above-mentioned example describes the founding of two imaginary Indian restaurants with a fast-food section: one based on causation, that is, the predictive logic of decision-making, and the other on effectuation logic. The traditional management paradigm (causation logic) indicates that founding the restaurant would require: "that we proceed inward to specifics from a larger, general universe – that is, to an optimal target segment from a predetermined market" (Sarasvathy, 2011, 246). This would require time- and often also money-consuming processes of segmentation, targeting and positioning.

In turn, in the effectual process, as Sarasvathy (2011) explains, the entrepreneur could, for instance, instead of expending extraordinary amounts of time and analytical effort, start with the assumption of an existing market and examine the particular set of accessible means or causes. As Sarasvathy (2001, 250) put it: "Entrepreneurs begin with three categories of 'means': they know who they are, what they know, and whom they know – their own traits, tastes, and abilities; the knowledge corridors they are in; and the social networks they are a part of." Therefore, with limited resources, the entrepreneur should think creatively (and as we see, playfully!), to bring the idea to market with as few resources as possible.

As Sarasvathy (2001, 247) outlines: "in using effectuation processes to build her firm, the entrepreneur can build several different types of firms in completely disparate industries. This means that the original idea (or set of causes) does not imply any one single strategic universe for the firm (or effect)." So, if the customers' real interest was, for instance, in the idea of ethnic entertainment instead of only food, the effectual entrepreneur might develop other products, such as catering services, party planning, and Indian food cooking courses. Thus, with the same starting point but a different set of contingencies, our imaginary entrepreneur might ultimately build a variety of businesses. This would involve listening to customers' needs, building networks, grasping serendipitous events, dealing with uncertainties, and entrepreneurial imagination (Sarasvathy, 2001).

Playful approaches, as we see them, can facilitate students' imagining of possibilities, and adopting new perspectives, thus leading to effectual thinking and behavior. Further, as early as 1933, Whitehead reminded us that drawing an exact line of distinction between educational institutions dedicated to abstract knowledge and those dedicated to application and to handicrafts is not sensible. Purposeful activity, intellectual activity, and the instant sense of rewarding achievement should be conjugated in a unity of experience. Similarly to Whitehead, we see that this doctrine should be implemented with discretion and according to other educational requirements.

In the following sections, we describe a pair of courses as case examples, which provide suggestions for how playful learning may be facilitated in the context of academic learning among young adults.

CASE EXAMPLES – A PAIR OF COURSES EMPLOYING PLAYFUL METHODS

This section describes playful learning in practice, *activation through playful approaches*. Next, a pair of courses linked together at a single Finnish university – one organized in the Faculty of Humanities, the other in the School of Economics – are described and discussed. We start by explaining the Faculty of Humanities' course, as it acted as the starting point and inspiration for employing playful methods at the School of Economics' course.

Case 1: "Playful Museum" Course at the Faculty of Humanities

In some disciplines, a case study is an ideal way to see how students can apply their knowledge and professional skills. It could be written up as a project or as an item for a portfolio, suggested Biggs and Tang (2007, 222). In the fall of 2021, the second author designed and ran the "Playful Museum" ("Leikillistyvä museotila") course delivered in Finnish at the Faculty of Humanities to a group of Finnish students. The motivation for the course was to plan student-centered, hands-on work accentuating playful learning pedagogy. The course employed the jigsaw group model, as presented by Biggs and Tang (2007, 141). The model sees the groups allocated sub-tasks and the plenary is to put the finished sub-tasks back together to complete the main task. In each class, the students performed sub-tasks related to the conceptual and physical design of a museum space that was "playified" in the process.

Steinert (1996, 204) advised pedagogues to "Try to make your session stimulating, interesting and informative." The "Playful Museum" course used theory, earlier research, case examples, and the like to create interest and inform the students, whereas activation via various tasks and tools aimed to stimulate their creativity and eagerness to solve design problems. Thus, students were asked to take more responsibility for their own learning, an approach also proposed by Knight and Wood (2005).

For the project-based course, there was a greater task to be completed at the end of the course. It was influenced by engagement with the theories and activities throughout the course, where the students were asked to work in their groups and develop one "playful dimension" for the common project, which was built up little by little as the course advanced.

Playful formation of groups

During the first session, everyone was asked to sit in a circle and say a few words about their own intended learning goals for the course, on which the teacher made notes and looked to incorporate appropriate tasks in the teaching. The goal of starting with a casual discussion was to create a positive atmosphere for learning, "establishing a productive classroom climate" (Biggs & Tang, 2007, 37).

Researchers have highlighted how the right climate to encourage creativity is where the students feel they can take risks, and feel free to ask "what would happen if?" without being ridiculed (Biggs & Tang, 2007, 147). This inspired the second author to set up not only a "magic circle for learning", but also of play (a concept introduced by cultural theorist Johan Huizinga, also discussed in Whitton, 2018), which makes for a trusting and safe environment. This was achieved in one way by the spatial arrangement of the classroom seating. Sitting in a circle quickly developed into a habit, as the students themselves started to ask when they entered the classroom whether or not they should start organizing the seating. This practice proved to be a good way of checking attendance and finding out how students were doing.

According to Steinert, "Small group teaching offers students an opportunity to discuss and refine their understanding of complex issues, to problem solve and apply their knowledge to new situations, and to reflect on their attitudes and feelings." (Steinert, 1996, 203) In this course, small groups proved to work well in terms of interaction and creative work. At the beginning of the course, the students were assigned to groups of three or four, not more than six, based on their "museum types" discovered using Finland's national broadcaster YLE's "Museum Machine" online application.

The flipped classroom task

Biggs and Tang argued that "students do their best work when given freedom and space to use their own judgment" (Biggs & Tang, 2007, 38), and that formative assessment means involving your students (Biggs & Tang, 2007, 191). In the Flipped Classroom Task (or "learning through teaching"), the students (some of whom had studied museology) were asked: "What are the main functions of traditional museums?" The resulting insights were then added to the lecture slides, and presented using Microsoft PowerPoint. This exercise was motivated by the goal of achieving the students' trust in the knowledge they had already gained, and their ability to teach their peers.

Measurement of goals

"The ultimate aim of any professional education course [...] is to improve their professional competence" (Biggs & Tang 2007, 50–51). Steinert (1996) saw teachers as group facilitators for whom it is important to vary the teaching methods. The present authors believe that by deploying different "invitations to play" as playful approaches, a teacher is better equipped to facilitate the use of creativity. How is that measured? Biggs and Tang (2007, 229) suggested that an important ingredient of creativity is the originality of the product. Many original ideas stemmed from the co-creative coursework, and in this way, it was also very rewarding for the author as a teacher to see how students created "something out of nothing", illustrating that a transformative process had taken place. "It does not seem that hard: Good teaching produces change: it is called learning" (Biggs & Tang 2007, 277).

Student feedback

Student feedback was collected from the students in the end of the course. Some examples of this feedback follow, describing students' responses to their intrinsic motivation and learning goals and the general atmosphere:

> At the beginning of the course, I set a goal for myself to learn how playification and gamification can be employed in the museum space, and how they could be used in other contexts and environments. The course content corresponded fully with my goals, and I felt I could make use of the knowledge and experiences gained earlier. Especially the "Playful Museum" concept functioned as a good "device" for learning, and brought together all the theory I learnt during the course. (Student 1)

> The teaching style of the course was really great, intensive but casual. Sitting in a circle probably awakened more conversation and eased the tension. The many different kinds of activities and tasks were instructive. The theoretical side of the course was interesting, and did not feel at all like "lecturing". I think the course had a safe atmosphere, which is really important everywhere, and I believe that I learned about communication, open-mindedness, how to listen to others and care about their opinions [more] than theory. This is a good thing! (Student 2)

> My learning goal was to understand more about how to enliven and playify, and in general to learn something new in the area of museology. The course corresponded well with these expectations and was really innovative and fun! A wonderful oasis among theoretical courses that are all the same. (Student 3)

Case 2: "Entrepreneurial Opportunities" Course at the School of Economics

Our second example of playful learning as a pedagogical method is a course given by the first author of this chapter at the School of Economics at Bachelor's degree level. The course (5 ECTs – European Credit Transfer System) was implemented in hybrid mode due to the COVID-19 pandemic, in the fall of 2021. It is a part of the university's minor studies in Entrepreneurship (25 ECTs), and is also open to exchange students at the School. In total, 25 Finnish, German, and French students participated in the course. The students were majoring in marketing, management and organization, or accounting and finance. Thus, the course was both multidisciplinary and multicultural. It ran under the title "Entrepreneurial opportunities", and ended with intensive days of study, when playful approaches were employed as a pedagogical method.

The aim of the course was to allow students to become familiar with the first phases of the entrepreneurial process, concentrating on ideation, business opportunities, evaluation, and enterprising behavior. The aim throughout the course was to encourage students to elaborate on how their ideas create value for others, and for themselves, and what kind of value that is: economic, enjoyment, social, harmony, or influence (Lackéus, 2018, see also Fayolle,

2007). The first three weekly course meetings focused on theories relevant to the course theme, and discussing them with students. The key theoretical themes were opportunity creation vs. discovery (Alvarez & Barney, 2007), and effectuation vs. causation (Sarasvathy, 2001).

The course comprised classroom exercises (or on Zoom), and independent learning, for example, reading journal articles weekly to complete pre-assignments for background, prior to course meetings where theoretical viewpoints were further discussed (Flipped Classroom). Since one of the key focuses of the course was how to develop ideas into opportunities with commercial potential, students were also asked, for example, to follow the news and social media to identify problems that customers might experience, in order to encourage ideation, and then bring the materials to class and discuss the ideas together.

As mentioned above, the course was inspired and implemented in collaboration with the "Playful Museum" course described earlier, which was running simultaneously at the Faculty of Humanities at the same university. Prior to the intensive study days, the course teacher at the Faculty of Humanities gave the business students a presentation on playification, play experience, and the customer journey concept. The presentation provided the students with background information on the "Playful Museum" concept. A Museum of Selfies and Museum of Ice Cream (Heljakka, 2023), for example, were described as examples of interactive and playful museum concepts.

At the beginning of the first intensive study day, the students were provided with some instructions. The groups were asked to come up with ideas they thought would be suitable as services and products at a fictional "Playful Museum" in the private sector. They were also asked to discuss these ideas in their groups, evaluate them, and turn the best into business opportunities. The student groups were encouraged to think about potential customers' needs, and how to satisfy them, to create innovative solutions, both physical and digital. At this stage, the students were also reminded that the ideas could be related to creating any type of value (Lackéus, 2018; see also Fayolle, 2007), and in their presentation to link practice with theories covered during the course. The groups were further expected to elaborate in their presentations how they evaluated the feasibility of their ideas in terms of: Is it doable? What will it take to do it? What kind of resources, financial and otherwise, as well as marketing would be needed?

Each group was provided with their own workspace, to create the coziest and most creative classroom settings available, and some of the groups also worked by turns in the so-called "Laboratory of Play", a creative, shared space in the university consortium (also see Heljakka & Blomberg, 2022). Those who joined in by Zoom worked in breakout rooms. There are, nevertheless,

Source: Photographed by Katriina Heljakka, 2021.

Figure 12.1 Students interacting with large scale Comicubes at Pori Laboratory of Play

no special requirements for classrooms when employing playful learning as a pedagogical method.

The participants in class were provided with stimulation in the form of cardboard *Comicubes* (Heljakka & Ihamäki, 2016), and those using Zoom received digitalized Comicube blanks (Figure 12.1). "The Comicubes is a creative prototyping tool, a hybrid combining images with a physical, three-dimensional cardboard cube. Hybridity means that the cube as a physical artefact can be given a digital layer or digital elements." (Ihamäki & Heljakka, 2020, 7). It has been suggested that the power of play with materials extends the realm of ideation and designing new experiences in combination with game elements to brainstorm and co-create concepts (Ihamäki & Heljakka, 2020).

Students were asked to take pictures while working with the Comicubes. They used the cubes in multiple ways, for example, one of the groups as a kind of three-dimensional post-it note, while another constructed something demonstrating activity at the Playful Museum. One group used Comicubes as a cartoon-type thought bubble by writing on the cubes, taking pictures of themselves with them, and then employing the pictures in their presentation.

Following this workshop day, there were two seminar days where student groups presented the results of their ideation. The students were informed in advance that in addition to the first author, the assistant professor responsible for the course, there would be a "Shark Tank" for every group, to evaluate and give feedback on their ideas. The "Sharks" comprised teachers and researchers from the School of Economics, as well as practicing stakeholders. The Shark Tank was remarkably multidisciplinary, representing the subjects of entrepreneurship, management, marketing, visual culture, digital culture, and arts management. Thus, students received versatile feedback. Referring to a well-known business reality television series verbally and visually in the student instructions looked, on the one hand, to add playfulness and fun to the learning, and on the other to motivate the students to do their utmost in their teamwork presentations and learn from the sharks' comments.

The students came up with a number of ideas for a Playful Museum, for children and adults alike. There were five groups in total, each of four to five students. Some groups concentrated more on the learning aspect of playful activities, while others focused on the amusement dimension, along with stress relief and bringing families together. Some emphasized ideas employing augmented reality and gamified experiences, and others concentrated more on physical toys and games, or a combination of the former and latter.

In the feedback process, students were asked among other things: "Which factors in this course helped you to learn?" The following answers were fairly typical:

> Group work! And the Shark Tank – the feedback of the Sharks. (Student 1)

> It was nice to do group work that allowed us to use our imagination. And great to have the possibility to design and to use your creativity. The Shark Tank was a workable concept, which made the work groups' presentations feel like an exam. In my opinion, the absence of a written exam was a valid solution. (Student 2)

The playful learning tools, techniques, and tactics used in the two courses and cases described above are summarized in Table 12.1.

SUPPORTING ENTREPRENEURSHIP COMPETENCIES BY PLAY COMPETENCIES

The pedagogic rationale for using playful approaches to learning in entrepreneurship education is grounded in the similarities that a playful mindset has to an "entrepreneurial mind". "Sense of initiative and entrepreneurship" has been listed as one of the eight key competencies for all citizens (European

Table 12.1 *Playful learning tools, techniques, and tactics (Whitton, 2018) combined with the playful approaches in our two case studies*

Playful learning	Playful approach	Description	Case study 1	Case study 2
Tools	Inviting play through materials	Objects, artefacts and technologies that signify a playful environment (e.g., games, toys, simulations, puzzles, virtual environments)	Comicubes	Comicubes
Techniques	Making room for play	Pedagogies and learning approaches that facilitate play (e.g., role play, making, performance, problems, quests)	Ideation, creation, and prototyping of a 'Playful Museum' through building a conceptual and physical model	Ideation, creation, and prototyping of a 'Playful Museum' through building a conceptual and physical model
Tactics	An allowing atmosphere	Mechanics and attributes that engender playfulness (e.g., surprise, humor, chance, competition, storytelling, mystery, badges)	Surprise, humor, storytelling	Shark Tank TV series

Parliament and the Council, 2006). "Sense of initiative and entrepreneurship" is referred to as: "the capacity to turn ideas into action, ideas that generate value for someone other than oneself. Sense of initiative and entrepreneurship is a transversal key competence, which every citizen needs for personal fulfillment and development, active citizenship, social inclusion and employment in the knowledge society." (Bacigalupo et al., 2016, 7). Accordingly, the understanding of entrepreneurship, including a "sense of initiative", forms the basis for the Entrepreneurship Competence Framework (EntreComp) developed by the European Commission with its learning outcome descriptors.

The framework is one of the measures to support entrepreneurship competence across the field of education and work. The framework comprises three competence areas, 15 competencies, and up to 442 learning outcomes (Bacigalupo et al., 2016). It tries to bridge the gap between education and work, while seeing entrepreneurship as a competence. The three competence areas of the EntreComp framework are entitled: (1) ideas & opportunities, (2) resources, and (3) into action. Each comprises five competencies. Ideas & opportunities consist of: spotting opportunities, creativity, vision, valuing ideas, and ethical and sustainable thinking. Resources comprise self-awareness and self-efficacy, motivation and perseverance, mobilizing resources, financial and economic literacy, and mobilizing others. Into action, in turn, is about taking the initiative, planning and management, coping with uncertainty, ambiguity, and risk, working with others, and learning through experience (Bacigalupo et al., 2016, 12–13). Table 12.2 demonstrates the connection between entrepreneurship competencies and play competencies, rooted in playful approaches.

Table 12.2 shows that entrepreneurship competencies have several similarities with play competencies and are thus intertwined. For example, creativity, self-efficacy, motivation, ambiguity, and collaboration are included in both concepts. Further, entrepreneurship competencies have counterparts in the context of play. For example, a parallel can be drawn between the vision of entrepreneurship competencies and imagination and fantasy of play competencies, and spotting opportunities is close to exploration. Thus, it can be seen that entrepreneurship competencies and playful competencies are, in fact, two sides of the same coin.

CONCLUSIONS

At the beginning of the chapter, we posed a question: How might playful learning as a pedagogical method support the development of students' entrepreneurship competencies? Table 12.2 parallels entrepreneurship competencies and play competencies and thus demonstrates the linkage between the two. As far as the present authors are aware, this is the first attempt to make explicit

Table 12.2 Interfaces of entrepreneurship competencies and play competencies

Entrepreneurship competence areas	Entrepreneurship competencies	Play competencies	Scholars linking competence in relation to play/playful approaches (examples)
Ideas & Opportunities	Spotting opportunities	Exploration	Sutton-Smith (1986); Hughes (2002)
	Creativity	Creativity	Lieberman (1977); Power (2011); Dearybury & Jones (2020)
	Vision	Imagination, fantasy	Sutton-Smith (2008); Smith (2010); Burghardt (2015)
	Valuing ideas	Resourcefulness	Heljakka (2021)
	Ethical and sustainable thinking	Sustainable thinking in play	Heljakka (2022)
Resources	Self-awareness and self-efficacy	Spatial and perceptual awareness Self-efficacy in play	Boehm (1986) Román-Oyola et al. (2018)
	Motivation and perseverance	(Intrinsic) motivation	Scott (2012); Gray (2015); Dearybury & Jones (2020)
	Mobilizing resources	Mobilizing tendency of toys	Heljakka & Ihamäki (2020a)
	Financial and economic literature	Playful tools, techniques and tactics	Whitton (2018)
	Mobilizing others	Mobilizing tendency of play	Heljakka & Ihamäki (2020b)

Entrepreneurship competence areas	Entrepreneurship competencies	Play competencies	Scholars linking competence in relation to play/playful approaches (examples)
Into action	Taking the initiative	Play as activism, toy activism	De Koven (2015); Heljakka (2020)
	Planning and Management	Organization fantasy	Jones (2008)
	Coping with uncertainty, ambiguity and risk	Playful resilience Ambiguity, 'Amphibolous' nature of play	Heljakka (2021) Sutton-Smith (1997); Whitton & Moseley (2019); Spariosu (1989)
	Working with others	Social play; collaboration as a playful approach	Hughes (2002), Franzén et al. (2020)
	Learning through experience	Playful learning	Whitton (2018); Whitton & Moseley (2019)

the linkage between entrepreneurship competencies and playful competencies rooted in playful approaches (Bacigalupo et al., 2016).

Since entrepreneurship competencies and play competencies share several similarities and counterparts, it indicates that by employing playful approaches in university pedagogy, it is possible to support not only play and related skills but also entrepreneurship competencies. Building entrepreneurship competencies is imperative as they are seen as drivers of transformation, innovation, and growth in nations (Bacigalupo et al., 2016).

Furthermore, as stated in earlier literature on playful learning: "We MUST advocate for students the right to play" (Dearybury & Jones, 2020), and "Encouraging a spirit of play among learners allows them to have space to imagine, explore and create in new, exciting and playful ways" (Whitton, 2018). It is then the educationalists' task to legitimize play in the work setting of an academic institution, and this chapter suggests it can be achieved by the deliberate playification of coursework offered to students.

Playful learning design must take into account the planning of physical space, and conceptual structure of the sequence of the learning process. Cable (2019, 58) suggested a sequence of experiences that take place during a playful event:

- The icebreaker or introduction, which is usually the first participatory activity for delegates.
- The group-builder, which is designed to help groups form quickly.
- The energizer, which happens after a lunch break or long task.
- Parting ways (Eggleston & Smith, 2004), which bring the event to the conclusion and celebrates what has been achieved.

To conclude, we provide a summary of playful approaches in entrepreneurship education. Playful methods in entrepreneurship education based on Gray's definition of play (2015, 125) are activities that are: (1) gamified or playified approaches to learning offered as "invitations to play" for the students, (2) motivated by the students' intrinsic goals, (3) guided by rules defined and interpreted creatively by the students themselves, and (4) call for the capacity to imagine and are conducted in an alert, but playful frame of mind.

Based on our course designs and findings, we suggest how Cable's playful event design can be combined with Gray's conceptual ideas of play and, consequently, be applied in designing learning experiences (see Figure 12.2).

The integration of playful practice in entrepreneurship education has just begun. The authors' interest in the potential of playful learning in this particular context was spurred by the observations of how the introduction of playful tools, such as Comicubes, provides an engaging way for students to participate in play to achieve learning goals set by courses in the humanities and entrepre-

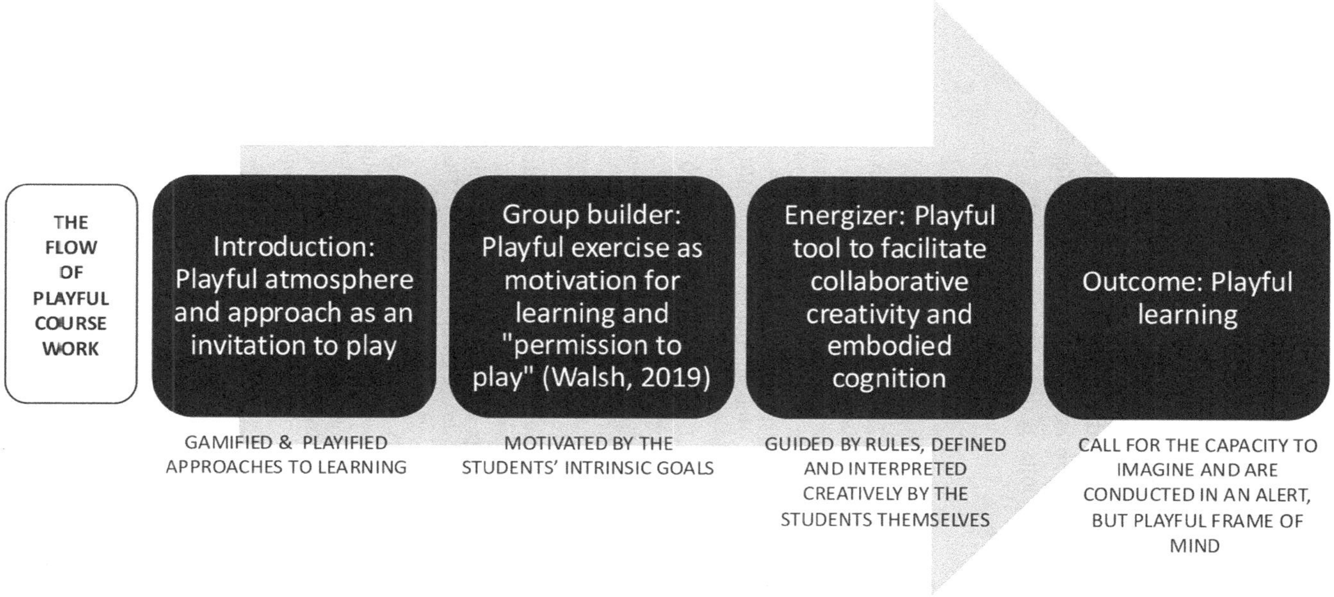

Source: Authors' own elaboration.

Figure 12.2 The flow of playful course work is based on Cable's (2019) concept of playful event design and Gray's definition of play (2015) neurship. We have aimed through our two case studies on playful learning in the higher education context to inspire readers to create their own designs for invitations to play in the context of learning situations.

Finally, it is essential to consider the sustainability of playful approaches in education. Whitton (2018) notes that it is crucial to appreciate that play is not equally accessible to all – "play is a privilege for those with the time, inclination, appreciation, confidence, social capital and ability to engage." To fully embrace the opportunities that play provides in learning situations, we must include considerations on how to construct and offer inclusive playful learning experiences for adults of different ages –useful for any current and future entrepreneur, too.

REFERENCES

Alvarez, S. A., & Barney, J. B. (2007). Discovery and creation: Alternative theories of entrepreneurial action. *Strategic Entrepreneurship Journal*, *1*, 11–26.

Bacigalupo, M., Kampylis, P., Punie, Y., & Van den Brande, G. (2016). EntreComp: The Entrepreneurship Competence Framework. Publication Office of the European Union. https://eige.europa.eu/resources/lfna27939enn.pdf.

Beichner, R. J., & Saul, J. M. (2003). Introduction to the SCALE-UP (student-centered activities for large enrollment undergraduate programs) project. *Proceedings of the International School of Physics "Enrico Fermi" Varenna, Italy.*

Biggs, J., & Tang, C. (2007). *Teaching for quality learning at university: What the student does.* 3rd ed. Society for Research into Higher Education & Open University Press.

Boehm, H. (1986). *The right toys: A guide to selecting the best toys for children*, Bantam Books.

Burghardt, G. M. (2015). Integrative approaches to the biological study of play. In Johnson, J. E., Eberle, S. G., Henricks, T. S., & Kuschner, D. (Eds.), *The handbook of the study of play, volume II* (pp. 21–39). Rowman & Littlefield.

Burke, A. (2011). Group work: How to use groups effectively. *The Journal of Effective Teaching*, *11*(2), 87–95.

Cable, L. (2019). Playful interludes. In Whitton, N., & Moseley, A. (Eds.), *Playful learning: Events and activities to engage adults* (pp. 58–70). Routledge.

Csikszentmihalyi, M., & Nakamura, J. (2014). The dynamics of intrinsic motivation: A study of adolescents. In Csikszentmihalyi, M., *Flow and the foundations of positive psychology: The collected works of Mihaly Csikszentmihalyi* (pp. 175–197). Springer.

Dearybury, J., & Jones, J. (2020). *The playful classroom: The power of play for all ages*. Jossey-Bass.

De Koven, B. L. (2015). Playing playfully in public is a political act. February 10. https://www.aplayfulpath.com/playing-playfully-public-political-act/.

Eggleston, T., & Smith, G. (2004). Building community in the classroom through ice-breakers and parting ways. Society for the Teaching of Psychology.

European Parliament and the Council. (2006). Recommendation of the European Parliament and of the Council of 18 December 2006 on key competences for lifelong learning. *Official Journal of the European Union*, L394/310.

Fayolle, A. (2007). *Entrepreneurship and new value creation: The dynamic of the entrepreneurial process*. Cambridge University Press.

Fayolle, A. (2018). Introduction. In Fayolle, A. (Ed.) *A research agenda for entrepreneurship education* (pp. 1–9). Edward Elgar Publishing.

Franzén, R., Heljakka, K., & Nieminen, N. (2020). Playful approaches to entrepreneurial competencies in university teaching: Introducing the 4Cs Model. In Markopoulos, E., Goonetilleke, R. S., Ho, A. G., & Luximon, Y. (Eds.), *Advances in Creativity, Innovation, Entrepreneurship and Communication of Design: Proceedings of the AHFE 2020 Virtual Conferences on Creativity, Innovation and Entrepreneurship, and Human Factors in Communication of Design*, July 16–20, USA (pp. 105–112). Springer.

Giddens, A. (1964). Notes on the concepts of play and leisure. *The Sociological Review*, *12*(1), 73–89.

Gray, P. (2015). Studying play without calling it that. In Johnson, J., Eberle, S., Henricks, T., & Kuschner, D. (Eds.), *The handbook of the study of play* (pp. 121–138). Rowman & Littlefield.

Guitard, P., Ferland, F., & Dutil, É. (2005). Toward a better understanding of playfulness in adults. *OTJR: Occupation, Participation and Health*, *25*(1), 9–22.

Hake, B. (1998). Lifelong learning and the European Union. In Griffin, C., Holford, J., & Jarvis, P. (Eds.), *International perspectives on lifelong learning* (pp. 32–43). Routledge.

Harter, S. (1978). Effectance motivation reconsidered: Toward a developmental model. *Human Development*, *1*, 661–666.

Hassinger-Das, B., Toub, T. S., Zosh, J. M., Michnick, J., Golinkoff, R. M., & Hirsh-Pasek, K. (2017). More than just fun: A place for games in playful learning. *Infanc. Aprendiz.*, *40*, 191–218.

Heljakka, K. (2014). *Comicubes*. A physical prototyping method and tool.

Heljakka, K. (2020). Pandemic toy play against social distancing: Teddy bears, window screens and playing for the common good in times of self-isolation. *Wider Screen*, 11 May 2020.

Heljakka, K. (2021). Liberated through teddy bears: Resistance, resourcefulness, and resilience in toy play during the COVID-19 pandemic, *International Journal of Play*, *10*(4), 387–404. https://doi.org/10.1080/21594937.2021.2005402.

Heljakka, K. (2022). On longevity and lost toys: Sustainable approaches to toy design and contemporary play. In Muthu, S. S. (Ed.), *Toys and sustainability: Environmental footprints and eco-design of products and processes*. Springer, Singapore. https://doi.org/10.1007/978-981-16-9673-2_2.

Heljakka, K. (2023). See me play! Self-portraiture in pseudo-museums as immersive playscapes for adults. *International Journal of Games and Social Impact*, *1*(1). https://www.doi.org/10.24140/ijgsi.v1.n1.01.

Heljakka, K., & Blomberg, A. (2022). Materializing playfulness: Developing a social play space for a multidisciplinary research community. In Anderson, K. (Ed.), *Participatory practice in space, place, and service design* (pp. 125–143). Vernon Press.

Heljakka, K., Harviainen, J. T., & Suominen, J. (2018). Stigma avoidance through visual contextualization: Adult toy play on photo-sharing social media. *New Media & Society*, *20*(8), 2781–2799.

Heljakka, K., & Ihamäki, P. (2016). Comicubes: A playful tool to stimulate (design) creativity. In Desmet, P. M. A., Fokkinga, S. F., Ludden, G. D. S., Cila, N., & van Zuthem, H. (Eds.), *Celebration & Contemplation: Proceedings of the 10th*

International Conference on Design & Emotion, 27–30 September, Amsterdam, the Netherlands (pp. 387–394). The Design & Emotion Society.
Heljakka, K., & Ihamäki, P. (2020a). Toy tourism. From Travel Bugs to characters with wanderlust. In van Es, N., Reijnders, S., Bolderman, L., & Waysdorf, A. (Eds.) *Locating imagination: Popular culture, tourism & belonging* (pp. 183–199). Routledge.
Heljakka, K., & Ihamäki, P. (2020b). Toys that mobilize: Past, present and future of phygital playful technology. In Arai, K., Bhatia, R., & Kapoor, S. (Eds.), *Proceedings of the Future Technologies Conference (FTC) 2019: Volume 2* (pp. 625–640). Springer International Publishing.
Henricks, T. S. (2015). Where are we now. Challenges for the study of play. In Johnson, J., Eberle, S., Henricks, T., & Kuschner, D. (Eds.), *The handbook of the study of play, vol. II* (pp. 381–391). Rowman & Littlefield.
Hewitt, K. (2001). Blocks as a tool for learning: A historical and contemporary perspective. *Young Children, 56*(1), 6–12.
Hjorth, D. (2005). Organizational entrepreneurship. With de Certeau on creating heterotopias (or spaces for play). *Journal of Management Inquiry, 14*(4), 386–398.
Hughes, B. (2002). A playworker's taxonomy of play types. 2nd Edition, Play Education.
Huotari, K., & Hamari, J. (2017). A definition for gamification: Anchoring gamification in the service marketing literature. *Electronic Markets, 27*(1), 21–31.
Ihamäki P., & Heljakka, K. (2020). Co-creating gamified service design – case gamified airport security workshop. In Veloso, A., Mealha, O., & Costa, L. (Eds.), *21st International Conference on Intelligent Games and Simulation*, GAME-ON 2020, September, Portugal (pp. 5–12). EUROSIS-ETI.
Jenson, E. (2005). *Teaching with the brain in mind.* ASCD.
Jones, G. (2008). *Killing monsters: Our children's need for fantasy, heroism, and make-believe violence.* Basic Books.
Khan, N., Oad, L., & Aslam, R. (2021). Entrepreneurship skills among young learner through play strategy: A qualitative study. *Humanities & Social Sciences Reviews, 9*(2), 64–74.
Knight, J. K., & Wood, W. B. (2005). Teaching more by lecturing less. *Cell Biology Education, 4*(4), 298–310.
Lackéus M. (2018). "What is value?": A framework for analyzing and facilitating entrepreneurial value creation. *Uniped, 41*(1), 10–28.
Lieberman, J. N. (1977). The role of playfulness in a theoretical framework for a relationship among play, imagination, and creativity. *Playfulness: Its relationship to imagination and creativity* (pp. 107–122). Academic Press.
Manzano-León, A., Camacho-Lazarraga, P., Guerrero-Puerta, M. A., Guerrero-Puerta, L., Alias, A., Aguilar-Parra, J. M., & Trigueros, R. (2021). Development and validation of a questionnaire on motivation for cooperative playful learning strategies. *International Journal of Environmental Research and Public Health, 18*(3), 960.
Nørgård, R. T., Toft-Nielsen, C., & Whitton, N. (2017). Playful learning in higher education: Developing a signature pedagogy. *International Journal of Play, 6*(3), 272–282.
Payne, B. K., Monk-Turner, E., Smith, D., & Sumter, M. (2006). Improving Group Work: Voices of Students. *Sociology & Criminal Justice Faculty Publications*, 441–448.

Penaluna, A., & Penaluna, K. (2021). In search of entrepreneurial competencies: Peripheral vision and multidisciplinary inspiration. *Industry and Higher Education, 35*(4), 471–484.
Play and Playground Encyclopedia (2019). https://www.pgpedia.com/.
Power, P. (2011). Playing with ideas: The affective dynamics of creative play. *American Journal of Play, 3*(3), 288–323.
Robinson, S., Neergaard, H., Tanggaard, L., & Krueger, N. (2016). New horizons in entrepreneurship: From teacher-led to student-centered learning, *Education + Training, 58*(7/8), 661–683.
Rogan, B. (1998). On collecting as play, creativity and aesthetic practice. *Etnofoor, 11*(1), 40–54.
Román-Oyola, R., Figueroa-Feliciano, V., Torres-Martínez, Y., Torres-Vélez, J., Encarnación-Pizarro, K., Fragoso-Pagán, S., & Torres-Colón, L. (2018). Play, playfulness, and self-efficacy: Parental experiences with children on the autism spectrum. *Occupational Therapy International*, October. https://doi.org/10.1155/2018/4636780.
Ryan, R. M., & Deci, E. L. (2000). Self-determination theory and the facilitation of intrinsic motivation, social development, and well-being. *American Psychologist, 55*(1), 68–78.
Sarasvathy, Saras, D. (2001). Causation and effectuation: Toward a theoretical shift from economic inevitability to entrepreneurial contingency. *The Academy of Management Review, 26*(2), 243–263.
Scott, A. (2012). Meaningful play: How play is changing the future of our health. IDSA Education Symposium, August 15, Boston. https://www.idsa.org/sites/default/files/Scott.pdf.
Silverman, S. (1993). Student characteristics, practice, and achievement in physical education. *The Journal of Educational Research, 87*(1), 54–61.
Smith, P. K. (2010). *Children and play: Understanding children's worlds.* Wiley-Blackwell.
Spariosu, M. (1989). *Dionysus reborn: Play and the aesthetic dimension in modern philosophical and scientific discourse.* Cornell University Press.
Steinert, Y. (1996). Twelve tips for effective small-group teaching in the health professions. *Medical Teacher, 18*(3), 203–207.
Stenholm, P., Ramström, J., Franzén, R., & Nieminen, L. (2021). Unintentional teaching of entrepreneurial competences. *Industry and Higher Education, 35*(4), 505–517.
Sutton-Smith, B. (1986). *Toys as culture*. Gardner Press, Inc.
Sutton-Smith, B. (1997). *The ambiguity of play*. Harvard University Press.
Sutton-Smith, B. (2008). Beyond ambiguity. In Brown, F. and Taylor, C. (Eds.), *Foundations of playwork*, Open University Press.
Vestergaard, L., Moberg, K., & Jørgensen, C. (2012). Impact of entrepreneurship education in Denmark 2011. The Danish Foundation for Entrepreneurship – Young Enterprise. Odense.
Walsh, A. (2019). Playful training. In Whitton, N., & Moseley, A. (Eds.), *Playful learning: Events and activities to engage adults* (pp. 72–84). Routledge.
Whitehead, A. N. (1933). The study of the past: Its uses and its dangers. *Harvard Business Review, 11*, 436–444.
Whitton, N. (2018). Playful learning: Tools, techniques, and tactics. *Research in Learning Technology, 26*. https://doi.org/10.25304/rlt.v26.2035.
Whitton, N., & Moseley, A. (Eds.) (2019). *Playful learning: Events and activities to engage adults*. Routledge.

13. Build, deconstruct, reconstruct an entrepreneurship tool in a Freirian pedagogical approach[1]

Alain Fayolle

WHAT WE CAN LEARN FROM THIS CHAPTER

- The pedagogical approach uses alternative construction sequences, deconstruction and reconstruction of a methodology and an evaluation tool of business plans in the context of new venture creation.
- Learning objectives focus on understanding the process development of an evaluation method in relation to a posture and a context of evaluation.
- During and at the end of the training, learners are encouraged to develop an awareness of the power and freedom available to them (and have) as to the choice (or design) and use of the tools of management, whatever the situations and problems to be dealt with.

INTRODUCTION

For more than 15 years at emlyon business school I designed and ran, with several colleagues[2] a seminar entitled "Learning to Entrepreneurship". It was positioned at the start of the programs,[3] teaching different audiences in continuing education and leading to a diploma. The objective of this short introductory seminar (lasting approximately two days) was, in addition to an original awareness of business creation, to enable learners, through an educational situation, to develop and apply a management tool intended to evaluate business plans in the context of new venture creation. This objective was rather paradoxical, even incongruous, insofar as all the learners, middle managers from companies of very different sizes and sectors, had enrolled in a management training program to acquire knowledge, tools and techniques useful for processing issues and problems relating to marketing, accounting, finance, human resources management, strategy, operations management, etc. However, what was offered to them at the start of their training had nothing to do with what they were seeking. Rather than presenting a particular management tool, then asking them to apply it through a case study, I urged them to build their own entrepreneurship tool to deal with a specific problem, the evaluation of entrepreneurial business plans, not ignoring the fact that most of them had very limited knowledge in the field of entrepreneurship as well as in fields relating to management in the broad sense. They therefore found themselves in a situation, often very uncomfortable, of having to, in teams of four to six people, develop a methodology and a tool for evaluating business creation projects. It is useless to say to what extent this pedagogical approach, which involved them in a learning process that ran counter to their traditional conception of education was, for them, destabilizing, even distressing. For me, it has always been essential that in training courses intended to prepare individuals for the exercise of high-level responsibilities, there may at one time or another be an approach to question and relativize management and entrepreneurship concepts and tools. Where do they come from, in what socio-historical context were they designed, for what purposes, what are they really used for, what are their fields of application, what are their limits, can we, must we adapt them, under what circumstances and conditions? All these questions seem important and legitimate, and one of the effects of this seminar was to be able to address them in the context of interactions between learners and educators. For years, I did not make the connection between the pedagogical model on which this seminar was based and the pedagogical approach advocated by Paulo Freire, which has been a source of inspiration for many educators and teachers worldwide.[4]

The main objective of Paulo Freire's educational model is the emancipation of learners – and indeed, in our case, it was a question of developing, during and at the end of the seminar, an awareness of the power and freedom that our learners have and will have with regard to the choice (or design) and the use of management tools, whatever the situations and the problems that need to be dealt with. As we will see later in this chapter, the approach we used has many similarities with the pedagogical pillars of Paulo Freire's model.

"LEARNING TO ENTREPRENEURSHIP" OR "LEARNING TO ASK (AND THINK ABOUT) THE RIGHT QUESTIONS"?

To date, more than 2,000 learners have experienced the educational model and the pedagogy of the "Learning to Entrepreneurship" seminar. To better understand what it aims to develop in learners and compare their pedagogy with the educational model of Paulo Freire, it seems necessary to us, first of all, to present our pedagogical practice in relation to its objectives and its methods of implementation.

The Objectives of the Educational Intervention

If the title of the seminar is "Learning to entrepreneurship", its main objective is far removed from what the title suggests. It is above all a methodological nature and logic, to enable one to learn to organize one's thoughts around a situational problem, by asking the right questions, and to implement a methodology aimed at developing a business plan assessment tool. More specifically, I state below the objectives as we have always explained them in one of our slides supporting the introductory remarks:

- Learn to develop an evaluation method in relation to objectives and a context.
- Understand the consequences of your choices on the method and results of the work.
- Learn to make a decision(s) without having all the useful data or information.
- Learn to "manage" your impressions and your intuitions (objective/subjective).

Among these objectives, only the third, refers to a situation characterizing entrepreneurial behavior and decision-making during uncertainty. The first objective is at the heart of the educational practice and links the assessment tool to the objectives and context of the individual or organization that develops, updates or uses it.

More specifically, with regard to the assessment of business creation projects, the objectives of a local authority, a foundation, an investment club, a business angel, a venture capital or a bank are very different. The same applies to the contexts of intervention of these actors. In a certain way, at one time or another the positions and roles of those who evaluate this type of project influence/determine the choice or the process of developing the tool as well as its use. The second objective aims to show that during a process of building a tool of management, the methodological choices, taken individually or collectively, have consequences on the construction process in progress (influence it, direct it) and can bias the results. The purpose of the fourth and last objective is to make participants aware of the need to be conscious, during the process of constructing the management tool and during its application, of what falls within the objectivity and what relates to subjectivity.

When learning about a problem-based situation, here a case study based on two real business plans, how do you check your first impressions? On the other hand, despite the degree of sophistication of an evaluation method, not everything can be "measured" in an objective way. Under these conditions, what place and what importance should be given to subjectivity and what type of arbitration between objectivity and subjectivity should be referred to?

The Teaching Process and Methods of Implementation

The pedagogical process starts on the first day at 9 a.m. with a short introduction, lasting no more than 30 minutes, which outlines, in an uncluttered way, the motivations and objectives of the seminar, the main actors (educators and learners), the learning levels (individual, working group, all of the participants), the problem to be investigated (building a business creation project evaluation tool and applying it to two real business plans), the roles and responsibilities of the educators and learners and the schedule for the next two days.

In this introduction, we insist on the fact that each group must quickly define its role, that is to say a position of investor willing to invest in business creation projects,[5] and the objectives attached to this position (for example, search for added value, job creation, regional development). We also present the expected results, the resources that can be mobilized and the role of the educators.[6] Then, we encourage them to join the rooms assigned to the groups, specifying that they have full freedom to organize collectively the work and to engage in the process of constructing their methodology and entrepreneurship tool to evaluate business plans in the context of new venture creation.[7] At the end of this launch sequence, we give each participant a copy of the slides presented as well as a document containing in extenso the two business plans which will be the subject of the application of the assessment tool.

The whole first day is made up of exchanges between the participants within a working group and between the latter and the educators.[8] The number of visits, and, therefore, of interactions, is variable, but, in general, at least two interventions are carried out during the morning and between 4 and 6 p.m.[9] The purpose of the interactions between educators and learners is to take stock of the current state of work (what has been done and how it has been done and what remains to be done) and to generate reflections and discussions on issues related to the construction and implementation of the assessment tool, based on questions that we, as educators, put to them, or by using a mirror effect.

The second day of the seminar takes place in two stages. The morning is dedicated to the presentation by each group of its methodology and its evaluation tool to all the participants of the same universe[10] (on average 25 people) and with the presence of the educator assigned to this universe. Each presentation lasts about 30 minutes and all the presentations allow learners to better understand both the similarities but also the differences between the methods.

More precisely, during the morning of day two, each learning group will have to present to other participants, in a professional, clear and coherent manner, its positioning, role and investment objectives, clearly focusing on the process and the method used to make sense of the investment decision. The analysis criteria used in the assessment tool must be relevant, operational, rational and applicable to projects other than those which were the subject of the evaluation (universality of the method for other projects falling within the chosen positioning). In addition, at the end of the presentation, "everyone" (including other participants and the educators) should be able to understand the process followed by the group and the modus operandi of the evaluation tool (transferability potential of the method).

The afternoon of day two is devoted to the synthesis and conclusion of the seminar with all the participants. During this last half-day, the educators manage a triple feedback, on both group decisions and projects that have been evaluated (what has happened with these projects), on the process experienced during day one with feedback from the participants and also from the educators, nourishing a dialogue rich in lessons and finally on the evaluation business creation projects (the only one theoretical contribution on the subject, during the seminar, is given at the end of day two and has a duration of approximately 45 minutes).

CONFRONTATION OF THE SEMINAR PEDAGOGICAL METHODOLOGY WITH PAULO FREIRE'S EDUCATIONAL MODEL

The main pillars on which Paulo Freire's educational model is based are the problem-based learning pedagogy, experiential learning, learner autonomy, dialectics and praxis, critical questioning and awareness. The fundamental objective of his model is the emancipation of learners, which amounts to giving them more power and possibilities to understand the "world" in which they find themselves and to act on this.[11]

In our pedagogical methodology, a first problem which is posed to the participants is in relation to their learning and professional stakes. They undergo training to complete and deepen their skills in the areas of administration and management. To this end, they are generally part of a classical and transmissive approach to education. Paulo Freire called this educational model "banking".[12] However, our learners find themselves in a business school and a classroom, where at the start of their training, from the first hour, the educators do not transmit to them any knowledge, any management technique, or any management or diagnostic tool. They are facing a problem that they are not sure how to approach or deal with. This problem is: "how to evaluate two business plans by building an evaluation tool that can be used beyond these two cases to evaluate under the same methodological conditions other business plans falling within the same contextual dimension (defined by the position of investor and the objectives attached to it". The problem is therefore in relation to the design, methodological elaboration and use of a management tool. Our objective is to arouse and raise the awareness of the participants of the seminar as to the relativity of the management tools (in this particular case and in general), the context and the conditions in which they were created and, consequently, their scope and their limitations. Such an objective aims to free the learners of a form of conditioning which could put them in a situation of excessive dependence vis-à-vis the universalism and absolutism (I would add to a certain extent, the magic power) of management tools. For this exercise to be successful, from the point of view of achieving the objective and the learning outcomes, it is necessary that great autonomy and freedom of action be given to the participants, with at regular intervals dialectical interactions between them and the educators, made up of questions, discussions and debates, intended to feed subsequent sequences of reflection and action (the praxis dimension).

During the two days of training, the participants go through phases of construction, deconstruction and reconstruction of the assessment tool that they must design and apply to the two business plans. These phases are preceded by a (first) awareness of the educational exercise, its objective and the problem posed to them.

Understanding the Problem

During their first visit to the working groups,[13] the educators first adopt the position of observer to get an idea of how the groups work and to grasp the content and logic of the activities in progress. They then question the participants to make sure that the objective has been assimilated and that the problem posed to them has been identified by all those present. Almost systematically, neither the objective nor the problem to be instructed were clearly understood by the learners. The latter, after a quick presentation of each of them, which does not always lead to a precise inventory of the skills and resources available to the group, very quickly began to read the business plans. The educators then engage in a discussion with the members of the group to make them aware of the objective of the seminar and the problem that they must "solve" collectively. This work of refocusing can take a little time, because it comes up against the representations of the participants as to their own conception of teaching and their biased understanding of the exercise which leads them to conceal the methodological component in order to retain only the evaluative dimension. In short, at this stage they are more interested in the result and practically are not in the process of achieving it, under the conditions described in the introduction phase of the seminar.

Constructing and Deconstructing

The first phase of construction is initiated immediately after the introductory session and, as we have mentioned previously, without the groups always fully understanding what the central objective and the problem at the heart of the educational system is. About nine out of ten groups, without sometimes having decided collectively, approach the exercise by reading the two business plans and trying to identify their strengths and weaknesses. Some groups or individuals apply, often incompletely, strategy tools such as SWOT or Porter's industrial analysis.[14]

In general, the construction phases follow passages, interventions and discussions with the learners, which, using almost exclusively questioning, make participants aware, in the course of their work, of the limits and weaknesses of their business plan assessment model and therefore of the need to deconstruct it to engage the group in a new construction.

The deconstruction phases are the consequence of highlighting the non-compliance with principles and rules in terms of the methodological design, elaboration and application of management tools.

Here, in the order in which they appear during the first day, are some examples of questions that are systematically at the center of the discussions inspired by educators.

1. Why did you start the exercise by reading the two business plans? Were there no other options? What are the advantages and disadvantages of the different options available? How do you take into account, in the continuation of the process, the fact of having started with the reading of the cases?
2. Why did you choose to apply this tool (SWOT or Porter's analysis) at this stage of the process? What is this tool really for? When was it created, for whom and why? Does this tool actually solve the problem you are facing? Does it make it possible to evaluate, in the most objective way possible, the two business plans?
3. How do you define an assessment tool? What does it mean for you? What are the components and operating methods on which it is based? What representation (descriptive, graphic) do you have of a new venture creation project?
4. Regarding the criteria of your assessment grid of business plans – are they relevant? Are they consistent? To what extent do the criteria you have selected take into account your investment objectives? Do you have veto criteria? Did you take note of some key criteria? How did you operationalize your evaluation criteria? Do you have enough criteria to evaluate the business plans (what is simple is wrong, what is complicated

is unusable!)? Where does the business plan data come from? What is their validity? Why do you think financial data are important? Are they really in the context of new venture creation projects?

5. You now have an evaluation grid of business plans, which will allow you to "score" business plans, how reliable is it? What margin of approximation and error are you willing to accept? How do you take into account the subjective dimension of your management tool when it is implemented? What is a priori your "best" decision-making rule with regard to your position and objectives as an investor?

Generally speaking, questions 3, 4 and 5 are those that generate the most discussion, debate, awareness and critical questioning of previous methodological approaches and work of participants.

Rebuilding a Contextualized Management Tool

The reconstruction phase corresponds mainly to the activities of day two of the seminar. Indeed, the latter offers each participant a diversity of points of view, through the different models and evaluation tools presented and discussed, in each universe, during the morning. There is therefore no single business plan assessment tool, but tools that are quite similar while being adapted to different contexts and investment objectives. The afternoon talks, the feedbacks that go over the difficulties encountered by the participants and the way in which they were overcome, and the general synthesis allow us to collectively consolidate a design and application methodology for a contextualized business plan evaluation tool.

EDUCATIONAL AND PEDAGOGICAL IMPLICATIONS: SET UP PROBLEM-BASED LEARNING, REFOCUS THE PURPOSE OF ENTREPRENEURSHIP EDUCATION AND RETHINK THE LEARNER–EDUCATOR RELATIONSHIP

The confrontation of our pedagogical practice with the educational model of Paulo Freire leads us to propose several educational and pedagogical implications valid for many higher education systems. They concern the way in which educators could redefine the object of education, its objectives, its dynamics and the relationship between learners and educators.

The teaching object could be constructed, whenever possible, from problem-based authentic situations, with a desire to give them meaning for the learners, in that they could echo the concerns which are immediate, daily, or even existential. Meaning also comes from their authenticity and their ability to faithfully translate real problems that arise for managers or entrepreneurs engaged in processes of reflection, decision and action. As we have shown in a previous work, the concept of situation inscribes the subject (the individual) and the object (the problem or the project) in a spatiotemporal context and places, de facto, importance on contextual variables and temporal dynamics (Fayolle, 2021).

Problem-solving and problem-based learning are based on four major learning principles (Dolmans et al., 2005): constructivism, self-direction, collaboration and contextualization. The problems raise questions, discussions and stimulate the learning of the learners; collaborative work energizes and enriches interactions, involves educators who facilitate learning and awareness processes. The choice of problems must be made taking into account their proximity to the learners, by bringing them to light in discussions or scenarios. Under no circumstances should they be too structured or too simple, which would reduce the space for dialogue and construction of knowledge about them.

As Paulo Freire suggests, the educator, in this type of pedagogy, must avoid being too directive and remain in its role as mediator. The dialogue and the contextualized learning around a problem situation make it possible to free oneself from methods favoring the imposition of ideas and knowledge that are meaningless and devoid of interest for the learners.

The teaching objectives or rather its aims should be refocused more on the intellectual autonomy of the learners and their personal development. I consider that all higher education students and adult learners confronted with an educator in an educational design and environment are exposed, in one way or another, to a form of conditioning, sometimes to an ideology, patterns of thought, corresponding to social and educational expectations and norms and constraints that society imposes. The seminar "Learning to Entrepreneurship" clearly shows us that training objectives falling within a critical perspective and an emancipatory aim have their place in higher education. Such objectives help students and learners to free themselves from taken-for-granted ideas, cooking recipes, ready-to-think, the doxa that sprinkle the fields of management and entrepreneurship, or, as we have done, to put them in interactive and iterative situations of deconstruction/reconstruction/creation of a field, in our case that of the evaluation of business creation projects, by opening up avenues of innovation in terms of educational purpose.

These objectives, centered on the learners, aim to develop a critical mindset and an ability to learn differently in order to prepare them to be more socially intelligent actors, in their spatiotemporal context, faced with uncertainty and dealing with the complexity of the world in which they project or operate themselves.

In our pedagogical design, it is the dialectic between learners and between educators and learners that establishes the learning dynamic.

The reciprocation of sequences, individual reflection, work in small groups, exchanges within the universes and in plenary sessions, promotes the involvement of each learner and maintains a dynamic learning process. Praxis and succession, in iterative loops, phases of reflection and action, construction and deconstruction, as well as the contributions generated by the educator, thus contribute to maintaining the dynamic, even to stimulate it. In the same vein, the mediation activities of educators vis-à-vis theoretical and empirical knowledge and of the "real world", in the context, in the broad sense, in which any action can take place, can, it seems to us, act as factors for increasing the commitment of learners in their learning process.

Finally, the seminar shows us how essential the relationship between educators and learners is and how much it is necessary to rethink it. In Paulo Freire's conception of education, educator and learner are at the same level and at a distance from any relationship of domination, of the first over the second, through knowledge or through any other form of legitimacy. Through dialogue, learners and educators become subjects. The knowledge needed to analyze a situation results from continuous dialogue, which takes place in mutual respect, from critical questioning and from fruitful interactions where the roles can sometimes be reversed. In this mode of relationship, the educator is neither a transmitter of knowledge, nor a coach or tutor. They are a facilitator, an awakener who designs and sets up the conditions and learning situations. The educator has a role of mediator vis-à-vis the context in which the learner evolves and with regard to the theoretical and empirical knowledge, which they might be able to use. It helps learners to improve their reading and their understanding of the problems, situations and world in which they live and where they will have to take a stand in order to act and transform it. This contributes to their awareness at all levels, of the realities and opportunities of their environment, but also of their ability to orient themselves in this world, to seize life opportunities according to their values and their aspirations. It seems to us, moreover, that one of the missions of the educator, thanks to qualities of listening, empathy, and questioning with a reflexive aim, is to help learners to improve the knowledge that they have of themselves, particularly with regard to their fundamental values, their personal and professional life aspirations and their ability to achieve them. This is true at the dawn of management training such as that followed by the learners of the seminar, but it is also true at other times in their professional lives. The last slide that closes the final summary of the seminar illustrates this idea in a certain way: "Live as if you were to die tomorrow. Learn as if you were to live forever".[15]

NOTES

1. This work was originally published in the French journal *Entreprendre & Innover, 2021/4*(51), 29–42. Article available online at https://www.cairn.info/revue-entreprendre-et-innover-2021-4-page-29.htm.
2. In particular, Bernard Calisti, Saulo Dubard Barbosa and Geneviève Le Normand.
3. This seminar is always offered, several times a year, to the various promotions of the General Management Program (PGM). It has also been offered in the past to participants in the institution's MBA programs.
4. Paulo Freire was born in 1921 in Brazil in Recife, he died at the age of 75 in Sao Paulo. Recife is the capital of one of the most disadvantaged regions of this country, the Northeast. This particular context immediately confronted Paulo Freire with social injustice, exclusion, discrimination, marginalization and the illiteracy of part of the population, and led very early on to his involvement in popular education movements and associations, in university, municipal and parish structures within which he gradually developed his conception of literacy for the emancipation of the people. Paulo Freire experienced arrest and imprisonment during the 1964 military coup in Brazil, then a very long period of exile, particularly in Chile. He has taught at Harvard, advised UNESCO and inspired educational programs in Africa and South America. Paulo Freire first studied law, while being interested in the psychology of language and philosophy, a discipline in which he was inspired by phenomenology, Christian personalism, existentialism and humanist Marxism. His best-known works are: *Pedagogy of the oppressed* (1970), Seabury Press, New York and *Education for critical consciousness* (1973), Seabury Press, New York.
5. Each group has €100,000 and must invest in at least one project.
6. Each educator interacts with 5 groups of 4 to 6 people, which constitute a universe; each working group has a room and exchanges between groups are prohibited. As presented in a slide, the educator: (a) does not provide specific technical advice or solutions; (b) is there to help you in your way of working/organizing and for the construction of your analysis method;(c) is there to make sure you get ahead. In this respect, the educator is attentive to your needs, helps develop a climate conducive to exchanges and debates, and feeds the process of reflection and construction of the method.
7. They have the whole day to carry out this work.
8. Although each educator was assigned to working groups, we never refrained from interacting with groups accompanied by another educator to offer a variety of points of view, using the diversity of educator profiles. In recent years, the specializations of the four main educators were entrepreneurship, strategy, marketing and human resource management.
9. The work within the groups generally continued very often after 8 p.m. and sometimes even after midnight. The participants organized themselves to

eat on the spot and had, of course, been warned that the exercise could be prolonged until a late hour.

10. In almost all cases one-third of a promotion.
11. See among other works: Freire, P. (1974), *Pedagogy of the oppressed followed by conscientization and revolution*, François Maspéro, Paris; Lenoir, Y., & Lizardi, A. O. (2007), *The concept of existential situation in Paulo Freire: At the heart of a critical and emancipatory pedagogy*, Documents du CRIE et de la CRCIE (new series), No. 3, Faculty of Education, University of Sherbrooke; Rugut, E. J., & Osman, A. A. (2013), Reflection on Paulo Freire and classroom relevance, *American International Journal of Social Science*, *2*(2), 23–28; Fayolle, A. (2021), Promouvoir une pédagogie émancipatrice de l'entrepreneuriat: Des idées clés du constructivisme critique au modèle éducatif de Paulo Freire, *Revue Interdisciplinaire Droit et Organisations*, *1*(1), 56–76. (Text adapted from the site Kindnessforbusiness.org.)
12. For Paulo Freire, a "banking" pedagogy is one where teachers, who hold knowledge, "deposit" knowledge in the minds of receptive and passive students who are supposed to assimilate it at the end of the educational process in order to reuse it afterwards.
13. As a general and key rule, we let the groups start the process on their own, for about 45 minutes.
14. The SWOT is a tool for strategic analysis which makes it possible to match the strengths (*Strengths*) and weaknesses (*Weaknesses*) of a company or an area of activity with the opportunities (*Opportunities*) and the threats (*Threats*) of its environment. Porter's model is a tool for analyzing the attractiveness of a sector of activity and the positioning of a company in this sector, which is based on a qualitative analysis of the competitive forces exerted on the business. These competitive forces come from the balance of power within the sector (negotiating power of companies in the sector with upstream (their suppliers) and downstream (their customers), threats of substitution products and technologies, threats from new entrants and the intensity of intra-sector competition.
15. This quote is from *Bhagavad-Gîtâ* by Mahatma Gandhi.

REFERENCES

Dolmans, D., De Grave, W., Wolfhagen, I., & Van der Vleuten, C. (2005). Problem-based learning: Future challenges for educational practice and research, *Medical Education, 39*, 732–741.

Fayolle, A. (2021). Promoting an emancipatory pedagogy of entrepreneurship: Key ideas from critical constructivism to the educational model of Paulo Freire. *Interdisciplinary Review of Law and Organization (RIDO)*, *1*(1), 56–76.

Freire, P. (1970). *Pedagogy of the oppressed*. Seabury Press, New York.

Freire, P. (1973). *Education for critical consciousness*. Seabury Press, New York.

APPENDIX: EDUCATOR'S TESTIMONIALS

Geneviève Le Normand

"And above all, do not make any commitments for tonight; you may be out late."

This last sentence of the instructions, before the learners return to their room, leaves them perplexed. Some are trying to get more details. Others report that they already have a commitment, or that they have to pick up their children …

"Well, you will arrange with your group. If you can make yourself available, that would be better."

And the groups begin to function, each in a room.

Floating of the groups both on the organization of the work and on the understanding of the objectives. Reaction: capture the facilitator to obtain clarifications, or even more. And this is where the chosen pedagogy comes in: not answering all the questions; letting them "wander", and find for themselves, and, above all, get off the rails … it can take time, a lot of time!

The afternoon of day one is often a bad experience for the participants. They feel that they are not moving forward, get bogged down in details, try to reassure themselves by going on the Internet; ask the facilitator for more figures and absolutely unnecessary details, and above all are faced with two difficulties: poor time management, and poor listening to each other. This of course refers to the classic phenomena of group work. As well as the question of the leader, the oppositions between the supporters of different theories on management, the rivalries for power, etc. …

And time passes … After a few hours, the learners have understood that their facilitator is not going to give them a solution, and that they must build, themselves, a new working method, different from what they have learned.

The facilitator must practice several skills (or competences):

- A very fine and discreet method of listening.
- A memorization of the stages and difficulties experienced by the group, in order to be able to explain them during the summary session.
- Interventions "at the right time" so as not to be discouraged.
- Show empathy, a little humor and no judgement.
- Rarely – but it could happen, settle a conflict between participants …

And the groups progress, at very different speeds.

Around 8 p.m., classic dinner time, they realize that they have been working for a long time, have not even been hungry, that they are starting to stick to a method, that they cannot stop there and … they look at the facilitator laughing: we understood why we shouldn't make a commitment! A few sandwiches, pizzas ordered at the local restaurant, and they get back to work.

Some groups worked until midnight or even longer, and the next day they were in good shape, happy with the work done, surprised to have exceeded their usual limits, and were proud of themselves.

Day two is more serene: they have understood the real objective, have the common thread, know how to divide up the work, go to the essentials, in short, be efficient.

The presentations of the last day are almost always good, creative, full of vitality. One could even say that there is a shared pleasure of this success between the learners and the facilitators. The faces are smiling, and all leave the seminar with regret.

The animators are of course the key to this success.

This seminar was led by a small team who knew each other well, enjoyed working together, trusted each other. And above all who loved this pedagogy, and just like the learners, did not complain about time taken or pain involved.

Go from group to group, for two long days, be attentive, feel the atmosphere of the group to help it move forward without doing it for them, be benevolent, understanding, stimulating, without being a demagogue, know how to provide contributions essential to their progress … rejoicing at the results, know how to show them their development, their achievements. Such is the attitude of the leader of this seminar.

During the last plenary session, learners, then facilitators, share their feelings, their discoveries, their conclusions.

Everyone expresses themselves simply, freely; without coercion or sycophancy.

Admittedly, this is a "hot evaluation"; and we must be clear about the enthusiasm of the participants. At the same time, experienced facilitators know how to decode comments and attitudes. The repetition, at each seminar, of the positive, laudatory opinions of learners is one response.

The team of facilitators sincerely believes in the effectiveness of this approach, and would have liked to be able to carry out another evaluation a few months later.

Saulo Dubard Barbosa

Always aim to help without doing the work for the learners, never imposing a point of view but always opening minds with a question, an observation, or a simple smile … Having facilitated this seminar for several years, I will always remember the sensation of the first day when I approached each group, always asking myself, "Should I intervene now?" and in most cases, I refrained. Why? Because in a pedagogy inspired by Paulo Freire, the journey traveled is always more valuable than the path shown or demonstrated. And this seminar designed by Alain was exactly in this spirit: we travel the path together, but I don't tell you about the path because, to a large extent, you will create it for yourself.

This very attentive but initially very silent posture (after the first half-hour of starting), implies a benevolent letting go and at the same time some profound questioning. For most participants, this had never been experienced before. I remember a participant who declared, at the end of the two days, that initially, she wondered, "What kind of teacher is this?" Indeed, the facilitator did not provide input and often responded to questions with another question, like "Is this really the most relevant question to ask now?" Or: "Do you know who you are and what you really want?"

A gradual, but not at all linear, transformation occurred during this first long day. The next day, the participants and their groups were truly transformed. They presented their journeys, full of pitfalls, but also their roles, evaluation methods, and investment decisions. Throughout a constant dialectic process, they also learned from others and questioned their methods and decisions. What a joy for me to see this transformation, to know that I had facilitated it in some way, through dialogue, silence, body language, and always trust in their own abilities.

The most sublime pedagogical magic for me is to teach without teaching. And this seminar always allowed for that.

The dialogue always continued in the plenary session, the second day, in a more structured manner. And there I would talk a lot and bring content, always adapted to the needs and questions of the participants. Very often, we were a team of facilitators, which made the conversation even more interesting. When pedagogical content is placed in a conversation and is directly related to the experience lived by the participants, then I think there is a much higher chance that it will be assimilated.

I remember emphasizing that a manager must make decisions, that it is often not easy, and that an entrepreneur must also build the decision-making environment for their own decisions. In a way, that was exactly what they had just done …

Sometimes a participant asked whether we had really engaged in entrepreneurship (besides evaluating business plans). Then I would ask them a series of questions:

- Did the method you used to evaluate these business plans already exist?
- No. We created it.
- You created it, and you did it as a team. Is this team now an organization? Did it exist yesterday morning?
- No. It's true; we also created an organization …

- So you created an evaluation method, an organization, and a working process to build your evaluation method and apply it … Bravo! And with a sincere smile, we would add, "Imagine if in business we worked as you have worked in this seminar!"

This led to a reflection on the factors contributing to the efficiency and the smooth functioning of the group, and how to reproduce them in their professional contexts.

Often participants highlighted the originality of the pedagogical approach, as well as its effectiveness. They also emphasized the difficulty of the task and the sometimes tortuous path they had taken … One of the factors that always stood out was the right to make mistakes.

I would ask, "Do you have children?" and I would add that I had a son who was my greatest teacher. When he was learning to walk, he often fell. But he always got up, without complaining. Can you imagine if he reproached himself every time he fell, doubted his ability, regretted trying …? He would never have walked!

Several months after these two days, I would encounter participants in the school corridors. They still remembered this seminar, even years later. Once, a lady told me, "Sir, what you said about your son changed the way I see my two daughters."

Thank you, Alain, for all these experiences.

14. Generative critical conversation: a method for developing reflexivity and criticality[1]

Jennifer Huntsley and Catherine Brentnall

INTRODUCTION

In this chapter, we introduce a novel method – Generative Critical Conversation – which we propose can help develop the reflexive capacity of educators and researchers in Enterprise and Entrepreneurship Education (EEE). The method was developed when we – a senior lecturer in university-based initial teacher education and a business advisor from a university enterprise support team – worked together to develop an EEE intervention for primary student teachers. Primary schools are a noticeable target in enterprise education policy pronouncements in England (Young, 2014; Department for Education, 2017; Hinds, 2019). However, in EEE, student teachers are simultaneously identified as having the opportunity to develop enterprise from the beginning of their careers yet lacking the conceptual understanding to do this (Lepistö & Ronkko, 2013; Deveci, 2016; Tiernan, McCracken & Matlay, 2016).

Inducting pre-service teachers to view enterprise as extra-curricular *schemes* (Holman, 2014), which can be outsourced to providers, some of whom will provide activity for free (Hanson, Hooley & Cox, 2017), follows a well-trodden route likely to grow the *quantity* of enterprise education in schools. However, *from our first meeting*, we both agreed that we wanted to offer the primary student teachers we worked with a critical introduction to enterprise education and provide space for them to question EEE, its purposes and practices.

As our professional work developed, we became more curious about *why* we were both inclined towards this critical approach. To explore this, during the process of planning, delivering, and evaluating the intervention, we began to record our conversations, capturing our personal and professional experiences and what we thought was influencing our practice. We would listen back to these recorded conversations separately and then, at our next meeting, make new recordings, reflecting on our previous conversations and expanding the conversation in new directions. Through using our recorded conversations as artefacts for reflection (Bullough and Pinnegar, 2001), we generated a deeper understanding of our motivations and assumptions and experienced moments of self-critical illumination (Schön, 1991). Furthermore, listening to ourselves forced us to recognise the self – our interpretations and internalised discourses – a necessary step in developing reflexivity as an educator or researcher (Alvesson & Sköldberg, 2018). Through this process, and emerging from our practical experience, the possibilities of purposeful conversation to develop reflection and reflexivity became more apparent. This is particularly important in EEE, where the field is said to lack, and need to develop, criticality (Fayolle, 2013). We argue that reflexivity is a pre-requisite to criticality, and therefore methods that develop educator-researcher reflexivity are needed to help strengthen criticality in EEE. We propose that Generative Critical Conversation (GCC) is such a method and offers an innovative and practicable route for educators and researchers to explore and reflect upon their practice and actions and develop reflexive insight.

Our chapter unfolds in the following steps. First, we summarise recent calls for criticality in the field of enterprise and entrepreneurship education. Then, we consider the significance of reflection and reflexivity in supporting the development of criticality in the field of educational practice. Following this, we describe the emergence of Generative Critical Conversation out of our practical experience working together to develop an enterprise education intervention for primary student teachers. Next, we lay the theoretical groundwork for GCC, drawing from literature in educational research and reflective practice to explore terms such as criticality and reflexivity, and suggest that reflexivity is a necessary pre-cursor for criticality. We introduce a framework by reflexivity scholars which describes levels of reflexive insight which we later use as a lens through which to (re)view our conversations. We ground GCC as a method, hybridizing from three methodological approaches in teacher education – self-study, co-generative dialogue and critical questioning. Then, we illustrate, through three conversational excerpts, how GCC facilitated us to develop reflexive insight within and between conversations. We discuss enabling conditions that facilitate GCC, and its potential transferability. We conclude by underscoring the potential GCC has to practically address calls for greater educator-researcher reflexivity, and, as a result, strengthen critical capacity in, and beyond, EEE.

Generative Critical Conversation is an innovative method which *practically addresses* the issue of educators and researchers lacking criticality and/or needing to develop reflexivity. In addition, by drawing from the world of education to theoretically ground this method, our approach also contributes to efforts to better connect the world of EEE with the world of education.

CALLS FOR CRITICALITY IN THE FIELD OF EEE

In the following section we provide a narrative literature review (Grant & Booth, 2009), to support the need for criticality in the field of EEE and to contextualise the usefulness of GCC. We start by pointing to long expressed issues about the contested and problematic nature of EEE in relation to schools, the setting we practice in, which implicitly require the development of educators and their reflective capacity. We then turn to summarising more recent and explicit calls for greater criticality in the field of EEE.

In the seminal paper "Schools and Enterprise", Jamieson (1984) asserted "There can be few school activities which raise quite so many educational, organisational, political, and economic questions." (p. 20). For schoolteachers, enterprise education raises questions regarding the relationship between enterprise related knowledge and subject knowledge, the usefulness of knowledge gained through an enterprise activity and the pedagogy needed in order for students to gain practical wisdom and skills through an activity (Jamieson, 1984, p. 26). Whilst Jamieson concluded optimistically that the spirit of enterprise could be a "radical irritant" to traditional assumptions in education (Jamieson, 1984, p. 27), other authors started to identify assumptions *within* enterprise education that could hold back its development. Authors discussed issues such as the problematic and contested meanings of enterprise education (Gibb, 1987; Grant, 1986), the potential to reproduce corporate hegemony and education for capitalism (Crompton, 1987), and ethical concerns re the development of negative entrepreneurial profiles (Caird, 1990). The engagement and training of educators and staff to be aware of, and work with, these issues was considered a crucial strand in effective policy programming (Gibb, 1987, p. 36). Teachers were seen as central to the design and delivery of enterprise education in order to encourage an "*educational* response to social and economic changes" (Crompton, 1987, p. 10, emphasis added). Acknowledging these issues also meant acknowledging that enterprise education did not (and does not), lend itself to value free study (Gibb, 1987, p. 12).

In terms of primary schools in academic literature, they were seen responding to the calls to develop enterprise in education, with case studies offering examples of the benefits and challenges (Crawshaw 1996; Raven-Hill, 1996; Iredale, 1996; Bishop, 1997). However, reviewing the progress of enterprise education in schools, many years later, Gibb (2008) was still arguing that teachers should "own" the development of enterprise, for example, familiarising themselves with concepts and outcomes, designing experiments and innovation and evaluating successes and failures (Gibb, 2008, p. 11). His ongoing concern was that there was limited exploration of the meanings of enterprise education, and its link (or not) to broader educational goals, which hindered its development (Gibb, 2008, p. 14). These discussions persistently underscore the role of teachers in the development of EEE, and the need for them to be involved in debating it as a concept and designing and reflecting on it in practice, *implicitly* articulating the importance of informed and critical educators.

Recently however, there have been more *explicit* calls for criticality in the field of EEE, and more direct illustrations of the issues which arise when educators and researchers lack criticality. First, EEE has been called a taken-for-granted professional domain, where practices and assumptions are handed over with little questioning or reflection (Fayolle, 2013; Fayolle & Loi, 2018; Berglund & Verduijn, 2018). This can be seen in research, where instructor narratives of pedagogies are often based in implicit assumptions, with little reflection and a "less-than-convincing" critical stance (Fayolle, Verzat & Wapshott, 2016, p. 2). This is then compounded by a lack of criticality in research approaches, where researchers in EEE tend not to question their unconscious philosophies and practices; therefore, they do not borrow concepts or methods from other fields. Such borrowed concepts or methods could help explain contradictory results of interventions or explore research issues that require out-of-the-box thinking (Fayolle, 2013). This lack of criticality limits the legitimacy of the field (Fayolle, 2013; Fayolle et al, 2016). Over time, this lack of criticality can be argued to have contributed to the "McDonaldization" of EEE (Hytti, 2018), where adoption of highly standardised practices (such as drafting business model canvasses, pitching exercises and competitions) means provision is oblivious to questions of gender, class and ethnicity and important axiological debates about "why?" are silenced. In this scenario, educators and researchers risk conveying the message that structures and context do not matter, and unintentionally and unreflectively, becoming tools of top-down agendas which have been left unexplored (Berglund & Verduijn, 2018; Hytti, 2018).

Reflection and reflexivity are both identified as a route to countering the taken-for-granted in entrepreneurship education (Fayolle et al, 2016; Kyrö, 2015; Berglund & Verduijn, 2018; Hytti, 2018). Reflective practices can help challenge the normative reproduction of beliefs and values that evangelise and cult-ify the field (Farny, Frederiksen, Hannibal & Jones, 2016). Indeed, increasing reflectiveness on the use of concepts and conceptualisations is the way we might better understand *others'* views on the meaning of EEE, as well as identifying our own view and understanding (Kyrö, 2018). Within education literature and research, concepts of reflection, reflexivity and criticality are well-developed. In the next section, we explore these ideas, before presenting a method – Generative Critical Conversation – that may practicably support educators in EEE developing criticality.

DEVELOPING CRITICALITY THROUGH REFLECTION AND REFLEXIVITY IN EDUCATION PRACTICE

Teachers in the UK are required to be critical practitioners; it is said they should both think critically and enact criticality in the classroom, scrutinising and evaluating claims made in education literature and through education practice (Door, 2014). Reflection and reflexivity are established in education literature as routes to developing criticality (e.g., Bulman, 2013; Door, 2014; Bolton & Delderfield, 2017). Teacher educator and scholar of critical practice Door asserts that "reflexivity is a prerequisite to criticality" (2014, p. 45), and that reflexivity and criticality are essential dispositions that underpin effective teachers' practice. The notion of the "reflective practitioner", first coined by Schön in 1983, has been particularly influential in a broad range of professional fields, including initial teacher education. Schön's work is underpinned by that of philosopher John Dewey (1910), who developed the notion that learning is brought about through experience and reflection. Hofer suggests "reflection and reflexivity are central to professional growth as educators" (2017, p. 299). As such, it is relevant to connect the fields of educational research and EEE. The qualities of an effective educator in EEE are likely to be aligned with the qualities of effective educators in other fields. To learn more about these qualities, in this section, we explore conceptualisations of key terms "criticality", "reflection" and "reflexivity" proposed in educational research.

Exploring Criticality in Educational Research

In educational research, criticality has been defined as a "human disposition of engagement where it is recognised that the object of attention could be other than it is" (Barnett, 1997, p. 179). This has close links to Dewey's belief that "uncertainty is the hallmark of the search for knowledge" (Hofer, 2017, p. 301). It may be inferred that through practising criticality, understanding might be deepened or expanded through being willing to think from different and sometimes uncomfortable perspectives. Both Door (2014) and Barnett (1997) draw distinctions between criticality related to formal knowledge or theory and criticality related to practice. Barnett describes the former as critical reason and the latter as critical action. He identifies a further third domain of criticality as critical self-reflection: "that form of criticality which finds expression in being directed towards the self" (1997, p. 179). More recent authors reinforce this, saying that a key quality of being critical is being able to: "[consider] … an issue from multiple perspectives, even when these involve self-critique" (Banegas & Villacañas de Castro, 2016, p. 455). In teacher education, it has been argued that asking critical questions should be central to teachers' development and curriculum making (McNiff, 2009). Criticality is perceived as a transformative act; by asking such questions as "What are we doing?", "Why are we doing it?", "What difference are we trying to make?", generative transformational capacity is developed, that is, the ability of any thing "to transform itself into a more developed form of itself" (McNiff, 2009, p. 5). This previous work in the field of education demonstrates that calls to strengthen criticality within the field of EEE may be addressed by exploring the established routes to criticality through reflection and reflexivity in the field of education.

Exploring Reflection and Reflexivity

In conceptualising reflexivity, we may first examine reflection. Scholar of critical thinking and higher education Moon (2006), suggests that authors writing about reflection come from a range of disciplines and backgrounds, but rarely move beyond their own field, which gives rise to multiple definitions and crossover in meanings. Conceptualisations of reflection are both many and competing; a commonality among much of the literature in teacher education is the recognition that there is a lack of an ultimate definition of terms in this area (e.g., Ryan 2012; Rogers 2001). Within teacher education literature, multiple terms are used to describe reflective processes (Rogers, 2001) and educators and/or researchers bring personal interpretations to the terms "reflection" and "reflective practice" (Russell, 2014). Russell and Martin (2017) argue that this implies a lack of understanding as to how or why reflective practice may be valuable for student teachers – a situation that may extend into other fields and scenarios, such as and including EEE.

Recognising the multitudes of definitions of the term, teacher educator Ryan (2012) broadly encapsulates *reflection* as "making sense of experience" and "reimagining future experience" (p. 208); a sense of first looking back and then looking forward. Rogers' work agrees but expands these ideas; he suggests that reflection is triggered by a specific event and that it is a transformative process through which new understanding emerges (2001). These aspects of reflection have strong resonance with Barnett's definition of criticality. Making sense of the triggering specific event may be seen as the "object of attention" and through re-imagining it as "other than it is", new understanding may emerge (Barnett, 1997, p. 179). Further support for this link is apparent in Barnett's description of critical thought as "potentially emancipatory for individuals" and "educationally radical" (1997, p. 4).

Building on this, *reflexivity* may be defined as a process of "critical self-reflection", where one must be simultaneously both "*involved* and *detached*" (Bates, 2014, p. 227). It involves recognising "the ways in which one may affect and be affected" (Cole and Masny, 2012, in Attia & Edge,

2017, p. 35). One adopts a reflexive position through "interaction and interpretation" by imagining "the other's viewpoint into one's sense of self" (Zienkowski, 2017, p. 4). While *reflection* might be seen as examining one's own experiences and reimagining them for the future, *reflexivity* could be seen as both one's own interpretation and *the lens through which one views* those interpretations. Through reflexivity, the researcher "takes responsibility for one's own situatedness within [research and practice] and the effect that it may have" (Berger, 2015, p. 220).

It is suggested that reflexivity is closely entwined with *interpretation*; through *acts of interpretation*, Alvesson and Sköldberg (2018) suggest that *we as researchers* construct both *research objects* and *ourselves* socially. They describe four aspects or levels of interpretation: (see Table 14.1).

The first level is the point at which the initial data is constructed, where researchers "make preliminary interpretations ... where the degree of interpretation is relatively low or somewhat unclear to the researchers themselves" (Alvesson & Sköldberg, 2018, p. 330). The second level is "guided by ideas that can be related to academic theories (scientific paradigms) or to other frames of reference (cultural ideas or taken-for-granted assumptions, implicit personal theories, and so on)" (2018, p. 331). The empirical material is likely to inspire, develop, and reshape theoretical ideas; at the same, the researchers' own interpretative repertoires will define the scope of possible interpretations to be made. Shifting to the third level, critical interpretation, the researchers' focus moves from considering the underlying meanings of the empirical data to noticing the presence of ideologies, power and social reproduction. The fourth level, reflection on text production and language use, represents interpretations that are the furthest away from the original interaction with the empirical material. Here, researchers are concerned with their own text, they question their and others' claims to authority in an informed manner, and they recognise the selectivity of the voices represented.

Table 14.1 Levels of interpretation from Alvesson & Sköldberg, 2018, p. 331

Aspect/level of interpretation	Focus
Interaction with empirical material	Accounts in interviews, observation of situations and other empirical materials
Interpretation	Underlying meanings
Critical interpretation	Ideology, power, social reproduction
Reflection on text production and language use	Own text, claims to authority, selectivity of voices represented in the text

These levels are not a hierarchy, nor something to be worked through in a linear manner; there is no "best" level of reflexive interpretation. Rather, Alvesson and Sköldberg suggest that reflexivity is developed by the researcher paying attention to their movement *through and between* these levels. Reflexivity arises in the "relations" and "interfaces" between these levels (2018, p. 330), it is in these moments that researcher recognises the ways in which *they may affect and be affected.*

In relation to EEE, authors have offered ways of thinking about reflexivity in entrepreneurial learning (Higgins, Smith & Mirza, 2013), and developing student reflexivity in entrepreneurship education (Achtenhagen & Johannisson, 2018). Thus, whilst reflexivity is positioned as an important concern for educators and researchers, it is less clear how they might go about developing it in a practical sense. Our contribution is in providing a method – Generative Critical Conversation – which aims to support educators and researchers in the field of EEE to develop reflexivity and criticality.

Whilst our chapter and this method responds to the call for deeper criticality in EEE, we ground its theoretical underpinning in existing practice from the field of education relating to critical reflection and theory from scholars of reflexivity. By doing so we simultaneously contribute to calls from Fayolle (2013; 2019) that EEE better reflect and connect. We offer a way that educators and researchers in EEE can critically *reflect* upon and question their practice, as well as *connecting* this method with research and practice from the field of education and reflexivity scholarship. Having set the scene by outlining calls for criticality in EEE and exploring key terms and conceptualisations from education and reflexivity scholarship, we will now describe the method of GCC and how it emerged from our practice.

THE EMERGENCE OF GENERATIVE CRITICAL CONVERSATION

Generative Critical Conversation was developed while planning and implementing an intervention – *A Critical Introduction to Enterprise Education* – for primary student teachers in a School of Education in a university in northern England. The purpose of, and reflections regarding, the intervention itself have been presented elsewhere as a conference paper (Brentnall & Huntsley, 2019). Following this, we set out the method which emerged from that process – Generative Critical Conversation – in a journal article (Huntsley & Brentnall, 2021). This chapter explores our reflections on both the intervention and the construction of the journal article.

Whilst developing the intervention for primary student teachers we enjoyed a rich dialogue between ourselves and shared our work and thoughts with colleagues within and beyond the institution where we were working. Following a suggestion from a colleague – "*you should record your conversations*" (Higgins, 2019) – we took the leap and made an audio recording of one of our meetings.

Once we recorded our conversation (using the audio recording function on a smart phone and sharing the file via WhatsApp), we listened back to this conversational artefact separately. Then, when we met again, we reflected on what we remembered and what struck us about the previous conversation. We discussed what was painful, what was valuable, what insight we had gained into ourselves and each other. We recorded this conversation, and again, we listened to it separately. This (re)listening allowed us to reflect on our original conversation and probe further into elements that might otherwise have been forgotten: "... *when you said ... it made me think about* ...". It prompted us to delve into a comment in greater detail because the tone of speech changed, or because we heard a pause or perceived some other conversational sign. Perhaps there was moment of shared laughter, an indication of some deeper agreement we could explore. Or there was an extended pause, or an "*mm* ..." that indicated confusion, uncertainty or dissonance between us, our experiences, values and beliefs. We continued to record and re-listen to our conversations over time; these are detailed in Figure 14.1.

These conversations were not just a personal exploration, they were connected to a practical and professional context. Initially, the purpose of our conversations was to develop an intervention for primary student teachers; then the purpose was to reflect on our motivations, experiences and sense-making of the intervention (the focus of the aforementioned 2019 paper); following this, our purpose shifted to constructing the journal article. As such, each conversation was strongly linked to considering *what we were doing in practice* and *why*. We came to recognise the potential of this approach to spark critical thought, uncertainty and the prompting of thinking multiple perspectives and sought to define it.

We developed the term *Generative Critical Conversation* (GCC) to describe this process. The conversations, the subsequent (re)listening, the subsequent conversation and joint reflection were generative (McNiff, 2009), in that they had a transformative impact on our thinking or practice, and they were critical (Banegas & de Castro, 2016), in that they also broadened, challenged and questioned our individual viewpoints on literature, practice and the wider world. We explore the terms generative and critical further in the next section. Having summarised how GCC emerged organically from our practice, we theorise GCC as a method connecting it to existing practice in reflective educational research and reflexivity scholarship.

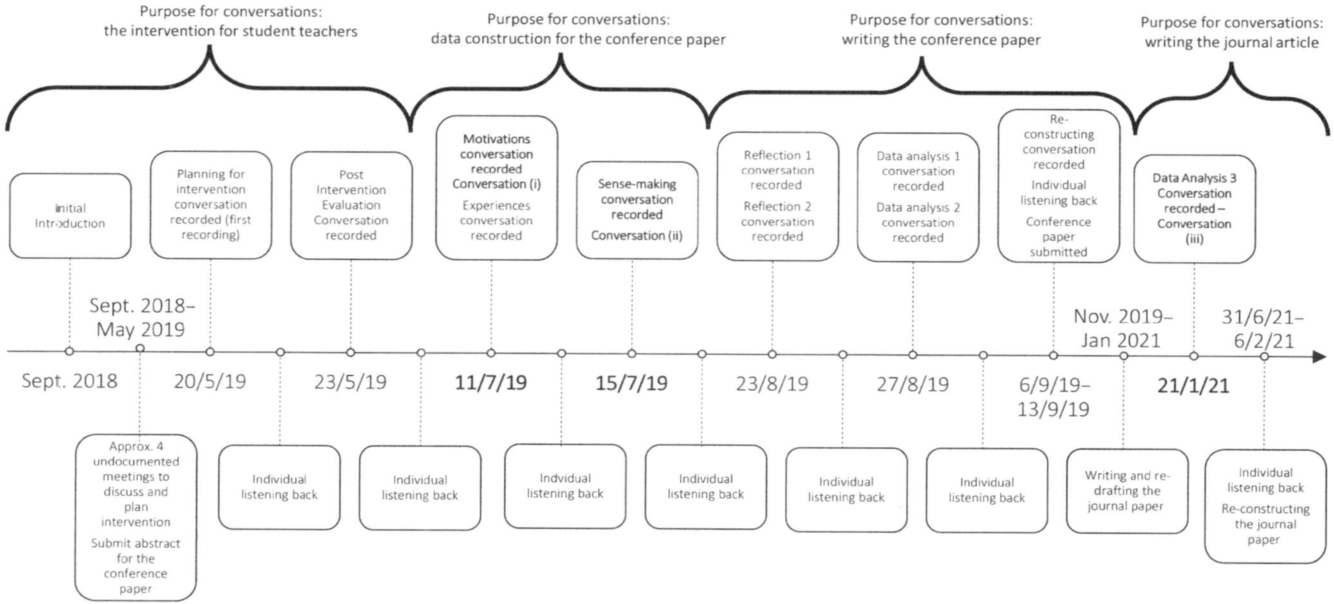

Figure 14.1 *Timeline showing our recorded conversations, individual listening back and purposes for meeting*

CONNECTING GCC TO EDUCATIONAL RESEARCH AND REFLEXIVITY SCHOLARSHIP

In this section, we draw from literature from the fields of educational research and reflexive scholarship to theorise GCC. We introduce existing practices from educational research to ground GCC in existing approaches and we introduce a framework of reflexive interpretation which will be used to illustrate how reflexivity is developed through GCC.

Through the course of our interactions and interpretations, in the process of our Generative Critical Conversations, we noticed how the opportunity to *reflect* on previous conversations (looking back and looking forward), enabled us to be more *reflexive* (recognising the ways in which one may affect and be affected). We began communicating about our communication, our "discourse" bending back on discourse (Zienkowski, 2017, p. 3). In doing so, we found that we were questioning ourselves and the worlds to which we were connected, considering issues from different perspectives and starting to recognise the different and competing discourses at play in our conversations and contained within our utterances (Bakhtin, 1986). Using Alvesson and Sköldberg's *levels of reflexive interpretation* as a lens through which to (re) view our conversations, we could see that we were moving between the levels both within and between our conversations. Thus, we suggest that GCC is a method that develops reflexivity by enabling researchers to become more aware of their own movement between levels of reflexive interpretation. Later in the chapter we provide excerpts from our recorded conversations to illustrate moments where we notice the relations and interfaces between the levels of interpretation. Next, we provide the theoretical grounding for GCC, hybridizing existing methods in educational practice and then summarising the terms "generative", "critical" and "conversation".

Grounding GCC: Hybridizing from Existing Methods in Educational Research

We now ground Generative Critical Conversation (GCC) in existing methods from the field of education. GCC blends the self-study approach of reflecting on recorded material (Bullough & Pinnegar, 2001), and the spirit of exploring lived experiences in co-generative dialogue (Roth, Lawless & Tobin, 2000), with a focus on critical questioning of McNiff (2009). We identify these as the three methodological elements of GCC. The process itself provides a practicable framework for developing educator and researcher reflexivity, and therefore offers a method to help strengthen criticality, of individuals and the field more generally. To connect our method to existing examples in education, we draw on self-study, co-generative dialogue, critical reflexivity and dialectical reflectivity to lay the theoretical ground for GCC.

Self-study

Self-study is a methodology often associated with teacher education, where researchers examine their own practices. Methods are mainly qualitative, the most common forms of data being correspondence and recorded conversations (Bullough & Pinnegar, 2001). The process is interactive and reflective and is closely tied to exploring and developing teacher educators' sense of identity (Loughran, 2018). The researcher records their responses to that which is being studied; returning to this record, they examine their initial processes at a deeper level. In this, self-study draws on the autobiographical, historical and cultural aspects of the subject-researcher's life (Hamilton & Pinnegar, 1998). Loughran (2018) asserts that a strength of collaborative self-study is that it facilitates the "questioning of taken-for-granted assumptions" and "the detailed analysis of alternative perspectives on pedagogical experiences" (p. 4). Self-study encompasses a drive for personal transformation – those engaging in self-study should seek to improve their practice (LaBoskey, 2004). But it also has a moral dimension, that of gaining understanding necessary to make interactions between self and other "increasingly educative" (Bullough & Pinnegar, 2001, p. 15).

Co-generative dialogue

Co-generative dialogue describes encounters where stakeholders "equitably participate in conversations about curriculum practice that they have enacted together" (El Kadri & Roth, 2015, p. 44). It provides a forum in which the lived experience of successes, failures, and (failed) opportunities are raised and analysed (Roth, Lawless & Tobin, 2000, p. 7).

Within *co-generative dialogue*, there are some fundamental assumptions about the purpose and position of educators, for example, that human beings live in (and under) certain conditions that determine their actions, but they also have "power-to-act" and change these conditions (Roth, Lawless & Tobin, 2000, p. 4). The purpose of inquiry is not just to understand the world, but to change it (for the better). The wider world, therefore, becomes part of the conversations about curricula and education. It is expected that stakeholders in such conversations have different experiences of the same (curricula) event, and that this provides in-roads to critically interrogate and understand differences as the result of biography and social and societal location. The act of sharing lived experiences provides "a common resource" from which shared explanations and new understandings can be forged (Roth, Lawless & Tobin, 2000, p. 7).

Table 14.2 *Summary of terms*

Generative	Critical	Conversation
Gaining and deepening understanding to improve practice and make interactions between the self and others increasingly educative.	Questioning the self, others, the wider world and objectivity itself to reveal assumptions and consider alternative perspectives.	Equitable conversation where successes and failures are analysed and critically interrogated in relation to personal and social contexts.
Helps to develop reflexivity, which supports criticality.		

Critical questioning

We include two concepts under the heading critical questioning. First, *dialectical reflectivity* relates the individual experience of the researcher to the broader socio-cultural context, whilst *critical reflexivity* is concerned with interrogating and questioning the self (McNiff, 2011). Teacher educator McNiff uses these terms to describe how educators and researchers might critically reflect upon and *critically question* both the historical, political *contexts* in which they work and *their own thinking*. McNiff (2009) asserts that we must "interrogate and transform our own epistemologies: our theories of what we know and how we came to know it" (p. 4). For McNiff, critical questions are central to educators' development and curriculum making. This is a strategy for exploring their values and experiences, by continually asking: What are we doing? Why are we doing it? What difference are we trying to make?

In Table 14.2 we provide a summary of terms to encapsulate the focus of "generative", "critical" and "conversation", informed by the three methodological elements discussed above.

Now we have grounded GCC as method and provided a summary of terms, in the following section we explore how the methodological elements of GCC support the development of reflexivity.

NOTICING THE THREE METHODOLOGICAL ELEMENTS WITHIN OUR CONVERSATIONS

In this section, we present three excerpts from our recorded conversations. In each, we notice the presence of the three methodological elements of GCC: the *self-study strategy of recording on reflective material, sharing lived experiences in co-generative dialogue* and *critical questioning.*

The first and second conversational excerpt are from relatively early in our GCC timeline, 11 and 15 July 2019 respectively. During the first excerpt, we are discussing our motivations for designing and delivering the EEE intervention for student teachers. In the second excerpt, we have listened back to the first conversation individually, and we share our reflections from this. The third excerpt is taken from a conversation recorded in the process of preparing the journal article, 21 January 2021, where we start to recognise some of the discourses present in our earlier conversations. For the sake of brevity and relevance, we present each excerpt as a combination of transcripts and summaries. Alongside each excerpt, we indicate where we notice the three methodological elements and discuss them below.

Additionally, we indicate where we notice Alvesson and Sköldberg's (2018) different levels of reflexive interpretation (R-L1, R-L2, R-L3 and R-L4). These are discussed in the next section.

Presentation of Conversation (i)

Here we present an excerpt from the conversation (Table 14.3), recorded on 11 July 2019, where we are discussing our motivations for designing and delivering the intervention. In this excerpt, we hear Jennifer (JH) and Catherine (CB) lost in conversation, a moment of shared understanding where both question the effectiveness of the school Enterprise Week. Such themed weeks are a common practice for delivering EEE in primary settings (Kashefpakdel, Rehill & Hughes, 2018), and prior to the intervention for student teachers, were Jennifer's only experience of EEE.

The Three Methodological Elements of GCC in Conversation (i)

There are aspects of self-study in this conversation; through interrogating our motivations, we are seeking to improve our practice and make our interactions with students increasingly educative (Bullough & Pinnegar, 2001). However, the main aspect of self-study that GCC draws upon is *reflecting on recorded material,* something we had not yet started to do consistently. Self-study is discussed to a greater extent in Conversation (ii).

A key element of *co-generative dialogue* is equitable participation of both parties. We see indications of equitable participation in Conversation (i) in various places. In the above excerpt, Jennifer is sharing her prior experiences of EEE in primary schools; listening to the full conversation, we hear Catherine doing the same. There is strong sense of "balance" in the conversation, a back-and-forth, where both researchers appear comfortable to share their motivations for taking part in the intervention. In addition to this openness to sharing, there are also indications of active listening – for example, Catherine agrees enthusiastically, or with an encouraging tone of voice.

Another key element of *co-generative dialogue* is that lived experience and the wider world become part of the conversation. In Conversation (i), we talked about our motivations for designing a *critical* introduction to enterprise educa-

Table 14.3 Presentation of Conversation (i)

Conversation Extract	Interplay between methodological element and levels of reflexive interpretation
CB: … what were your experiences of enterprise, as a teacher?	*Co-generative dialogue* – equitable participation and lived experiences/ the wider world becoming part of the conversations. *Self-Study* – examining own and colleagues' practice.
JH: Err, enterprise fairs, enterprise weeks, make something and at the enterprise fair, a local business comes to judge … and it tends to be a vehicle for middle leaders to show what they've led in school, that kind of thing, y'know – CB: Right	**R-L1** – interaction with empirical data – an account of previous experience of EEE.
JH: So it was always "make a bookmark", "make a water carrier", sell it to your parents because no one else is going to buy your water carrier! (*Both laugh).* It was just like an add-on, it was really … "this looks good," y'know, "let's do this," kind of thing, and um, it was *never ever* embedded. I tried	*Critical questioning* – interrogating practice
to embed it and it was really complicated because I thought we'll do some maths around working out our profits and explaining the difference between price and cost as different things, to the children – these are 9-year-olds – they really struggled … I was like "surely …?" – I did not appreciate how much they would struggle with the idea that the price of something isn't necessarily the cost of something –	**R-L2** – interpretation – use of word "embed" and "embedded" – a significant (and loaded) word in Jennifer's primary setting. *Self-study* – examining own practices. *Critical questioning* – critically reflecting on own practice and thinking.
CB: (*enthusiastically agreeing*) Yeah, yeah, yeah –	
JH: And y'know, to me I was like, "well, you know that it cost this much to make so if you sell if for this much, you make so much profit"	**R-L1** – observation of personal experience.
CB: (*encouraging*) Mmmm!	

Conversation Extract	Interplay between methodological element and levels of reflexive interpretation
JH: And they [the pupils] were like "… what?!", y'know, and they had no … I just … it really made me realise it's quite complicated in what can – I just questioned "what are we getting out of this [the school enterprise week]?"	*Critical questioning* – what are we trying to achieve? What difference is it making?

tion. Although we started by considering our motivations, we quickly started to naturally make links to the wider world – for example, Jennifer brings in her experiences of EEE as a primary teacher. In other parts of the conversation Catherine recalls meetings with Head Teachers or school partnerships where she felt she was "selling" enterprise and the discomfort that generated.

These ideas are closely linked to *critical questioning*. Jennifer's criticism of EEE practice in primary schools implies that she is starting to question both the context in which she worked and her own thinking. An indication of this questioning might be the way Jennifer seeks affirmation from Catherine ("*y'know?*"). Indeed, at one point, Jennifer remembers the question she asked herself as a teacher, "*What are they [the children] getting out of this?*"; this draws a close parallel with McNiff's assertion that educators should critically question themselves and their practice by asking "*What difference am I trying to make?*" (McNiff, 2009).

Presentation of Conversation (ii)

Next, we present an excerpt from the conversation recorded on 15 July 2019 (Table 14.4). We had each listened back to the full recording of the conversation above and we were sharing our reflections.

The Three Methodological Elements of GCC in Conversation (ii)

The process of *self-study* frequently involves listening back to recorded conversations and is closely tied to the researcher's sense of identity. Here, the transcribed discussion grows from Catherine's *reflection on recorded material*. Listening back to recorded conversations is essential for GCC as it enhances the participant's memory of what was said and how they felt; their interpretations of past conversations are therefore likely to be deepened and expanded than if they were based on memory alone.

Similarly, we summarise above how Jennifer notices the discomfort she experiences when *reflecting on the recorded material*. At various points in all

Table 14.4 Presentation of Conversation (ii)

Conversation Excerpts	Interplay between Methodological Element and Levels of Reflexive Interpretation
Jennifer noted intense discomfort when listening back to the excerpt from the previous conversation, afraid she was revealing a lack of competency as a primary teacher, and that her reflection on her experience was obvious or naïve.	*Self-study* – listening back to recorded conversations, researcher sense of identity **R-L1** – observation of experience
CB: There was a bit in one of the conversations where you were talking about cost and price – JH: *(Confirming)* Mmm.	*Self-study* – reflecting on recorded material
CB: – and it was a really good point – like, having basic concepts – I must admit that at one point in the conversation I started to think "what is the point of enterprise?"	**R-L2** – underlying meanings, critical interpretations.
JH: *(Laughing)* God! Oh no, don't! *(Calmer)* No, that's good because we're being critical – CB: Yeah. JH: – So what conclusion did you come to?	**R-L4** – a hint of reflection on text production – this conversation should be critical because we're reading McNiff.
CB: Erm … I don't know if I came to a conclusion, I was just more thinking … no, it was just like the question was *hanging* over me –	**R-L2** – grappling with underlying meaning
JH: Was it a bit scary? CB: – like, er … yeah, kind of like in a dark cloud – JH: Yeah. CB: – like, "*what* is the point of it?"	*Co-generative dialogue* – interrogating understanding
JH: What was making you think that, what was feeding that?	*Critical questioning* – questioning practice and impact
CB: I think that, erm, cos I was thinking about … the – the – these are basic economic concepts that we're talking about – JH: Mm hm.	**R-L1** – observation of experience
CB: the difference between what it costs and the price of it, and you're dead right, like, if you do an enterprise project and you don't come out with that basic understanding kind of knowledge … was it actually an enterprise project?	*Critical questioning* – questioning practice and impact

the conversations, Jennifer and Catherine note their discomfort when listening back, questioning the validity or relevance of their own contributions. Had we been working alone, this may have been a barrier to developing reflexivity. However, we were able to overcome this because of the way the process of GCC unfolded. We listened back individually (safely) and experienced the uncomfortable emotions alone. When we met again for the next conversation, we often laughed about how uncomfortable we felt at listening to our own reflections, which went some way to dissipating the discomfort. Further to this, we both articulated how much we saw in *each other's* reflections, which served to reassure and encourage us in future conversations.

Aspects of *co-generative dialogue* are also present in the conversation. Jennifer interrogates Catherine to build joint understanding around Catherine's experiences of listening back to Conversation (i). Similarly, Catherine makes links to the wider world, drawing on her own experiences of other EEE projects. Notably, when listening back (and re-living) the excerpt from Conversation (ii), Jennifer and Catherine have very different experiences; Jennifer feels intense discomfort whereas Catherine appears to articulate some criticism regarding, or discomfort about EEE practice.

Critical questioning is evident during this conversation, particularly in Catherine's dialogue. She repeatedly questions the legitimacy of EEE projects, struggling to decide on their purpose and meaning, and suggesting that a focus on enterprising skills and competencies often takes precedence over learners gaining an understanding of "*basic economic principles*". Later, at end of the conversation, Catherine starts to consider her pre-occupation with "*all the cognitive science people*" and "*what they [the student teachers we were providing the intervention for] will remember*". Within this conversation, Catherine is grappling with both her experiences of practice and her own preoccupations with the nature and focus of learning (as remembering content, concepts and knowledge or the development of skills and competencies).

The "spark" of Catherine's critical questioning first emerged *in-between* conversations when she was listening back to recorded material. However, it was in the next conversation, through the co-generative dialogue with Jennifer, that her critical questions were voiced explicitly and explored in more depth. Hence, the excerpts from the above conversations provide an example of how this method gives rise to conversation that is both *critical* and *generative*. It is *critical* because it facilitates the questioning of taken-for-granted assumptions and reveals alternative perspectives. It is *generative* because it deepens understanding and makes interactions between the self and others increasingly educative.

Presentation of Conversation (iii)

Here we present the third excerpt (Table 14.5), from a conversation recorded on 21 January 2021. This was a significant time after the above conversational excerpts (although we had recorded and reflected upon several conversations within this time). As shown on the timeline, the reason we met was to discuss the development of the journal paper.

The Three Methodological Elements of GCC in Conversation (iii)

The practice of self-study is evident in this conversation as we refer back to our previous recorded conversations; indeed, before we recorded Conversation (iii), we both had returned to listen to some of the earlier conversations. Aspects of co-generative dialogue are apparent in that we are interrogating and seeking to understand our practice as educators, questioning our earlier shared assumption that learning must involve either the demonstrable acquisition of knowledge *or* the demonstrable acquisition of skills. Inherent throughout the conversation is a sense of critical questioning of ourselves and our practice. However, we noticed more significant reflexive moments in this conversation, and we now turn to these.

DEVELOPING REFLEXIVITY THROUGH GCC

This section explores how Generative Critical Conversation can support the development of reflexivity. Over time our conversations created space and opportunities for us to move between the reflexive levels of interpretation set out by Alvesson and Sköldberg (2018), including accessing levels of interpretative reflexivity we consider more difficult to access, such as critical interpretation and reflection on text production and language use.

Alongside the above excerpts, we indicate where we notice the different levels of reflexivity. For the sake of clarity, we use the following abbreviations (Table 14.6).

The numbers are not intended to imply the "value" of the levels, or that they exist as "steps", we use them simply to aid us in noticing the levels within each conversation. The conversations have not been systematically coded for the reflexive levels; such an endeavour would be at odds with the interpretative methods that inform GCC. We used the levels to review our conversations and think about where we could see their presence. In doing this, we are able to discern that it is reflexivity that is happening, as opposed to simply reflection. Finally in this section, we present an abstracted figure of GCC, illustrating how the three methodological elements contribute to developing reflexivity, which is evidenced by noticing the levels of reflexive interpretation.

Table 14.5 *Presentation of Conversation (iii)*

Conversation Excerpt	Interplay between Methodological Element and Levels of Reflexive Interpretation
Catherine recalls Jennifer's suggestion that learning could be viewed as some addition or alteration which might not be actioned for years to come.	*Self-study* – reflecting on recorded material
Jennifer suggests that theoretical grounding for this second view on learning might be latent learning (Tolman, 1951).	**R-L3** – critical interpretation – ideology
Catherine recognises that she has been reproducing a particular binary discourse in relation to the nature of learning.	**R-L4** – selectivity of the voices represented in the text.
CB: One of the things that I'm taking out of this is … is that me talking about skills versus knowledge … is … it's much, erm … it's much more complex than that. And there's competing discourses about what learning is. And that might be skills or knowledge, or latent learning or surface and depth … even me going "skills versus knowledge," that's discourse, that there's skills versus knowledge, whereas that we recognizing, now, in this conversation, a multiplicity of voices …	**R-L4** – reflection on text production **R-L4** – selectivity of the voices represented in the text. *Co-generative dialogue* – critically interrogate and understand practice
JH: Yes, yeah. I like that multiplicity. And there's a multiplicity like … it's really easy, isn't it to get into, it's so tempting to get into a conversation or work with a framework that is something versus something for like knowledge versus skills. It's really, it's like you're saying in previous conversations, it's like seductive because you understand it, and you can hang your hat on it, can't you? It's like, you know, is it knowledge? Or is it skills? Or is it both? But actually, it's, you know, it's some knowledge and it's some skills and it's something else entirely. There's, there's some … there's something else that … there's erm … language, I suppose, maybe like language is the … language is restricting our understanding of it …	*Self-study* – reflecting on recorded material **R-L3** – critical interpretation – articulating educator internalisation of educational discourses **R-L4** – reflecting on language use

Conversation Excerpt	Interplay between Methodological Element and Levels of Reflexive Interpretation
CB: I think that is what Bakhtin is trying to get people to appreciate though … JH: Right …	
CB: That instead of this … there being this kind of authoritative "well, it's skills versus knowledge" even in this conversation, it has demonstrated to me that I've just so internalised that skills versus knowledge thing, that when I come to write a text, I just simplistically put, "oh, well, this is a competing discourse about skills versus knowledge" … rather than saying, "but there's this one thing, which is skills versus knowledge." No, no, no, no, no. It's much more complicated than that and that we're doing ourselves a disservice by pretending that there's not that complexity …	**R-L4** – pre-occupation with authors in recently expanded theoretical repertoire **R-L3** – critical interpretation – recognising power of education discourses **R-L2** – uses new acquired language regarding internalisation to construct meaning **R-L4** – critically reflects on one's own production of text

Table 14.6 Abbreviations and levels of reflexive interpretation (Alvesson & Sköldberg, 2018, p. 330)

Abbreviation	Aspect/level of interpretation	Focus
R-L1	Interaction with empirical material	Accounts in interviews, observation of situations and other empirical materials
R-L2	Interpretation	Underlying meanings
R-L3	Critical interpretation	Ideology, power, social reproduction
R-L4	Reflection on text production and language use	Own text, claims to authority, selectivity of voices represented in the text

The Levels of Reflexive Interpretation in Conversation (i)

In Conversation (i), how do we notice ways that we are affecting and being affected? Jennifer is giving an account of her own experience – underlying meanings are implied, but not fully realised. This indicates first level of reflexive interpretation (*interaction with empirical material*). This account was prompted by exploring motivations for designing and delivering a critical intervention – so again, an implication of looking for underlying messages, but relatively little relation or movement between the reflexive levels. That said, there are some hints at the second level, *interpretation*. For example, the use of the term “embedded” relates back to Jennifer’s experiences in school where the term was a buzzword – for learning to be effective, it had to be *embedded*, the implication being through repetition, revisiting, rigour. Perhaps one of the underlying meanings that Jennifer is implicitly communicating here is “if EEE is so important to this school, why are we not *embedding* it?”

The Levels of Reflexive Interpretation in Conversation (ii)

In Conversation (ii), we see a greater presence of the third level, critical interpretation. In particular, Catherine discusses the ideologies that inform her beliefs about learning, contrasting the learning of skills with the learning of knowledge. Similarly, in places her words indicate an awareness of power and status within educational research (e.g., “all the cognitive science people”). We notice other levels of reflexive interpretation as well. In describing their listening back to the previous conversation, both Catherine and Jennifer provide observations, accounts of their experience. They are “interacting with empirical material” (the first level). In asking “what is the point in enterprise?”, Catherine is searching for underlying meanings to her practice, indicating the second level, interpretation. We notice a brief indication of the fourth level where Jennifer says, “that’s good because we’re being critical”. In saying this, Jennifer is reflecting on text production, implying that our own text (in this case, the recorded conversation) needs to have a degree of criticality. It is interesting to note that in our first conversation, there appears to be a greater presence of the first and second levels. However, in the second conversation, after we have reflected upon recorded material, we are starting to be more critically interpretative (the third level).

The Levels of Reflexive Interpretation in Conversation (iii)

Within this excerpt, we notice the third level, *critical interpretation*, in various places. For example, Catherine revisits previous conversations where we discussed the nature of learning. Jennifer, with a background in educational research, has a broader interpretive repertoire on which to draw. Through conversation, Jennifer expands Catherine’s conception of learning suggesting the theory of latent learning (Tolman, 1951) as possible grounding for some of the ideas we were discussing.

As well as more frequent instances of critical interpretation within Conversation (iii), we also notice the fourth level, *reflection on text production and language use*. Conversation (iii) was recorded in preparation for the journal article, and again, our ideas about the nature of learning resurface. However, we now reflect on our earlier conversations in relation to the meta-theoretical perspective of dialogism (Bakhtin, 1986; Bauman, 2005). We start to recognise the voices or discourses that we ourselves are reproducing (e.g., "… *even me going 'skills versus knowledge', that's discourse*"; "*I've just so internalised that skills versus knowledge thing*"; "*we're doing ourselves a disservice by pretending that there's not that complexity*"). In turn, this prompts reflection on language use (e.g., "*I like that [term] multiplicity*"; "*language is restricting our understanding of it [the nature of learning]*").

Although we recorded Conversation (ii) on 15 July 2019, our deeper understanding of the discourses present did not emerge until we returned to the recorded artefact in January 2021, which was driven by the practical purpose of constructing our own text. We were signposted towards dialogism by a reviewer of the original paper; additionally, we had seen the theory introduced at a conference (Higgins & Refai, 2019). These instances broadened our interpretative repertoire, and we gained deeper reflexive insight by recognising the discourses inherent in Conversation (ii).

In the latest conversation, there are more instances of the fourth level of reflexive interpretation (*Reflection on text production and language use*) than in the earlier conversations. Alvesson and Sköldberg (2018) are clear that levels of reflexive interpretation are not worked through in a linear process. However, the conversations above suggest that the third and fourth levels appear less likely to be accessed in initial stages of reflection. Engaging in constructing our own text facilitated us in reaching the fourth level of reflexive interpretation. The level did not lead us to the text, the text led us to the level. This indicates the importance of *using one's own academic constructions as empirical material* to prompt reflexivity.

The Abstracted Form of GCC

Above, we have presented excerpts of our conversations, indicating the presence of the three methodological elements and the emergence of the levels of reflexive interpretation. In Figure 14.2, we present the abstracted form of GCC. The central circle represents the first recorded conversation, where the researchers discuss their chosen focus (in our case, our motivations and experiences of our practice). Each circle moving outwards represents a subsequent recorded conversation, where the researchers reflect upon what they each noticed in the previous recording (drawing upon the method of *self-study*). The researchers engage in *co-generative dialogue* and *critical questioning* in order to look for underlying meanings, question taken-for-granted assumptions. Throughout this, the different levels of reflexive interpretation may be noticed in their conversations. We suggest that the first and second levels are likely to be more present in the early conversations, and the third and fourth levels are

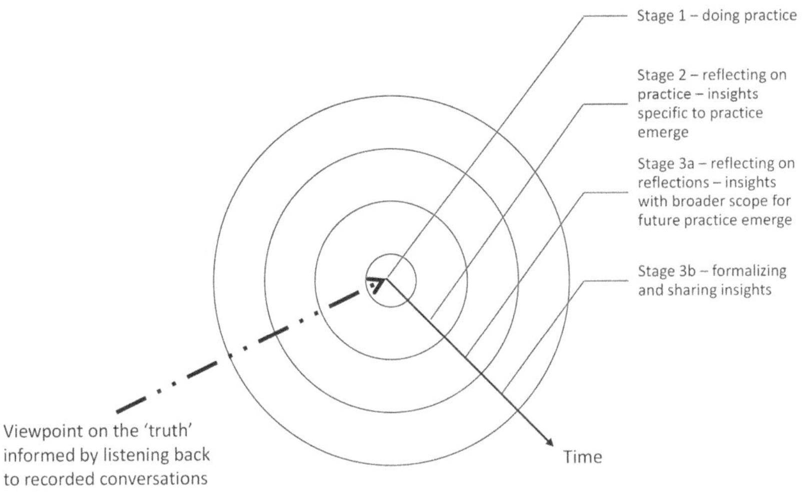

Figure 14.2 *The method and the outcome in generalised/abstracted form*

more likely to be noticed in the later conversations, especially when reflecting on one's own text construction.

Having presented the abstract figure, we now go on to describe the conditions that enable GCC and consider its transferability within and beyond EEE.

DISCUSSION – ENABLING CONDITIONS AND TRANSFERABILITY

This chapter's contribution is in offering a practicable method that facilitates deepening reflexivity for educators and researchers. We consider there are enabling conditions for GCC to develop fruitfully: a shared purpose, willingness to question, and temporality. We then explore the potential transferability of GCC.

Shared Purpose

As it is a collaborative process, a shared purpose between the participating educator-researchers is important to give focus and practical relevance to conversations. In our case, we were initially designing and delivering an EEE intervention together; as shown in the timeline, our shared purposes shifted to writing a conference paper and later the journal article. Our shared purposes contributed to the sense of investment that we felt during and between conversations, and in the way we thought of the conversations as supporting us to realise our shared purposes.

Willingness to Question

Another important enabling condition for GCC is that educator-researchers are willing to question themselves, others, the wider world and *objectivity itself* in order to reveal assumptions and consider alternative perspectives. As well as having a shared purpose which facilitated such questioning, the role of trust – in terms of asking questions of each other sensitively, recognising their own/others' preoccupations and actively listening to the other – was important. In addition, being from similar but ultimately different fields (Catherine is from the world of EEE; Jennifer has a background in primary teacher education) contributed to our ability to question each other's assumptions. We had enough shared language to understand each other (e.g., both being familiar with "enterprise weeks" in primary schools), but there was also enough difference between our initial perspectives to question, challenge and interrogate *each other*. In turn, we found that this encouraged us to question, challenge and interrogate *ourselves*. We recognise that being able to work with educator-researchers from other fields is not always practicable. With this in mind, we provide a selection of questions that we found ourselves asking each other throughout our conversations (see Table 14.7). Educator-researchers working with someone in the same field could use these questions as prompts to notice each other's taken-for-granted assumptions.

Temporality

As Alvesson and Sköldberg (2018) assert, movement can occur between any or all of the levels of reflexive interpretation, at any time. While the excerpts of conversation suggest that this is indeed the case, we also suggest that the third and fourth levels (*critical interpretation* and *reflection on own text production and language use*) are harder to access in the initial stages of reflection. We noticed these levels with greater frequency in the later conversations. We are not suggesting that time alone can bring about deeper reflexivity, however, there is a temporal aspect. Listening back to the recorded material, revisiting and sharing our ideas in subsequent conversations; this happened over a period of days, weeks and months. The time between the recordings, the listening back, and the next conversation allowed for introspective reflection. Individually, we were coming to terms with uncomfortable feelings or questions about our contributions to the conversation; we were making links between those ideas and other aspects of our practice; we were making links back to previous conversations. This led to more open and more critical dialogue in subsequent conversations.

Table 14.7 *Conversation prompts for developing reflexivity*

Levels of Reflexive Insight (Alvesson & Sköldberg, 2018)		Conversation prompts (abstracted from our experience)
R-L1	Interaction with empirical material	*Procedural questions and responses.* For example: What are the educational aims for this intervention? What are our aims for our students? What is the context for this intervention? (For example, what have students already learned/ experienced?) What resources do we already have that can support us in meeting our aims? How might we make our practice engaging for different students? *Evaluative conversations.* For example: Were we successful in achieving our aims? What are our first impressions of student engagement? How successful were individual aspects of the intervention? (For example, a specific resource or activity) What unintended reactions or outcomes did we observe or perceive?
R-L2	Interpretation	*Questions probing, exploring and illuminating educators' motivations and experiences, inviting links to academic theory, cultural references, taken-for-granted assumptions and personal theories.* For example: "What were we doing?", "Why were we doing it?" or "What difference were we trying to make?", What led you to working on this intervention? What have been your prior experiences relating to this subject? In your practice, what has made you uncomfortable, what have you questioned? What were your motivations for putting this intervention together? What do you remember about teaching the intervention? What did students learn (or not)? How do you think you know this? How do you think this will affect the students in the future? What do you think they will have taken away from the experience of this intervention (or not) and why?

Levels of Reflexive Insight (Alvesson & Sköldberg, 2018)		Conversation prompts (abstracted from our experience)
R-L3	Critical interpretation	*Questions inviting educators to share their reflections on the recorded conversations, inviting links to broadening academic theory, noticing ideology, power and social reproduction* What stood out to you when you listened back to the recordings? Why do you think that was? Why do you think you said …? What surprised you about the conversation? Why? What did you notice listening back that you hadn't noticed at the time? Does what you said at this point in the conversation relate to what you said at this second point?
R-L4	Reflection on text production and language use	*Own text, claims to authority, selectivity of the voices represented in the text* What would happen if I hadn't read that paper then? What if we were from different fields?/What if we were from the same field? Have we lost our criticality? Did we lose it in a previous conversation? How strongly do you believe this? Is this an idea you are constructing through the conversation, or is this an idea that you can link to theory? Whose voice is speaking here? What/whose language am I using? How am I using language to legitimise ideas or make claims to authority? What discourses am I reproducing?

Transferability

We have both taken action towards and considered possibilities for applying GCC within our respective roles in teacher education and enterprise education. In teacher education, within a module developing reflective practice, students were formally introduced to the idea of GCC and asked to record a series of four conversations, and then to reflect back in order to look forward. In enterprise education, the approach has been more organic, spotting an opportunity here or there where collaborating students might benefit from having the chance to converse, listen, reflect and converse again.

Given the enabling factors discussed in the preceding section, it is important to avoid viewing GCC as a magic pill that people can take to develop their reflexivity. We discussed that it might be possible to feel anxious, inadequate and threatened in the process of listening back, in particular to one's self. In offering GCC as a method, we also recognise that *we brought ourselves* to this process and that our willingness to challenge and be challenged, by ourselves and each other, contributed to the value we perceived. Yet, for those looking for a way to develop reflexivity, and create a space to question and interrogate their practice and assumptions, it provides a practicable route towards that.

Whilst our attention has been more directed towards the reflexive potential of GCC, we believe it also holds interesting possibilities in terms of developing insights into moments of creation that happen when two educators negotiate and work together to create something new, whether that be research or educational provision. In one conversation, we strayed into talking about a future session we were going to plan; listening back to this conversation, we heard ourselves trying to build understanding between our different disciplinary knowledge and co-construct mutually appealing activity that served out different needs and interests. With this intentional focus, GCC becomes a method to "capture it as it happens" (Brundin, 2007), when educators negotiate and decide how they piece together their professional and personal pre-occupations.

We perceive GCC as transferable to many research and practice situations, either a specific focus or open-ended investigation, both in education and in EEE, and, indeed, more importantly, bringing both together. While our text has reflected our experience in one-to-one exchanges and individual reflections in between conversations, the process could be used in group and collective inquiry. The value of interdisciplinary collaboration was highlighted in our previous work (Brentnall & Huntsley, 2019). Indeed, a practical way to better connect the fields of education and EEE, as advised by Fayolle (2013), would be to work more closely together *as colleagues*, developing research and practice *together*. GCC could both capture and support reflection upon such developments, which may help build understanding and break down barriers, facilitating stronger connections between people and their respective disciplines and the development of thoughtful research and practice. If methods are "concrete techniques or procedures that are used to gather data" (Crotty, 1998, p. 6) and a methodology is a research "strategy or plan of action" (Crotty, 1998, p. 6), then GCC could potentially be either, depending on how an educator or researcher chooses to use it.

In relation to our experience of using GCC as a method to develop reflexivity, we have abstracted a list of question prompts which may guide conversation. Equally, we acknowledge that at the start of our process, we did not have such a list, but were guided by the spirit of McNiff (2009) and overarching critical questions such as: what are we trying to achieve and what difference are we making (intended and unintended)? Indeed, it may be the willingness to explore the *unintended* as well as the intended consequences and implications of our research and practice that might yield the most critical insight.

CONCLUSION

In this chapter, we summarised how a lack of criticality has been seen as a factor limiting the field of EEE. Uncritical educators may unquestioningly reproduce handed down activities, with insufficient concern for structures and context and which silence axiological debate. Uncritical researchers may unquestioningly reproduce taken-for-granted research approaches and practices, undermining the exploration and explanation of research issues that require out of the box thinking. Authors in EEE are clear that *reflexivity* is required, from both educator and researcher, to address this lack of criticality, however, it is less clear *how* one should start, practically, to develop one's reflexivity. This chapter contributes a method that enables that development. By hybridizing three methodological elements from educational practice – the self-study strategy of *reflecting on recorded material; exploring lived experiences through co-generative dialogue* and a focus on *critical questioning* – we provide a method for the development of educator-researcher reflexivity. We use a framework from reflexive scholars (Alvesson & Sköldberg, 2018), to recognise movement between levels of reflexive interpretation. And we recognise a move in our conversations from reflection (examining one's own experiences and reimagining them for the future), to reflexivity (recognising the ways in which one may affect and be affected). Whilst the concept of reflexivity has been positioned as important to the quest for legitimacy in EEE, without concrete ways of doing it, it is likely to remain a theoretical rather than a practical concern. Generative Critical Conversation is a practical contribution, offering a feasible method and a process to enhance educator-researcher reflexivity. The method we offer may strengthen not only the contribution an individual makes, but also the field itself, through its potential to enable more reflexive educators and researchers with increased capacity for criticality, a lack of which is said to limit the legitimacy of EEE. There is interesting potential in the transferability of the approach, into different contexts, with different stakeholders and for different purposes; not just within education or enterprise and entrepreneurship, but between – and beyond – these two disciplines, in circumstances where educators or researchers wish to explore their practice and assumptions.

NOTE

1. This chapter comes from an article published in the *Journal of Small Business Management* (Huntsley, J., & Brentnall, C. (2021) Generative critical conversation: A method for developing reflexivity and criticality, *Journal of Small Business Management*, DOI: 10.1080/00472778.2021.1938096, © 2021 International Council for Small Business). Reprinted by permission of

Taylor & Francis Ltd, http://www.tandfonline.com on behalf of International Council for Small Business.

REFERENCES

Achtenhagen, L., & Johannisson, B. (2018). The reflexivity grid: Exploring conscientization in entrepreneurship education. In Berglund, K., & Verduyn, K. (Eds.), *Revitalizing entrepreneurship education: Adopting a critical approach in the classroom* (pp. 62–81). Routledge.

Alvesson, M., & Sköldberg, K. (2018). *Reflexive methodology: New vistas for qualitative research*. 3rd edn. SAGE.

Attia, M., & Edge, J. (2017). Be(com)ing a reflexive researcher: A developmental approach to research methodology, *Open Review of Educational Research, 4*(1), 33–45. https://doi.org/10.1080/23265507.2017.1300068.

Bakhtin, M. M. (1986). *Speech genres and other late essays*. University of Texas Press.

Banegas, D. L., & de Castro, Luis S. Villacañas. (2016). Criticality. *ELT Journal, 70*(4), 455–457. https://doi.org/10.1093/elt/ccw048.

Barnett, R. (1997), *Higher education: A critical business*. Open University Press.

Bates, A. (2014). Reflections from a tarnished mirror: An application of Alvesson and Sköldberg's "reflexive interpretation" to a study of curriculum design in higher education. *International Journal of Research & Method in Education, 37*(3), 227–241. https://doi.org/10.1080/1743727X.2013.822858.

Bauman, R. (2005). Commentary: Indirect indexicality, identity, performance: Dialogic observations. *Journal of Linguistic Anthropology, 15*(1), 145–150. https://www.jstor.org/stable/43104044.

Berger, R. (2015). Now I see it, now I don't: Researcher's position and reflexivity in qualitative research. *Qualitative Research, 15*(2), 219–234. https://doi.org/10.1177/1468794112468475.

Berglund, K., & Verduijn, K. (2018). *Revitalizing entrepreneurship education: Adopting a critical approach in the classroom*. Routledge.

Bishop, P. E. (1997). Bridging school and industry: A role for the trainee teacher. *Education + Training, 39*(5), 176–183. https://doi.org/10.1108/00400919710169481.

Bolton, G., & Delderfield, R. (2017). *Reflective practice*. Sage.

Brentnall, C., & Huntsley, J. (2019). Creating space to question. Paper presented at the ISBE – Institute of Small Business and Entrepreneurship Conference, 15 November, Newcastle. https://www.researchgate.net/publication/351451139_Creating_Space_to_Question.

Brundin, E. (2007). Catching it as it happens. In Neergaard, H., & Ulhøi, J. P. (Eds.), *Handbook of qualitative research methods in entrepreneurship* (pp. 279–307). Edward Elgar Publishing.

Bullough, R.V., & Pinnegar, S. (2001), Guidelines for quality in autobiographical forms of self-study research, *Educational Researcher, 30*(3), 13–21. https://doi.org/10.3102/0013189X030003013.

Bulman, C. (2013). An introduction to reflection. In Bulman, C., & Schultz, S. (Eds.), *Reflective Practice in Nursing* (pp. 1–22). Wiley-Blackwell.

Caird, S. (1990). What does it mean to be enterprising? *British Journal of Management, 1*(3), 137–145. https://doi.org/10.1111/j.1467-8551.1990.tb00002.x.

Crawshaw, L. (1996). Developing an "education business partnership" through placement. *Education + Training*, *38*(7), 8–15. https://doi.org/10.1108/00400919610130727.
Crompton, K. (1987). A curriculum for enterprise: pedagogy or propaganda? *School Organization*, *7*(1), 5–11. https://doi.org/10.1080/0260136870070102.
Crotty, M. (1998). *The foundations of social research: Meaning and perspective in the research process*. Sage.
Department for Education. (2017). Careers strategy: making the most of everyone's skills and talents. Department for Education. DFE-00310-2017.
Deveci, I. (2016). Perceptions and competence of Turkish pre-service science teachers with regard to entrepreneurship. *Australian Journal of Teacher Education*, *41*(5), 10. http://dx.doi.org/10.14221/ajte.2016v41n5.10.
Dewey, J. (1910). *How we think*. Boston: D.C. Heath & Co.
Door, V. (2014). *Developing creative and critical educational practitioners*. Critical Publishing.
Farny, S., Frederiksen, S. H., Hannibal, M., & Jones, S. (2016). A CULTure of entrepreneurship education. *Entrepreneurship & Regional Development*, *28*(7–8), 514–535. https://doi.org/10.1080/08985626.2016.1221228.
Fayolle, A. (2013). Personal views on the future of entrepreneurship education. *Entrepreneurship & Regional Development*, 25(7–8), 692–701. https://doi.org/10.1080/08985626.2013.821318.
Fayolle, A. (Ed.) (2019). *A research agenda for entrepreneurship education*. Edward Elgar Publishing.
Fayolle, A., & Loi, M. (2018). Enhancing entrepreneurship education and practice: Challenging taken-for-granted assumptions and dominant perspectives. *Journal of Management Inquiry* Developmental Conference and Dialogue Call for Papers, July. https://entrepreneuriat.com/cfp-journal-of-management-inquiry-developmental-conference-enhancing-entrepreneurship-education-research-and-practice/.
Fayolle, A., Verzat, C., & Wapshott, R. (2016). *In quest of legitimacy: The theoretical and methodological foundations of entrepreneurship education research*. International.
Gibb, A. A. (1987). Enterprise culture: Its meaning and implications for education and training. *Journal of European Industrial Training*, *11*(2), 2–38. https://doi.org/10.1108/eb043365.
Gibb, A. (2008). Entrepreneurship and enterprise education in schools and colleges: Insights from UK practice. *International Journal of Entrepreneurship Education*, *6*(2), 101–144.
Grant, B. (1986). Capability, enterprise and entrepreneurship. *The Vocational Aspect of Education*, *38*(100), 55–66. https://doi.org/10.1080/10408347308002701.
Grant, M. J., & Booth, A. (2009). A typology of reviews: An analysis of 14 review types and associated methodologies. *Health Information & Libraries Journal*, *26*(2), 91–108. https://doi.org/10.1111/j.1471-1842.2009.00848.x.
Hamilton, M. L., & Pinnegar, S. (1998). Conclusion: The value and the promise of self-study. In Hamilton, M. L. (Ed.), *Reconceptualizing teaching practice: Self-study in teacher education* (pp. 235–246). Falmer Press.
Hanson, J., Hooley, T., & Cox, A. (2017). Business games and enterprise competitions. What works? The Careers & Enterprise Company. https://www.careersandenterprise.co.uk/sites/default/files/uploaded/careers-enterprise-what-works-report-business-games-enterprise-comps.pdf.
Higgins, D. (2019). Personal correspondence. WhatsApp Message, sent 15 May.

Higgins, D., & Refai, D. (2019). Talking into space: Dialogical reflexivity and social poetics in the entrepreneurial educators "polyphonic" classroom. Being able for knowing (être capable de savoir (savoir for pouvoir). Institute for Small Business and Entrepreneurship Conference.
Higgins, D., Smith, K., & Mirza, M. (2013). Entrepreneurial education: Reflexive approaches to entrepreneurial learning in practice. *The Journal of Entrepreneurship, 22*(2), 135–160. https://doi.org/10.1177/0971355713490619.
Hinds, D. and the Department for Education (2019). Ministerial announcement. https://www.gov.uk/government/speeches/education-secretary-sets-out-five-foundations-to-build-character.
Hofer, B. (2017). Shaping the epistemology of teacher practice through reflection and reflexivity. *Educational Psychologist, 52*(4), 299–306.
Holman, J. (2014). Good career guidance. The Gatsby Charitable Foundation, London. https://www.gatsby.org.uk/uploads/education/reports/pdf/gatsby-sir-john-holman-good-career-guidance-2014.pdf.
Huntsley, J., & Brentnall, C. (2021). Generative critical conversation: A method for developing reflexivity and criticality, *Journal of Small Business Management, 61*(6), 2788–2817. https://doi.org/10.1080/00472778.2021.1938096.
Hytti, U. (2018). Epilogue: Critical entrepreneurship education: A form of resistance to McEducation? In Berglund, K., & Verduijn, K. (Eds.), *Revitalizing Entrepreneurship Education: Adopting a critical approach in the classroom* (pp. 228–235). Routledge.
Iredale, N. (1996). School/industry links at the primary level: Engaging the small business. *Citizenship, Social and Economics Education, 1*(3), 236–249. https://doi.org/10.2304/csee.1996.1.3.236.
Jamieson, I. (1984). Schools and enterprise. *Education for Enterprise, 1*(1), 7–18.
El Kadri, M. S., & Roth, W. (2015). Co-teaching/co-generative dialogues in a teaching education program as room for agency and new forms of participation: "I found Jesus in [writing] the paper". *Teacher Development, 19*(1), 40–58. https://doi.org/10.1080/13664530.2014.976715.
Kashefpakdel, E., Rehill, J., & Hughes, D. (2018). *What works? Career-related learning in primary schools*. The Careers and Enterprise Company.
Kyrö, P. (Ed.) (2015). *Handbook of entrepreneurship and sustainable development research*. Edward Elgar Publishing.
Kyrö, P. (2018). The conceptual contribution of education to research on entrepreneurship education. In Fayolle, A. (Ed.), *A research agenda for entrepreneurship education* (pp. 164–186). Edward Elgar Publishing.
LaBoskey, V. K. (2004). The methodology of self-study and its theoretical underpinnings. In Loughran, J. J., Hamilton, M. L., LaBoskey, V. K., & Russell, T. L. (Eds.), *International handbook of self-study of teaching and teacher education practices* (pp. 817–871). Springer.
Lepistö, J., & Ronkko, M. L. (2013). Teacher students as future entrepreneurship educators and learning facilitators. *Education + Training, 55*(7), 641–653. https://doi.org/10.1108/ET-05-2012-0055.
Loughran, J. (2018). Learning about self-study of teacher education practices. In Ritter, J. K., Lunenberg, M., Pithouse-Morgan, K., Samaras, A. P., & Vanassche, E. (Eds.), *Teaching, learning, and enacting of self-study methodology: Unravelling a complex interplay* (pp. 1–7) Springer.
McNiff, J. (2009). How I/we contribute to the development of new institutional epistemologies of educational knowledge for sustainable social practices. British Educational Research Association Annual Meeting, September, University of

Manchester. https://www.jeanmcniff.com/userfiles/file/Publications/Bera09/JMBERA09individualopt.pdf.
McNiff, J. (2011). New cultures of critical reflection in Qatar, *Educational Action Research, 19*(3), 279–296. https://doi.org/10.1080/09650792.2011.600548.
Moon, J. A. (2006). *Learning journals: A handbook for reflective practice and professional development* (2nd ed.). Routledge.
Raven-Hill, D. (1996). Introducing economic and industrial understanding: The primary school. *Education + Training, 38*(7), 30–36. https://doi.org/10.1108/EUM0000000004284.
Rogers, R. R. (2001). Reflection in higher education: A concept analysis. *Innovative Higher Education, 26*(1), 37–57. https://doi.org/10.1023/A:1010986404527.
Roth, W. M., Lawless, D. V., & Tobin, K. (2000). {Coteaching|cogenerative dialoguing} as praxis of dialectic method. *Forum Qualitative Sozialforschung/Forum: Qualitative Social Research, 1*(3). http://dx.doi.org/10.17169/fqs-1.3.1054.
Russell, T. (2014). Paradigmatic changes in teacher education: The perils, pitfalls, and unrealized promise of the "reflective practitioner". In Bruno-Jofre, R., & Johnston, J. (Eds.), *Teacher education in a transnational world* (pp. 158–176). University of Toronto Press.
Russell, T., & Martin, A. (2017). Reflective practice: Epistemological perspectives on learning from experience in teacher education. In Brandenburg, R., Glasswell, K., Jones, M., & Ryan, J. (Eds.), *Reflective theory and practice in teacher education.* ProQuest Ebook Central.
Ryan, M. (2012). Conceptualising and teaching discursive and performative reflection in higher education. *Studies in Continuing Education, 34*(2), 207–223. https://doi.org/10.1080/0158037x.2011.611799.
Schön, D. (1991). *The reflective practitioner: How professionals think in action.* Ashgate.
Tiernan, P., McCracken, M., & Matlay, H. (2016). Enterprise education in initial teacher education in Ireland. *Education + Training, 58*(7/8), 849–860. https://doi.org/10.1108/ET-03-2016-0053.
Tolman, E.C. (1951). *Behaviour and psychological man: Essays in motivation and learning.* University of California Press.
Young, L. (2014). Enterprise for all: The relevance of enterprise in education. Department of Business, Innovation & Skills, UK Government. https://www.gov.uk/government/publications/enterprise-for-all-the-relevance-of-enterprise-in-education.
Zienkowski, J. (2017). Reflexivity in the transdisciplinary field of critical discourse studies. *Palgrave Communications, 3*, 17007. https://doi.org/10.1057/palcomms.2017.7.

Adopting Paulo Freire's great answers: a review of "Generative critical conversation: a method for developing reflexivity and criticality"

R. Duncan M. Pelly

This chapter addresses an overarching question in entrepreneurship by exceeding the boundaries of descriptive research – and diving into prescription. Not only does it narrate the importance of conversations, introspection, criticality, and reflection, it embraces the spirit of Paulo Freire (1970) to engage these processes in the face of the "banking model" found in entrepreneurship and enterprise education. The empirical setting of entrepreneurship in primary schools is paramount for educators because it is the period when young minds can be molded to think of and plan for future business opportunities (Brüne and Lutz, 2020). This review will converse upon three cruxes contained within the chapter and explicate their relevance to this volume. First, generative critical conversation fills a gap in criticality in entrepreneurship that is often overlooked in entrepreneurship education. Second, it not only advocates for additional reflexivity in entrepreneurship education, it serves as a practical and convincing example. Last, this methodology could be relevant for educators across multiple disciplines and levels.

With respect to criticality, entrepreneurship pedagogy struggles because there is a lack of reflection of instructors' underlying values, the rise of unconvincing narratives, and the prevalence of implicit assumptions in the classroom (Fayolle et al., 2016). The authors respond to these deficits by intertwining perspectives from teacher education and entrepreneurship education, which promotes intellectual diversity. The authors – one with a background in business and the other in education – serve as intellectual archetypes for those who "borrow boldly" from other disciplines (Herron et al, 1992), and support not only the rich intellectual diversity of entrepreneurship research and practice, but also its pedagogy.

The criticality that flows as a result of exchanging practices between disciplines enhances reflexivity because these conversations force participants to engage with potentiality, questioning ways in which familiar perspectives may be altered, whilst respecting fundamentally different viewpoints (Kakouris, 2015). The reflexivity dialogued in the chapter goes beyond reflecting and interpreting text in a detached sense; it involves active co-construction and fabulation in concert with colleagues (Hjorth, 2011). Their struggles, as recorded in the interview excerpts and analyses, demonstrate that neat concepts and hierarchies found in reflexivity literature are queried during the interplay of generative critical conversation.

The final rationale that substantiates inclusion of generative critical conversation within this text is that its implications extend beyond the scope of entrepreneurship. This chapter reflects the precept that entrepreneurship is a mentality that encourages original ways of cogitation (Daspit et al, 2023). Generative critical conversation is a pathway for scholars from differing disciplines to engage in a process of intellectual bricolage that can birth ideas to enhance a world beyond the halls of academia. This chapter was scribed to inspire the next generation of entrepreneurial endeavors. Moreover, other disciplines could use this same technique to create innovations that positively impact primary schools and expand the frontiers of education.

REFERENCES

Brüne, N., & Lutz, E. (2020). The effect of entrepreneurship education in schools on entrepreneurial outcomes: A systematic review. *Management Review Quarterly*, *70*(2), 275–305.

Daspit, J. J., Fox, C. J., & Findley, S. K. (2023). Entrepreneurial mindset: An integrated definition, a review of current insights, and directions for future research. *Journal of Small Business Management*, *61*(1), 12–44.

Fayolle, A., Verzat, C., & Wapshott, R. (2016). In quest of legitimacy: The theoretical and methodological foundations of entrepreneurship education research. *International Small Business Journal*, *34*(7), 895–904.

Freire, P. (1970 [2017]). *Pedagogy of the oppressed.* Penguin Modern Classics. Penguin.

Herron, L., Sapienza, H. J., & Smith-Cook, D. (1992). Entrepreneurship theory from an interdisciplinary perspective: Volume II. *Entrepreneurship theory and Practice*, *16*(3), 5–12.

Hjorth, D. (2011). On provocation, education and entrepreneurship. *Entrepreneurship and Regional Development*, *23*(1–2), 49–63.

Kakouris, A. (2015). Entrepreneurship pedagogies in lifelong learning: Emergence of criticality? *Learning, Culture and Social Interaction*, *6*, 87–97.

15. Future suggestions for dealing with big questions in entrepreneurship research: towards great answers

Alain Fayolle, Sandrine Le Pontois and R. Duncan M. Pelly

CURRENT STATE AND LIMITATIONS OF RESEARCH METHODS USED IN THE FIELD OF ENTREPRENEURSHIP

The chapters included in this volume highlight several implications for entrepreneurship scholars and communities of research in management. The contributors argue that there is a need for scholars to be more aware of the contributions and limitations of the most commonly used methods in entrepreneurship research.

It is well documented that a wide array of research methodologies is available to entrepreneurship scholars, all of which are grounded in various epistemological approaches and sustained by different scientific reasoning. The two most common are deduction and induction. Even if research methods are oriented in deduction or induction, they do not conform exclusively to either approach (Eisenhardt, 1989). In our opinion, a useful starting point is to be aware of the need to combine and mix methods with rigor and scientific relevance in an integrative way to build new avenues for knowledge creation.

While quantitative methods form the foundation of the majority of articles published in top entrepreneurship journals, it seems necessary to remember that entrepreneurship is not a linear process. A substantial challenge is to consider the temporal and practical specificity of each entrepreneurial process/experience on a large scale (as can be achieved through ethnographies). One proposition is to adopt Experience Sampling Methodology (ESM) to collect primary data and include more analyses of nonlinear effects. Another avenue is promoting awareness of the fact that accessing a plethora of data enhances our capacity to do more research but doesn't automatically improve the relevance and appropriateness of this research. Saulo Dubard Barbosa's (this volume, Chapter 7) four main stages of the research process is a powerful guideline to render quantitative research as relevant and accessible as possible to inform entrepreneurs, policy makers, and other stakeholders. "Exploring the asymmetries between gains and losses offers an opportunity to further drive our piles deeper and question conventional knowledge through more refined quantitative research" (p. 124).

A second challenge is confronting the ability of qualitative research to be insightful and creative in order to follow a teleological perspective, attract more attention, and be published in top-level journals. Four pathways are proposed (Hlady-Rispal, Fayolle & Gartner, this volume, Chapter 8): exploring "entrepreneurial action" in action, embracing co-design and collective intelligence, revealing a constructive critical attitude, and joining a phenomenon-driven conversation. The aim is to design and apply new methods of data collection to boost novel theoretical contributions in the link between paradigms and research designs.

Indeed, entrepreneurship scholars are being warned that increasing access to more and more data (big data, AI) means a complete redefinition of our ways of working, of the scopes and criteria of methodologies, and of the philosophical background of methods – be they quantitative or qualitative. In fact, many research questions and issues need creative mixed methods to reach a deeper understanding of complex phenomena, especially in the face of the incredible quantity of data available. Mixed-methods research seems more effective in addressing the urgent questions arising from our modern times of transition (Gruber, 2023). Using an appropriate research method linked with an insightful research question may be the first step in this daunting task. For these reasons, it is crucial to be aware of the key issues in entrepreneurship research methods to produce robust, interesting, and useful new knowledge.

KEY IMPLICATIONS OF UP-TO-DATE PHILOSOPHICAL AND METHODOLOGICAL DIRECTIONS FOR ENTREPRENEURSHIP RESEARCH

Defining Our Own Entrepreneurship Scholarship Voice and Identity

Writing a research paper also means participating in a scientific conversation. This dialogical dimension of research encourages introspection, the pursuit of paths that have already been pursued, and sometimes advocating for deviant alternatives: "Take the road less traveled, because that may well make all the difference" (Pelly, this volume, Chapter 4, p. 70). Researchers must make their voice heard in order find a home in their research communities, starting with their doctoral studies. The methodological and epistemological choices underpinning doctoral research must therefore correspond to the part of the identity that is being shaped to align with a PhD student's career aspirations (Le Pontois & Foliard, this volume, Chapter 10).

Reading Alain Fayolle's tribute to Mike Wright (this volume, Chapter 2) invites each of us to reflect upon which entrepreneurship scholar we wish to emulate by reviewing three potential archetypes: Darwinian, Communitarian, and Missionary. Darwinians focus primarily upon their level of research performance (e.g., impact factor, publications, etc.) and devote their resources to activities that will increase their own reputation and that of their university in a highly competitive environment. Communitarians are team builders of stakeholders in their research communities, where they produce innovative research that they share and diffuse with the support of their peers. Missionaries believe they can be powerful agents of change in the research community, and even in society, while being aware of the limits of change management. Even if most of us can identify with one of these social identities, being aware of the characteristics of all three would enable us to strike a balance between relevance, meaning, and rigor in research.

Examining Our Research Questions with a Critical Lens

Entrepreneurship research appears to be one of those phenomena where action and intervention have raced far ahead of the theory, ontology, and methodology.[1] Stratos Ramoglou (this volume, Chapter 3) gives us a good example of this discrepancy by analyzing the way in which research has been built around the question "Who is the entrepreneur". Entrepreneurial stories are based upon the fallacy of possibilism in a world where some people have characteristics that predetermine their entrepreneurial success. It is this flawed theoretical assumption that underpins this position of the "guilty", and "deterministic" characteristics underlying entrepreneurial success or failure. As a corollary, for over 20 years, positive thinking about the entrepreneur has fueled entrepreneurialism discourse (Eberhart et al., 2022; Caliskan & Lounsbury, 2022) in a body of research that struggles to capture the full range of entrepreneurial realities around the world: "this agent-centric story leaves no room for interventions that can help make the opportunities in our economies more accessible to more people" (Ramoglou, this volume, Chapter 3, pp. 41–2). This oversight is especially germane in a context where various forms of entrepreneurship are needed to overcome the challenges of the Anthropocene era.

The big question could be why and how do we perform research in our field? How do we augment the legitimacy of our discipline? As entrepreneurship scholars, we need to examine our research questions more carefully before embarking upon a research design potentially built around the wrong questions. A question can be flawed if it does not correctly and fully address the right context. For instance, there is no article discussing the impact of increased cardiovascular circulation upon the stress and decision-making of high-level squash players (e.g., a loss of lucidity). Two possibilities could be discussed here: (1) it is a gap to be filled; and (2) this situation does not concern high-level players (but rather amateurs). Indeed, professional players have acquired the physical and mental skills to avoid (or very rarely experience) this zone of lucidity loss. This serves as an example of a question developed from observation (players sometimes lose their lucidity) but disconnected from the reality of professional players and coaches. When addressing a research question, we must adopt a critical approach to help us understand possible judgement errors and psychological biases in previous research as we redirect our thinking towards more promising issues.

Examining Our Methodological Choices with a Critical Lens

Entrepreneurship scholars may reflect upon their own experiences (Ramoglou, this volume, Chapter 3) as well as why their careers as entrepreneurs are not seen as empirically robust by using autoethnography. As Duncan Pelly (this volume, Chapter 4, p. 68) writes: "the goal of composing an autoethnography is not to write for its own sake, but to be able to ask different types of research questions" that ask us about entrepreneurial identities/individuals and the story behind the formation of a new business, because struggles make the story believable (Pelly, 2020).

Using practice-based theories to study entrepreneurship as a social phenomenon allows us to move from an individual perspective in economic systems, to theorizing what entrepreneurs do in social practices and spaces, as well as how they (re)shape theses spaces (Teague & Tunstall, this volume, Chapter 5). Adopting a critical approach, such as a critical constructivist perspective, enables us to approach the reality of entrepreneurial practice, which includes cultural, social, economic, political, cognitive, and emotional dynamics (Hlady-Rispal, Fayolle & Gartner, this volume, Chapter 8).

Drawing Robust Research Designs: (Re)thinking the Links between Ontology, Methodology, Methods, Theories, and Context to Tell a Story

Future research needs to continue to examine the role and potential impact of methodologies, methods, and philosophical positioning in research because they shape our knowledge of entrepreneurship. To explain this link, we reflect upon the Sapir-Whorf hypothesis. This socio-linguistic hypothesis is based upon the problem posed by the variability of representations and categorizations of the world in different languages (as introduced into linguistics by W. von Humboldt). In brief, the language in which an individual thinks and lives determines their representation of the world.

Entrepreneurship research is based upon methodologies, methods, and philosophical assumptions which form a conventional language for entrepreneurship scholars. Being a scholar in entrepreneurship first requires adopting the knowledge, representations, and categorizations produced by previous entrepreneurship researchers, most of whom write in English. Afterwords is the integration into a community and engagement in previous conversations. Thus, entrepreneurship research, to a certain extent, constitutes a form of language conditioning and representation. When the vast majority of published entrepreneurship research is produced in Western countries with their accompanying perspective on what entrepreneurship is and the types of activities and entrepreneurs to support or study (e.g., start-ups, deep-tech companies, unicorns, multinationals, family entrepreneurship, etc.), the vision of what entrepreneurial practice is may not be representative of the worldwide reality. Historically, entrepreneurship research has fueled the entrepreneurialism discourse: the entrepreneur is initially seen as a self-employed risk-taker, and as an innovative super (wo)man in charge. After adopting a personalized approach to the entrepreneur (Pelly, this volume, Chapter 4), the researchers looked at them through a practice-oriented lens to gain a better understanding of the micro-level processes involved in entrepreneurial activities (Teague & Tunstall, this volume, Chapter 5).

Entrepreneurial practices and situations around the world are highly diverse, as well as culturally, socially, economically, and environmentally rooted because "entrepreneurship as a phenomenon is highly context dependent" (Laveren et al. 2021). Since intentions, characteristics, activities, structures, and contexts are so divergent, innovative investigative methods are required. We cannot study different objects with the same assumptions and the same body of commonly accepted knowledge due to diverse cultural influences. The first question we must investigate seems to be: what are the ontological aspects of entrepreneurship? Key issues in entrepreneurship research methods are linked with contextual components (contextualizing the entrepreneurial phenomena), methodological stances (the changing nature of entrepreneurship research methods), and theoretical constructs (theorizing and theory building) (Dana & Salamzdeh, this volume, Chapter 6). As all the contributors of this book have stated, it is time to stop and rethink the building blocks in entrepreneurship research methods.

Finding the Right Outlet for Publication

Another important issue concerns selecting the appropriate publication venue. Researchers are aware that there is often limited space in A-rank journals for highly original contributions that use novel designs and topics, innovative methods, or that challenge taken-for-granted assumptions through intuition.

Such research is often published in less prestigious journals than internationally A-ranked ones or is found in "grey" literature. However, limiting oneself to A-rank journal datasets can contribute to a form of cultural endogeneity in entrepreneurship research. Allowing for the exploration of "grey" literature, methods from other fields, and rigorously combining contextual, methodological, theoretical, and ontological elements can lead to the development of innovative research methods. It is about inviting us, as scholars, to adopt playful approaches (Suomi & Heljakka, this volume, Chapter 12) in entrepreneurship research to learn to ask (and think about) the right questions in a process of enlightened emancipation (Fayolle, this volume, Chapter 13). For example, recent video-based research offers benefits such as accessing the interactive, emotional, material, and embodied nature of entrepreneurial action (Ormiston & Thompson, this volume, Chapter 11).

Developing Professional Skills through the Career: Learning to Apply New Tools

Task automation tools that facilitate data collection are becoming increasingly numerous and effective; however, one must learn how to use them. For instance, data scraping provides a broad, precise, and relevant collection of data already available online, provided that the researcher is trained to program this automated collection. For example, several software options are available for mapping literature reviews (e.g., Connected Papers, Inciteful, VOSviewer, LitMaps, ...). Now more than ever, it is essential to work collaboratively on mixed-methods research projects, learn to use increasingly numerous and powerful tools, and benefit from complementary skills (including the choice of methods and epistemological positioning), to generate new knowledge. Another valuable tool for improving theoretical alignment involves "storyboarding", or multimethod research projects before the collection, compilation, and analysis of data (Knight, 2020).

CONCLUSION

This volume focuses upon methodological and philosophical issues in entrepreneurship research to achieve relevance and rigor in research. The chapters in this volume hail from a number of different perspectives that highlight the methodological diversity and the emerging trends in entrepreneurship research. In this final chapter, we have argued that there is still much research work needed to reveal the strengths, weaknesses, and limits of our methodological and philosophical choices.[2] The diversity and sometimes the complexity of approaches needed to design a robust research project were discussed to integrate critical and novel thinking.

The main implications of this book are mainly (but not exclusively) to provide readers with critical approaches of methodological and philosophical issues in entrepreneurship research and to propose new ways of thinking and performing research. This goal aligns with the global competitiveness of entrepreneurship research that is confronted with significant challenges (i.e, an exponential increase in available data and tools, entrepreneurship in the transition era, … etc.). In this context, researchers need to stress the meaning of research and how this will influence policy makers and society. A way to do this is to encourage scholars to work within teams and to place professional development at the core of their activity to enhance their ability to formulate the "right" questions.

There are research gaps surrounding the literature about methodological and philosophical issues in entrepreneurship that need to be addressed. As indicated in the chapters of this book, there is also more research needed on how to improve our contributions as scholars embedded in a dynamic and collective process of knowledge production.

Future research needs to be more creative and integrative, without compromising the quality of the epistemological stance, methodological choices, theoretical framework, and research context. Like a Nietzschean philosopher, the entrepreneurship researcher must not only equip themselves with a hammer, pliers, and a screwdriver but also learn from and with others on how to use them to construct robust and exemplary research projects and papers (e.g., multimethod research, Wellman et al., 2023).

Finally, we hope that this volume contributes to and extends the research on methodological and philosophical issues in entrepreneurship research. In that way, our conclusion is not the end of the story but rather a new and stimulating chapter in the history of entrepreneurship as a field of research.

NOTES

1. This sentence is a reference to a Rideout and Gray article (2013): Rideout, E. C., & Gray, D. O. (2013). Does entrepreneurship education really work? A review and methodological critique of the empirical literature on the effects of university-based entrepreneurship education. *Journal of Small Business Management*, *51*(3), 329–351.
2. The authors were delighted to see that in January 2024 the Academy of Management Journals (AMJ) expanded the Manuscript Portfolio to include Research Methods articles.

REFERENCES

Caliskan, K., & Lounsbury, M. (2022). Entrepreneurialism as discourse: Toward a critical research agenda. In Eberhart, R. N., Lounsbury, M., & Aldrich, H. E.

(Eds.), *Entrepreneurialism and society: New theoretical perspectives.* Research in the Sociology of Organizations, Vol. 81 (pp. 43–53). Emerald Publishing Limited.

Eberhart, R. N., Lounsbury, M., & Aldrich, H. E. (Eds.). (2022). *Entrepreneurialism and society: New theoretical perspectives.* Research in the Sociology of Organizations, Vol. 81. Emerald Publishing Limited.

Eisenhardt, K. M. (1989). Building theories from case study research. *Academy of Management Review, 14*, 532–550.

Gruber, M. (2023). From the editors: An innovative journal during transformational times – embarking on the 23rd editorial term. *Academy of Management Journal, 66*, 1–8.

Knight, A. P. (2020, May 20). Enhancing theory–method alignment in *AMJ* submissions. *AMJ* paper development workshop. Online (held virtually).

Laveren, E., Ben-Hafaïedh, C., Kurczewska, A., & Jiang, Y. D. (2021). An introduction to *Contextual Heterogeneity in Entrepreneurship Research.* In Laveren, E., Ben-Hafaïedh, C., Kurczewska, A., & Jiang, Y. D. (Eds.), *Contextual Heterogeneity in Entrepreneurship Research: Frontiers in European Entrepreneurship Research* (pp. 1–14). Edward Elgar Publishing.

Pelly, R. D. M. (2020). Sadism in foreign lands: the burn pit atrocity. *Academy of Management Proceedings, 2020*(1), 18217. https://doi.org/10.5465/AMBPP.2020.18217abstract.

Wellman, N., Tröster, C., Grimes, M., Roberson, Q., Rink, F., & Gruber, M. (2023). Publishing multimethod research in AMJ: A review and best-practice recommendations. *Academy of Management Journal, 66*(4), 1007–1015.

Index